STAFFORDSHIRE PARISH REGISTERS SOCIETY founded 1901

President

Col. I.S. Swinnerton

Chairman

Dr. P.D. Bloore

Hon. Secretary

Mr. I. Wallbank,
82 Hillport Avenue,
Newcastle-under-Lyme,
Staffs.,
ST5 8QT

The Society has pleasure in placing in the hands of members a further volume of printed Staffordshire Parish Registers consisting of the registers of the parish of Kinver.

Enquiries concerning copies of registers already printed and still available for sale should be addressed to the Hon. Secretary.

ISBN 978-0-9551159-6-7

Copyright © Staffordshire Parish Registers Society 2008

No part of this publication may be reproduced or transmitted in any form or by any means, electronically or mechanically, including photocopying, recording or any information storage or retrieval system, without the prior permission in writing from the publisher.

British Library Cataloguing in Publication Data
A catalogue record for this book is available from the British Library

Acknowledgements

An initial partial transcript of the early register of Kinver was made by Johnson Ball in the 1950's. This transcript was then checked against the original register and Bishop's Transcripts by Peter D. Bloore, and then the coverage extended to produce the final document here.

The Bishop's Transcripts cover the period 1655-1880 but with significant gaps from 1755-58 and 1762-1773, as well as other minor gaps. A photograph of two of these submissions to the Bishop is included in this publication which clearly show the variation in presentation.

The Society would express it's thanks to the Revd. David Blackburn for permission to publish this register. The Society is also indebted to Mrs Thea Randall, Head of Archives Service, Staffordshire County Record Office, for permission to use the microfiche for transcription purposes. Also to Mr. Andrew George, Area Archivist at Lichfield Record Office, for permission to include the photographs of two of the original Bishop's Transcripts covering this parish.

This volume covers the following:
   Baptisms and Burials 1560 to 1775
   Marriages 1560 to 1754
The later registers are covered in a separate volume, namely Part 2.
The Index to both Part 1 and Part 2 is included in Part 2

© Staffordshire Parish Registers Society 2008

All Rights are Reserved.

No part of this publication may be re-produced or transmitted in any form or by any means electronically or mechanically without prior permission from the Society.

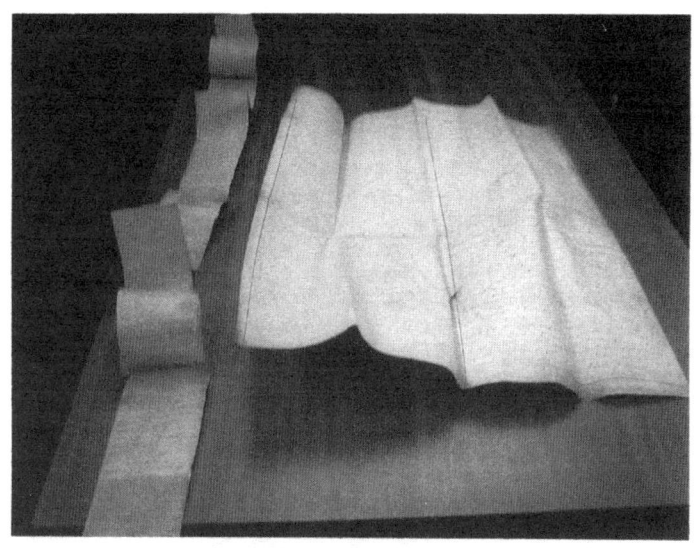

Example of two of the Bishop's Transcripts
The one on the left, a narrow but long document, covers 1701-3, whilst the larger document on the right covers 1721-3

© Staffordshire Parish Registers Society 2008

KINVER AND ITS CHURCH

William White writing in 1834 in his "History, Gazetteer and Directory of Staffordshire" describes Kinver as:

KINFARE, or, as it is commonly called, Kinver, is a large and pleasant village, consisting of one long street, with many good houses, on the declivity of an eminence called Kinfare Edge, on the west bank of the river Stour, near the borders of Worcestershire, four miles W.S.W. of Stourbridge, and 11 miles S. by W. of Wolverhampton. It was anciently a borough and market town of some importance, but the weekly market and two annual fairs on May 1st and Dec.14th, have long been obsolete, though the market-house or town-hall still remains. It was formerly noted for the manufacture of both coarse and fine narrow woollen cloth, and it has now several forges for the manufacture of bar, rod, and sheet iron; and one of them at a place called Hyde, is said to be the first rolling and slitting mill erected in England, being founded by one Brindley, who went into Germany, and there "acted the part of a fool," until he had obtained a complete knowledge of all the machinery, &c., used in the iron works of that kingdom. The parish is intersected by the Stour river and the Staffordshire and Worcestershire canal, and contains about 9000 acres of fertile land, and 1831 inhabitants. It consists of two manors, viz., Kinfare, (including Compton, Dunsley, Iverley-hay, and Stourton Castle,) of which John Hodgetts Hodgetts Foley, Esq., M.P., of Prestwood Hall, is lord; and Whittington, on the east side of the Stour, of which the Earl of Stamford is lord. These lords are likewise owners of most of the land; but here are a few small freeholders and copyholders, the latter of whom pay small chief rents, and a fine equal to two years' rent, on the change of lord or tenant. On the south side of Kinfare-edge, is a small plain covered with sand, where there are the remains of an ancient encampment, of an oblong form, 300 yards long and 200 broad, which tradition says was the work of the Danes; but Shaw imagines it to have been constructed by Wulfere, one of the Kings of Mercia;- Kin-vaur, signifying in the Anglo-Saxon language, the great edge or ridge. Just below the camp appears a tumulus, surrounded by a narrow ditch, and supposed to cover the ashes of a Celtic warrior. Near it is a large stone of a square figure, two yards in height and four in circumference, but tapering towards the summit, on which there are two notches. It is called Bastone, or Bolstone. On the north side of the hill is a remarkable cavern, called Meg-o-fox-hole. The Church holds a lofty situation upon the same hill, on the west side of the village, and is an ancient fabric, dedicated to St. Peter. From the form of an arch over the principal window, Bishop Lyttleton supposed it to have been erected even prior to the Norman conquest; but the chapel adjoining the chancel, he ascribes to the time of Henry the third, when the Hamptons were lords here, and resided at Stourton Castle. Here are some fragments of painted glass, and several antique monuments of the families of Grey, Hampton, Hodgett, Foley, and Talbot. The benefice is a perpetual curacy, vested in trustees, and now enjoyed by the Rev. Howell Davies. The lord of the manor, J. H. H. Foley, Esq., is impropriator of the tithes, and pays thereout the yearly sum of £43. 6s. 8d. to the officiating curate, who also receives the following yearly payments, viz., £5. 6s. 8d. from the Leather Sellers' Company of London, pursuant to the bequest of Wm. Moseley, in 1617; and £47, from a house at Shadwell, in Middlesex, and three small tenements at Kinfare.

The Free Grammar School, of Kinfare, was endowed before the 13th of Elizabeth; but the date of its foundation is unknown. Of the benefactors of land, only two appear to be known, viz., Wm. Vynsent, in 1592, and Roger Jeston, in 1605. The yearly income now amounts to about £130, of which £6. 13s. 4d. is an annuity charged on the tithes of Kinver, in consideration of £50 left in 1595, by John Jorden; and £2. 13s. 4d. is paid by the Leather Sellers' Company of London, pursuant to the will of William Moseley, in 1617. The rest arises from land and buildings in this parish. The school was rebuilt in 1819, after having lain dormant for several years, during which the funds were employed in repairing the buildings on the school lands, and in erecting four new cottages. It is only free for the classics. The present master, the Rev. George Wharton, M.A., is allowed to take boarders.

Benefactors to the Poor - In 1625, Roger Jeston left £5 a-year to be paid to by the Haberdashers' Company of London. In 1624, £28 given by the Jorden family, was laid out in the purchase of two houses with gardens, in Kinfare, now let for £13 a year, including the rent of an allotment made at the enclosure in 1800. In 1649, Thomas Keyghtley, Esq., left a yearly rent charge of £5, out of land at Bromsgrove, to be distributed on St. Thomas's day amongst twenty aged poor. The sum of 50s. is paid yearly out of the Bible Meadow, to purchase bibles, testaments, and catechisms, pursuant to bequest of the Rev. Roger Kimberley, in 1659. The yearly sum of £2. 16s., being the interest of £70 arising from the gift of Robert Bird, in 1689, is distributed in apprentice fees and donations to young women. Five cottages, with gardens to each, at Whittington, were derived from the gifts of Longworth Crosse, Mary Newey, and others in 1717, and are now occupied, rent free, by poor families. In 1659, George Brindley gave 20s. to be distributed in bread out of the Burgage field. The poor have also 20s. yearly out of as estate at Dunsley, left by John Grove, in 1698; £2, from a house and garden at Stourton, left by John Cook, in 1770, and £2. 10s. as the interest of £50, bequeathed by Margaret Comber, in 1777. They also receive, as their portion of

William Seabright's charity, of Alveley, in Shropshire, £3. 7s. 4d., in bread, yearly.

Compton is a hamlet of scattered houses, 2 miles W. of Kinfare, near the borders of Shropshire.

Stourton Castle, nearly two miles N. of Kinfare, on the west bank of the Stour, is a venerable mansion, which has recently been repaired, and is occupied by James Foster, Esq. an extensive iron-master. At an early period it was the property of the Hamptons, and Leyland says, "I heard there was a Lord Storton, a baron of this Storton." It was fortified for the King at the commencement of the civil wars, but surrendered to the Parliament in 1644. The celebrated Cardinal Pole was born in this castle, in 1500. His descent was illustrious, being younger son of Lord Montague, (cousin german of Henry VII.) by Margaret, daughter of George Duke of Clarence, brother of Edward IV. He received many marks of royal favour from Henry VIII. but his court influence was of short duration; for having vigorously opposed the divorce of Catherine of Arragon, he became so obnoxious to the lascivious King, that he was obliged to seek shelter in Italy, where he wrote his celebrated piece, intituled "De Unitate Ecclesiastica," which so exasperated Henry, that he caused an act of attainder to be passed against him, which however was repealed when the Catholic Mary ascended the throne. On his return to England, the Cardinal's first act was to absolve the kingdom from the papal interdict under which it laboured, on account of the apostacy of Henry VIII. He was now advanced to the Archbishropic of Canterbury, but he died shortly after, on Nov. 17th, 1558, the same day on which the Queen herself expired. Whilst in Italy, he was twice elected to the Papal See, after the death of Pope Paul the third, but he declined the honour, because one election was too hasty, and the other was made in the night.

Whittington, on the opposite side of the Stour, 1 mile E. of Kinfare, and 4 miles S.W. of Stourbridge, is a small village and ancient manor belonging to the Earl of Stamford, as has already been seen.

Kinver Clergy

The following list of the Kinver Clergy is taken from the "History of the Church of St. Peter, Kinver" by Herbert Grainger, published in 1951.

1511	Thomas Rondell, Priest and First Grammar School master
1553	Richard Blockley, Vicar when Eccl. valuation was declared.
1563	John Cooke, Curate
1570	Richard Mansell
1577	Frank Symkis
1593-1610	Wm. Selborne, M.A.
1595	J. Jordan, a local vicar
1620	Edward Jones, M.A.
1624	Gerald Whorwoode, Incumbent
1625	Richard Blockley
1646	Rev. John Cross
1649	Wm. Kimberley, Minister and Schoolmaster
1652	Rev. S. Smith
1655	Roger Kimberley, B.A., Minister and Schoolmaster
1662	Rev. Thos. Morton, ejected
1664	During this stormy period of Church History, Jonathan Newey was Curate and Vicar for 54 years and is recorded as a good and brave man.
1676	A. Thornburgh
1741	W. Yates, Curate and Vicar
1743	Richard Bate, Minister
1746-1776	Paul White, Curate and Vicar for over 30 years.
1759	Rev. John Comber Raybould, a Local Vicar
1764	Rev. John Worrall, a Local Vicar
1774-1783	Rev. J. Fox, Curate and Vicar
1779	Rev. Edward Hill
1781	Rev. G. Lewis
1786	Rev. H. Downing
1782-1786	Rev. H. Davies
1795-1828	Rev. J. Davies during the first quarter if this century
1803	Rev. James Stokes
1810	Rev. Thos. Homfrey
1828	Rev. James Taylor
1817-1826	Rev. T. Houseman, Curate and Vicar
1833	Rev. Geo. Wharton
1867	Rev. John Hodgson

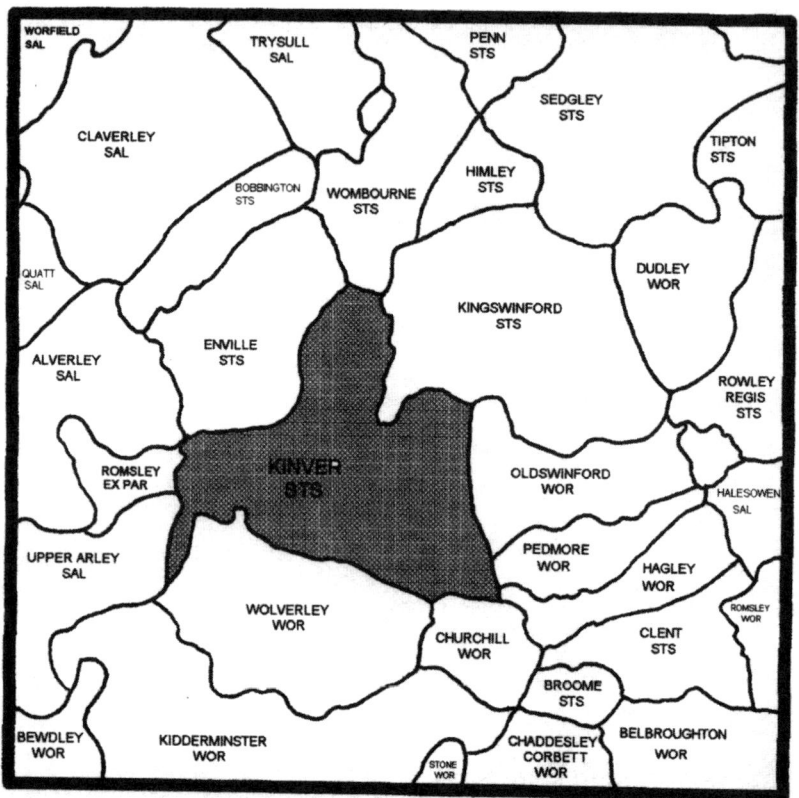

Map of Kinver and Adjacent Parishes

(SAL – Shropshire; STS - Staffordshire; WOR – Worcestershire)

Kinver Parish Register, 1560 - 1649

[On the inside is written the following paragraph which appears to be a more modern copy of the start of the original text:]

This Register book for Kynver made the - -. Daye of May and in the year of Our Lord God 1598 at the charges of the parish these Humfrey VINCENT and Humfrey KETLEY being then the Church wardens in which book is truly recorded all that is in the olde Register book from the year of our Lord God 1560 to this present year of Our Lord God 1598.

[What appears to be the original text starts at the top of the first page:]
This Register booke for Kynver made the .... Daye of Maye and in the yeare of O^r Lord God 1598 at the charges of the pish there Humfrey VINCENT and Humfrey KETLEY being then the Church wardens in wch book is truly recorded all that is in the olde Register booke from the years of O^r Lord God 1560 to this p^{r}sent yeare of O^r Lord God 1598.

[On the lower part of this first page in faint characters are the following words and names]
The Register of Kinvar ....
Weddings ....

Humfrey VINCENT
    laurea
                       Jonathan NEWEY

   Hale G ....[?]

Edward JONES[?]

            John BARTON

            Edward ....[?]

William KIMBERLEY Minis^{ter}

William WHORWOOD
Esqr Received
   this thinge
   from ....
     you

William WHERRET [very faint]

Jo MOSELEY

Edward ADDENBROOKE

     [Starting then on the next page which is severely marked:]

Ano Dni 1560

The 14th of September was baptized at Envilde Margery the daughter of Robert BATE of Comton
The same day was Baptized Elizabeth the daughter of Nycholas DARBYE
The 24th of September was baptized Roberte the sonne of Robert VINCENT and buried the same daye
[On the opposite (preceeding) page in more modern writing:] Thomas HYLLMAN and John COOKE

The 8th of October was baptized and Buryed ....FRECKLETON
The 12th November Roger ....John COLE
The same day was baptized Roger the   Catherine BOWLAND
November 25 was baptized Elyzabeth   FLETCHER
The 9th December was baptized John MONCKE
The 24th December was baptized Chrystabel PSONS[?]
The 3rd March was baptized Humfrey HARRIS[?]
The 20th March was baptized Rychard SYGTHE[?]
The 24th March was baptized Izabell SWYVEN[?]

Weddings in Ano 1560

Jul 25 Denis CASTELLDON & Cristabell ATKYS widdo
Nov 5   John COOKE & Joyce TOYE
Dec 3   Nycholas SAUNCER & Joyce HAUSE
Dec 23 Thomas GRAVENOR & Joane BATE
[On the opposite (preceeding) page in more modern writing:] William the sone of William UDERWOOD[?]

Jan 21 John SYSTON & Isabel SERGANTE

Buryings in Ano 1560

Jul 9   Margarett wife of John SYSTON
Aug 19   Elynor the bastard of Thomas SHINTON
Aug 28   Anne BATHE & Willyam RYDER were buryed
Aug 31   Edward HACKET
Sep 5   Thomas HACKETT father of the same Edward HACKETT
Dec 2   John MONKE
Jan 5   John ROBINSON of Storton
Jan 12   John EVERYE[?]
Jan 30   Elizabeth NOUCKE[?]
Feb 23   Christabell PSONS

Christenyngs in Ano 1561

Mar 31   Joyce d of Richard LUCE by his servant Ane PERRYE
Dec 15   Margarett the daughter of Denis CASTELLDON
Oct 6   Edward s of George HILMAN
Oct 6   Mary d of Thomas COMBER
Feb 16   Margaret d of Edward BLOCKLEY
Mar 8   Francis s of Hugh SHADWALL
Mar 13   Mary d of William KEMSTONE

Weddings in Anno 1561

- Jan 26 John DAVIES & Elyzabeth
- Jan 30 Edmond WANERTON & Joane HACKETTE
- Jan 31 Robert GARRETT & Annes COMBER

Burials 1561

- Jan 17 John MOSLEYE
- Feb 14 John SPARRYE
- Mar 19 Blanche BATTE

Christenyngs in Ano 1562

- May 25 Thomas s of Roger BRADLEYE
- Jun 12 Richard s of Willyam FLETCHER
- Jun 30 John s of John SYSTON
- Jul 15 Julyan d of Robert BATE
- 20 Humfrey s of Humfrey LYTHALL
- Aug 12 Dorothye d of John NEWPORT jun'[?]
- Aug 15 Margery d of Thomas NORRIS
- Aug 25[?] Thomas s of John SANDES
- Aug 25[?] Humfrey s of Henry HICKMANS
- Aug 31 Mary d of Hugh LAWE
- Sep 10 Isabel d of Thomas GROVE
- Dec John s of Edmond WANERTON
- Dec 21 Anne d of John MAYRE
- Feb John s of William FORDE
- Feb Francis s of John PERRYE
- Feb John s of John SCRIVEN
- Mar 10 Elizabeth d of John COCKE
- Mar Richard s of Edward PHILLIPS
- Mar Humfrey s of Humfrey BATE

Weddinges in Ano 1562

- May 4 Nicholas HILL & Elizabeth FOWKE
- May 8 Alixander COOLE & Joane WANERTON
- Jun 1 Humfrey BATE & John[sic] WARROLE
- Jul 14 Thomas MOSLEYE & Isabell LYNE
- Nov 15[?] Humfrey HOPE & Joyce WEBB
- Nov 24 Willyem CAUXIE? & Annis GARRETT
- Nov 27 Rychard GOLDE & Frances WINDELL
- Jun 1 Richard REDLEGGE & Margaret RYDER
- Sep 27 John SMYTHE & Elizabeth FRECKELLTON
- Jan 31 Humfrey YATE [?BATE] of Whittyngton & Margery SYLVESTER
- Feb 2 Willyam HAULE & Joyce BARKER
- Feb 3 John JONES & Isabell WATKYS
- Feb 7 Thomas GRANER & Catheren WILKES

Buryinges Ano 1562

- Apr 4 Alis

May 1	[?]
Jun	Elyzabeth d of
Jul 4	Margaret SMITH[?]
Oct	Elizabeth
Oct 20	Alis d of Richard ATKYS
Dec 2	John s of John PERRYE
Dec 11	Alis d of Robert GARRETT
Dec	Francis d of George SHERWOOD[?]
Dec 18	Edward s of Richard TOYE
Dec 22	Willyam HANDYE
Dec	Jane d of Robert SHAXTONE
Feb 26	Annis KETLEY
Feb	John s of William FORDE

Chrystenynges 1563

Apr	John s of Roger COCKE
Apr	Edward s of John COOLE
May 10	Isabell d of Nicholas PYTT
Jun 14	Jane d of Humfrey FRECKELTON
Jun	Roger s of Roger WESTON
Aug 24	Joane d of Thomas TYTHE
Aug 30	Christabell d of Rychard KIRKAM
Sep 16	Joane d of Robert GARRETT
Sep 24	Joane d of Rychard COTTON
Sep 30[?]	Thomas s of John JOONES
Oct	Humfrey s of Humfrey HOPE

Weddings 1563

Jun 13	John CAYMES[?] & Elynar HAUDYE
Aug	Thomas HOLLAND & Margarrett HIGHWAY
Oct	Willyam SMYTH & Margarett WILLAT
Nov 7	Richard WINALL & Catherine NEWNAM
Nov 28	John NEWNAM & Margerye ELCOXE
Jan 26	John TOYE & Alice WALTON
Jan 26	John TEARNE & Ane CATARDE
Feb 4	Francis WILKYNSON & Alis OSLANDE

Buryinges in Ano 1563

Mar 25	Elynor d of William BARBER

Christenyngs in Ano 1564

I finde in the olde Register booke the yeare 1563 to be twizce put downe I have therefor put downe the same under the same tytle as I here find it.

Apr 8	Mary d of Willyam FOORDE
Apr 24	Elyzabeth d of Willyam WORDELL
May 2	Dionis s of Willyam FREEMAN
May 2	Humfrey s of Thomas MOSLEY
May 9	Francis s of Thomas COMBER
May 17	John s of Humfrey LYTHALL

May 19	Dorothye d of Nycholas DARBYE
Jun 27	Joane d of Edmond WANERTON
Sep 5	Anne d of Thomas KEETLEYE
Sep 8	Joyce d of Nycholas HILL
Sep 21	Anne d of Thomas HYLMAN
Sep	Francis s of John SYSTON
Oct 10	Dorothye d of John BADGER
Oct 18	Joyce d of Thomas GRAVENOR
Nov	Humfrey s of Geordge HYLMAN
Nov 23	Isabell d of Thomas MANOX
Dec 10	Alis d of Robert GARRETT
Dec	Francis s of Edward BLOCKELEY
Feb 3	Anne d of Harry HYCKEMANS
Feb 8	Mary d of John SYSTON the elder
Feb 20	Humfrey s of John HYLL
Feb 24	Alis d of Roger COOCKE
Mar 4	Joane d of Humfrey MOSLEY
Mar 4	Isabell d of Robert SHAXTON
Mar 17	Joan d of John PERRYE
Mar 17	Isabell d of Rychard CERKAM
Mar 28	Joyce d of Humfrey WILKES
Apr 23	Humfrey s of Denis CASTELLDON
May 11	Anne d of Hughe OSLANDE
May 21	Ane d of Humfrey BATE
May 21	Isabell d of Humfrey NYCHOLES
May 21	Willyam s of John YORKE
Jun 4	Margarrett d of Willyam FLETCHER
Jul 16	Martha d of Hughe SHADWALL
Jul 16	Thomas s of John JONES
Jul 30	Denis s of William HYLL
Aug 30	Dorothye d of John COOKE
Sep 3	Margaret d of Thomas GROVE
Sep 29	Margery d of Thomas NORRIS
Oct 3	Thomas s of Thomas HILMAN
Oct 28	Agnes d of John SCRIVEN
Nov 19	Elinor d of Rychard BIRDE
Nov 26	Elynor d of John TEARANE
Dec 24	Sara d of John MAYRE
Jan 22	Elizabeth d of John SMYTHE
Feb 6	Edward s of Thomas MOSLEY
Feb 6	Margarett d of John TOYE
Feb 7	Elinor d of Rose BARBER
Feb 26	Richard s of Robert GARRETT
Feb 29	Mary d of Humfrey HARRIS
Mar 6	Robert s of John COOCKE
Mar 8	Elynor d of David ap HOWELL

Weddings in Ano 1564

Jun 5	Richard EVANS & Anne CHAMBERS
Jun 18	Humfrey WHITE & Margarett PRICE

Oct 17	Willyam YORKE & Margery HILMAN
Oct 22	George NEWNAM & Agnis BURDE
Nov 12	Robert BATE & Anne HAMONDE

Buryinges in Ano 1564

Jan 15	Robert BATE of Compton
Jan 19	Humfrey FRECKELTON
Feb 10	Elizabeth GROVE
Feb 12	John COMBER

Christenyngs in Ano 1565

Apr 1	Thomas s of Wm FORDE
Jul 22	Henry s of Edward ALCHURCHE
Sep 2	Margaret d of Roger BRADLEYE
Sep 8[?]	Thomas s of Robert BATE
Sep 30	Rychard s of Humfrey LYTHALL
Sep 20[?]	Rychard s of John KIRKAM
Nov 3	John s of Humfrey MOSLEY
Nov 12[?]	John s of Willyam WILLATE
Dec 2	Joyce d of John NEWNAM
Dec 20	Joane d of Francis BROWNE
Mar 13	John s of Roger WACKELAM

Weddinges in Ano 1565

Feb 5	Willyam WILLATE & Elynor JORDAYNE
Jul 1	Richard CLERKE & Joyce HOPE
Sep 2	David ap JOHN & Annis FYDKYN
Sep 30	Geordge PERRY & Elizabeth COTE

Buryinges in Ano 1565

Mar 26	Elinor d of Willyam BARBER
Apr 14	Robert BURDE of Compton
Apr 30	Julyan HAULE
May 7	John COMBER
May 30[?]	John HACKETTE
Jun 12	Isabell d of Nycholas HYLL
Jun 27	Elynor wife of Robert BATE
Jul 1	Joan d of Humfrey MOSLEY
Jul 10[?]	Judith d of Willyam WIDALL

Christenyings in Ano 1566

Apr 13	John s of Jhon TOYE
Apr 13	Richard s of Hughe SHADWALLE
Apr 20	Isabell d of Thomas GRAVENOR
Apr 20	Alis d of Thomas HILMAN
Apr 22	Richard s of Harry HYCKEMANS
May 10	Isabell d of John YORKE
Jul 22	Isabell d of Humfrey HARRIS
Jul 22	Edward s of John HILL
Aug 17	Maude d of John COOKE

© Staffordhire Parish Registers Society

Sep 13   John s of Geordge PERRYE
Oct 19   Margaret d of Willyam TOYE
Oct 22   Dorothie d of John LYNGAM

Weddings in ano 1566
Oct 21   John SPARRYE & Rose WILLATE
Nov 12   Robert MYLES & Alis FURNISALL
Nov 20   Willyam TOYE & Joyce BUTLER

Burynges in Ano 1566
Aug 7   Thomas s of Richard ATKIS
Sep 21   Joane wife of Thomas GARRETT
Oct 25   Elynor wife of John JOONES
Oct 27   Margarett wife of Thomas HOLLANDE
Nov 22   Thomas s of John JOONES
Mar 7   Willyam JORDAYNE

Christenyings in Ano 1567
Jan 13   Joane d of Humfrey BATE
Feb 5   Francis d of Edmond WANERTON
Feb 6   Alis d of Deonis CASTELLDONE
Feb 11   Anne d of Richard CLERKE
Feb 11   Joane d of William BANESTER
Mar 2   Thomas s of Willyam YORKE
Mar 9   Sara d of Hughe SHADWALLE
Mar 9   Thomas s of John JOONES
Apr 10   Jane d of Edward JURDEN
Apr 11   Margarett d of Roger COOCKE
May 19   Elenor d of Thomas HILMAN

Weddings in Ano 1567
Jan 27   Thomas CLARKE & Elizabeth SHEMELL
Jan 27   Thomas ELCOXE & Elenor WILKYNSON
Feb   John HILL & Joyce TOYE
Nov 3   Thomas WARRANE & Isabell MOSELEY

Buryals Anno 1567
Apr 20   Marie d of William FORDE
Apr 11   Richard s of Henry NEWNAM
May 8   Humfrey s of Thomas MOSELEY
May 9   Francys s of [blank] COMBER
Jun 1   Thomas HAULE
Jun 11   Margarett HIGGES
Jan 28   Margery d of Thomas NORRYS

Christenings 1568
May 20   Isabell d of William FISHER & Isabell his wife
Jul 2   John s of William SMYTH & Margaret his wife
Aug 11   Alyce d of Edward BLOCKLEY & Dorothye his wife
Sep 29   Elizabeth d of John SPARRYE

© Staffordhire Parish Registers Society

Oct 13   Thomas s of Willm TOYE & Joyce his wife
Oct 20   Richard s of John MERE & Margeret his wife
Oct 28   Elenor d of Thomas KETLEY & Agnes his wife
Oct 28   Thomas s of John VINCENT & Mary his wife
Nov 10   William s of Francys WILKENSON & Alice his wife
Dec 2   Anne d of Willm CLARKE & Agnes his wife
Dec 12   William s of Robert GARRETT & Agnes his wife
Dec 14   Thomas s of Thomas [blank]

Weddings 1568

Jan   John LINGAM & [blank]
Jan 23   Richard MANSELL Clarke & Anne PHILLIPS

Buryings in Ano 1568

Feb 13   Dorothy d of John BADGER
Feb 13   Elenor SELVESTER
Jun 10   Margaret BRADLEY
Jun 20   Jhoane the s'vant of Humfrey BATE
Aug 3   Rose WATKYS

Christenings in Anno 1569

Jan 5   Richard s of Robert COXE & Elinor his wife
Jan 5   Isabell d of John PYRRYE & Margaret his wife
Jan 30   Thomas s of John SMYTH & Elizabeth his wife
             Thomas s of Edward JONES baptized last day of January
Feb 1   Jane d of Thomas ARROWSMYTH & his wife
Feb 6   William s of Thomas MOSELEY & Elizabeth his wife
Feb 20   Elenor d of Robert SHAXTON & Elenor his wife
Feb 13   John the s of Roger WAKELEY & Jhoane his wife
Apr 23   John s of John TOYE & Elenor his wife
Apr 13   Richard s of Edward SHADWALL & Dorothye his wife

Weddings in Anno 1569

Apr 27   Thomas VINCENT & Jane HYEWAY
Jul 20   Henry PERRYE & Jhoane HACKET
Sep 28   Willm HEPWOODE & Anne WEBBE
Oct 17   Humfrey WEBBE & Isabell GRANER

Buryings in Anno 1569

Aug 10   Isabell d of Thomas KETLEY
Oct 3   Thomas NORRYS buried
Oct 29   Humfrey HOPE
Nov 20   Margaret SHISTON
Dec 29   Thomas BYRD

Christenings in Anno 1570

Feb 26[?]   Richard s of Richard MANSELL Clarke & Anne his wife
Nov 28   Margaret d of John MERE
Dec 4   Elenor d of Thomas LUSE & Margaret his wife
Dec 28   Thomas s of Willm SMYTH & Margaret his wife

© Staffordhire Parish Registers Society

Feb 2   Humfrey s of John TERNE & Anne his wife
Feb 2   Mary d of Willm FISHER & Isabell his wife
Mar 22   Francys d of John NEWNAM
Mar 22   William s of Edmond WANNERTON & Jhoane his wife
Mar 23   Elizabeth d of Willm CLARKE & Agnes his wife

Weddings in Anno 1570
Aug 17   Thomas HART & Katheryne HIGHWAY
Aug 26   John DICKYNS & Katheryne HILL

Buryings in Anno 1570
Apr 7   Richard s of Robert GARRET
Jul 11   Isabell FYDKIN
Jul 21   Katheryne WHITE
Dec 9   Margarett PHILLIPPS

Christenings in Anno 1571
Apr 14   Rebecca d of Hugh SHADWELL & Dorothy his wife
Apr 20   Richard s of Nicholas DARBY & Elenor his wife
Apr 20   Julyan d of Humfrey ELCOXE & Elenor his wife
May 9   Thomas s of Henry HICKMAN & Anne his wife
May 9   Robert s of Robert COXE & Elenor his wife
May 9   Joyce d of Willm BANNESTER & Baterich his wife
May 16   Thomas s of Edward JURDEN & Elenor his wife
Jun 3   Margaret d of John JONES & Isabell his wife
Jun 12   Radulpe s of Radulpe BROWNE & Joyce his wife
Aug 1   Edward s of Humfrey WEBBE & Isabell his wife

Weddings 1571
[None]

Buryings in Anno 1571
Sep 10   Isabel LUSE
Nov 10   Walter s of Franncys WILKINSONNE
Nov 26   Richard WEBBE
Dec 23   Jhoane d of Franncys BROWNE
Dec 5   Thomas s of William YORKE
Mar 24   John LARANCE

Christenings in Anno 1572
Sep 12   Agnes d of Richard BYRDE & Jhoane his wife
Sep 19   Isabell d of Humfrey LYTHALL & Margery his wife
Sep 19   Christabell d of Thomas HILMAN & Elizabeth his wife
Sep 29   Rober s of Robert GARRET & Anne his wife
Dec 12   Elenor d of Margaret REGNOLD
Dec 25   Rose d of [blank] KYRCKAM & Alice his wife
Jan 1   Jane d of John COOCKE & Jhoane his wife
Jan 23   Elenor d of Thomas CLARKE & Elizabeth his wife
Feb 7   Alice d of Edward JONES & Agnes his wife
Feb 21   John s of John SMYTH

Feb 25   Anne d of Willm YORKE
Feb 28   Richard s of Willm ATKYS & Anne his wife
May 18   Jhoane d of Willm SMYTH & Margaret his wife
May 23   Margaret d of John TERNE

Weddings in Anno 1572
Sep 5   Thomas LYTLEFORDE & Elizabeth UNDERELL
Nov 10   Willm POTTER & Jhoane BEE
Oct 16   Thomas LANGMORE & Anne JORDAYNE
Nov 6   Edward HOLYMAN & Jhoane WAKMAN

Buryings in Anno 1572
Jun 16   Elizabeth d of Robert BRYBBES
Jul 10   Anne MAYRE d of John MAYRE
Aug 5   Thomas s of Willm YORKE
Nov 10   Edward s of John GREY
Dec 10   Richard s of John MERYE
Dec 28   Margaret d of Thomas NORRYS

Christenings in Anno 1573
May 23   Richard s of Thomas MOSELEY & Isabell his wife
May 23   Thomas s of Thomas LYGHT & Agnes his wife
Jun 12   Agnes d of John PYRRYE & Margaret his wife
Jun 12   Katheryne d of Henry PENNYE & Jhoane his wife
Jun 26   Alyce d of Thomas LYTLEFORD & Elizabeth his wife
Sep 13   Isabell d of Elizabeth SYMONS - patre ignoto
Sep 14   Edward s of Edward BLOCKLEY
Sep 16   [blank] the child of John KEMPSTONE
Sep 17   Jhoane d of Thomas SPARRYE
Sep 23   Margaret d of Franncis [blank]
Nov 24   Willm s of Richard MANSELL Clarke & Anne his wife
Dec 31   Anne d of Humfrey HARRYS & Anne his wife
Jan 6   Elenor d of Willm SMYTHE

Weddings in Anno 1573
Nov 20   Humfrey ROBYNSON & Margaret WARROLL
Nov 26   Richard HORTON & Alyce UNDERHILL
Jan 21   Richard WEBBE & Agnes SCRYVEN

Buryings in A° 1573
Jan 4   Elenor YMNONS buried
Jan 8   Elenor SELVESTER
Jan 10   Anne d of Willm CLARKE
Jan 22   Jhoane d of Richard LYTHALL
Jan 25   Jhoane d of ELCOCKE
Apr 1   John CLARKE
Apr 12   Jhoane MASIE

Christenings in Anno 1574
Jan 10   Pernell d of Thomas WARRAND & Isabell his wife

Mar 5	Denyse the sonne of Dionyse CASTELON
Mar 10	Joyce d of John LINGHAM
Apr 30	Agnes d of Richard TOYE
Apr 30	Elizabeth d of ye same Richard TOYE baptised the same day
May 11	Humfrey s of Thomas GROVE
May 21	Edward s of Margaret WILKENSON
May 28	Thomas s of Thomas KETLEY
Sep 5	Elizabeth d of Edward HILMAN & Jhoane his wife
Sep 10	Jhoane d of Robert GARRET
Sep 16	[blank] the child of Franncys WILKENSON
Sep 21	Thomas the s of Willm CLARKE
Sep 23	Elizabeth d of John JONES

Weddings in Anno 1574

Jan 28	Roger DAWSON & Elizabeth [blank]
Jan 30	John ARCHE & Anne DEYCE
Aug 2	Edward TEYLOR & Elenor LYTHOLL

Buryings in Ano 1574

Jun 10	Richard HUBBOLE
Aug 2	Richard s of Henry HICKMAN
Oct 8	Agnes NEWNAM
Feb 6	John WILLATHE
Mar 2	Christabell [blank]
Mar 16	Richard TOYE

Christenings in Anno 1575

Nov 10	Edward s of John DICKYNS & Katheryne his wife
Nov 21	Anne d of Thomas LYTLEFORD
Jan 6	Edward s of Henry HICKMAN & Anne his wife
Jan 23	Richard s of Henry HENE & Jhoane his wife
Jan 24	Richard s of Margaret FYDKYN, patre ignoto
Aug 26	[blank] child of Thomas HILMAN
Sep 3	Thomas s of Thomas GRANER
Sep 9	Robert s of Thomas MOSELEY
Sep 3	Rose d of Humfrey WEBBE
Sep 9	Elizabeth d of John MERE

Weddings in Anno 1575

Oct 19	Thomas HALL & Anne WAKEMAN
Nov 11	Humfrey KYRKHAM & Katheryne HILMAN

Buryings in Anno 1575

Apr 9	Thomas s of Willm SMYTH
Apr 12	Richard s of Hugh SHADWALL
Apr 14	Thomas HASELWOOD
Oct 20	Edward SADLER
Oct 30	Humfrey SYMONS
Jun 29	Alyce d of Thomas LYTLEFORD
Jun 29	Margaret d of Willm ATKYS

Christenings in Anno 1576

Mar 8	James s of John PIRRYE
Jan 4	Anne d of John GRAZELEY & Elizabeth his wife
Mar 10	Willm s of Richard WEBBE & Anne his wife
Jan 9	Isabell d of Humfrey WHITE & Margaret his wife
Mar 11	Margaret d of Thomas LYTLEFORD
Mar 20	Thomas s of Richard MANSELL & Anne his wife
Mar 29	Humfrey s of Edward JURDEN & Elenor his wife
Apr 5	Gabriell s of Henry LYECOCKE
Apr 18	W........... d of John TERNE
Apr 18	Elenor d of Humfrey HARRYS
Sep 26	Humfrey s of Richard BATE
Sep 26	Anne d of John LINGHAM
Jan 22	Richard s of Richard HORTON

[The following entry is written lengthwise in the margin]

May 9	Elizabeth d of Edward & Margaret SILVESTER

Weddings in Anno 1576

Nov 22	Nicholas HOLLYS & Elizabeth BYRD
Jan 13	John WARROLL & Elizabeth ETERSALL
Jan 23	John PENNELL & Julyan WEBBE
Feb 4	Leonard HILL & Margaret LYNE

Buryings in Anno 1576

Aug 5	Thomas LYTLEFORD
Aug 5	Agnes SMYTH
Aug 10	Roger WESTON
Aug 10	Thomas LITH
Nov 15	Edward HILMAN
Nov 20	Thomas HAMPSON
Jan 22	Humfrey LYNE

Christenings in Anno 1577

Mar 26	John CLARKE the base sone of John CLARKE
Mar 27	Anne d of Richard BANKES
Mar 28	Edwarde ONGAR the s of Thomas ONGAR
Apr 3	Alice BATE d of Humfrey BATE
Apr 22	Thomas s of John SPARRYE
Apr 22	Willm s of Willm WYLLOT
May 1	Willm s of Thomas HAULE
May 7	Jane d of Thomas DIXFILD
Mar 3	Edward s of Thomas WARRENE & Isabell his wife
Mar 4	Willm s of John CHAPMAN
Mar 10	John s of Thomas DIXFILD
Mar 10	Jane d of Thomas LYTLEFORD
May 4	John s of Willm SMYTH
Jun 8	John s of John DYCKENS
Jun 9	Franncys d of Humfrey HARRYS
Jun 30	Margaret d of Richard WEBBE

Aug 11   John s of Edward HILMAN
Sep 1   Jane d of John NEWNAM
Sep 8   Elenor d of Thomas ONGAR
Oct 6   Willm s of Wm ATKYS
Oct 14   Anne d of Richard LYNE
Jan 11   Mary MOSELEY bapt & buryed
Jan 28   Alyce HICKMANS
Feb 4   Richard s of George WATKYS
Feb 20   Magdalen WYLKENSON
Feb 24   Margaret d of Richard HORTON
Mar 24   Martha WATTELL[?]

Weddings in Anno 1577

May 28   Thomas SMYTH & Agnes CLANT
Jul 6   Richard HIPKYS & Franncys BOWLAND
Jun 12   Christopher FRANNCYS & Alyce HIPWOOD
Jul 7   Willm TAYLOR Clarke & Elenor SHADWELL
Jul 10   Thomas HUDSONE & Jhoane ARROWSMYTH
Dec 6   John COOCKE & Jhoane BRUCKHOWSE
Feb 5   Humfrey COOCKE & Agnes DYCKENS
Mar[?]   Willm PRATT & Elenor WALTER
May 7   Willm DARBY & Dorythe BOWLAND

Buryings in Anno 1577

Apr 25   Richard BYRD
Jun 1   Jhoane JURDEN widowe
Jul 7   Dennys s of John TERNE
Jul 7   Alyce ROBYNSON
Jul 18   Richard HAWES
Aug 14   John s of John SPARRY
Dec 2   John WALTER
Feb 12   Robert SHAXTON
Mar 4   Franncys SYMKYS Clarke
Jun 8   Alyce WYNDELL
Jun 18   John WEBBE
Oct 18   Richard MOSELEY
Feb 15   John s of Humfrey COOCKE
Jan 14   Jane HADDOCKE

Christenings in Anno 1578

Apr 26   Bridget d of Thomas LANGMORE
Apr 29   John s of Richard BRADLEY
May 4   Elizabeth d of Thomas BACHE
May 11   Elizabeth d of Thomas WARRANE
Jul 4   Richard s of Richard CLARKE
Jul 27   Richard s of John JONES
Sep 3   Anne d of Willm CLARKE
Sep 12   Alyce d of Edward SELVESTER
Sep 14   John s of Humfrey TAYLOR & Margery his wife
Oct 18   Thomas s of Edyth ELLYOTTE

Nov 26   Joyce d of Humfrey BATE
Jan 25   Thomas s of John MERE
Jan 30   Jane d of Thomas GROVE & Alyce his wife
Feb 2   Agnes d of John DICKENS & Katheryne his wife
Feb 12   Anne d of Leonard HILL & Margaret his wife

Weddings in Anno 1578

Apr 28   Nicholas COURTE & Alyce BYRD
Apr 28   John CATERALL & Katheryne GROVE
Sep 28   Jevon ap CUDWALITER & Isabell CLARCKSON
Dec 7   Richard COWDALL & Elenor SHAXTON
Dec 16   John KIGHTLEY & Elizabeth DAWSON

Buryings in Anno 1578

May 11   John s of Richard BRADLEY
Jul 27   Richard s of Richard CLARKE
Jul 27   Richard s of John JONES
Nov 17   Lattes wife of Thomas COOKE
Dec 15   Margery wife of Roger BUTLER
Dec 17   Isabell wife of Thomas MOSELEY

Christenings in Anno 1579

Feb 22   Sara d of Richard LYNE & Alyce his wife
Feb 26   Jefferye s of Humfrey COOKE & Anne his wife
Feb 28   Humfrey s of Richard WYLLET his wife
Apr 11   Edward s of Edward JURDEN & Elenor his wife
May 3   Margaret d of Thomas GENNES & Anne his wife
May 10   Humfrey s of Richard BRADLEY & Elizabeth his wife
May 10   Elizabeth d of Edward HALE & Anne his wife
May 16   Joyce d of Thomas HILMAN & Elizabeth his wife
May 18   Edward s of Edward OLDNALL & Elenor his wife
Jun[?]20 Garrard s of Richard BYRD & Elizabeth his wife
Jul 23   Elizabeth d of William ATKYS & Anne his wife
Sep 17   Jane d of Franncys HIMBLOCKE[?] & Margaret his wife
Oct 18   Isabell d of Thomas HAULE & Anne his wife
Nov 9   Thomas s of Thomas BATE & Fortune his wife
Nov 29   Elizabeth d of Thomas MOSELEY & Joyce his wife
Dec [?] Edward s of Thomas LYTLEFORD & Elizabeth his wife
Jan 21   Thomas s of Thomas LEVER & Joyce his wife
Feb 1   Richard s of Thomas WARRANE & Isabell his wife
Feb 2   Thomas s of Richard LUSE & Isabell his wife
Feb 12   Dyonise s of Edward SELVESTER & Margaret his wife
Feb 12   Margery d of Robert POTTER & Anne his wife
Feb 17   Mary d of Jhoane SHACKSPERE - patre ignoto
Feb 25   Richard s of Thomas ELCOCKE & Margery his wife
Feb 25   Fortune d of George WATKYS & Anne his wife
Feb 25   Alyce d of John CATERALL & Katheryne his wife
Feb [?] Elizabeth d of Richard BAKER & Alyce his wife
Mar 13   Dyonise s of Thomas ONGAR & Anne his wife
Feb 10   Jane d of John SPARRY

Mar 13	John s of Richard DICKENS & Rose his wife
Mar 20	1580 Margery d of John MADSTERDE & Johane his wife
Mar 27	Thomas s of John KIGHTLEY & Elizabeth his wife
Apr 29	Jhoane d of Arthure BUCKNALL & Margaret his wife
May 8	Jhoane d of Willm YORKE & Margaret his wife

Weddings in Anno 1579

May 21	Robert BRISCOE & Julyan UNDERHILL
Sep 4	Thomas MOSELEY & Joyce EVANS
Sep 5	Leonard ADDENBROKE & Margaret FORD
Jan 24	Jefferey GARRET & Anne CLARKE
Jan 30	John HILL & Isabell BOWLAND
Feb 12	Arthure BUCKNALL & Margaret DASFILD

Buryings in Anno 1579

Feb 14	Margaret wife of Nicholas FLECHER
Feb 20	Jane d of Thomas & Alyce GROVE
Mar 7	John COOKE of Compton
Mar 10	Dorothe d of John COOKE
Mar 21	Margery wife of Thomas BYRD
Apr 12	Elizabeth COOKE widowe
Apr 16	Henry HICKMANS
May 12	Roger COOKE
May 13	Agnes the wife of John COOKE
May 14	Willm WILLETTE
Jun 28	Joyce wife of Wm HAULE
Jan 12	Jhoane WILLET widowe
Jan 30	Elenor wife of Richard COWDALL
Feb 20	Agnes d of Nicholas DARBY
Feb 25	John WILLET
Feb 26	Margery d of Franncys WILKENSON

Christenings in Anno 1580

[?]	Anne d of Humfrey TEYLER & Margery his wife
May 22	Margaret d of John GRANER & Elizabeth his wife
May 29	Henry s of John TERNE & Anne his wife
Jun 12	Humfrey s of Robert BRISCOE & Julyan his wife
Jun 16	Magdalen d of Leonard ADDENBROKE & Margaret his wife
Jul 31	Sara d of Richard WOOLLASTON & Elenor his wife
Aug 7	Dyonise s of Willm PRATT & Elenor his wife
Aug 12	John s of Humfrey ROBINSON & Margaret his wife
Aug 23	Jane d of Richard BRADLEY & Elizabeth his wife
Sep 28	Henry s of Humfrey BATE & Jhoane his wife
Oct 7	Humfrey s of John WILLET & [blank] his wife
	Dyonise s of Thomas HILMAN & Elizabeth his wife baptized the last day of October
Jan 11	Richard s of Richard WILLET & Elizabeth his wife
Jan 13	Thomas s of Thomas LANGMORE & Anne his wife
Jan 29	John s of Humfrey COOKE & Anne his wife
Mar 5	Dorothe d of John CAPMAN & Anne his wife

Weddings in Anno 1580

Sep 19 Sampson MEWCRELL & Elizabeth HOPTON
Sep 27 Thomas DEWES & Jhoane WILLET
Nov 6   William HAGLEY & Alyce WARDE
Nov 8   Edmund WANERTON & Jane BARCROSTE
Jan 16 Thomas WARROLL & Rose BATE
Jan 21 Henry TEYLOR & Agnes COURTE
Jan 29 James BURTON & Agnes PEARSON

Buryings in Anno 1580

May 10 Margaret PHILLIPPS widowe
May 17 Joyce DICKENS
May 28 Henry BENNET
Jul 23 James POTTER
Aug 10 Roger HINSHAWE
Aug 12 Elizabeth wife of Henry TEYLER
Aug 12 Willm HEEDES
Aug 20 Margaret wife of Robert WEBBE
Oct 14 Elizabeth WILLET widowe
Nov 4   Nicholas BENNET
Nov 22 Elenor LYDDYAT
Nov 13 Isabell wife of John HILL
Jan 22 Agnes d of Thomas KETLEY & Anne his wife
Mar 27 Jhoane HILMAN

Christenings in Anno 1581

May 14 Magdalen d of Thomas HAULE & Anne his wife
May 15 Richard s of Edward OLDNALL & Elenor his wife
Jun 11 Philipp s of Thomas BATE & Forten his wife
Aug 27 John s of Robert BRISCOE & Julyan his wife
Oct 15 Alice d of Richard WEBBE & Agnes his wife
Oct 1   Elizabeth d of Thomas HUTCHENS & Joyce his wife
Oct 22 Edward s of Humfrey WHITE & Margaret his wife
Oct 22 Thomas s of Thomas WARROLL & Rose his wife
Nov 12 John s of Franncys HIMBLOCKE & Margaret his wife
Nov 19 Joyce d of Leonard ADDENBROKE & Margaret his wife
Dec 9   Elizabeth d of John DYCKENS & Katheryne his wife
Feb 11 Thomas s of Richard BRADLEY & Elizabeth his wife
Feb 11 Edward s of Richard WILLET & Elizabeth his wife
Mar 3   Isabell d of Richard HILL & Anne his wife
Mar 9   Elizabeth d of Richard LYNE

Weddings in Anno 1581

Apr 9   Richard POTTER & Anne MOSELEY
Apr 4   William JONES & Joyce COOKE
May 4   Willm LEVINGTON & Jhoane PYPER
Jul 16 Edward VINCENT & Agnes BRADLEY
Jul 18 Richard BATE & Rose SPARRYE
Jul 23 John SPITTULL & Elenor PSONS

Aug 22	Thomas COLE & Mary MEIRE
Aug 29	Richard BYRD & Jane HARRYS
Aug 29	John COOKE & Jhoane HOLLYMAN
Sep 3	Richard YEOMAN & Jhoane GRENEWOOD
Sep 10	John WHITE & Elizabeth HILL
Sep 17	William WEBBE & Jane MARKE
Oct 22	Philipp PHILIPPS & Elizabeth TEYLOR
Nov 4	Arthure BUCKNALL & Margery DERETONE

Buryings in Anno 1581

Mar 27	Jhoane HILMAN
May 29	William s of Willm ATKYNS & Anne his wife
Jun 28	Margaret wife of Arthure BUCKNELL
Feb 11	Thomas CLARKE

Christenings in Anno 1582

Mar 26	Margaret d of Edward COMBER & Anne his wife
Apr 8	Johanne d of Edward SELVESTER & Margaret his wife
Apr 15	John s of Thomas ONGAR & Anne his wife
Apr 25	Margery d of Henry TAYLER & Anne his wife
Apr 29	Alice d of John KIGHTLEY & Elizabeth his wife
May 1	Jane d of Robert POTTER & Anne his wife
May 20	Humfrey s of Thomas WARRANE & Isabell his wife
May 20	Joyce d of Edward HALE & Anne his wife
Jun 14	John s of Thomas MOSELEY & Joyce his wife
Jul 16	Richard s of Philip PHILIPPS & Elizabeth his wife
Aug 19	Margery d of Richard BAKER & Alice his wife
Sep 9	Magdalen d of Richard BYRDE & Elizabeth his wife
Oct 28	John s of John COTERALL & Katheryne his wife
Dec 24	Isabell d of Thomas WARROLL & Rose his wife
Jan 13	Michaell s of Sampson ALLEN & Alice his wife
Jan 23	Elizabeth d of Thomas COLT & Mary his wife
Jan 25	Richard s of Elenor BATE patre ignoto
Feb 17	Katheryne d of Thomas HANCOX & Anne his wife
Feb 2	Anne d of John MADSTARDE & Johane his wife
Feb 2	Elizabeth d of Thomas ELCOCKE & Margaret his wife
Mar 3	Jane d of Humfrey BATE & Johane his wife
Mar 18	Anne d of Richard BATE & Rose his wife

Weddings in Anno 1582

Sep 9	John ETON & Elizabeth SLANYE
Oct 8	Thomas WILKES & Jane SHISTON
Nov 5	Thomas RUDGE & Margery NEWNAM
Nov 20	Sampson ALLEN & Alice HASELWOOD
Nov 28	Roger SELVESTER & Elenor TEYLER

Buryings in Anno 1582

Apr 18	William HILL of Compton
May 14	Anne ROBYNSON widowe
Dec 24	Katheryne BROWNE widowe

Christenings in Anno 1583

Apr 15	Franncys s of Humfrey TEYLER & Margery his wife
Apr 25	William s of Leonard ADDENBROKE & Margaret his wife
May 5	Elizabeth d of John CHAPMAN & Anne his wife
May 12	Michaell s of Arthure BUCKNALL & Margery his wife
May 12	Isabell d of Richard WILLET & Elizabeth his wife
Jun 9	John s of Edward OLDNALL & Elenor his wife
Jun 9	Johane d of Humfrey COOKE & Anne his wife
Jul 22	Alice d of Thomas COOKE & Elizabeth his wife
Sep 16	Alice d of Thomas LYTLEFORDE & Elizabeth his wife
Sep 28	Anne d of Richard HILL & Anne his wife
Nov 29	Margaret d of Robert BRISCOE & Julyan his wife
Dec 1	Jane d of Franncys HIMBLOCKE & Margaret his wife
Dec 8	Magdalen d of Thomas BATE & Forten his wife
Dec 17	Robert s of Philip & Elizabeth PHILIPPS & Elizabeth his wife
Dec 22	Rose d of Edward VINCENT & Agnes his wife
Dec 26	Alice d of John WARRALL & Elizabeth his wife
Oct 27	Robert & William sons of Richard DICKENS & Rose his wife
Jan 12	Josyantye d of Edward TRUXTON & Blandyna his wife
Jan 19	Margaret d of Edward SELVESTER & Margaret his wife
Feb 9	Humfrey s of Richard BYRDE & Jane his wife
Feb 16	Garrard s of Thomas WARRANE & Isabell his wife
Feb 23	Martha d of Thomas LEVER & Joyce his wife
Mar 20	William s of John ETON & Elizabeth his wife
Mar 22	Margaret d of Richard BRADLEY & Elizabeth his wife

Weddings in Anno 1583

Jul 16	Humfrey VINCENT & Margery BATE
Jan 27	Humfrey KETLEY & Isabell NICHOLLS
Feb 14	Richard COXE & Rose YATE
Mar 2	John MALPAS & Elizabeth GURTH

Buryings in Anno 1583

Oct 20	Richard s of John CHAPMAN & Agnes his wife
Oct 21	Richard YATE
Oct 26	Thomas LANGMORE
Oct 29	Katheryne wife of Walter BLUNT Esq
Oct 30	John s of Thomas HALL & Anne his wife
Nov 2	Garrard s of Thomas RIDGE & Margery his wife
Mar 13	Alyce d of Thomas COOKE & Elizabeth his wife
Mar 15	John JURDEN
Mar 20	John MOSELEY

Christenings in Anno 1584

Apr 5	Samuel s of Thomas MOSELEY & Joyce his wife
Apr 19	Isabell d of Evan CADWALLETER & Isabell his wife
May 1	Henry s of Thomas & Mary COLE & Mary his wife
May 3	Margaret d of John KIGHTLEY & Elizabeth his wife
May 3	Katheryne d of Thomas GROVE & Alice his wife

May 27	Samuell s of John MALPAS & Elizabeth his wife
Jun 28	Margaret d of Humfrey VYNCENT & Margaret his wife
Jun 29	Robert s of Jeffery GARRET & Anne his wife
Aug 2	Margery d of Humfrey ROBYNSON & Marga his wife ret
Aug 19	Hugh s of Robert POTTER & Anne his wife
Aug 22	Elizabeth d of William HALL & Anne his wife
Oct 4	Blandyna d of Richard LYNE & Alice his wife
Nov 29	Jane d of William PRAT & Elenor his wife
Nov 29	Thomas s of Henry TAYLER & Agnes his wife
Dec 6	Nicholas s of Edward OLDNALL & Elenor his wife
Dec 26	Elizabeth d of William MICHELL & Agnes his wife
Jan 3	Thomas s of Richard BAKER & Alice his wife
Jan 17	Margery d of John CATEWALL & Katheryne his wife
Jan 17	Humfrey s of William CLARKE & Agnes his wife
Jan 30	Johane d of Thomas HALL & Anne his wife
Feb 5	Henry s of Richard BYRDE & Elizabeth his wife
Feb 21	Elenor d of Humfrey KETLEY & Isabell his wife

Weddings in Anno 1584

Jun 8	Humfrey NEWNAM & Alyce LEWES
Jun 15	Thomas MORRICE & Agnes SCRIVEN
Aug 30	Henry HALMER & Magaret PERESON
Nov 27	Edward HILL & Isabell HALE
Jan 28	Richard WALLYS & Johane BATE

Buryings in Anno 1584

Apr 24	Edward COMBER
Jun 25	William FLETCHER
Jun 26	Margaret wife of Leonard HILL
Aug 1	George WATKYS
Nov 6	Thomas CAKE
Jan 19	Alice wife of Richard WHITTINGER

Christenings in Anno 1585

Mar 29	Jane d of Edward HALE & Anne his wife
Apr 25	Magdalen d of John GRANER & Elizabeth his wife
Jun 6	Christabell d of Humfrey COOKE & Anne his wife
Jun 27	Isabell d of Richard BRADLEY & Elizabeth his wife
Sep 4	Sara d of John DICKENS & Katheryne his wife
Sep 16	John s of Meridith ap GRIFFEN & Gwen[?] his wife
Sep 21	Agnes d of John ETON & Elizabeth his wife
Sep 26	Richard s of Edward HILL & Isabell his wife
Oct 10	William s of Richard LUCE & Elizabeth his wife
Oct 28	Johane d of John WARRALL & Elizabeth his wife
Dec 6	John s of Philip PHILIPPS & Elizabeth his wife
Jan 9	Isabell d of John MADSTARD his wife
Jan 16	Jane d of Thomas LEVER & Joyce his wife
Feb 2	Edward s of John CHAPMAN & Anne his wife
Feb 13	Richard s of Richard HANCOXE & Anne his wife
Feb 20	Thomas s of Humfrey LYTHALL & Johane his wife

Feb 27 Thomas s of Richard HILL & Anne his wife
Feb 27 Agnes d of Franncys HIMBLOCKE & Margaret his wife
Mar 13 Johane d of Robert BRISCOE & Julyan his wife
Mar 13 Elizabeth d of Richard WALLYS & Johane his wife

Weddings in Anno 1585
Jan 17 Richard CORKER & Elizabeth COMBER

Buryings in Anno 1585
Apr 19 Thomas CLARKE bur
Jun 9 Alyce WALKER
Aug 22 Agnes LYNE widowe
Oct 10 Robert BATE of Stourton
Dec 26 John s of John & Elizabeth COPPAM
Jan 7 Humfrey MOSELEY
Mar 13 Thomas s of Humfrey & Margery TEYLOR

Christenings in Anno 1586
Apr 17 Elenor d of Roger MICHELL & Anne his wife
Apr 17 Katheryne d of Thomas WARREN & Isabell his wife
Apr 17 John s of Thomas ONGAR & Anne his wife
Apr 24 Meriall d of Richard BATE & Rose his wife
May 15 Thomas s of Thomas COLT [possibly COLE] & Mary his wife
Jul 1 Susanna d of Humfrey NEWNAM & Joyce his wife
Sep 4 Martha d of Thomas BATE & Forten his wife
Sep 25 Humfrey s of William TRENT & Edith his wife
Sep 25 Johane d of Gefferey GARRET & Anne his wife
Oct 2 Martha d of Humfrey VINCENT & Margery his wife
Oct 30 Anne d of Richard WEBBE & Anne his wife
Nov 9 William s of Evan ap PRICE & Elizabeth his wife
Nov 11 Meriall d of Richard HARRYS & Meriall his wife
Jan 29 John s of James ARDEN & Mary his wife
Jan 29 John s of Geffroey GRIFFEN & Dorothy his wife
Feb 19 Alice d of Richard COXE & Rose his wife
Feb 25 Meriall d of Richard WYLLOTT & Elizabeth his wife
Mar 5 Henry s of Thomas MOSELEY & Joyce his wife
Mar 10 Thomas s of John CATTERALL & Katheryne his wife
Mar 12 Thomas s of Richard ARDEN & Anne his wife

Weddings in Anno 1586
May 1 William SYMONS & Margery YATE
Jun 27 John BANNESTER & Isabell SHISTON
Aug 1 William DECON & Alice GARRET
Oct 2 Thomas MOSELEY & Anne BURMAN
Oct 10 Geffrey GRIFFEN & Dorothe GREENELESE
Oct 17 Franncys KETLEY & Johane MORYS
Jan 22 Robert CLEMSON & Margaret BRUCKHOUSE
Jan 30 John CLARKE & Johane WANERTON

Buryings in Anno 1586

Apr 4	Jane d of Thomas LYTELFORDE & Elizabeth his wife
Apr 10	Elizabeth d of Richard BAKER & Alice his wife
Jun 19	Robert VINCENT
Oct 1	Richard DARBY
Oct 18	John TERNE
Nov 16	Meriall d of Richard HARRYS & Meriell his wife
Jan 8	Elenor wife of John CLYMER
Jan 18	Henry NEWNAM the elder
Mar 21	William CLARKE

Christenings in Anno 1587

Mar 26	Henry s of John COPPAM & Margaret his wife
Apr 5	Mary d of Thomas DIXFILD & Mary his wife
Apr 17	John s of Garrard WHORWOOD gent & Dorothe his wife
Apr 18	Thomas s of Humfrey COOKE & Anne his wife
May 6	Humfrey s of Richard LYNE & Alice his wife
May 7	Edward s of Thomas HALL & Anne his wife
May 24	Johane d of William DECON & Alice his wife
May 28	Isabell d of Thomas LYTELFORDE & Elizabeth his wife
Jun 6	Richard s of John BANESTER & Isabell his wife
Sep 10	Elizabeth d of John ETON & Elizabeth his wife
Sep 13	Emanuell s of Richard BRADLEY & Elizabeth his wife
Oct 1	Dorothy d of Richard HARRYS & Meriell his wife
Oct 12	Edward s of John SHISTON & Anne his wife
Oct 8	Margaret d of Richard VINCENT & Elinor his wife
Oct 15	Jane d of Humfrey TAYLER & Margery his wife
Oct 21	William s of Humfrey FOORDE & Margery his wife
Nov 26	Thomas s of John SMYTH & Katheryne his wife
Dec 10	Alice d of Richard BYRD & Elizabeth his wife
Dec 30	Alice d of Richard DICKENS & Rose his wife
Mar 24	Elizabeth d of Robert BRISCOE & Julyan his wife

Weddings in Anno 1587

Jun 19	John SHISTON & Anne WARREN
Jun 26	William MICHELL & Elizabeth PERRY
Oct 15	Edward WALLES & Margaret FLUDE
Oct 23	John RISE & Ann COTES
Nov 5	Roger DEVAIS & Elizabeth SMYTH
Nov 6	William HALL & Elizabeth TROWE
Nov 19	Richard WEBBE & Alice POOLE

Buryings in Anno 1587

Apr 6	Nicholas ARCHBOLD
Apr 18	John s of Garrard WHORWOOD gent & Dorothye his wife
Apr 29	Thomas son of John CATTERALL & Katheryne his wife
May 15	Agnes wife of William MICHYLL
May 22	Alice d of Richard COXE & Rose his wife
Jul 6	Elenor BENNET
Sep 11	Agnes wife of William HALL

Oct 9	Franncys d of Dorothie EDWARDS
Nov 17	Alice wife of Richard KYRKHAM
Nov 18	Joyce COWLEY of the pish of Wolverhampton
Dec 18	Richard KYRKHAM
Dec 27	Anne COOKE
Dec 30	Richard COOKE
Jan 9	Richard ELLETTE
Jan 12	Humfrey COOKE
Jan 18	Richard s of William CLARKE
Jan 23	Elizabeth wife of John GRANER
Jan 25	John s of Thomas WILDE & Franncys his wife
Feb 2	Elizabeth wife of Will'm MICHELL
Feb 5	Edward OLDNALL
Feb 6	Margery WESTON
Feb 13	Thomas RIDGE
Feb 15	Margaret wife of Thomas HOLLAND
Feb 21	Humfrey LYTHALL the husband of Margery
Mar 5	John COOKE the elder
Mar 14	Margarett wife of John MERE

Christenings in Anno 1588

Apr 17	Elizabeth d of Thomas DIXFILD & Mary his wife
Apr 21	John s of Edward HALE & Anne his wife
Apr 21	Edward s of Humfrey LYTHALL & Johane his wife
Apr 21	Thomas s of John CHAPMAN & Agnes his wife
May 21	Edward s of Garrard WHORWOOD gent & Dorothe his wife
Jun 23	John s of Roger SELVESTER & Elenor his wife
Aug 10	Robert s of John RICE & Alice his wife
Aug 25	William s of Henry TEYLOR & Anne his wife
Sep 1	Richard & Joane the children of Roger MICHELL & Anne his wife
Sep 14	Marie d of Thomas COLE Clarke & Mary his wife
Sep 29	Jane d of John LYTHALL & Johane his wife
Oct 6	John s of Jefferey GARRET & Anne his wife
Oct 6	Anne d of Thomas BANNESTER & Agnes his wife
Oct 13	Thomas s of Humfrey KETLEY & Isabell his wife
Oct 13	Johane d of Richard BARNET & [blank] his wife
Nov 10	Johane d of Richard HILL & Agnes his wife
Nov 17	Humfrey s of Thomas WESTLEY & Joice his wife
Nov 24	Thomas s of John MADSTARD & Johane his wife
Dec 1	William s of Humfrey HARRYS & Dorothe his wife
Dec 8	Richard s of Roger DEVOES & Elizabeth his wife
Dec 1	Elizabeth d of Roger MOYSES & Katherine his wife
Dec 13[?]	Jane d of John CATTERALL & Katherine his wife
Jan 9	Isabell d of Thomas HOLLAND & Johane his wife
Jan 19	Thomas s of Thomas WILDE & Franncys his wife
Jan 19	Anne d of Humfrey HOPE & Elenor his wife
Jan 19	Humfrey s of Franncys BOULTE & Mary his wife
Jan 26	Edward s of Humfrey FOORDE & Margery his wife
Feb [?]	Thomas s of William SELVESTER & Rose his wife

Weddings in Anno 1588

Apr 10	Thomas HOLLAND & Johane ARCHE
May 12	John WHITE & Agnes HILL
Jun 1	Franncys BOLTE & Mary KEMPSTOWE
Jul 1	Thomas HACKET & Margery SHELDON
Oct 3	Thomas PALMER & Isabell HARRYS
Oct 7	Richard WEBBE & Margery BURMAN
Oct 26	Edward ERE & Mary MANSELL
Jan 13	Humfrey VINCENT & Marie SHISTON
Jan 25	Humfrey WEYRE & Elizabeth COOKE
Jan 25	Humfrey HILL & Marie FISHER
Apr 3 1589	Humfrey HOPE & Ellinore KETLEY [entry appears to have been partially crossed through]

Buryings in Anno 1588

Mar 28	Katherine wife of John DICKENS
Apr 2	Thomas s of John COOKE
Apr 5	George NEWNAM
Apr 9	Elenor wife of Wm PRATT
Apr 11	Anne wife of Thomas KETLEY
Apr 11	John DICKENS
Apr 17	Margery wife of Humfrey VINCENT
Apr 19[?]	Elizabeth HILL widowe who was the wife of Edward HILL
Apr 19	William PRATT husband of Elenor PRATT
Apr 27	Jane WEBBE widowe
Apr 30	Thomas DIXFILDE(DITCHFIELD) gent
Apr 30	Isabell d of Robert POTTER
May 8	Richard FITTER s'vant to Richard BRADLEY
May 11	Margery wife of Humfrey BATE
May 13	John CLARKE the husband of Johane CLARKE
May 15	Thomas GROVE the husband of Alice GROVE
May 18	Edward HUGHES
Jun 14	Elenor d of Foulke BROWNE
Jun 14	Alice SCRIVEN widowe
Jun 22	Agnes wife of Richard WEBBE
Jul 3	Henry PENNY
Aug 13	Margaret wife of William ETON
Aug 16	Edward s of Garrard WHORWOOD gent & Dorothe his wife
Aug 19	Alice d of Richard & Elizabeth BYRDE
Sep 6	Alice d of Richard & Agnes WEBB
Sep 14	Anne d of Richard & Agnes WEBB
Sep 17	Johane d of Robert & Julyan BRISCOE
Sep 28	Jane d of Humfrey ROBYNSON
Nov 4	Johane d of Roger & Agnes MICHELL
Oct 6	Martha BATE widowe
Oct 20	Thomas MARSHALL wch was slayne by Richard FLETCHER
Oct 24	Anne d of Thomas BANNESTER
Nov 28	Richard s of Roger & Anne MICHELL
Dec 11	Margaret wife of Richard TOYE

Dec 15   Jane d of John LYTHALL
Oct 25   Jane d of Humfrey TAYLER
Oct 24   Elenor wife of Edward TAYLER
Mar 15   George HILMAN

Christenings in Anno 1589

Mar 30   Franncys d of Richard BAKER & Alice his wife
Mar 30   Philip s of Gefferye GRIFFEN & Dorothe his wife
Mar 31   Thomas s of Thomas HACKETT & Margery his wife
Apr 19   Rose d of Thomas BATE & Forten his wife
Apr 25   Thomas s of William SELVESTER & Rose his wife
Apr 27   Roger s of John WHITE & Anne his wife
May 8   Thomas s of Guy PIXELL & Petronil his wife
May 18   Alice d of Leonard ADDENBROKE & Margaret his wife
May 20   Humfrey s of Richard HARRYS & Meriell his wife
Jun 9   Edward s of Humfrey BOUCKLEY & Ann his wife
Jun 11   Thomas s of Humfrey HILL & Mary his wife
Jun 15   Elizabeth d of Thomas ONGAR & Anne his wife
Jun 15   Theodosia d of Garrard WHORWOOD gent & Dorothe his wife
Jul 20   Richard s of Thomas LEVAR & Jane his wife
Aug 17   Marie d of John ETON & Elizabeth his wife
Sep 29   John s of John LYTHALL & Johane his wife
Oct 12   Elizabeth d of Thomas WARRANE & Isabell his wife
Oct 9   William s of John WILLET & Johane his wife
Nov 26   Richard s of Richard WEBBE & Alice his wife
Nov 29   William s of Richard BYRDE & Jane his wife
Jan 6   Agnes d of Thomas JENNES & Elizabeth his wife
Jan 11   John s of John COPPAM & Margaret his wife
Jan 19   Edward s of John SUTTON als DUDLEY gent & Elizabeth his wife
Mar 8[?] Joyce d of Thomas BANNESTER & Agnes his wife
Mar 20   John s of John SHISTON & Agnes his wife

Weddings in Anno 1589

Apr 10   Griffen JOHNES & Anne CLARKE
May 2   Thomas TIGHE & Margery BANNESTER
Nov 23   Thomas SMYTH & Elizabeth SPARRYE
Feb 7   Roger WESTON & Isabell BICKERSTAFE

Buryings in Anno 1589

Apr 24   Rose d of Thomas BATE & Forten his wife
Jun 10   Edward s of Humfrey BOUCKLEY
Aug 23   Isabell wife of Richard CLARKE
Oct 13   Edward SELVESTER
Oct 25   Mawlde ALDERSEA
Nov 29   An infant the sonne of Agnes HICKMAN wch died wthout the outward sign of baptisme
Nov 30   William WEBBE
Dec 27   Roger MUNDEY

Dec 31	John MERE
Jan 9	Johane PENNY widowe
Feb 1	Thomas WILDE
Feb 28	Edward ALCHURCH

Christenings in Anno 1590

Mar 29	Richard s of John RISE & Anne his wife
Apr 5	Judith d of Richard LYNE & Alice his wife
Apr 12	Anne d of Richard HARRYS & Meriell his wife
Jun 24	Margaret d of Richard KETELSBYE Esquier & Marie his wife
Jul 12	Anne d of Thomas TIGHE & Margery his wife
Jul 26	William s of Griffen JOHNS & Ann his wife
Jul 26	Edward s of Richard BYRDE & Elizabeth his wife
Aug 2	William s of William ADDAMS & Isabell his wife
Aug 9	Robert s of William DECON & Alice his wife
Sep 20	Elenor d of Robert BRISCOE & Julyan his wife
Sep 27	John s of Thomas SMYTH & Elizabeth his wife
Oct 3[?]	Samuell s of Richard ARDEN & Anne his wife
Oct 4	Samuell s of Robert POTTER & Anne his wife
Oct 11[?]	John the sonne of Garrard WHORWOOD gent & Dorothe his wife
Oct 25	Robert the s of Edward VINCENT & Anne his wife
Nov 17	William s of John WARROLL & Elizabeth his wife
Nov 25	Lettys d of John DUDLEY gent & Elizabeth his wife
Nov 29	Mary d of Humfrey VINCENT & Mary his wife
Dec 6	John s of Roger & Elizabeth DEVYES his wife
Dec 13	Margaret d of Edward HALE & Anne his wife
Dec 23	Magdelen d of Thomas ELCOCKE & Margaret his wife
Jan 1	Thomas s of Richard DICKYNS & Rose his wife
Jan [?]	Humfrey s of Richard WEBBE & Alice his wife
Jan 10[?]	Rose d of Humfrey HOPE & Elenor his wife
Jan 14[?]	Richard s of Thomas HOLLAND & Johane his wife
[?]	John s of Thomas HOLLAND & Johane his wife
Jan 27	Elizabeth d of Richard WYLLET & Elizabeth his wife
Jan 27	Anne d of Richard WILLET & Elizabeth his wife
Jan 27	Johane d of Franncys BOLT & Mary his wife
Jan [?]	Katherine d of John COTTERALL & Katherine his wife
Feb 3	Mary d of Richard VINCENT & Elinor his wife
Feb 13[?]	Thomas s of Thomas LYTLEFORD & Elizabeth his wife
Feb 28	John s of Richard HARRYS & Merill his wife
Mar 7	Thomas s of Jeffere JOHNS & Dorothe his wife
Mar 15	Garrard s of John SHISTON & Anne his wife

Weddings in Anno 1590

Apr 25	Lawrence GROVE & Elenor BATE
Jun 12	Humfrey MILLIES & Isabell WALKER
Jan 19	William DOVERDALE & Margaret COOKE

Buryings in Anno 1590

Apr 2	Agnes STEWARD

May 18	Johane wife of Humfrey BATE
May 31	Blandyna d of Richard LYNE & Alice his wife
Jul 13	John ap ROBERT the S'vant of Mr KETLESBYE
Jul 31	Agnes wife of George HILMAN
Oct 5	Robert s of William DEKON & Alice his wife
Oct 18	Anne ELLIOTTE
Oct 18	John s of John COPPAM
Oct 26	Elizabeth wife of Humfrey NYCHOLLE
Nov 10	Thomas s of (blank) CLARKE
Jan 1	Magdalen d of Thomas ELCOCKE & Margaret his wife
Feb 1	An infant the sonne of Thomas WILDE & Franncys his wife
Feb 3	Thomas WATTES
Feb 10	Mary d of Richard VINSENT
Feb 19	Richard s of Thomas HOLLAND & Johane his wife
Feb 26	William FORDE
Mar 12	Johane BYRDE
Mar 16	An infant the sonne of John WILLETT & Johane his wife
Mar 17	Anne d of Richard WILLETT & Elizabeth his wife
Mar 20	Elizabeth READE
Mar 23	Thomas RUMNEY

Christenings in Anno 1591

Mar 28	Richard s of Richard HILL & Anne his wife
Mar 28	Richard s of John CORBET & Elizabeth his wife
May 14	Margaret d of William DOVERDALE & Margaret his wife
[?] 015	Richard s of Thomas MOSELEY & Jone his wife
Jun 27	Jone d of Richard BARNET & [blank] his wife
Aug 28	Richard s of John LYTHALL
Sep 19	James s of William DEKON
Sep 24[?]	Richard s of Roger WESTON
Nov 28[?]	Isabell LYTHALL was baptised
Feb [?]	Richard s of Humfrey & Margaret FORDE
Feb 21	Magdalen d of Thomas KEV [KEY?]
Mar 12	Anne d of Richard VINCENT
Mar 20	Margaret d of Richard WEBBE

Weddings in Anno 1591

Jul 21	Thomas BACHELER & Johane STEVENS
Aug 1	John STILLYN & Johane MOSELEY
Oct 10	John TAYLER & Margery HOLLOWAY
Oct 30	Franncys BATE & Joyce SHELDON
Nov 12	Humfrey LUCE & Alice READE
[?]	David ap SHINKEN & Margaret COPPAM

Buryings in Anno 1591

Mar 26	Edward s of John CAPMAN & Anne his wife
Apr 9	John INGELEY
Apr 14	Anne TUNKES a poore woman was buryed
Apr 18	Mary d of Humfrey VINSENT & Mary his wife
Apr 25	Elenor NEWNAM

Apr 26	Johane d of Gefferey GARRET & Anne his wife
May 17	Thomas HORSELEY Baylyffe
May 25	Two infants s & d of Lawrence GROVE
May 28	Humfrey BATE
Jun 16	An infant the d of Edward PAYNE & Anne his wife
Jun 23	Katherine GRAVENE the wife of Thomas GRAVENER
Jul 6	Isabell wife of Franncys BATE
Aug 13	Margaret PRAT
Aug 19	Isabell wife of Humfrey WEBBE
Aug 20	John s of Richard HARRYS
Aug 31	John GRAVENER
Sep 13	Rose ARCHBOLD widowe
Dec 3	William KEMPSTOWE & Roger WAKELEM
Dec 25	Johane BATE
Jan 29	Elizabeth WILLET

Christenings in Anno 1592

Apr 2	Richard s of Richard MOSELEY
Apr 2	Elenor d of John WILLET
Apr 9	Garrard s of Humfrey HILL
Apr 23	Anne d of Leonard ADDENBROKE
May 14	William s of William ADDAMS
Jun 4	Alice d of John ETON
Jun 11	Joyce d of Thomas HOLLAND & Johane his wife
Jun 17	Eliz d of John MADSTARD
Mar 4	Richard s of Humfre KETLEY [Added in black ink at bottom of page]
Jul 16	John s of Lawrence GROVE
Jul 23	Magdalen d of Garrard WHORWOOD gent & Dorothe his wife
Aug 14	John s of John PURSLOWE
Sep 24	Richard s of David ap JENKEN
Oct 2	[Blank] s of Isabell GRAVENER Spurius
Oct 15	Anne d of John SMYTH & Katherine
Nov 1	William s of John WHITE & Anne
Nov 5	Alice d of Humfrey TEYLOR & Margery his wife
Dec 10	William s of Humfrey VINSENT & Mary his wife
Dec 17	Joyce d of Thomas SMYTH & Elizabeth his wife
Dec 30	An infant of John CORBETTE
Jan 6	Anne d of Edwarde WEBBE
Feb 13	John s of Richard BYRDE
Mar 11	Margaret d of John SHISTON
Mar 18	Daniell s of William DAVERDALE
Mar 18	Elizabeth the d of a ztaine poore woman

Weddings in Anno 1592

May 6	Humfrey WEBBE & Grace WAKELEM
May 22	William GODDARD & Anne HARRYS
Sep 6	Nicholas WOODDALL & Alice KETLEY
Oct 8	William BYRCH & Johane FRECLINGTON
Oct 15	Richard RAYBOULD & Margery BLOCKLEY

Oct 30   Leonard SHISTON & Anne BYRDE

Buryings in Anno 1592
Apr 1   Franncys wife of Thomas WILDE
Apr 7   Johane KETLEY
May 2   Anne d of Leonard ADDENBROKE
May 18   Anne wife of Robert GARRET
May 20   Anne wife of Robert BATE
         Bryan UNDERHILL was buryed the 15th day of 25th day of May [sic]
Jun 2   Isabell wife of John SELVESTER
Jun 23   Elizabeth wife of Philip PHILIPPS
Jul 3   Henry TAYLER
Jul 15   John PHILIPPS
Jul 18   Margaret d of Richard WEBBE & Alice his wife
Aug 18   Elizabeth d of John MADSTARD
Dec 13   Margery wife of John TEYLOR
Dec 29   John ANDREWES
Feb 17   Humfrey WHITE

Christenings in Anno 1593
Apr 8   Zacharias s of William RUMNEY
Apr 8   Franncys s of Geffery GARRET
Apr 8   Anne d of Robert BRISCOE
Apr 8   Humfrey s of Richard WEBBE
Apr 9   Margery d of Guy PIXELL
Apr 17   Nicholas s of Richard WEBBE
Apr 17   Elizabeth d of Humfrey HOPE
May 11   Charles s of Richard HARRYS
May 13   Meriell d of Thomas BYRDE & Margery his wife
Jun 10   Anne d of Edwarde WEBBE
Jul 8[?] Roger s of Roger WESTON
Jul 15   Johane d of John COOKE
Jul 23   (Blank) the s of William BYRCH
Oct 4   John s of Richard MOSELEY
Nov 9   Isabell d of Richard BYRDE
Jan 27   Abell s of William SHELBURNE
Mar 10   Edwarde s of Richard BARNET
Mar 13   Jane d of Humfrey GROVE

Weddings in Anno 1593
[None]

Buryings in Anno 1593
Apr 10   Elenor MOSELEY widowe
Apr 11   [Blank] BERE widowe
Apr 12   Elenor wife of Nicholas DARBYE
May 13   Elenor wife of Edwarde TAYLER
Jun 12   Elizabeth wife of Richard BRADLEY
Jul 24   Anne d of Edward WEBBE

Jul 28	Johane d of John COOKE
Aug 5	Isabell wife of John SANDE
Aug 9	Isabell wife of Richard HAWES
Aug 10	Thomas s of Edwarde TEYLER
Nov 21	Thomas MOSELEY
Feb 10	Robert GARRET

Christenings in Anno 1594

Apr 11	Mawde d of John DUDLEY gent & Elizabeth his wife
May 7	William s of Garrard WHORWOOD gent & Dorothe his wife
May 20[?]	Garrard s of Richard HARRYS & Merill his wife
Jun 7	John s of Humfrey WEBBE & Grace his wife
Jul 21	John s of Edward WOOD & Christabell his wife
Jul 28	Humfrey s of John LYTHALL & Johane his wife
Jul 28	Elenor d of John TEYLER & Agnes his wife
Aug 18	Johane d of Richard WEBBE & Alice his wife
Sep 15	Donsable d of Margaret NORRYS
Oct 20	John s of John ETON & Elizabeth his wife
Oct 20	William s of William DEACON & Alice his wife
Oct 27	Elizabeth d of Richard HILL
Nov 3	William s of John PURSLOWE & Elizabeth his wife
Nov 3	John s of John BANNISTER
Nov 24	Joyce d of Edward HILL & Isabel his wife
Nov 19	[Blank] s of Franncys BOLT
Jan 6	Humfrey s of Richard VINSENT & Elenor his wife
Jan 6	Rose d of Richard VINSENT & Elenor his wife
Feb 16	Henry s of Humfrey FORDE & Margery his wife
Feb 23	Margery d of Edward HALE
Feb 23	Johane d of John SMYTH
Mar 2	Thomas s of John WILLET
Mar 2	Richard s of William GARRET
Mar 2	Johane d of William BYRCH
Mar 2	Johane d of Franncys FRECLINGTON

Weddings in Anno 1594

May 6	William GARRET & Anne LANGMORE
Oct 28	Richard HOTCHKYS & Anne COOKE
Oct 29	Richard STURMY & Jane GARRET

Buryings in Anno 1594

Apr 5	Agnes wife of William ATKYS
Jun 7	Joyce wife of Richard COPPAM
Jun 27	Alice d of Thomas MOSELEY
Aug 1	Elenor d of John TAYLER & Agnes his wife
Sep 28	Thomas CLARKE
Sep 29	Donsable d of Margaret NORRYS
Dec 3	William ETON

Christenings in Anno 1595

| May 11 | Humfrey s of Humfrey VINCENT |

Jun 29   Marie d of Richard HARRYS
Jul 10   Johane d of Guy PIXELL
Sep 29   Edward s of William MOSELEY
Oct 5   Josias s of John SHISTON
Oct 19   Thomas s of Thomas KEY
Nov 2   Thomas s of William RUMNEY
Nov 16 Martha d of John RICE
Feb 15   Richard s of Richard WEBBE
Feb 22   Jane d of Thomas SMYTH
Feb 22   Robert s of Richard BYRD & Jane his wife
Mar 7   Richard s of Thomas GRYFFEN
Mar 21   Marie d of Thomas WAKELEM
Mar 21   Anne d of Richard MOSELEY
          [Written along the margin in different ink:]
          Anne d of Homfre KETLEY was baptised one lamas daie

Weddings in Anno 1595
Sep 28   Thomas BAKER & Anne MICHELL
Oct 6   John TAYLER & Cicelye FISHER
Feb 23   John FOULER & Alice BAKE

Buryings in Anno 1595
Feb 23   Margaret WHITE
Mar 22   Anne wife of John SHISTON the yonger

Christenings in Anno 1596
May 15 Elenor d of Edward WOOD & Christabell his wife
May 24 Sara d of Richard WILLET & Elizabeth his wife
Jun 3   An infant of Henry STRANGE & Franncys his wife bapt & buried
Jun 20   Anne d of Richard ARDEN & Anne his wife
Jun 20   Isabell d of James TYRPEN & Elenor his wife
Aug 1   Margaret d of Richard HARRYS & Merill his wife
Aug 1   Johane d of [blank] BLUCKE & Mary his wife
Aug 2   Mary d of Richard RAYBOULD & Margery his wife
Aug 8   Humfry s of Roger WESTON & Isabell his wife
Aug 8   Isabell d of John WHITE & Anne his wife
Aug 29   Barnabas s of Mr FRENSHAM & Anne his wife
Sep 12   John s of Humfrey VINCENT & Mary his wife
Sep 14   John s of Thomas HACKET & Margery his wife
Oct 17   Richard s of Franncys FREGLINGTON & Joane his wife
Jan 2   Elenor d of Richard LYTHELL & [blank] his wife
Feb 13   John s of William RUMNEY & Joyce his wife
Mar 20   Richard s of John PURSLOWE & Isabell his wife
Mar 24   [blank] s of Franncys BOULT & Mary his wife

Weddings in Anno 1596
May 3   Dennys HILL & Elenor LUCE
Jun 22   Humfrey LUCE & Joyce BATE
Jun 28   John TAYLER & Joyce MOSELEY

Buryings in Anno 1596

Apr 24	[Blank] the wife of John WAKELEM
May 14	Margaret INGLISH widowe
May 27	[Blank] d of Humfrey HOPE
Jul 20	Anne TIGH widowe
Aug 26	Isabell wife of John SHISTON the eldest
Sep 19	Humfrey HARRYS
Sep 20	Sara s of Richard & Elizabeth WILLET
Oct 27	Joane BLUCKE
Nov 10	John SMYTH
Nov 19	Lewes (blank)
Dec 29	[Blank] the wife of Thomas LUCE
Jan 19	Richard COPPAM
Mar 9	William HALL
Mar 12	An old woman in Compton was buried

Christenings in Anno 1597

Apr 17	Edward s of Mr Garrard WHORWOOD & Dorothe his wife
Apr 17	(Blank) the dau of (blank) & his wife
Apr 29	Henry s of Richard VINSENT & Elenor his wife
May 8[?]	Elizabeth d of John LYTHALL & Johane his wife
Jul 17	Elizabeth d of Richard HARRYS & Merill his wife
Sep 4	Isabell d of Humfrey HOPE & Elenor his wife
Sep 25	Anne d of William BYRCH & Jone his wife
Sep 29	Mary d of Humfrey LUCE & Joyce his wife
Oct [?]	Merill d of Thomas CLARKE & [blank] his wife
Nov 28 [?]	Margaret d of Richard WEBBE & Alice his wife
Dec 11	Humfrey s of John ETON & Elizabeth his wife
Dec 11	Elenor d of Dyonise HILL & Elenor his wife
Feb 5	Abigall d of William SHELBURNE & Elizabeth his wife

Weddings in Anno 1597

Nov 14	Edward MOSELEY & Elizabeth BRETTEL

Buryings in Anno 1597

Apr 15[?]	Richard s of Richard LYNE
Apr 17	Widowe WAKELEM & a poore strange childe were buryed
Apr 28	Richare WYLLET
May 1[?]	Josias SHISTON
Apr 30[?]	Dorothe DARBY
May 5	Henry VINCENT
May 2[?]	John SHISTON the elder
Jun 29	John HALE
Jul 2[?]	Alice GROVE widowe
Jul 30	Clement ORDYMERE widowe
Sep 23	Joyce d of Thomas HOLLAND
Oct 8	Elizabeth d of Richard HARRYS
Oct 21	Richard s of Edward HILL
Oct 23	Dorothe the wife of Edward BLOCKLEY
Nov 2	Anne d of Edward HILL

Nov 12[?] Isabell FOORD widowe
Dec [?] Margaret BOLAND
Dec 19 Johane COOKE
Jan 18 David JOHNS
Feb 11 Nicholas DARBY
Feb [?] Jane d of Thomas ONGAR
Feb 13[?] Anne FYDKYN
Feb 17[?] Thomas HIGGES
Feb 23 Dyonise SUGAR & John SUGAR
Mar 15 Humfrey BATE of Whittington

Christenings in Anno 1598

Jun 4   John s of Richard HARRYS & Merill his wife
Jun 15 Richard s of John WILLET
Jul 4   Franncys s of John BANNISTER
Jul 16 William s of William DAVERDALE
Jul 25[?] Richard s of Stephen WEDGE
[?]   Humfrey s of Humfrey FOORDE
        [The next entry is at the foot of the page in a different ink:]
        Elizabeth d of Hamfree KETLEY was baptised the sevent daie of March
Aug 2   Mary d of William DECON
Aug 10 William s of Edward WOOD
Oct 17 Richard s of John SMYTH & Katherine his wife
Oct 22 Thomas s of Thomas WAKELEM
Nov 15 John s of Richard WEBBE
Dec 2   Elizabeth d of Edward COMBER
Dec 10 Richard s of Humfrey GROVE
Nov 9   Merill d of Humfrey HILL
Jan 21 Humfrey s of Franncys FRECKLINGTON & Johane his wife

Weddings in Anno 1598

Oct 22 Edward COMBER & Agnes ROBYNSON

Buryings in Anno 1598

Mar 30 Elenor HILL widowe
Apr 3   Elizabeth wife of John KIGHTLEY
Apr 9   Richard s of Humfrey FORD
Jun 7   Thomas s of Richard HANCOXE
Jun 7   Elizabeth wife of William COOCKE
Jul 19 Johane SPARRY
Oct 14 John s of John SHISTON
Oct 28 John s of Richard HARRYS
Nov 19 Franncys BATE
Jan 26 Christabell d of Thomas HILMAN
Feb 28 George KIGHTLEY

[Many of the following pages are badly stained and difficult to read]

Christenings in Anno 1599

Apr 25[?]	Edward s of Edward MOSELEY & Elizabeth his wife
May [?]	Isabell d of Humfrey WEBBE & Grace his wife
May 10	Jane d of Richard BYRDE & Jane his wife
Jul 4	Amy d of John RICE & Anne his wife
Jul 8	Elienor d of Franncys BOLT & Marie his wife
Aug 21	Agnes d of John DUDLEY Esq & Elizabeth his wife
Sep [?]	William s of John MOLE & Isabell his wife
Sep 10	Edward s of Roger WESTON & Isabell his wife
Oct 21	Mary d of John STYLLEN & Johane his wife
[?]	John s of John KIGHTLEY & [blank] his wife
Nov 10	Marie d of Alice BLOCKLEY his wife
Dec[?] 7	John s of John TEYLOR & Joyce his wife
Dec 8	Margaret d of Edward WEBBE & [blank] his wife
Jan 26[?]	Elizabeth d of Thomas GRYFFEN & Elizabeth his wife
Jan 26[?]	Felice d of Henry STRANGE & Franncys his wife
Jan 26[?]	Elizabeth d of Edmond NOXAN & Anne his wife
[?]	Richard s of Richard HARRYS & Merill his wife
[?]	Katherine d of Thomas SMYTH & Elizabeth his wife

Weddings in Anno 1599

[?]	Thomas HILMAN & Amy HILL
[?]	Hughe WESTON & Elizabeth HOPKYS
[?]	John TOMMAS & Joyce BANNISTER
[?]	Edmond NOXON & Anne BURGEN
[?]	John SMYTH & Elizabeth LOVE
[?]	Humfrey TIGH & Joyce BATE
Oct 28	Thomas HICKMAN & Lucie OCLEY
Feb 4	William ARCHE & Alyce BLOCKLEY
Mar 25	Edward COMBER & Elizabeth LANGMORE
May 16[?]	John BAKER & Jane SPARRY [Entry inserted later]

Buryings in Anno 1599

Mar 28	Thomas BUTLER
Apr 21	Anne HALL widowe
May 1	Elizabeth d of Edward COMBER & Agnes his wife
Apr 10	Franncys WILKENSON
Jul 16	Amy d of John RICE & Anne his wife
Nov 3	John RYDER
Jan 7	Thomas HILMAN
Feb 11	Elenor SPARRYE
Mar 10	Elizabeth SMYTH
[?] 12	Thomas CHILTON

[The next two entries are added on the stained & otherwise blank lower half of the page]

Christenings in Anno 1600

	Thomas s of John & Mary LONGMOORE
Nov 16	Elizabeth d of Thomas & Amye HILLMAN

© Staffordhire Parish Registers Society

[Top of new page and in a different hand]
Feb 17   Elizabeth d of William ARCHE
Feb 23   Mary d of Richard LITHALL & Cathern his wife
Mar 1   Meriall d of Edward COMBER & Elizabeth his wife
Mar 1   Marye d of John WILLET & Joane his wife
Mar 7   Humfrey s of Richard MOSELEY
Mar 2   Edward s of John POWELL
Mar 21   Anne d of Willm DEKON
Apr [?]   Joane d of John BAKER

[Entries below this are very badly stained in the middle of the page]
Weddings in Anno 1600
[?]   Roger SAXONE & Alce MANSELL
[?]   Richard GESTE & Mary PHILLIPES

Buryings in Anno 1600
Dec 28   M[?] ASTELLON widowe
Oct [?]   John s of William WILKINSON
Feb [?]   Margaret wife of John SHISTON
[?]   Thomas HULLANND
Feb 23   Jane wife of Foulke BROWNE
[?]   Isabell d of Willm D....
Mar [?]   Elizabeth CLARKE widowe
Mar [?]   Edward s of John LYTHALL

[Page stained with ink]
Christenings in Anno 1601
[?]   Edward s of John RICE & Anne[?] his wife
[?]   Ancarer d of Richard WEBBE & [?] his wife
Jun 3   Marye d of John SMYTH & Elizabeth his wife
Jul 7   Elizabeth d of John SMYTH & [?] his wife
Sep 27   John s of Roger WESTON & Isabell his wife
Sep 27   Mary d of Edward MOSELEY & Elizabeth his wife
[blank]   Judeth d of Thomas WAKELAM
Nov 30   George s of Edward COMBER & Anne his wife
Dec 28   John s of Edward SYCH
Jan 2   Humfrey s of Humfrey KETLEY
Jan 18   Jane d of Humfrey LUSE
Jan 28   Rose d of Margret BAKER – Patre ignotam
Mar 15   John s of Franncys FRECKELLTON
Mar 15   Humfrey s of Edward WEBBE

Buryings in Anno 1601
Jul 20   Mary d of John WILLET
May 4   Elizabeth d of Humfrey HALL
Oct [?]   Johane LONERT [letter O altered; might be LENERT]
Jan 10   Elizabeth d of Willm DEAKON

Christenings in Anno 1602

Aug 22 Humfry s of John BAKER [Entry inserted at beginning in different ink]
Oct 24 Jane d of Humfrey FOORD
Nov [?] Humfrey s of Thomas HILLMAN

[The following entries continue with no heading]

Nov [?] Margery wife of Humfrey FOORD buried
Dec 3 Humfrey FOORD
Dec 24 Johan wife of Thomas DEONRS[?]
Apr 30 Alice d of John KITLEY
May 3 Willm s of M WHITTBROKE
May 13 Lettice d of John DUDELY Esq was buryed the 13th daie of Maie

Christenings in Anno 1603

[?] 26 Edwart s of Richard RAYBOULD was bapt Mar [This entry inserted in different ink under title]
Jul 17[?] Dorothy d of John MOLLE
Jul 25 John s of John WILLET
Aug 8 Johan d of Mr SHELBURN

Buryings in Anno 1603

Aug 5 Johan wife of John WILLET

Christenings in Anno 1603

[There appears to be one entry unreadable]

Aug [?] Jone d of Richard BYRD
Sep 5[?] Isabell d of Willm DAVARDALE
Sep 19[?] Magdalen d of Edward NOXON
Dec [?] Willm s of Willm POWELL
Oct 7 John s of Robert CLARKE

Buryings in Anno 1603

Aug 24 Richard s of Richard HARRIS
Sep 1 Mary d of Mr WHITTBROKE
Aug 5 John s of John WILLET
Jan 29 Anne COPPAM
Aug 25 Willm ATKISSE

Weddings in Anno 1603

Jul [?] John TYBBUT & Anne LYNE
Nov 2 Humfrye LANGMORE & Elinor BATE

Christenings in Anno 1604

Isabell the dau of Dionys MEIS(?) & Catherine his wife was baptised the 25th of December [Inserted under title in different ink]
Dec 25 Elizabeth d of Roger WESTON & Isabell his wife
Sep [?] Willm s of Thomas AGBOROW & Elizabeth his wife

© Staffordhire Parish Registers Society

Sep [?]   Elizabeth d of Edward MOSELEY & Elizabeth his wife
May [?]   Richard s of Humfrey HILL
Jul [?]   Thomas s of Thomas CLARKE & Johan his wife
Jul [?]   Thomas s of Richard MOSELEY & Anne his wife

Weddings in Anno 1604
Aug [?]   George SILLITO & Margaret COMBER
[?]   Richard BATE & Anne CLARKE widow

[The next entries have no heading]
Oct 21   Garrard s of Willm RUMNEY & Joyce his wife
Nov 4   Mary d of Willm BROOKE & Johan his wife
Nov 11   Joyce d of William DAVERDALE & Margaret his wife
Nov 18   Richard s of John MOLLE & Isabell his wife
Dec 2   Thomas s of Thomas HILLMAN & Amye his wife
Dec 16   Elizabeth d of Humfrey JURDEN & Jane his wife
Jan 6   Martha d of Roberte KINSON
Feb 4[?] Anne d of Stephen WEDGE & Jane his wife
Mar 10   Joyce d of Humffrey ROBINSON & Isabell his wife
Mar 17   Joyce d of Edward COMBER & Anne his wife

Buryings in Anno 1604
Sep 7   Phillip PHILLIPS
Nov [?]   Margaret d of Edward COMBER
Dec [?]   Margery LANGMORE
Feb [?]   Jane wife of Stephen WEDGE

Christenings in Anno 1605
[All of this section is very badly stained]
Apr 2   Joyce d of Edwarde SITCH
[?]   Richard s of William MOSELEY & Jane his wife
[?]   John s of John POWELL & Magdalen his wife
May 30   Isabell d o of One APPEWE & Elizabeth his wife
Aug 4   Elizabeth d of Richard BATE & Anne his wife
Aug 25   Theadotia d of John WILLET & Beatridg his wife
Sep 1   Elizabeth d of Humffrey BICHE(?) & Brydget his wife
[?]   Richard s of Edward CUMBR & Elizabeth his wife
[?]   John s of Henry LANGMORE & Margery his wife
[?]   Humfrey & Robert sons of John PURSLOWE & Isabell his wife
Feb [?]   Elizabeth d of John BAKER & Jane his wife
Feb [?]   Johane d of John POWELL & Margaret his wife
[?]   Anne d of Richard BYRD & Jane his wife
[?]   Franncys s of Geffery CARKE & Margery his wife
[?]   James the s of [blank] & [blank] his wife
[?]   Humfrey s of Humfrey LUCE & Joyce his wife
[?]   [?] s of John DAVIS & Elizabeth his wife

Weddings in Anno 1605
Jun   Nathanyell & Margaret the dau of Margaret SELVESTER

Dec   Franncis [?] & Elnours dau of Thomas HILLMAN

Buryings in Anno 1605
- Aug 10   John HOLLYDAYE bur
- Aug 18   M GOJARD
- Oct 1   Richard s of Thomas CLARKE
- Dec 27[?] Robert CROSS
- Jan 4   Humfrey WORRAT
- [?]   Elizabeth d of Robert BRISCOW
- Mar [?]   A base child of Edward SYTCH
- [?]   Humfrey VINCENT
- [?]   Willm DICKYNES

[The next entry is hidden under a blot but the first part seems to read:]
    John & Elizabeth [Blank]

Christenings in Anno 1606
- Jul 6   Jane d of William ARCHE & Allice his wife
- Aug 3   Jane d of John LANGMORE & Marye his wife
- Aug 10   Richard s of Edward WEBBE
- Sep 19   Margaret d of Franncys FRECKELLTON & Johan his wife
- Oct 5   Mary d of Thomas HILLMAN & Amy his wife
- Oct 5   Richard s of Richard TEARNE
- Oct 23   Humfrey s of Thomas CLARKE
- Dec 7   John s of Robert KINGSTON
- Feb 6   Jeffery s of Jeffery MASON

Weddings in Anno 1606
- Jun 15   Samuell CUMBR & Magdalen WILKINSON
- Jun 22   William CURTLER & Allice RAVENHILL
- Jul 6   Richard TEARNE & Margery YORKE
- Aug 19   Thomas WAKLAM & Anne PATCHET
- Aug 20   William HALE & Anne HILL
- Sep 29   William SMYTH & Anne PEARSON

Buryings in Anno 1606
- Sep 19   Elizabeth wife of Thomas SMYTH
- Sep 28   Edward LITLEFORD
- Dec 26   Martha d of Thomas BACH & Jone his wife
- Mar 6   John DICKINS

[In a different hand from this point]
The Christenings in Anno 1607
- Jul 19   Humferie the s of Dennis HILLMAN & Anne his wife
- Jul 19   Jone d of Richard BATE
- [?]   Robt s of Humferie WEBBE
- Aug 23   John s of Edward HILL
- Aug 23   Isabell d of John MOULE
- Dec 6   Henrie s of Allen WEBSTER
- Dec 13   Margaret d of John WILLET
- Jan 30   Humpherie s of Edward COMBER

Feb 21　Edward s of Richard LYTHALL
Mar 11　Marie d of Hercules LOûTTON

Marriages 1607

Apr 16　John WOOLEY & Marie VINCENT
Dec 17[?]　Franncis BIRCHE & Elizabeth CLIFFORD
Jan 21　John PITCHFORK & Marie HILLMAN
Feb 11　John KINNERSLEY & Janne JOWIS

Buryings in Anno 1607

May 15　Magdalyn Ladie WHORWOOD
May 18　Franncis LANGHLEY
May 19　Thomas CLARKE
Dec 26　Margerie ORDYMER
Feb 17　John GIRTH
Apr 10　John s of Edward HILL & Eliner
[?]　John SYMONS

Christenings 1608

Jun 12　Thomas s of Jefferie COOKE
Jun 19　John s of Edward SITCHE
Jul 24　Richard s of Humphrie LUCE
Aug 21[?]　Joyce d of John LITHALL
Sep 11　John s of Edward WATKISS
Oct 23　Joane d of Willm SHELBURNE
Oct 30　Richard s of Willm POWELL
Dec 11　Edward s of Roger DEVIS
Feb 20　Elizabeth d of Edward BAMBURIE

Marriages 1608

Oct 12　Rychard EVANS & Joanne BAKER

Burialls 1608

Jun 26　John s of Edward SITCHE
Jul 26　Thomas KETLY
Oct 4　Margerie d of John SMITHE
Nov 11　Marie d of Thomas WAKELYN

Christenings 1609

Jun 11　John s of John LONGEMORE
Jun 18　Franncis s of Edward HILL
Jul 9　Anne d of Thomas HILLMAN
Jul 18　Marie d of Richard BATE
Aug 13　Thomas s of [blank] NEWMAN
Aug 27　Willm s of Willm CURTLER
Nov 12　Jane d of John SMITHE
Nov 19　Humfrie s of John WILLET
Nov 19　Dina d of Hugh POTTER
Nov 19　Merriall d of Richard WHITE
Nov 19　Anne d of Edward MOSELEY

Jan 21   Magdalyn d of Humfrie HILL
Mar 10   Elizabeth d of Edward BAMBURIE   [This entry squeezed in]
Mar 23   Sara d of Edward WATKIS
Apr 23   Abigal JURDEN
Jun 12   John s of Walter THATCHER
Jun 12   Margaret d of John POWELL
Jul 15   Nicholas s of Humfry LUCE
Jul 15   Isabell d of Allyn WEBSTER
Aug 30[?] [Blank] d of Humfry LYNE
Sep 2   Beteridge d of Humfry BACH

Burialls 1609

Oct 24   Grace wife of Humfrie WEBBE
Oct 27   Edward BLOCKLEY
Jan [?]   Anne d of Willm DEACON
Jan 24   Joyce wife of John TAYLOR
Jan 29   Meriall d of Richard WHITE
Feb 2   [Blank] LITHALL widow
Feb 16   Margaret WALLIS
Mar 20   Thomas LITHALL
Mar 22   Thomas CRIPPIN buried
Mar 24   William [Blank] Servant to Thomas WARREN

Burialls 1610

Apr 20   Merriall SMITH
May 23   John YORKE
May 27   John JONES
Aug 28   Richard HANCOX
Nov 2   Richard ARDEN
Nov 22   Anne wife of Richard WARROLE
Nov 24   Richard ARDEN
Jan 19   Robt BRISCOE
Feb 20   Joane TAYLOR

Christenings 1610

Nov 4   John LOWTON
Dec [?]   Charles s of Richard WHITE
Dec 23   John s of John THOMAS
Dec 30   Jane CURTLER baptised being the daughter of Willm CURTLER
Jan 17   Joyce d of Jeffery COOKE
Jun 18   Robert s of William BROXHOLME & Isabell his wife

Marriages 1610

Nov 3   John TAYLOR & Martha BATE

Marriages 1611

Apr 2   John CORBET & Margery TAYLOR
Apr 15   Richard WARROLE & Anne JUNELY[?]
Oct 22[?] Thomas HILL & Marie HILL

Nov 16 Edward WALLIS & Christian BANNESTER
Nov 16 Edward WALLIS & Christian BANNESTER [entered twice]
Nov 25[?] Edward CLARKE & (blank)
Jan 20 John HARRIS & Elizabeth WILKINSON

Christenings 1611

Apr 18 Willm s of John BROOKE
May 7 Willm s of Willm BROXAM
May 22 Janne d of Edward WATKIS
Jul 7 Isabell d of Thomas SMITH
Jul 21 John s of Thomas HILLMAN
Jul 28 Mary d of John BADGER
Sep 14 Mary d of John COOKE
Sep 29 Thomas s of Humfrey HOPE
Oct 13 Roger & Humfrey sons of John MOLE
Oct 20 Joyce d of [blank] WHITCOM [Entry written around a hole in the page]
Oct 27 Isabell d of John LUCE
Dec 8 Sara d of John WILLET
Dec 12 John s of William SHELBURNE
Dec 20 [Blank] d of John SILVESTER
Mar 9 Olyver PAYNE bapt
Mar 10 Willm s of Edward COMBER

Burialls 1611

Apr 15 Anne wife of Humfrey BATE
May 4 Elizabeth wife of Richard BIRD
Jul 7 Anne GIRTH
Jul 26 Thomas SYMKIS
Sep 2 Margaret d of Humfrey VINCENT
Oct 8 Alice WILKINSON widdowe
Oct 4 Willm s of John BROOKE
Oct 6 Isabell d of Thomas SMITH
Sep 26 Joanne HARRIS
Dec 6 Humfrey s of Richard BIRD
Dec 8 Mary wife of Humfrey HILL
Dec 25 John WORROLE
Mar 12 Franncis BIRCH

Christenings 1612

Apr 13 Margery d of Jephrey COOKE & Margery his wife
May 31 Humfrey s of John LONGMORE & Mary his wife
Apr 12 Edward s of William BROXHOLME & Isabell
  [At this point there is a gap which may contain faded entries]
Aug 13 Jane d of John TOYE & Merriall his wife [written around a hole in the page]
Sep 20 Edward s of Humfrey JURDEN & Jane his wife
Nov 19[?] John the s of George WOOLRIGE & Jane his wife
Nov 22 Marie d of Arthure SWANNEWICK & Dorothee his wife
Dec 6 Jane d of Edward MOSELEY & Elizabeth his wife

Dec 13   Edward s of Humfrey LYNE & Elizabeth his wife
Dec 13   Jane d of John COOKE & Joyce his wife
Jan 24   Humfrey s of John CORBETT & Margery his wife
Jan 30   Anne d of William TAYLER & Anne his wife
Mar 4   John s of Richard HULLE & Elizabeth his wife
Mar 9   Susanna d of Humfrey DICKENS
Mar 13[?]   James s of William BROXHOLME & Elizabeth his wife

Weddings 1612

Apr 26   William TAYLER & Anne MARSHE
May 24   William JOHNSONNE & Catherine CATERALL
Jun 8   William BAYES & Margett VINCENT
Jun 21   John HOLLAND & Joan HARRISON
Sep 28   Walter LEYTON & Catherine HANCOXE
Jun 8   Humfrey DICKENS & Jane BATE

Burialls 1612

Apr 2   Joes NEWNA
Apr 14   Franncis TOY
Jul 22   Thomas s of John BROOKS & Myrriall his wife
Aug 13   John s of Thomas RUMNEY & Anne his wife
Aug 18   Franncis YONGER
Sep 24   Leonard ADENBROOKE
Oct 20   Roger CESTAR
Nov 27   Willia GRIFFIN
Nov 28   Elizabeth a spinner at SISTONS
Dec 16   John CATERALL
Feb 21   Catheren wyfe of William JOHNSONNE
Mar 8   John HARRIS
Mar 22   Susanna DICKINS

Christenings 1613

Apr 8[?]   Richard s of John BAKER & Jane his wife
Apr 11   Samuell s of Richard BATE & Anne his wife
Apr 18   Jane d of Thomas HILL & Mary his wife
May 2   Susanna d of John BRISKOWE & Mary his wife
Jul 25   Susanna d of John BROOKE & Isabell his wife
Feb 20   George WATKIS was baptized being the sonne of Edward WATKIS & Margerie his wife
         [The above entry is crossed through with an "X" at the beginning & the end of the two line insertion]
Aug 22   Richard s of Walter LEIGHTON & Catherine his wife
Aug 24   John s of Richard WORROLL & Eve his wife
Oct 31   Alen s of Arthure SWANEWICKE & Dorothee his wife
Nov 28   Anne d of Humfrey BATES & Bridget his wife
Feb 20   George s of Edward WATKIS & Margery his wife
Mar 20   Humfrey s of John HOLLEYS & Alice his wife
Apr 10[?] 1613 [3 altered to 4] Jane d of Richard BANNISTER & Margret his wife
Apr 27 1613/4 Judith d of John SILVESTER & Alice his wife

Weddings 1613

May 27	Richard BANISTER & Margaret NORIS
Jun 20	John HOLLIES & Als CATHERALL
Jul 20	John PHILLIPS & Judith LYNE
Jul 20	Humfrey TYGHE & Elinor SUGER
Oct 7	Thomas TAYLOR & Anne BENNET
Oct 28	Francis TOMASIN & Fortune TOYE

Burialls 1613

Mar 30	Margaret YORKE
Apr 2[?]	John ORDIMER
Apr 5	Joyce TYGHE
Apr 30	Richard PHILLIPS
May 6	Maudlen BATE
May 16	Richard BARNET
Jun 6	Margaret BARNET
Aug 8	Margery DARBIE
Aug 15	Als ARCHE
Sep 19	Margery BROWNE
Sep 24	Thomas RAYNOLDS
Dec 2	Humfrey BATE
Dec 5	Richard BATE
Dec 9	Margery TEARNE
Jan 4	Anne wife of William GARRIT
Jan 7	Isabell wyffe of Humfrey ROBINSON
Jan 11	Sisley RYDER
Feb 24	Margret CRYPPIN
Apr 9 1614	Pearce EVANS

Deare and looving father my most humbel duti first of all [...?...] Son sed unto you hopping that you are in good [An unfinished message written at the foot of page]

Christenings 1614

Churchwardens Edward WATKYS & Humfrey DICKINS

May 2	Elinor d of Humfrey DICKINS & Jane his wife
Jul 10	Als d of William CUTLER & Als his wife
Jul 14	Anne d of Thomas BATE & Susanna his wife
Jul 17	Walter s of Thomas WHITECOME & Elizabeth his wife
Aug 7	Anne d of Martin BLOUDWORTE & Mary his wife
Aug 8	Jane d of Thomas TAYLOR & Anne his wife
Sep 12	Mary d of William BROXHOLME & Isabell his wife
Oct 2	Humfrey s of John RAVENELL & Margery his wife
Mar 12	Mary d of John BRISCOWE & Margery his wife

1615

Apr 2	Anne d of Richard & Elizabeth HALE
Apr 2	Mary d of John & Elenor WILLETTS of Whittington
Apr 10	Richard s of Richard & Elizabeth GARRETT

1614

Nov 23   Jane d of John & Jane WILLIAMS
Dec 4   Elizabeth d of John & Margery CORBETT
Jan 8   Humfrey s of John & Judith PHILLIPPS
Jan 14   Edward childe of Joan BOULTE Illegitimate
Jan 20   Catherine dau of Als WORRALL Illegitimate

Weddings 1614

Sep 17   George WHITE & Anne JONES
Nov 28   John FILIAN & Margaret GREENE

Burialls 1614

May 12   Als WILKINSON
May 15   Thomas BADGER
May 18   Maudlen POWELL
Dec 16   Elizabeth wife of Richard BRADLEY
Dec 28   Isabell WILLETT
Jan 8   John RAVENILL
Jan 10   A childe of Edward WEBBS
Jan 31   Elizabeth CORBETT
Feb 3   Joan CUTLER
Feb 4   Catherin WARRALL an illegitimate childe was buried
Jul 11   Catherin FARMORE of Clibery was buried
Aug 10   An infante daughter to Franncis THOMASIN & Fortune his wife
Aug 12   Fortune the wife of Francis THOMASIN
Aug 21   Wydow BARNET
Sep 28   Laurence RIDLEY
Oct 27 [28?] George WATKIS
Feb 13   Evan CADWALADER
Feb 15   Humfrey RAVENELL
         Edward WATKIS, Humfrey DICKENS Churchwardens

Christenings 1615

Apr 23   John s of Thomas AGBOROWE & Elizabeth his wife
Apr 16   William HORTON als BAKER s of Thomas BAKER & Jane his wife
May 21   John s of John COOKE & Joyce his wife
May 23   John s of John BADGER & Margett his wife
Jun 4   Als d of George WHITE & Anne his wife
Jun 11   Edward s of Thomas HILLMAN & Amy his wife
Jun 18   Mary d of Humfrey JURDEN & Jane his wife
Jun 16   Edward s of Humfrey LUCE & Joyce his wife
Jul 16   Edward s of John TOYE & Mirriall his wife
Aug 6   Richard s of Thomas KETLEY
Aug 20   Betridge d of John WANERTON & Mary his wife
Aug 25[?]   John s of Richard EVANS & Joan his wife
Sep 3   Richard s of Humfrey LYNE & Elizabeth his wife
Sep 24   Margerie d of Phillippe BATE & Hester his wife
Dec 26   Humfrey daughter[sic] of Henry BATE & Weavelen his wife

Dec 28   George s of Maurice NEWNAM & Mary his wife
Jan 20   Henry s of William TAYLOR & Anne his wife
Jan 28   Thomas s of Edward WATKIS & Margerie his wife
Mar 25[?]   Robert s of Geffrey COOKE

Weddings 1615
Apr 17   William MOORE & Jane HALLE
Jun 9   William GARRETT & Isabell MARSHE
Jun 5   Roger PATCHET & Elizabeth BARNET
Jun 5   Edward BATE & Joane BLAKEMOORE
Aug 21   Thomas TAWNY & Alice ADENBROOKE

Burialls 1615
Apr 19   Richard GARRETT
Apr 23   Elinor TEARNE
May 24   Richard TEARNE
Jul 26   Richard BATE
Jul 26   Miriall TOYE
Jul 30   Edward BATCH
Aug 5   Richard LUCE
Sep 2   Humfrey BATE
Sep 15   Elizabeth LITLEFORD wydowe
Sep 21   Guy PIXELL
Dec 27   Elinor PHILLIPPS wydowe late wyfe to Phillippe PHILLIPPES
Jan 18   Roger DEVYS
Jan 27   Richard TAYLOR
Feb 25   Elinor JURDEN widow
Mar 30   Anne BAKER

Christenings 1616
Apr 14   Margaret d of Robert HILLMAN & Joan his wife
Apr 28   Whorwood d of Henry LONGE & Jane his wife
May 24   [Blank] s of William PURSELL & Elizabeth his wife
Jun 2   Joan d of George RICHARDS & [blank] his wife
Jun 11   John s of Wiliam & Margot [blank] his wife
Jul 20   Em d of Richard WARROLL & Em his wife
Oct 12   Elizabeth d of George PERKES & Alice his wife
Oct 13   Marget d of Thomas HACKET & Joan his wife
Nov 10   Richard s of Richard BANISTER & Margit his wife
Dec 8   Elizabeth d of Thomas HILL & Mary his wife
Dec 15   Humfrey s of Humfrey DICKINS & Jane his wife
Dec 30   Jane d of John WILLETT & Elnor his wife
Feb 24   William s of John POWELL & [blank] his wife
Mar 9   Edward s of Humfrey TIGHE & Elinor his wife
Mar 16   Denys s of Denys HILLMAN & Anne his wife

Weddings 1616
[blank]   Thomas FORREST & Betridg BANISTER
Oct 24   John DAVIES & Isabell SYMONS
Feb 4   Thomas BAKER & Anne HADNE

Burials 1616

Apr 8	Richard TOYE
Apr 12	John RICE
Apr 28	Anne SPITLE
May 1	Thomas WILLETT
May 5	Sir Thomas WHORWOOD Knight
May 10	Joan WANERTON
May 27	Edward CLARKE
Jun 13	John PHILIAN Junior
Jun 14	Elizabeth LONGEMORE
Jul 7	Mary BOULTE
Aug 21	Hughe HIGLEY
Sep 29	Richard VINCENT
Oct 12	Mary BAKER
Dec 7	[Blank] d of Richard HALE & Elizabeth his wife
Dec 11	An infante of Thomas BATTE & Susanna his wife
Jan 10	Elinor DEKON
Mar 17	Joan wife of Richard BAKER

Christenings 1617

Apr 6	Mary d of John FREEMAN & Mary his wife
Apr [?]	Richard s of John PHILLIPS & Judith his wife
Apr 20	Edward s of Phillip BATTE & Hester his wife
	[Change of writing here.]
May 18	Anne d of Walter LEIGHTON & Catherine his wife
Aug 10	Anne d of John SELVESTER & Allyce his wife
Aug 17	Roger s of Roger PAGGET & Elyzabeth his wife
Aug 17	Mary d of Thomas AGBORROWE & Elyzabeth his wife
Oct 5	Henry s of Willm TAYLLER & Anne his wife
Dec 7	Rychard s of Richard PAYTON
Dec 20	Rychard s of Thomas BAKER
Dec 28	Elyzabeth d of Rychard HALLE & Elyzabeth his wife
Jan 11	John s of Humfrey LYNE
Dec 28	Margery d of Richard WHITE & Allyce his wife
Feb 8[?]	Meryall d of Humfrey NEWNAM

Weddings 1617

Jun 15	Richard WESTONE & Elizabeth LEAE
Sep 16	William SMITHE & Jane BROWNE
Sep 21	Richard BRADELEY & Mary LOWSONE
Nov 17	William ADDENBROKE & Jane GROVE
Nov 17	Thomas PYXELL & Elizabeth HILL
Jan 20	John TOYE & Martha VINCENTE
Jan 24	Richard WONLEY & Anne EATONE
Jan 27	William JOHNSONE & Catherine WARREN
Feb 13	Stephen HARRYSON & Margrett SISTONE
Feb 17	Robert GARRETT & Margrett BRISCOE

Burials 1617

May 4	Anne HANCOXE widowe
May 10	Richard GRAVENOR
May 13	Ane infante of Richarde GARRETTE & Elizabeth his wife
May 18	William LAWSONE
Jun 8	Margrett of the foxe earthe
Jun 25	Margery d of Willm DAVERDALE
Jul 10	John CORBERT
Sep 23	The wife of John CORBETT
Nov 26	Mary d of Thomas AGBORROWE
Nov 7	Margery RUDGE widowe

[The next page is damaged at the top and only "mfray" readable]

Jan 11	Nichollas s of Thomas LYLLYE & Joane his wife
Feb 1	Edward HILL of Kinvare
Feb 3	Margery d of Richard WHITE & Allice his wife
Feb 22	Elyzabeth FOORDE
Mar 18	Ellyne wife of John SPILTELL

Christenings 1617

Feb 16	Elyzabeth d of John COOKE & Joyce his wife
Feb 23	Henry s of Morys NEWNAM
Feb 18[?]	Henry s of John BRISCOE
Mar 15	Humfrey s of Thomas BATE & Shusane his wife
Mar 21	John s of Humfrey JURDEN & Jane his wife
Mar 21	Meryall d of Richard WESTONE & Elyzabeth his wife

[The next two entries are at the bottom of a an otherwise blank page]

Christenings 1618

Apr 12	Elizabeth d of Thomas BAKER als HORTON & Jane his wife
May 9	William s of John CORBETT & Margery his wife

Christenings 1618

Mar 26	Richard s of Jeffrey COOKE & Margery his wife
Mar 26	Thomas s of Richard WARRALL & Em his wife
Mar 28	Elizabeth d of Thomas TAYLER & Anne his wife
Apr 23	Edward s of John WANCTON & Mary his wife
May 25	Mary d of Thomas BAKER & Jane his wife
Jul 1	Antony s of Henry BACHE & Maudlen his wife
Jul 24	Elizabeth d of [blank] OWENS a stranger yt lay at Thomas HICKEMANS – Illegitimate
[?]	Anne d of Edward WATKIS & Margery his wife
[blank]	Henry s of Richard GARRETT & Elizabeth his wife
Nov 8	Humfrey s of John TOY & Martha his wife
Nov 15	Anne d of Thomas FOREST & Betrice his wife
Nov 29	Marget d of Richard OVERLEY & Anne his wife
Dec 27	Mary d of Thomas HACKET & Joan his wife
Jan 10	Henry s of Henry LONGE & Jane his wife
Feb 14	Richard s of Richard HALL & Elizabeth his wife
Feb 21	Als d of Phillip BATTE & Hester his wife
Feb 21	Anne d of Thomas PIXELL & Joyce his wife

Weddings 1618

Apr 21	Thomas TONGUE & Margery CATTERALL
Nov 3	William BENNET & Mary CAUDRICKE
Sep 21	Richard LEVER als BATCH & Joyce ADDENBROOKE
Jan 4	John HULLAND & Anne GILLE
Jan 14	John GARRETT & Margery RAUNELL

Burials 1618

Mar 5	Elizabeth BATTE d of Richard BATE & Anne his wife
Oct 25	Thomas BATE
Oct 17	An Infante of Thomas STRETE & Als his wife
Jun 30	Roger a heatheane
Aug 1	An Infante of Thomas KETLEY
Nov 9	Richard BRADLEY
Nov 1	Anne FOREST
Oct 11	Rose COXE
Feb 2	Anne COMBER
[?] 7	Mary LONGEMORE [This entry has been inserted]
Feb 18	Edward RICE
Feb 19	An Infante of John GARRETT & Margery his wife
Mar 19	Elizabeth WARRALL

Christenings 1619

Apr 4	Thomas s of William JOHNSONNE & Catherine his wife
Apr 18	Mary d of William FOORDE & Anne his wife
Apr 25	Richard s of Richard BATCH & Joyce his wife
Apr 25	Marget d of Robert LOWE & Anne his wife
May 2	Joan d of Robert RICE & Joan his wife
May 18	Francis s of Roger PAGETT & Elizabeth his wife
May 18	John s of John BANISTER & Felix his wife
Jun 20	Richard s of Richard HALE & Elizabeth his wife
Jun 20	Edward s of Richard BANISTER & Marget his wife
Jul [?]	John s of Morice BLAYNE & Als his wife
Aug [?]	Arthur s of George WOLRICH & Jane his wife
Aug 22	Humfrey s of Thomas KETLEY & Elizabeth his wife
Sep [?]	John s of Thomas BAKER & Anne his wife
Sep 22	Obadiah s of John CROSSE & Margett his wife
--- 29	Stephen s of Stephen HARRYS & Marget his wife
Nov 2	John s of Edward JOHNES & Anne his wife
Dec 1	Phillippe s of Thomas ATKIS & Als his wife
Nov 7	Margett d of Thomas STREETE & Als his wife
Jan 16	John s of John CLARKE & Anne his wife
Jan 23	Vincent s of Richard PAYTINGE & Anne his wife
--- -	Margery d of Thomas HILL & Mary his wife
Feb 23	Richard s of Richard BATE & Anne his wife
Mar 15	John s of Edward MOSELEY the yonger & Margrett his wife
	[This last entry written vertically in the margin in a different hand]
Mar 20	James s of Humfrey BRADLEY & Johane his wife

Weddings 1619

- Apr 30   William BOYER & Elizabeth ATKIS
- May 4   Thomas FOWNES & Jane GRAVENOR
- July [?]   Thomas JOHNSONNE & Sibell WONLEY
- Jul 25[?]   Edward MEREDEN & Als KENT

[The next entry is written in a different ink & the date not given]

- [blank]   Thomas ATKIS & Als HARRYSONE

Burials 1619

- Apr 22   William SMYTH
- Apr 23   Edward OKELEY
- Apr 30   Anne LONGER
- May [?]   Marget PAYTINGE
- May 16   William CORBETT
- May 19   [blank] was buried
- May 19   Thomas SUGAR
- May 28   Joan SLEWANS
- Jun 30   Als BAKER
- Aug 8   Marget RIDER
- Sep 18   Thomas HUNTE als YEOWLE
- Oct 8   Anne wife of Roger MICHELL
- Oct 19   Gillian BRISCOWE wydowe
- Nov 7   Edward WEBBE
- Nov 9   Leonard ECCLES
- Jan 20   Edward HALE
- Jan 30   Richard BIRD of Dunsley

Christenings 1620

- Apr 1   Margaret d of William ADDENBROOKE & Jane his wife
- Apr 14   Elizabeth d of William BOWYER & Elizabeth his wife
- May 7   Miriall d of John HORTON als BAKER & Jane his wife
- May 21   Elizabeth d of Richard WOLVRLEY & Anne his wife
- Jul 9   Elnor d of John SILVESTER & Als his wife
- Aug 6   William s of William HADOCKE & Joan his wife
- Aug 20   Elizabeth d of William HILL & Anne his wife
- Aug 30   Margaret TAYLER illegitimate d of Emanuell BRADLEY & Betrice TAYLER
- Sep 18   Abigall d of John WHORWOOD Esq & Abigail his wife
- Oct 22   Mary d of Lancelot WILDE & Amy his wife
- Oct 23   William s of Richard BATCH & Joyce his wife
- Nov 3   Maudlen d of Henry BATE & Maudlen his wife
- Dec 3   John s of Edward JURDEN & Joan his wife
- Dec 22   Richard s of Richard WARRALL & Emlen his wife
- Dec 21   Edward s of Richard HALE & Elizabeth his wife
- Dec 30   William s of John BANYSTER & Foelix his wife
- Jan 11   William s of Williams FOORDE & Anne his wife
- Jan 30   Longeworth s of John CROSSE & Marget his wife
- Feb 24   Mary d of Robert HILMAN & Joan his wife
- Mar 18   Oliver s of William GARRETT & Isabel his wife

Feb 24 ~~James s of Humfrey BRADLEY & Joane his wife~~ [Entry crossed out]
Mar 18 Phillip BATTE s of Phillip BATE & Hester his wife
Mar 20 Richard s of Morice NEWNAM & Mary his wife

Weddings 1620
Oct 23 Thomas WALLIS & Margery DICKINSON
Feb 6   John HACKET & Joyce PHILLIPPS
[The following, apparant. signature occurs at the bottom of the page]
Mary BIRD

Burials 1620
Apr 14 Elizabeth BOWYER
Aug 10 Fortune BATE wydowe
Aug 20 Richard HILL of Compton
Aug 20 Elizabeth HILL
Nov 1[?] Robert POTTER
Dec 24 Humfrey HILLMAN
Jan 9   Edward WALLIS

Christenings 1621
Mar 29[?] Abigall d of William TAYLER & Anne his wife
[The above entry appears to have been inserted later]
Apr 3   Elizabeth d of Edward JOHNES clerck & Anne his wife
Apr 8   Elizabeth d of Richard GROVE & Miriall his wife
Apr 8   Humfrey [written over erasure] sonne [written over erasure] of John BRISCOWE & Margery his wife
Apr 15 Elizabeth d of Thomas PIXELL & Joyce his wife
Apr 19[?] Elizabeth d of Mary FOWLER – illegitimate by Richard HAWES the reputed father
May 10 William s of Humfrey JURDEN & Jane his wife
Apr 22 [May crossed out and April inserted above] Elizabeth d of Walter LEIGHTON & Catherine his wife
May 29 Elen d of Richard BANISTER & Margaret his wife
Nov 5   Mary d of Edward MOSELEY & Margaret his wife
Feb 17 Humfrey PAYTINGE s of Richard FAYTINGE & Anne his wife
Feb 17 Edward s of Edward WATKIS & Margery his wife
Mar 8   Dorothee d of John WHORWOOD gentl & Abigail his wife

Weddings 1621
Jun 18 Robert JOHNSONNE & Jane BENBOWE

Burials 1621
May 2   Walter LEIGHTON
May 10 Cicely KESTAR
May 16 Anne LEIGHTON
May 20 Jane JORDEN wife of Humfrey JURDEN
Jun 22 William HEATH
Dec 12 Henry NEWNAM
Feb 8   Rice ap HUGHE

Christenings 1622

Apr 28	Elizabeth d of John CORBET & Margery his wife
May 12	Margeret d of Lancelot WYLDE & Amy his wife [Entry squeezed in]
Jun [?]	John s of Thomas LONGEMORE & Joan his wife
Jun 11	Elizabeth d of Thomas KETLEY & Elizabeth his wife
Jun 16[?]	John s of Robert JOHNSONNE & Jane his wife
Jun 22	Edward s of William BOWYER & Maudlen his wife
Jul 28	John s of Richard RICE & Margery his wife
Aug 25	John s of Elizabeth ROBINSONNE – illegitimate
Sep 1	Anne d of Richard GARRET & Elizabeth his wife
Sep 15	John s of John SILVESTER & Als his wife
Sep 29	John s of John BROOKES & Isabell his wife
Oct 6	Raphe s of Francis GARRET & Anne his wife
Oct 13	William s of Richard HALE & Elizabeth his wife
Oct 13	John s of Richard WARRALL & Jane his wife
Nov 20	William s of Thomas HILL & Mary his wife
Dec 6	Edward & William twynnes the sonnes of Robert RICE & Joan his wife
Dec 27	Joan d of Thomas NOTTE & Elizabeth his wife
Dec 30	Edward s of John BANISTER Junr & Foelix his wife
Jan 5	Elenor d of John PAYNE & Anne his wife
Jan 13	Elizabeth d of Robert HILMAN & Joan his wife
Jan 20	Anne d of John POWELL & Elizabeth his wife
Jan 27	Elizabeth s of John CLARKE & Anne his wife
Feb 3	Thomas s of Michael WEBBE & Jane his wife
Feb 9	Thomas s of Richard BATE & Anne his wife
Feb 18	John s of William SMYTHE als CANAPIE
Mar 17	Elizabeth d of Thomas HACKET & Joan his wife
Mar 18	William s of Phillip BATE & Hester his wife
Mar 22	Margery d of Thomas LYONS & Joan his wife

Weddings 1622

Jun 17	Edward WALLIS & Elizabeth WALLE
Jul 23	Thomas LYONS & Joan HACKET
Aug 6	Thomas BATE & Als TOMPSONE

Burials 1622

Jun 10	Thomas s of Thomas BAKER
Jun 28	Thomas HILLMAN of the hill
Aug 3	Anne wife of Richard PAYTINGE
Aug 13	Thomas HACKET the elder
Jul 17	Roger SILVESTER
Dec 14	Richard WALLIS
Jan 20	Joan HIPKIS
Feb 10	Parnell PIXELL wydowe
Feb 25	Thomas HAULE
Mar 8	John SILVESTER an Infante

Christenings 1623

Apr 20	Elizabeth d of Humfrey BRADLEY & Johane his wife (This above entry was inserted under the heading)
Apr 12	Elizabeth d of Humfrey LYNE & Elizabeth his wife
Apr 13	Anne d of Richard FREMINGE & Mary his wife
Apr [?]	Abigail d of Edward MOSELEY & Margaret his wife
Apr 27	Maudlen d of William ADDENBROOKE & Jane his wife
May 25	John s of Humfrey DICKINS & Jane his wife
Jun 7	Edward s of William FOORDE & Anne his wife
Jun 13	Judith d of Humfrey JONES & Catherine his wife
Jul 22	Elizabeth d of John WHORWOOD gentl & Abigail his wife
Aug 10	Elizabeth d of William VINCENT & Margaret his wife
Aug 24	Richard s of Thomas EDWARDS & Anne his wife
Aug 31	Elizabeth d of Michael WEBBE & Jane his wife
Sep 26[?]	Als d of Thomas SMYTH & Marget his wife
Oct 5	Mary d of Thomas PIXELL & Joyce his wife
Oct 10	John SMYTH illegitimate s of Catherine SMYTH by Ilsley BALL the reputed father
Oct 18	Elizabeth d of Thomas ATKIS & Als his wife
Oct 24	William s of John SOUTHALL & Dorothea his wife
Nov 1	Richard s of Arthur KETLEBY & Mary his wife
Dec 14	Elizabeth d of John BIRDE & Isabell his wife
Feb 1	Marget d of Morice NEWNAM & Mary his wife
Feb 1	Elizabeth d of John SILVESTER & Als his wife
Feb 15	Edward s of Richard GROVE & Miriall his wife
Feb 15	Anne d of Richard BANISTER & Marget his wife
Feb 22	Elizabeth d of John HACKET & Joyce his wife
Feb 29[sic]	Elizabeth d of Richard GARRET & Elizabeth his wife
Mar 7	Anne d of Robert LOWE & Anne his wife

Weddings 1623

Jun 23	Robert RIDLEY & Susanna LOWEWATTER
Jul 17	Gerard SISTON & Elizabeth EATON
Aug 4	Gabriel BURNESTUNNE & Kestabell WALLIS
Nov 1	John BUCKNELL & Margery PEARSON

Burials 1623

Apr 8	Anne POTTER wydowe
Apr 28	Elizabeth wife of John LUCE
May 8	John SPITTULL
Jul 16	Henry BATE
Aug 11	Als LYNE wydowe
Sep 19	Anne JORDEN
Oct 10	An Infante of Catherine SMYTH – Illegitimate
Nov 3	Richard HALE
Dec 3	Elizabeth BIRDE
Dec 16	Richard EDWARDS
Dec 12	Edward KELSIE
Dec 23	Thomas BANISTER
Dec 29	Anne JOHNS

Feb 8	An Infante of William HILL
Feb 10	An Infante of William JOHNSONS
Feb 12	Joan WESTON
Feb 16	Widowe RICE
Feb 25	Marget ADDENBROOKE
Mar 3	John SMYTH
Mar 4	Dorothea MOLE

Christenings 1624

Apr 4	Elizabeth d of Walter LEWKNAR & Elizabeth his wife
Apr 18	William s of John ROBINSONNE & Mary his wife
May 16	Edward s of Edward JOHNES cleric & Anne his wife
May 17	Abigal d of Gerard SISTONNE & Elizabeth his wife
	[The next entry appears to have been inserted under the heading at top of the page]
Jun 27	Margery d of Roger PAGET & Elizabeth his wife
Jun 27	Richard s of Richard WILDINGE & Alice his wife
Jul 10	Anne d of Clement MEBRYE & Mary his wife
Aug 1	Elizabeth d of Edward HEATH & Elizabeth his wife
Oct 3	Richard s of Richard BURFORD & Elenor his wife
Oct 17	John s of Thomas BAKER & Jane his wife
Nov 1	Anne d of Geffrey COOKE & Margerie his wife
Nov 22	Miriall d of William VINCENT & Margaret his wife
Nov 26	Thomas s of John CORBET & Margaret his wife
Dec 16	Edward s of Gawen AMBLETON & Mary his wife
Dec 19	Sussanna d of Richard RICE & Margerie his wife
Jan 1	Henry s of Thomas LONGEMORE & Joan his wife
Jan 9	Anne d of Mary MATHEWS Illegitimate
Jan 16	Jane d of William TAYLOR & Anne his wife
Feb 2	Mary d of Humfrey LYNE & Elizabeth his wife
Feb 13	Hester d of Thomas NOTT & Elizabeth his wife
Feb 15	William s of John WHORWOOD Esquier & Abigall his wife
Mar 8	Abigal d of William JOHNSONNE & Catherine his wife

Weddings 1624

May 18	William JOHNSONNE & Margerie ROYLE
Feb 10	Humfrey HOPE & Margerie PIXELL

Burials 1624

Apr 8	Humfrey CORBET
May 4	Anne LOWE
May 8	Anne HILL wydowe
May 27	Robert JONNES
May 25	Anne KNYGHTE late wife of Richard KNYGHTE
May 29	Dionys ATKIS
Jun 3	William BIRCH
Jun 12	Richard FREMINGE
Sep 10	Thomas WARREN Junior
Oct 24	John MORDEN
Nov 7	Richard KETLEBY

© Staffordhire Parish Registers Society

Nov 15	Thomas HICKEMANS
Nov 30	Thomas CORBET
Dec 6	John HOPKIS
Dec 21	Edward BAKER
Sep 29	Marget MOSELEY
Oct 11	Joyce COOKE
Oct 17	John PURSELOWE
Oct 15	Richard COMBER
Dec 21	Catherine SMYTH of Whittington
Dec 23	William POWELL
Dec 28	Richard WARROLL
Jan 2	Elinor LYNE
Jan 23	John NESTE
Jan 27	Humfrey TEARNE
Feb 8	Anne COOKE
Feb 14	John BAKER
Feb 21	Thomas BAKER, Mary HACKET, Isabell JOHNSONNE were buried
Mar 20	John RICE

Christenings 1625

Apr 3	Nicholas BOWYER & Maulen his wife were bapt 3rd Apr
May 18	George s of Edward POWELL & Mary
May 30	Penelope d of Lancelot WYLDE & Anne
Jun 2	Seabrighte s of Richard NASHE & Marget
Jun 25	Edward s of Edward MOSELEY & Marget
Jul 10	Thomas s of Robert HILLMAN & Joan
Jul 18[?]	John s of Richard HAULE & Elizabeth
Aug 17[?]	Richard s of Edward JURDEN & Joan
Sep 18	Marget d of John CLARKE & Anne
Nov 13	Henry [over an erasure] s of William FOORD & Anne
Nov 20	Mary d of John BAKER & Miriall
Dec 10	John s of Gerard SISSON & Elizabeth
Jan 15	Thomas s of Thomas KETLEY & Elizabeth
Jan 15	Anne d of William SMYTH & Jane
Jan 15	Hester d of John BRISCOWE & Margery
Feb 12	Robert s of Nicholas PARKER & Marget
Mar 12	John s of John CROSSE & Marget
Mar 5	Thomas s of William ADDENBROOKE & Jane
Mar 12	Beatrice d of John BANISTER & ffelix
Mar 12	Anne d of Robert JOHNSONNE & Anne

Weddings 1625

Jul 21	John BAKER & Miriall HILL
Aug 22	Richard KETLEBY gent & Mary PETTY
Sep 19	Robert LOWE & Joyce BARNET
Oct 23	John COOKE & Elnor NORRIS
Jan 17	Humfrey PRETY & Anne PAYNE

Burials 1625

Apr 27	Rose WARROLL
Apr 29	Anne NURTHALL
May 16	Maudlen ADDENBROOKE
May 23	John WILLET
May 23	Henry GERMAN
Jun 16	John DICKINS
Jun 23	Elizabeth BACHE
Sep 5	Thomas HILLMAN
Sep 20	John SMYTH
Sep 21	Penelope WILDE
Nov 2	Elizabeth RABON
Dec 18	Lucie HICKEMANS
Feb 2	Rose DICKINES
	Elizabeth KETLEY & Elnor SILVESTER were buried the 24th day of February
Mar 1	Raphe GARRET

Christenings 1626

Apr 12	Thomas the son of Thomas PIXELL & Joyce his wife
Apr 21	John s of Morice NEWNAM & Mary his wife
May 12	Marget d of Humfrey MOSELEY & Als his wife
May 29	Theodocea d of Richard WOLVRLEY & Anne his wife
Jun 8	Elizabeth d of Oliver BAKER gentl & Maudlen his wife
Jun 13	Hester d of John BRISCOWE & Margery his wife
Jun 20	Theodocea d of John WHORWOOD Esq & Abigal his wife
Jul 10	Samuell s of William VINCENT & Marget his wife
Jul[?] 30	[Illegible] s of Lancelot WYLDE & Amy his wife
Aug 8	Abigal d of John HACKET & Joyce his wife
Aug 13	William s of Richard GARRET & Elizabeth his wife
Sep 7	Anne d of Hughe HOLYMAN & Anne his wife
Sep 10	Richard s of John BIRDE & Issabell his wife
Sep [?]	John s of Richard PURSLOWE & Elizabeth his wife
Nov 5	Roger s of Robert LOWE & Joyce his wife
Nov 5	John s of Richard KETLEBY & Mary his wife
Dec 27	John s of Antony ADAMS & Margery his wife
Jan [?]	William s of John RABOLD & Anne his wife
Jan 21	Meriall d of Richard GROVE & Meriall his wife
Feb 18	Mary d of Richard RICE & Margery his wife
Feb 25	Roger s of Robert SEMUR & [blank] his wife

Weddings 1626

Oct 5	Thomas HOBY & Joan WEDGE
Oct 28	John FEREDAY & Betrice TAYLOR
Oct 30	John CLARKE & Elizabeth NAULE

Burials 1626

Apr 12	Anne TAYLER wydowe
May 15	An infante of Hierome LOWE
Aug 18	Thomas BATE

Jul 29	Humfrey BOULTE
Aug 13	Susanna BRISCOWE
Nov 9	Anne the wife of Griffin JOHNS
Nov 28	Mary MILLES[?]
Feb 19	Francis EVANS

Christenings 1627

Mar 30	Mary [altered to Thomas] d [altered to son] of Humfrey LYNE & Elizabeth his wife
Apr 3	William s of Edward JOHNES & Anne his wife
Apr 8	Joseph s of Hierom LOWE & Anne his wife
Apr 15	Thomas s of Thomas HILLMAN & Elinor his wife
May 10	Joan d of Phillip BATE & Hester his wife
Jun 7	Thomas [altered to John] s of Thomas SMYTH & Marget his wife
May 27	William s of Edward WESTON & Isabell his wife
Aug 12	Matheu s of Matheu SHOUGHE & Elnor his wife
Aug 15	Marget d of George BRINELEY & Isbell his wife
Sep 20	Francis d of John WHORWOOD & Abigal his wife
Sep 23	Elizabeth d of Humfrey BAKER & Alice his wife
Oct 1	Richard s of Francis GARRET & Anne his wife
Oct 7	John s of Edward MOSELEY & Elizabeth his wife
Oct 7	Richard s of John BROOKES & Dorothy his wife
Oct 15	William s of William CARTER & Agnes his wife
Oct 27	Walter s of John CLARKE & Anne his wife
Oct 26	John s of Gerard WARREN & Elinor his wife
Nov 11	Sarah d of Edward HURST & Sarah his wife
Dec 16	John s of Hughe HOLYMAN & Anne his wife
Jan 28	Susanna d of William DUNN & Joyce his wife
Feb 1	Joan [altered to Hannah] d of William BOWYER & Maudlen his wife
Feb 9	Sarah d of Richard PURSLOE & Elizabeth his wife [Entry squeezed in]
Feb 12	Thomas the s of [illegible] ATKYS & Alce his wife
Mar 12	Mary d of Richard SMYTH & Elizabeth his wife
Mar 1	Ilsley the s of [illegible] MEBRY & Elizabeth his wife

Weddings 1627

May 4	William CARTER & Agnes ATKIS
Apr 17	William DUNNE & Joyce SYCHE
Jun 27	William SYCHE & Isbell DOVRDALE
Dec 27	William PINSON & Elizabeth JURDEN

Burials 1627

Apr 13	Joan CHADBURNE
Jun 10	Gerard WHORWOOD Esqr
Jun 12	Joan BROOKE wydowe
Jul 10	Ales TAYLER
Jul 26	John BAKER als HORTON
Aug 10	John CLARKE

Aug 16   Ales HARINGTON
Aug 18   Jane BAKER als HORTON
Sep 23   Margery wife of Richard RICE
Oct 12   Phillip ATKIS
Nov 12   Richard BIRDE of Compton
Dec 12   Dionys HILLMAN
Dec 12   Elnor TAYLER
Jan 16   John HOLYMAN
Feb 4   Thomas MARRALL
Feb 26   Edward VINCENT

Christenings 1628

Mar 29   Mary d of Thomas KETLEY & Anne his wife
Mar 30   Elizabeth d of Edward MOSELEY & Marget his wife
Mar 30   Marget d of John BRISCOWE & Margery his wife
Apr 8   Elizabeth d of William FOORD & Anne his wife
Apr 5[?] Richard s of Richard NASH [entry inserted in same hand]
May 26   Abigall d of William VINCENT & Marget his wife
May 4 Apr 17 [date altered] Stephen s of Thomas HILL & Mary his wife
May 4   Anne d of Morice NEWNAM & Mary his wife
Jun 15   Marget d of Thomas HOBY & Joan his wife
Jun 22   Isabell d of William SICH & Isabell
Jun [?] Olivr s of William HILL & Anne his wife [entry inserted in same hand]
Jul 4   Stephen s of Richard GARRETT & Elizabeth his wife
Jul 27   Anne d of Walter LEWKNAR & Elizabeth his wife

[On an otherwise blank page:]
Verte Duo follia et ibi invenies reliqua
The Copie of Mr William SEABRIGHT Esq.
his Letter to the parish

[followed on the next page by:]
After my[?] hertie commendacone wheras myn purpose and intent by the helpe and assistance of Allmightie God is to give & bestowe upon the poore of yor parrishe of Kinvarre and likewise upon divers other parishes wthin that coutrie the quantitie of thirteene penny worth of white or wheaten bread to be distributed upon everie Saboth day for ever hereafter p^{e}sentlie after the ending of morninge prayer & the Sermon (if any shalbe) in penny loaves to thirteene of the most poorest & neediest persons of yor parrishe such as the parson or minister wth the Churchwardens and parrishe Clarke for the tyme being or the most part of them, shall in their good discretions thinke meet & to have most need. And wth all that if any such poore wthin yor parrish shallbe so weake and sick or impotent of their bodies, as they cannot be able in their owne persons to come to yor parrishe Church to receive such bread, as they shall be thought fitt to have in respect of their infirmities Then my desire is that such order may be taken that such allowance of bread may from tyme to tyme bee sent them by some of their neighbours to their dwellinge houses or places of their abode. And to

the end that this devise of mine and the like contributen to divers other parrishes and the errectinge of a free grammar Schoole wthin the parrish of Woolverley the place of my birth may bee insthe[?] and trulie pformed for ever hereafter.   I have allreadie taken order & assured lande of Inheritance of a sufficent value to divers feoffees that at everie feoff of all Sainte for ever heareafter there shalbe paid & delivered, as well to the Churchwardens or parrish Clarke of Kinvarre as also to divers other parrishes wthin that contrie the some of fiftie six shill-inge fower pence a peere, for one whole yeare then to come wherewth the shalbe provided by the said Churchwardens or parrish Clarke or by some of them against everie Sabath day hereafter for ever the quantitie of thirteene penny worth of good sweet and wholesome bread of wheat the same to bee set upon the communion table at the begininge of morninge prayer, and at the end thereof to be distributed as aforesaid And for that this distribution of mine may be better performed hereafter, I have taken such order that such of ye Churchwardens or parish Clarke or any other pson as yo^u the said parrishioners shall therafter appoint to take the paines in buyinge & providinge the said bread and seeinge it truly & orderlie wthout partiallitie distributed shall have & receive for their paines the some of five shillings to their own use at the end of everie yeare paid them by my feoffes there unto appointed. And for that, I ame very desierous to be advertized[?] from yo^u of that parrish whether that yo^u seeketh re-[?] the said yearly payment before hand   to see this bequest & Devise of mine p'formed in all points hereafter which out of my inter[?] & .... I write ye willinglie & freely that I may receive from ye Mr Garrad WHORWOOD the Curate & some or more of the most substantiall Inhabitants of that parrish by letter under yor hand at your convenienc to remaine for ever wthme and mine as a testimony of y^o willinge consente and promises for performance on yor behalf, whereupon I shall then prepare my self for the pformance of that coc^h on my part is fit to be done.   And wthall my ernest request & desire is that yo^u wilbee pleased not onelie to pay xv and safelie keepe this txt of myne amongst the wrytings and evidents belonging to yor parrishe, there to remaine to posteritie but alive to cause the contents therefore to bee truly entered word for word into yor Churchbooke whereby it may afterards trulie appeare hereafter how & in what sort this bequest was mynt ought in all things to be pformed, all wch if yo^u shall refuse then shall my purpose bee otherwise to dispose therefore to some other parrish thereabout wch upon the like condirant will thankfullie & most willinglie accept of it   And so leavinge the care and performance hereof to yo^u good consideractions wth my hartit re'mondacons. Soe end and bid yo^u farewell.

    Lombard Street London)   You^r verie lovinge
friende the xijth day of July   )   1618)   Wm SEABRIGHT

This the true copie of Mr William SEABRIGHTs his Letter the original w^h is in the pishe chest ....
....   Edwardus JOHNES

Christenings 1628

- Sep 14 Anne d of John CLARKE & [blank] his wife
- Sep 14 John s of Edward POWELL & Mary his wife
- Oct 28 Jane d of William PINSON & Elizabeth his wife
  [The next entry appears to have been inserted later]
- Oct [?] Sara d of Thomas HILLMAN & Elenor his wife
- Nov 8 Edward s of Richard KETLEBY gent & Mary his wife
- Nov 8 Elnor d of John HEDGER & (blank) his wife
- Nov 9 Anne d of Hierom LOWE & Anne his wife
- Nov 20 John s of John WHORWOOD Esqr & Abigal his wife
- Nov 23 William s of John BAKER & Miriall his wife
- Feb 4 Anne d of Lancelot WYLDE & Amy his wife
- Mar 11 Joan d of Nicolas & Marget PARKER his wife
- Mar 15 Richard s of Robert SEMUR & Joyce his wife

Weddings 1628

John NORTON & Elinor BURFORD weare married by Lycence upon Shrove-mooneday 1628

Burials 1628

- Apr 10 Anne BATE
- Apr 10 Richard BURFORD
- May 12 Als ATKIS
- Jun 22 Isabell wife of William SYTCH
- Jul 4 Elizabeth wife of Richard GARRET
- Jul 9 Issabell WARREN
- Jul 17 Stephen GARRET
  [signed at the bottom of the page:]
  John WALLIS, John CLARK Churchwardens
- Jul 29 John COOKE
- Aug 6 Humfrey LUCE
- Aug 28 Catherine wife of John CATTERALL
- Nov 28 William CARTER
- Dec 4 Edward PAYNE
- Jan 29 An Infante of William JOHNSONNE
- Feb 9 Marget HALE

Christenings 1629

- Apr 12 Abigal d of John SMYTHYARD & Anne his wife
- Apr 26 William s of Richard PURSLOWE & Elizabeth his wife
- Apr 28 William s of Gerard WARREN & Margery [crossed out] Elinor [both names in different inks] his wife
- May 26 Issabell d of John BIRDE & Issabel his wife
- May 27 John s of Edmund HURSTE & Sarah his wife
- May 28 John s of William YATES & (blank) his wife
- May 30 Joan d of Richard MOLE his wife
- Jul 28 John s of John HACKET & Joyce his wife
- Aug 5 John s of William VINCENT & Marget his wife
- Oct 1 Jane d of Robert JOHNSONNE & Jane his wife
- Nov 1 Edward s of Antony ADDAMS & Margery his wife

Nov 1	Edward s of William ADDENBROOKE & Marget his wife
	[Signed at the bottom of the page:]
	John WOLLES John CLARK Churchwardens
Dec 6	William s of Roger PAGET & his wife
Dec 6	Sarah d of Humfrey LYNE & Elizabeth his wife
Dec 13	Samuell s of Hughe HOLYMAN & Anne his wife
Dec 20	John s of John RABOLD & Anne his wife
Jan 4	Thomas s of ~~Thomas~~ [crossed out] Richard KETELBY & Mary his wife
Jan 6	Marget d of Humfrey MILNER & Joan his wife
Jan 6	Emanuell s of Wydowe ECCLESHAULE a stranger
Jan 10	William s of Thomas KETLEY & Anne his wife
Jan 10	Thomas s of John NORTON & Elno^r his wife
Jan 24	Anne d of William DUNNE & Joyce his wife
Feb 6	Mary d of John CROSSE & his wife
Feb 8	Joan d of John CLARKE & his wife
Feb 14	James s of William DEACON & his wife
Feb 14	Thomas s of Thomas LONGEMORE & his wife
Feb 16	Antony s of Richard RICE & his wife
Mar 6	William s of William BARTON & his wife
Mar 6	Paule s of Richard COOKE & his wife
	John WOLLES John CLARK Churchwardens

Weddings 1629

Apr 29	Thomas ATKIS & Marget YORKE

Burials 1629

Apr 10	Wydowe BANISTER of Stourton
May 7	William s of Wm FOORD
Jun 29	Gerard SHISTON
Aug 15	John HACKET a childe
Aug 20	Thomas MADSTART
Sep 7	Joyce wife of William WEDGE
Sep 7	Catherine wife of Thomas YORKE
Sep 10	Elinor wife of Humfrey HOPE
Sep 12	John WRIGHTE
Oct 25	Two infants of a stranger
Dec 20	Anne wife of John WHITE
Jan 9	Edward BAKER gentl
Mar 19	John HOLLAND
	John WOLLES John CLARKE Churchwardens

Christenings 1630

Apr 7	Thomas s of Robert LOWE & his wife
Apr 9	Sarah d of William BARTON & his wife
Apr 18[?]	Thomas s of Morice NEWNAM & Mary & his wife
Apr 25	Thomas s of Humfrey MOSELEY & Als & his wife
May 16	Edward s of William SYTCH & Joan & his wife
May 17	John s of John BRISCOWE & Margery & his wife
May 27	Elizabeth d of Henry GOSHOE & Elinor & his wife

Jun 10	Sarah d of George BRINLEY & his wife
Jun 13	Joyce d of Edward JOHNES cleric & Anne his wife
Jun 27	Anne d of Humfrey HOPE & Margery & his wife
Aug 1	Thomas the wyfe[sic] of Phillip BATTE & Hester his wyfe
Aug 26	Marget d of Thomas SMYTH & Marget his wife
Oct 7	Samuell s of William FOORD & Anne his wife
Oct 21	Seabright & John twyns the sonnes of Olivr BAKER gentl & Maudlen his wife
Nov 7	Anne d of John YORKE & Mary his wife
Nov 23	Elizabeth d of Gerard WARREN & his wife
Dec 4	Anne d of John HACKET & Joyce his wife
Dec 5	Thomas s of Thomas CLARKE & his wife
Dec 5	William s of Edward MOSELEY & Marget his wife
Dec 20	Thomas s of John BANISTER & Felix his wife
Jan 2	Richard s of Thomas HOBBY & Joan his wife
Jan 4	Abigal d of William PINSON & Jane his wife
	[the next entry is written along margin in a different hand]
Sep [blank]	John s of Thomas HILLMAN & Elnor his wife
Feb 5	Richard s of Richard PURSLOWE & Elizabeth his wife
Feb 13	Elinor d of Robert WEBBE & Ursula his wife
Mar 1	[Blank] s of Robert HODGETS & Anne his wife

Weddings 1630

Sep 28	Richard GARRET & Anne HULLAND
Nov 2	John ASPLE & Marget WALDERNE
Feb 3	Owen FOSTER & Judith FREEMAN

Burials 1630

Apr 4	Richard BATCH
Apr 4	Richard WHITE
Apr 10	Maudlen BOWYER
Apr 12	Wydowe PACHETT
May 13	Thomas NEWNAM
Jun 3	Elizabeth GOSHOR
Jun 7	Catherine SMYTH widowe
Jun 8	Thomas LOWE
Jun 8	Joan BOWYER
Jun 18	Gryffin JOHNS
Jun 18	William MOSELEY of Kinfare
Jul 14	Humfrey TIGHE
Aug 8	Isabell PURSLOWE wydowe
Aug 29	Marget SMYTH
Sep 3	Elinor VINCENT
Nov 22	Francis TALBOT
Dec 13	Phillip KELSIE
Jan 16	Francis PACHET
Feb 6	Richard PURSLOE
Feb 15	An Infante of Richard NASHE
Feb 18	Richard RICE
Feb 19	Anne WEDGE

Henry LONGMORE   John SOUTHALL   Churchwardens 1630

Christenings 1631

Mar 27	Thomas s of Lancelot WYLDE & Anne his wife
Apr 2	Elizabeth d of Francis LYNE & Catherine his wife
Apr 17	Gerard s of Morice NEWNAM & Mary his wife
Jun 4	John s of Phillip HEYCOCKE & Catherine his wife
Apr 25	Theodocea d of Richard POWNTENEY & Anne his wife
Jun 4	Margery d of Roger LOWE & his wife
Aug 7	Edward s of Richard GARRET & Anne his wife
Aug 14	Hester d of Wm VINCENT & Marget his wife
Aug 21	Richard s of Richard RICE & his wife
Aug 28	Thomas s of John ASPLE & Marget his wife
Sep 7	Theodocea d of Richard KETELBY & Mary his wife
[?]	[?] d of [?]
[?]	Catherine d of John WHORWOOD Esq & Abigal his wife
Jan 10	John s of Morice BLAYNE & Als his wife
Feb 6	Thomas s of Richard PURSLOE & Elizabeth his wife
Mar 12	Jane d of Hughe SMYTH of Staffs & Thomasin his wife (a stranger)
Mar 16[?]	Robert s of John BIRD & his wife

Weddings 1631

Sep 9	John HASSELWOOD & Joyce BANNISTER

Burials 1631

May 2	Gerard NEWNAM
Jul 2	Dorothea wife of John BROOKE
Nov 8	Judith SILVESTER
Nov 20	Issabell wife of Roger WESTON
Feb 6	William YATES
Feb 7	Thomas s of Richard PURSLOE
	Elizabeth WILLETS als GUEST was buried upon Shrove Tuesday

Harry LONGEMORE   John SOUTHALL   Churchwardens

Christenings 1632

Mar 29	Richard s of Richard HORTON & his wife
Apr 21	Fortune d of Jane LANE Illegitimate
Apr 22	Mary d of William PINSON & Elizabeth & his wife
May 20	Elizabeth d of William DEACON & his wife
Jun 1	Joan of John HACKET & Joyce & his wife
Jun 16	Maudlen d of Olivr BAKER gentl & Maudlen his wife
Jun 17	Margaret d of Antony ADAMS & Margery & his wife
Jul 6	Sarah d of Jane WESTON a stranger illegitimate by one PARTRIDGE the reputed father
Jul 8	Jane d of Richard GROVE & Miriall & his wife
Aug 4	Anne d of Richard MOSELEY & Marget & his wife
Sep 2	Elizabeth d of Tymothy HAYES & Joyce & his wife
Sep 19	Edward s of John WHORWOOD & Abigal his wife gent

© Staffordhire Parish Registers Society

Sep 20	Mary d of Richard KETLEBY & his wife & his wife
Sep 23	Thomas s of Thomas SMYTH & Marget & his wife
Sep 30	William s of Thomas LONGEMORE & his wife
Sep 30	John s of John GIBBES & his wife
Nov 25	John s of John FINISHE & Anne & his wife
Dec 2	Andrewe s of William SYTCH & his wife
Dec 9	William s of William VINCENT & Marget & his wife
Dec 9	Als d of Wm DUNNE & his wife
Dec 16	Elnor d of Richard SMYTH & Elizabeth & his wife
Dec 26	Edward s of Thomas HILLMAN & his wife
Dec 30	Mary the dau [altered to "John the s"] of Thomas KETLEY & his wife
Jan 1	Thomas s of Thomas POWELL & Elnor & his wife
Jan 9	William s of John NORTON & his wife
Jan 27	Mary d of Thomas ATKIS & Marget & his wife
Feb 3	Humfrey s of Humfrey LYNE & his wife
Feb 3	Richard s of Robert JOHNSON & Anne & his wife
Feb 4	Humfrey s of Humfrey HOPE & Mary & his wife
Mar 10	Joan d of Thomas CLARK & Elizabeth & his wife

Weddings 1632

May 5	John WILLSONNE & Jane HASSELWOOD
Jul 9	John TOY & Issabell GRAVENOR
Feb 12	Richard COOKE & Marget WILLET

Burials 1632

May 3	Fortune d of Jane LANE
May 4	Mary [crossed out] Theodocea KETLEBY
May 8	Rose BATE wydowe
May 20	Robert COOKE
Jun 2	John CATTERALL
Jun 2	Joan HACKET
Jun 11	An Infante of John ROBERTS & his wife
Jul 6	Als SYTCH
Jul 12	Michael TAYLER
Jul 29	An Infante of Humfrey MILLNER & his wife Jevan[?]
Aug 10	Richard HORTON
Sep 20	Edward WHORWOOD
Oct 7	Harry HARBOROWE
Oct 12	Issabell BANISTER
Oct 26	Richard JONES
Nov 3	[Blank] BANISTER
Nov 18	Marget SILVESTER
Nov 23	Anne CLARKE wydowe
Nov 23	An Infant of John BANISTER
Dec 26	Jane WYLLETTS
Jan 28	Thomas HILL

Christenings 1633

Apr 21	Mary d of John RABOLE & Anne

Apr 21	Mary d of William COOKE & his wife
Jun 2	Richard s of Richard PURSLOWE & Elizabeth
Jun 23	Edward s of Edmund HURST & his wife
Jun 30	Constance d of Daner NEVYE & Constance his wife
Jul 8	Abigal d of Oliver BAKER gentl & Maudlen his wife
Jul 21	John s of Richard HORTON & Jane
Jul 28	John s of William RUSSELL & his wife
Aug 18	John s of John HACKET & Joyce his wife
Sep 1	Margaret d of Richard GARRET & Anne his wife
Sep 8	Richard s of Phillip BATE & Hester his wife
Sep 8	John s of John TAYLER & Elinor his wife
Sep 20	Charles s of John WHORWOOD Esqr & Abigal his wife
Nov 23	Abigal d of Richard COOKE & Marget his wife
Dec 24	Elizabeth d of James CLARKE gentl & his wife
Dec 1	Joseph s of Henry ECCLESHALL & Elinor his wife
Dec 1	Edward s of William DUNNE & Joyce his wife
Dec 8	Anne d of William DEACON & Sarah his wife
Dec 15	Catherine d of Thomas HOBY & Joan his wife
Dec 21	Issabel d of Richard KETLEY & Anne his wife
Dec 22	John s of William FOORD & Anne his wife
Jan 4	John s of Humfrey MOSELEY & his wife
Jan 9	William s of Catherine SMYTH Illegitimate
Jan 12	John s of Richard MOLE & his wife
Feb 2	Anne d of Rice TAYLER & his wife
Feb 9	Dorothea d of Hugh NORCOTE & Elinor his wife
Feb 16	Mary d of John WATKIS & Mary his wife
Mar 2	Elizabeth d of William ADDENBROOKE & his wife
Mar 4	John s of John BAKER & Miriall his wife
Mar 9	Thomas s of Thomas RICHARDS & his wife
Mar 16	Margery d of Antony ADAMS & Margery his wife
Mar 23	John s of Adam STOKES & Mary his wife

Weddings 1633

May 16	Rice TAYLER & Mary LUCE
May 27	Edward WINDLE & Elizabeth PRICE
Jul 13	Christopher ROWLEY & Catherine DOVY were married by Licence
Jul 20	Edward SYTCH & Anne CATTERALL
Aug 6	John RICE & Joyce WHITE
Sep 25	Richard KETLEY & Anne LEIGHTON
Oct 17	John BARTON & Jane MOSELEY
Nov 9	Richard ALLEN & Marget BAGSHEWE
Nov 26	John SYMCOXE & Abigal JURDEN
Jan 13	Francis HAYES & Marget THATCHER

Burilas 1633

Mar 28	Edward HODGETTS
Mar 29	Richard HARRYS
Mar 31	Edward TAYLER
Mar 31	Robert HODGETTS

Apr 13	An Infant of Gerard WARREN
May 4	An Infant of John BRISCOWE
May 4	Hughe MORICE
May 15	Mary WOLLEY
May 18	Wm WILKINSONNE
May 21	Marget GROVE
May 26	Anne OCKELEY
Jun 2	Anne HOPE
Jun 3	John NEWNAM
Jul 8	Anne GARRETT
Aug 13	Robert DICKINS
Sep 20	Richard COXE
Sep 22	Charles WHORWOOD
Nov 7	Jane SILVESTER
Dec 21	Anne SYTCH
Jan 5	William COMBER
Feb 2	Elizabeth NEWNAM
Feb 4	Anne TAYLER
Feb 15	Geffrey GARRETT
Feb 24	Gabriel BURNSTON
Feb 28	Joyce BEAVEN

William WEDGE, William HILL – Churchwardens

Christenings 1634

Apr 27	Joseph s of William PENNE & Anne
May 11	William s of Francis LYNES & Catherine
May 18	Priscilla d of Thomas CRUNISHE & his wife
May 18	Mary d of Thomas GIBBES & Jane
May 21	Grace d of Edward WYNDLE
Jun 8	John s of Roger OLDNALE & Elizabeth
Jul 18	Jane d of Richard MOSELEY & his wife
Jul 19	Edward s of John JUGINS & his wife
Jul 29	Roger s of Humfrey MILLNER & his wife
Aug 2	Richard s of Gerard WARREN & his wife
Aug 3	Humfrey s of William SYTCH & his wife
Aug 28	Edward s of John BARTON & Jane his wife
Sep 14	Issabell d of John BANISTER & his wife
Sep 28	Mary d of John BIRD & his wife
Oct 15	Judith d of John CLARKE & his wife
Nov 16	Jane d of Thomas PIXELL & Joyce his wife
Jan 26	Seabright s of Oliver BAKER gentl & Maudlen his wife
Feb 7	Humfrey s of William SARBUTT & Anne his wife
Feb 8	Richard s of Thomas ATKIS & Margett his wife
Feb 9	Mary d of Edmund PETTY & Anne his wife
Feb 15	Anne d of Francis GARRETT & Anne his wife

Weddings 1634

Apr 28	Edmund PETTY & Anne KETLEBY
Jul 10	William SARBUTT & Anne BAKER
Oct 26	John TAYLER & Marget SAUNTES were married by Lycence

Nov 18	Robert HAULE & Issabell WHITE
Jan 15	George GIBBES & Anne BATE

Burials 1634

Apr 27	Meriam d of Richard GROVE
May 26	John HASSELLWOOD
Jun 9	John BRISCOWE
Jun 11	Humfrey KETLEY
Jun 19	Thomas [Blank] the huntesman was buried
Jul 21	Roger MILLNER
Aug 2	Elnor wife of Gerard WARREN
Oct 26	Kestabell BURNESTON wydowe
Jan 18	Mary MANTLE
Jan 24	Als BATE
Jan 26	Wydowe PHILLIPPS
Feb 9	Edward HURST
Feb 14	Elizabeth EATON

[The next page is badly stained]

Christenings 1635

Apr 1	John s of John YORKE & Mary his wife
May 19	William s of William TAYLER & Anne his wife
Jun 7	Anne d of John ASPLE & Marget his wife
Jun 7	Thomas s of Thomas HILLMAN & Elnor his wife
Jul 24	John s of Antony TEARNE & Mary his wife
[?]	George s of Timothy PAITEN & Frances his wife [entered in a different hand at the bottom of page]
Jul 22	Richard s of John TEARNE & Letice his wife
Jul 30[?]	John s of Richard COOKE & Marget his wife
Sep 7	Mary d of Richard PURSLOE & Elizabeth his wife
Oct 9	Edward s of James CLARKE gentl & Dorothea his wife
Oct 12	Richard s of Humfrey & Margerie HOPE
[?] 18	George s of Rice TAYLER & his wife
Oct 26	Thomas s of Thomas CLARKE & Elnor his wife
Nov 22	Anne [written over a name crossed out] d of Charles HARRYSONNE & Marget his wife
Nov 29	Elnor d of William HILL & Elnor his wife
Dec 6	Mary d of Hugh HOLYMAN & Anne his wife
Dec [?]	Francis s of Thomas KETLEY & Anne his wife
[?]	Ambrose s of Ambrose RAYNSFORD & Sarah his wife
Mar [?]	Mary d of Richard KETLEBY gentl & Mary his wife
Mar [?]	John s of William DUNE & Joyce his wife
Mar [?]	Richard s of Richard SMYTH & Elizabeth his wife

Weddings 1635

Nov 3	Thomas HOPE & Anne LYNE
----	John LONGEMORE & Anne WATKYS married by Lycence
----	William HALE & Anne COLE married by Lycence

Burials 1635

Jun 2	William s of Wm TAYLER
Jun 6	Als PAYNE
Jul 22	Thomas WALKER
Sep [?]	Jane PAYTINGE
Sep 15	Als wife of Humfrey MOSELEY
Dec 15	Margerie DAVIES [Entry squeezed in]
[?]	Mary RICE
Jan 20	Richard JOHNSONNE
Feb [?]	George WEBBE
Mar 23	An Infante Illegitimate of a strange harlot
Mar [?]	Richard HAULE
Mar [?]	Anne DOLASTON

Christenings 1636

Apr 3	Richard s of William FOORD & Anne his wife
Apr 3	Humfrey s of William PENNE & Anne his wife
May 1	John s of Richard MOSELEY & Anne his wife
[?]	Thomas s of Edward WYNDLE & [blank] his wife

[Page very badly stained with spilled ink on this next section]

Jun 3	Anne d of Richard KETLEY & Anne his wife
[?]	Marget d of Thomas HOBBY & Joan his wife
Aug [?]	Bridget d of John WHORWOOD Esq & Abigal his wife
[?]	Jane d of John TOMPSON & Issabell his wife
[?]	Humfrey s of John BANISTER & Felix his wife
[?]	Sarah d of Thomas CRANISHE & [?] his wife
[?]	Elizabeth d of [?]
Dec 18	John s of John SILVESTER & Dorothea his wife
Dec 25	Joseph s of Thomas GIBBES & Jane his wife
Feb 8	Mary d of John HACKET & Elizabeth his wife of the pishe of Clent
Mar 11	Jane d of John REBOLE & Anne his wife [Entry squeezed in]
Feb 18	Joseph the sonne of Thomas CLUCH & Marget his wife (A stranger yt came out of Cheshire)
Mar 5	[Blank] of Humfrey HOPE the younger & Marget his wife
Mar 12	William s of Adam STOKES & Elnor his wife
Mar 18	Thomas s of Thomas HOPE & Anne his wife

Weddings 1636

------	John TOMSONNE & Issabell MOLE by Lycense
Oct 20	John SMALEMAN & Joan POWELL
Nov 22	John BILLINGESLEY & Margery COOKE
Jan 24	Humfrey KETLEY & Jane LUCE

Burials 1636

Mar 28	Anne HALE
Apr 1	Thomas BATCH
	[Inserted at bottom of page in a different hand]
	Margaret d of William & Margaret VINCENT was baptized[sic] in July 1638

1639   Thomas HILLMAN & John COOKE Churchwardens

[Note: There are now no more entries until 1639 and when the handwriting changes]

Christenings 1639

Apr 21	Charles & Anne s & d of John REBOLE & Anne
Jun 6	Edward s of Edward JURDEN & Margret
Jun 16	Judeth d of William PENY & Elizabeth
Jun 30	Phelix s of Edward BATE & Elizabeth
Aug 11	William s of Thomas CRANNIDGE & Anne
Dec 8	Joseph s of Danner NEVIE & Constance his wife
Sep 15	Mary d of Thomas HOPE & Anne his wife
Sep 29	Frances s of Thomas KETTLEY & Anne his wife
Oct 13	Margret d of John RICE & Joice his wife
Nov 27	Elizabeth d of John DOLASTON & Dyna his wife
Nov 19	Mary d of William DUN & Joyce his wife
Nov 30	Richard s of Richard KETTLEY & Anne his wife
Dec 1	John s of John LYE & Alce his wife
Dec 3	William s of Hugh NORENT & Elenor his wife
Dec 28	Mary d of Richard COOKE & Maragret his wife
Jan 12	Elizabeth d of Edman PETTY gentl & Anne his wife
Jan 9	Mary d of Humfrey BATE & Jane
Jan 26	Mary d of John PICHFORTE & Sarah
Feb 2	John s of Richard SMITH & Jane
Feb 2	Richard s of Richard MOSELEY & Margett
Feb 16	Robert s of Robert WEB & Ursula
Mar 22	Elizabeth d of Richard BARRET a stranger borne at ADDAM'ses
Mar 2	Edman s of Edman KETTLE & his wife
	[Bad ink stain at top of page - 2 entries illegible]
Mar 22	Theodotia d of John HACKET & Elnar his wife

Weddings 1639

Apr 22	Edman HURST & Margret JONES
Oct 10	John POWELL & Elnar EVANS
Nov 23	William SOUTHALL & Elenor d of Humfrey DICKENS by Lycence
Jan 28	Humfrey s of Humfrey DICKENS & Elizabeth GROVE by Lycence

Burials 1639

Apr 28	Widdow FREMING
May 28	Old William YORKE
May 30	Elizabeth d of John TERNE
May 29	John TOMSON
Aug 25[?]	Anne BRYNLEY widdow
Sep 9	Obadiah s of John CROSSE Minister
Oct 3	William s of William SITCH
Nov 7	Margery d of Frances LYNES

© Staffordhire Parish Registers Society

Nov 16 Widdow BURCH
Jan [?] Thomas LANE
[?] [Illegible] RABON bur
[?] Widdow [Illegible] bur
         1639 Thomas HILLMAN Churchwarden

Christenings 1640

May 17 Mary d of Thomas HOBBY & Joane his wife
Jun 21 Elnor d of Richard MOLE & Anne his wife
Jul 12 Dorothy d of John WESTON & Joane his wife
Sep 27 William s of William VINCENT & Elenor his wife
Sep --- Jane d of Richard RICE & Mary his wife
Aug 30 Edward s of William SICH & Joane his wife
Oct 4 Elizabeth d of Thomas COMBAR & Dorothy his wife
Oct 1 Mary d of John CORBIT & his wife his wife
Oct 1 Mary d of Edman HURST & Margret his wife
Nov 1 Margret d of Addam STOKES & Elnor his wife
Nov 15 Joseph HILLMAN
Nov 29 Richard s of Roger OLDNOLE & Elizabeth his wife
Dec 6 George s of George LOWE & Sara his wife
Dec 20 Shusana d of Humfrey BATE & Mary his wife
Jan 7 Elizabeth d of Robart JOHNES & Margret his wife
Feb 7 James s of Diones HILLMAN & Elenor his wife
Feb 8 John s of John TEARNE & Elizabeth[?] his wife
Feb 10[?] William s of John BIRD & Isable[?] his wife
Feb 14 Thomas s of John LYE & Alce his wife
Feb 28[?] Thomas s of Robart[?] JOHNSON & Jane his wife
Mar 4[?] Elizabeth d of Edward JORDEN gent & Margret his wife

Weddings Anno Domini 1640

May 26 Richard GROVE & Kathrin RABON by Lycence
Jun 10 Thomas HILL & Elnor PRICHETT
--------- John HILLMAN & Meriam NORBON by Lycence
Oct 6 Thomas MOSELEY & Elizabeth OULEY by Lycence
Oct 22 Thomas BERRY & Izable TOMSON (Lycence)
Feb 2 Edward LYNE & Jane BARBAR by Lycence

Burials Anno Domini 1640

Apr 10 Sisle wife of John HILL
Apr 17 Widow HARRIS
May 15 Widow CLARKE
May 25 Anne WARREN
May 26 Edward HILL
Jun 12 Isable BUYCHER
Jul 14 John COOKE
Jul 29 Humfrey LUCE
Aug 4 Humfrey JORDEN
Oct 24 Robert WEBS mother in law, a stranger
Sep 24 Anne d of John & Anne REBOLD
Dec 17 Mary d of John & Jane CORBIT

Feb 7	Joseph s of William PEN Junior
Feb 8	Elnor wife of Thomas POWELL
Feb 18	John BANISTER Senior
Mar 10	Phebe son[sic] of Mary DEACON Illegitimate
Mar 17	William HILL of Checkhill

[Another hand begins here]

Christenings 1641

Apr 4	Margaret d of Willm HARRISON & Anne his wife
Apr 18	Isabell d of Edward BATE & Elizabeth his wife
May 2	Martha d of Hercy PATE gent & Anne his wife
Jun 6	Anne d of Thomas MOSELEY & Elizabeth his wife
Jun 6	Anne d of John PRATT & Mary his wife
Jun 13	Humfrey s of Humfrey DICKENS & Elizabeth his wife
Jun 21	Anne d of William PENNE & Margaret his wife
Jul 11	James s of Thomas BERRY & Isabell his wife
Aug 1	Elizabeth d of Thomas FLOYD & Anne his wife
Aug 8	John s of John HUBBALL & Jane his wife
Aug 8	Thomas s of James LEONARD & Jane his wife
Sep 11	Anne d of Thomas CRANNIGE & Anne his wife
Sep ---	Marie d of William VINCENT & Margaret his wife
Nov 7	Thomas s of Frances BENNET & Constance his wife
Dec 3	John s of Thomas HOPE & Anne his wife
Dec 5	Katherine d of Richard HORTON & Jane his wife
Dec 27	Henry s of Francis WOOLDRIGE & A: his wife
Jan 4	John s of John COOKE & Anne his wife
Jan 12	Elizabeth s of Richard KETTLEBY gent & Margaret his wife
Jan 16	Hanna d of Thoms ATKYS & Margaret his wife
Feb 13	Margery d of John BILLINGSLEY & Margery his wife
Feb 13	Martha d of Hugh NORCOT & Elenor his wife
Feb 27	Abigail d of Robert WEBB & Urselah his wife
Mar 13	Margery d of Richard MOSELEY & Margaret his wife
Mar 20	John s of John HILLMAN & Mirriall his wife

Burials 1641

Jun 12	Katherine ATKYS widow bur
Jul 11	Anne SMITH widow
Aug 29	Joyce wife of John THOMAS
Aug 30	Elizabeth wife of John BROOKE
Oct 16	John s of Thomas LONGMORE
Nov 28	Humfrey HOPE
Nov 30	[Blank] s of John HUBBALL
Dec 31	Dorothie d of John WESTON
Jan 18	John WHITE
Mar 18	Jane wife of Humfrey DICKENS
Apr 28	Elenor WILLETT widdow
May 4	Elizabeth COMBER widdow

[The whole of next page has been smeared with ink & most of the entries are quite indecipherable. A portion only of each of the entries has been recovered]

Weddings 1641

.... & Joyce RICHARDS
John KIRKHA of pish of Row....... & Mary BATE of ye pish of Kinver
Francis BAKER of ye pish of Kingswinford & Mary ....
.... of ye pish of Womborne & Elenor ....
.... COOKE & Mary BARBER of the pish of Woeverley

Thomas LONGMORE   Humfrey BATE   Churchwardens

Christenings 1642

[There are 28 baptismal entries on this page but those entered below are all that have been deciphered.]

.... the son of John & Anne REBOLD bapt
.... the s of Humfrey & Anne BATE bapt
... . the d of Thomas & Eliz MOSELEY bapt
.... of Roger & Eliz OLDNAL bapt
Constance d of Edward & Anne .... bapt
.... the d of Dennice & Elenor HILLMAN bapt Feb
.... the d of Francis & Katherine LYNE bapt Feb
.... the s of Wm & .... CRUNDALL bapt Feb
.... the s of Edward & Margaret JORDEN bapt Feb
George the s of George & Elizabeth WEBB bapt Mar
.... the d of Hercy & Anne PATE bapt Mar

Weddings 1642

.... CRANIGER [or GRANGER] of Seisdon & Joane DANNCER of .....swinford

[The next page is still badly stained]

Burials 1642

Jul 11	Martha d of Hugh NORCOT & Elenor his wife
Jul 18	Widow EVANS
Jul 27	Elizabeth DEVIS widdow
Aug 3	Widdow TEEK
Aug 26	John s of Thomas POWELL & Joyce his wife
Sep 20	George DEVIS
Oct 21	Elizabeth wife of Henry WHEELER
Oct 26	Richard OSBOURNE
Nov 26	William PENNE
Feb 1	Elenor HILL widdow
Feb 12	Margari d of William HARRISON & Anne his wife
Feb 25	Joyce HILL widdow
Mar 23	Thomas GUY

Thomas LONGMORE Humfrey BATE Churchwardens

Christenings 1643

Apr 9	Richard s of John HACKET & Elenor his wife
Apr 9	Anne[?] d of Thomas KETLEE & Anne his wife
Apr 25	John s of John HUBBAL & Jane his wife
May 22	Thomas s of Humfrey BATE & Mary his wife
Jun 11	John s of Thomas COMBER & Dorothie his wife
Jun 12	John s of John SMALLMAN & [blank] his wife
Aug 6	George s of Richard BRINDLEY & Esther his wife
Sep 29	Mary d of Normon YORKE & Margaret his wife
Oct 15	Thomas s of John HILLMAN & Mirrial his wife
Oct 29	Sarah d of Edward HILLMAN & Elizabeth his wife
Nov 1	John s of William VINCENT & Elenor his wife
Nov 19	Elizabeth d of Anthony BATE & Theodosea his wife
Dec 17	Edward s of William LAVENDER & Elizabeth his wife
Dec 17	Humfrey s of Richard LUCE & Jane his wife
Dec 31	Katherine d of Richard SMITH & Joane his wife
Jan 21	Thomas s of Thomas GIBS & Jane his wife
Feb [?]	Anne d of Adam STOKES & Elenor his wife
Feb 25	Jane[?] d of John BIRD & Isable his wife
Mar 3	Edward s of Edward LINE & Jane his wife

Weddings 1643

Sep 15	Jonas HOLLOWAY & Elizabeth WHOOP

Burials 1643

Mar 25	Edward MOSELEY the elder of Whittingtonn
Mar 24	Richard s of John & Anne REBOLD
May 7	Isabel d of ye Widdow GUY
May 8	An Infant of Richard HALL Jun.
May 26	Anne wife of Herfie PATE
Apr 14	Elenor wife of John HACKET
Jun 11	Widdow FURLONG
Jun 26	Two infants of Thomas POWELL
Sep 27	[?] wife of Thomas WARRALL
Sep 30	Robert BRINDLEY
Oct 11	Widdow RICE
Oct 15	William ADDENBROOKE bur 1st Oct
Oct 16	Anne GUY
Oct 21	Mary d of Norman & Margaret YORKE
Nov 13	John HILL & Anne MADSTART
Nov 20	Widdow JONES
Dec 8	Richard BACH
Dec 22	Mary d of Thomas CRANNAGE
Dec 29	Elizabeth wife of Edward MOSELEY of Kynvar
Jan 1	Thomas KETLE
Jan 2	John HOLLYS
Jan 27	Margaret wife of Robert JONS
Jan 3	John EATON
Mar 13	Robert LOWE

Christenings 1644

Mar 31	Elizabeth d of John REBOLD & Anne his wife
Mar 31	Robert s of Thomas BURY & Isabel his wife
Apr 7	Elizabeth d of Jonas HOLLOWAY & Elizabeth his wife
Apr 7	Elizabeth d of John DEANE & Katharine his wife
Apr 21	John s of Henery BAYLIS & Jane his wife
May 19	Constance d of Francis BENNET & Constance his wife
Jun 12	Elizabeth d of Richard [crossed out] Thomas HALL jun.
Jun 11	Elizabeth d of John LYE & Alice his wife
Aug 4	Humfrey s of Thomas HOPE & Anne his wife
Aug 18	Elizabeth d of Thomas POWELL & Joyce his wife
Oct 11	Esther d of Thomas ATTKIS & [blot] his wife
Oct 20	John s of Richard M......[?] & Elizabeth his wife
Nov 17	Dorothie d of Norman YORKE & Margaret his wife
Nov 22	William s of Walter ELDERSHAW & Anne his wife
Dec 4	Elizabeth d of John SPRUCER & Jane his wife
Dec 4	Richard s of Anthony BATE & Theodosea his wife
Dec 15	John s of Edward BATE & Elizab: his wife
Dec 15	Edward s of John COOKE & Jane his wife
Dec 15	Elizabeth d of Thomas MOSELEY & Elizabeth his wife
Dec 22	Dorothie d of Richard TRAUNTER & Elizabeth his wife
Dec 22	Thomas s of Danner NEVILL & Constance his wife
Dec 22	Francis s of William KETLEE & Elizabeth his wife
Dec 22	Richard s of John HACKET & Barbara his wife baptized same day
Jan 19	John s of Humfrey BATE & Joane his wife
Feb 9	Thomas s of Edmund HUST & Margaret his wife
Feb 23	John s of Dennis HILLMAN & Elenor his wife
Feb 23	Mary d of John BANNISTER & Anne his wife
Mar 11	John s of John RICE & Joyce his wife
Mar 16	Humfrey s of Hugh JONES & Elizabeth his wife

Weddings 1644

Jun 4	John MASON & Bridget HURST
Jul 1	Edward PIKE & Anne BALL
Nov 25	John SMITH & Margaret FREEMAN
Jan 30	Thomas HILL & Margaret WEBB
Feb 17	Edward WINDLE & Alice EATON

Burials 1644

Mar 28	Captaine PENNE
Apr 4	Richard MOY
Apr 9	An Infant of Robert WEBB
Apr 10	An Infant of Henery BRISCOES
Jun 20	John POWELL
Jun 24	An Infant of Thomas HILLS
Jun 25	Elenor wife of Thomas HILL
Jul 6	Elizabeth d of Jonas HOLLOWAY & Elizabeth his wife
Jul 9	Thomas SMITH
[?]	Isabell d of Richard & Margery BANISTER

[?]   John s of Richard & Margery BANISTER

[The whole of the last page of the register has been smeared over with ink. None of the top third of the page is decipherable, but since the last burial on the previous page is dated July 1644 the missing entries are probably the remaining burials for that year, i.e. August 1644 - March 1644/5. The next entry which can be read part way down this page is headed "1649".]

.... the sone of William KIMBERLEY by Elizabeth his wife was baptised the 26th of September. Wittnesse John? Floo?
William KIMBERLY minister & Scoolemaster
Wittnes Roger KIMBERLY

.... dau of Richard HALL   bapt Feb 1648
Richard the son of Richard BATE   bapt Sept

Richard BIRD

.... the .... of Angus MACE & Elizabeth his wife bapt Sept 1649

Wm VINCENT? & ....? MOSELEY

The .... day of July was buried Gerrard HILL of Aulde Swinforde Anno Dom 1644

End of Register

Kinver Parish Register, 1653-1710

[On the flyleaf are various scribblings:]
Jonathan NEWEY
Jonathan NEWEY was never [remembered]
by me   H. BATE
Minister

..........FORREST of Bobington   Kinver
..............ish & Anne WYGGAN   Jonathan
.... is parish were marryed
26 1703
Jonathan NEWEY
Minister of Kinver

[On reverse:]
Jonathan NEWEY
Minister of Kinver was a little
man but a Brave one
Jonathan

[The register now starts properly on the next page. The page is divided into two columns, but the writing is very faint:]

Baptisms 1653

Margaret the daughter of Richard BROOKES & Jane his wife was borne the 28th Sept. bapt Oct. 8th

Elizabeth the daughter of Edw. BATE & Elizabeth his wife was borne Novemb^r 20th, bapt 27th Nov

[Bridget] the daughter of Humphry PERRY & Elnor his wife was born ye 3rd Decemb. Baptized 10th

[?]ry the daughter of Thomas BACH als LEVIE & Isabel his wife was born Jan 9th baptized 15th January

[?   ] the daughter of Thomas HOPE & An. his wife was born the 7th of January & baptized ye 21th

.....ard son of Francis GRIFFITH & Mary his wife was borne the 13th February & baptized March 4th

Sarah the daughter of William KETTLE & Katharine his wife was born ye 17th February baptized the 19th

Margaret the daughter of Richard BANISTER & Margery his wife was born the 23th December bapt. Jan. 6th

Margaret the daughter of Thomas MOSELY & Elizabeth his wife was borne Feb. 19th & baptz^d ye March 11th

Burials

Richard FRANCIS was buryed October 8th
Mary the wife of Thomas SMITH bury^d Feb 20th
Jane COOK widdow was buryed October 12th
Eliza[?] LOWE widdow buryed October ye 27th
Sarah the wife of Mr John KINESSLY buryed January 7th

William JABASEY[?] buryed January ye 15th 1653
William COOK was buryed February 25th
    the daughter of Edward YORKE buryed March 1st
John TAYLER was buryed the 9th March
Thomas sone of Jon NORTHALL buryed ye 5th March
Richard WORRALL was buryed the 14th March
Mrs Ann ROPER daughter to Cath.[?] ROPER was buryed 15th April 1654

Marriages
William TAYLOR son of Widdow TAYLOR of Kinver & Margery SMITH were marryed March 6th 1653
Richard PURSLOE & Lydia WEBB both of this parish were marryed the 4th September 1654

Births & Baptisms 1654
Mary the daughter of John WYER & Ann his wife was bapt. here thr 20th April bapt 8th May

Buryalls 1654
Margery FRANCIS widdow was buryed May 6th
Elizabeth[?] ye wife of Wm WEBB was buryed 28th Sept

[At the bottom of the page]
Marriages 1654
Michell SPARRIE & Abigayle SYSTON were married ye 15th day of May And were forgott to be registered.

[In the otherwise blank, next column opposite to the previous baptisms]
Baptisms 1654
Elizabeth the daughter of Edward BURTON & Abigail his wife Baptized September the 9th 1653

[Also entered in this column very faintly:]
Eliz the daughter of John LAN[?] and – his wife

[New page]
Baptismes that were not Set down in their proper places Anno Dom 1664

Elienr d of Mr Richard BIRD & Elienr his wife Baptized Jan 22 1664
Edward s of Richard HARRICE was Bapt. also ye Jan 22d 1664
Katherine d of Bartholomew KETTELL was Bapt. Feb. 4 1664
Jane d of Edward ADENBROOK & Hester his wife Bapt. Feb. 6th
Elizabeth d of Richard GARRETT & Elienor his wife Bapt. ye Feb 15
William s of Richard BROOK & Jane his wife Bapt. Feb 12th
Benjamin s of Elias PUTTERFIELD was Bapt & buryed Feb 27th
Jane d of Richard HOPE Bapt March 18 1664

[New page The next paragraph stretches across the width of the page which is otherwise divided into two columns:]

The xiii[th] off January ao 1654
Edward MOSELEY gent. was Approved off for Register and Admitted to have the Keeping of the Register Booke And was Sworne before John WHORWOOD Esq. one of the Justices of the Peace for the Countie of Stafford as by this Certificatt under his Hand and Seale it doth and may Appeare

ao: 1654 Marriages

Humfrey LOWE & Marie TEARNE 9th day of January
Francis JORDEN & Margarett HILLMAN d of Robert HILLMAN were marryed the 9th Day of Jan

Births & Baptisms 1654

Robert the sonn of Robert POWELL & Susan his wyfe was borne the xi[th] day of January and was Baptized the 28th of the same.
Edward the sonn to Thomas COMBER & Dorothie his wyfe was borne the 10th Day of January and baptized the 30th day of the same
William the sonn off Will: TAYLOR & Margery his wyfe was borne the 17th of January and was baptized the 4th off February

Burialles Ao: 1654

Feb 2   John KYTELEY
Feb 6   Mrs Elizabeth TALBOTT d of Mr Will. TALBOTT gent and Marie his wife
Mar 18 Robert HILLMAN

Burialles Anno 1655

Jan 20 Mary the wyfe of Fowke GRIFFIN
Feb 20 Elizabeth the wyfe of Richard WESTON

Births & Baptismes A° 1654

Joseph the sonn of Thomas BACHE & Issabel his wyfe was borne the 9th day of February & was baptized the 13th of the same
John the sonn of John HART & Margret[?] his wyfe borne the 13th January & was baptized the 5th day of February & was buried the 12th day of the same month
Harry the sonn of Will. GARRETT & Sissley his wyfe was borne the 22th day of January & was baptized the 5th day of February
Hester the daughter of Humphrey PERRY & Ellinor his wyfe was borne the 12th day of March & was baptized the 18th of the same
Elizabeth the daughter of Henry LONGMER & Elizabeth his wyfe was borne the 4th day of March & was baptized the 24th of the same
William the sonn of John PURSLOW & Margery his wyfe was borne the 8th of March & was baptized the 26th of the same

Burialls 1655

Apr 13 Benjamin s of Francis WORRALL [BT's: "WARRALL"]
Apr 14 Katharine d of Jane HORTON [BT's: "widdow"]
Apr 17 John BRISCOE the elder

Apr 28	[BT's: "Sir"] William WHORWOOD Esq
Apr 30	Gerrard WARREN
May 3	John[crossed out] Thomas STREET
Jun 30	Stephen WEDGE
Jul 7	Katherine LINES
Jul 9	Richard DAVIS
Jul 31	Robert s of William TALBOT Esq.
	[blank] COOXY of Hales-Owen[inserted above] drowned Oct: 27 found Nov 5th buried Nov 7th 1655
Nov 15	Mrs Francis GRAVENOR
Dec 18	The wyfe of Humfrey JONES
Dec 19	Sarah KETTLE
[BT's:	"Marie the wyfe of Foulk GRIFFEN was buried the 20th day of Januarie"]

[In the opposite column at the top of the page:]
Births & Baptismes 1655

May 5	Henry s of Henry HUTT borne April 18
May 13	John s of Richard BIRD born April [?]
Aug 8	Elizabeth d of John & Elizabeth PENN born July 16
Oct 8	Thomas s of Edward HALE was born Oct^r [?]
Dec 14	Sarah d of John & Ann WYRE born December 3
[blank]	Elizabeth d of John & Elizabeth PENN born 16th day of July
Jan 21	Hunfrey s of Henry & [blank] BAYLIS born Jan 14
Feb 4	John s of Richard & Jane BROOK borne 30th of Jan
Sep 23	Thomas s of Humphrey KETLEY & Susan his wife

[Written under the above two sections:]
This above Registeres was bapt. by me Roger KYMBERLEY

Births & Baptismes Anno 1655

May 13	John s of John SPENSER & Jane his wyfe born the second day of May
May 22	Robert s of William TALBOTT gent. & Mary his wyfe borne the 9th day of May
May 28	William s of Willm GREAVES & An his wyfe borne the 13th day of May
Jun 17	William s of Robert COOKE & Mary his wyfe born the 7th day of June
Oct 7	Richard s of John WARRALL & Sarah his wyfe borne the 14th day of September

Births & Baptismes 1655

Aug 13	Hannah d of John MOSELEY & Ann his wyfe born the 6th day of August
Aug 30	Suttonn s of Mr William WHORWOOD & Dame Katherine his wyfe borne the [?] day of July
Sep 2	John s of Mychell SPARRY & Abigaile his wyfe born the 18th day of August

| Sep 6 | Kathrine d of Robert LEMSON Esq & Hannah his wyfe born 18th of August |
| Aug 23 | Anne d of William WHALDEN & Jane his wife |

Birthes & Baptismes Ano 1655

Sep 23	Thomas the sonn of Mr Richard BRYNLEY & Hester his wyfe born the 12th day of September
Sep 23	Margrett the daughter of Harry HACKETT & Mary his wyfe
Sep 2	John the sonn of Benedict BELL & Dorothy his wyfe born the 22 daye of August
Mar 3	Erssille[?] the daughter of Richard HALL & Elizabeth his wyfe
Mar 17	John the sonn of Humphey DAVIS & Anne his wyfe borne the 3rd daye of March
Mar 24	Margerie the daughter of Anthony BATE & Marie his wyfe borne the 19th day of March
Mar 25	Ann the daughter of Richard KETTLEY the elder & Ann his wyfe borne the 7th Day of March
Mar 31	Ellinor[?] the daughter of Thomas PIXELL & Ellinor his wyfe borne the 8th day of March

Anno 1655 Marriages

May 17	Thomas PIXELL & Ellinor GOODYER
Mar 13	Foulke GRIFFEN & Isabell SITCHE
Mar 18	William WARRENN & Jane KETLEY
Mar 22	Thomas HEMING of Olde Swynford & Elizabeth RUSSELL

Anno 1656 Marriages

Mar 25	John WHERRIT & Elizabeth LAYTON
Mar 25	Josiah RAYBOULD of Olde Swyforde & Jane BEDDARD
Apr 22	Richard SPITTLE & Jane BARNSLEY
May 22	George HARDING & Katherine WHEELER
May 27	George GARNER [BT's: "GARNOUR"] & Jane JOHNSON the younger
Jun 10	Richard HARRIS & Elizabeth LYNES
Jun 12	Thomas HUNT & Martha OAKLEY both of the psh of Sedgeley
Jun 23	Thomas SMITH & Mary GYBS
Jun 24	John JOHNES & Margrett STREETE
Aug 25	Joseph LAVENDER & Mary WESTON
Sep 1	Addam PARKSHOUSE & Margrett HATTONN of the psh of Sedgeley
Sep 15	John BOWRNE & Jane BROOKES
Sep 25	Roger HICKMAN &Sarah LYNE
Sep 29	Raphe RAWLISSON & Margrett ROUND
Oct 3	Edward HARVIE & Margrett HOBBIE
Oct 7	John WARTER & Mary SYMKYS
Oct 9	George COMBER & Ann LOWE
Oct 9	John GAUDIN & Allice BATE

Anno 1656 Births & Baptisms

Apr 18	Ann the daughter of George COMBER & Ann his wyfe borne 12th Aprill
Apr 27	Joseph the sonn of John SMITH & Margrett his wyfe borne the 16th April
Apr 27	Thomas s of Thomas MOSELEY & Elizabeth his wyfe borne the 19th Aprill
Apr 8	Thomas s of Edward LYNE & Jane his wyfe borne 26th March
Apr 10	Allexander & Richard the sonnnes of John LYNE & Elizabeth his wyfe being twyns were borne the 2th daye of Aprill
May 18	Ann the daughter of John CLARKE & Mary his wyfe borne 23 Aprill
Jun 2	Thomas s of Mr Edward JORDEN & Margrett his wyfe borne 23 May
Jun 1	John the sonn of Richard FEREDE & Frances his wyfe borne 24th May
Jul 3	Thomas s of John BRADELEY & Margrett his wyfe borne 22th June
	A female Infant one Mary ALLERSOMS a travelling woman coming out of Cheshier was borne the 4th Julie but was not baptized in third of [?]

Marriages 1656

Oct 31	Thomas MOSELEY & Callibria SMITH
Dec 4	Thomas HOWTONN & Margrett GARRETT
Dec 6	Olliver HILL & Amye LYE
Dec 24	William KETTLEY & Mary WHITTMORE
Dec 27	Thomas BROOKE & Ann MOWSELL both of the psh of Over Areley

Births & Baptismes Ano 1656

Jul 8	Ann d of John SMITH & Jane his wyfe borne 26th June
Oct 18	Isabel d of Thomas BACHE & Isabel his wyfe borne 29th September
Oct 18	Edward s of Edward JORDON[?] & Isabel his wyfe borne the 8th October
Dec 2	John s of William TALBOTT gent. & Mary his wyfe borne 19th November
Dec 5	Thomas s of Roger DAVIS & Prisilla his wyfe borne 23 November
Dec 9	Joan d of John TEARN & Elizabeth his wyfe borne 21 November
Dec 10	Thomas s of Edward HILLMAN & Elizabeth his wyfe borne 30th November
Jan 29	Thomas s of Thomas CORBYN Esq & Margrett his wyfe was borne the 17th Januarie
Feb 7	Jane d of Humphrey BATE & Jane his wyfe borne the 17th Januarie
Feb 7	[...ane?] d of Thomas SMITH & Mary his wyfe borne the 20th Januarie

Feb 21	[?] s of Richard DAVIS & Ann his wyfe borne the 10th off February
Mar 9	John s of Edward GROVE & [blank] his wyfe borne the 14th February
Mar 1	George s of William TAYLOR & Margery his wyfe borne the 5th Feb.
Mar 22	Thomas s of Edward BATE & Elizabeth his wyfe was borne the 13th March
Mar 24	Elizabeth d of Richard HARRIS & Elizabeth his wyfe borne the 10th Maij

Burialls ao 1656

Jul 16	William s of William BENNETT & Elienor his wyfe
Aug 8	Hughe POTTER
Nov 30	[?] GRIFFIN
Dec 9	Thomas DAVIS, sonn of Roger DAVIS & Priscilla his wyfe
Jan 7	[?] CORBITT, d of John CORBITT
Feb 12	Humphrey DICKENS
Feb 9	Joane KYNERSLEY illegitimate
Mar 21	Edward WEAVER a stranger dyed att the White Hart
Mar 23	Amie HILLMAN wyddow

Burials ao 1657

Apr 8	Margery the wyfe of Jeoffrey COOK
May 2	Talbott WHORWOOD the sonn of Will[m] WHORWOOD & Katheryne his wyfe
May 13	Henry LONGMORE
Jun 16	Elizabeth the wyfe of Will. FEILD
Jun 28	Edward LYNE
Aug 10	Ann HUBBALD the daughter of Jane BAKER
Aug 11	Hannah the daughter of John SMITH & Jane his wyfe
Aug 26	Francis GARRETT
Aug 31	John BYRD
Sep 4	John the sonn of Will: TALBOTT gent & Mary his wyfe
Sep 24	John BROOKE of the Rock
Oct 10	Ann the wyddow of John CLARK the elder
Nov 28	John SMYTH of Whittington
Dec 21	Mary the daughter of Robert POWELL & Susan his wyfe
Dec 30	Henry BRYSCOAE [BT's: "BRYSCOE"]
Jan 8	Thomas GROVE
Jan 23	Sutton WHORWOOD sonne of the Lady Katheryne WHORWOOD
Jan 28	Alice WHITE wyddow
Jan 17	Hester d of Humphrey PERRY & Ellinor his wyfe
Feb 13	Ann the wyfe of Thomas TAYLOR
Feb 17	Samuel the sonn of Mr Richard BRYNLEY & Hester his wyfe
Feb 24	Peeter the sonn of John SMYTH & Jane his wyfe

Marriages ao 1657

| May 18 | Edward BAGNALL & Margery BROOKHOUSE |

May 18	Richard BAXTER & Ellinor COXE
May 19	Allexander LAWDER Schoolmaster & Ann HACKETT
Aug 31	William ROBBINSON & Rebecke JEAVON
Oct 19	Richard WESTONN & Ann POTTER
Dec 26	Richard GARRETT & Ellinor THOMAS

Birthes & Baptismes 1657

Jun 17	Mary d of Richard BAXSTER & Margery his wyfe born 8th June
Jul 4	Humphrey s of Anthony BATE & Mary his wyfe born the 17th June
Jul 4	Margrett d of Thomas [BT's: "Junior"] MOSELEY & Callibria his wife born 30th June
Aug 9	Jane d of William WARREN & Jane his wyfe born the 18th July
Sep 12	Thomas s of Henry LONGMORE & Elizabeth his wyfe born the 6th September
Sep 29	Samuell s of Mr Richard BRYNLEY & Hester his wyfe born 20th September
Oct 5	Edward s of Edward HARVIE & Margrett his wyfe born the 18th September
Mar 28[sic]	Ann the daughter of Elmer HILL & Anne his wyfe was born 22 March
	John RAYBOLDE s of Thomas RAYBOLD & Ann his wyfe born the 30th September & was baptised 1st October and buried the 4th of October
Oct 20	John the sonn of Will. GREAVES & Ann his wyfe born 4th October
Oct 26	William the sonn of John PENN & Elizabeth his wyfe born the 10th October
Nov 14	Mary the daughter of Robert POWEL & Susanna his wyfe born 17 October
Dec 6	Benedict the sonn of Benedict BELL & Dorothie his wyfe born 14th Novemb:
Nov 28	Sarah the daughter of William WHEELDON & Ann his wyfe
Jan 4	William the sonn of Allexander LAWDER Schoolemaster & Ann his wyfe born 11th December
Jan 2	[?]nn the daughter of Henry BRISCOAE & Margrett his wyfe born 23 December
Jan 24	Elizabeth the daughter of William KETTLEY & Mary his wyfe born the 17th of January
Feb 22	Thomas the sonn of John PURSLOWE & Margery his wyfe born 25 January

Burialles ao 1657

Mar 1	Humphrey JOHNES
Mar 10	Margrett the daughter of Denyse HILLMAN & Ellinor his wyfe
Mar 13	Ann the daughter of George COMBER & Ann his wyfe
Mar 16	Ann EDWARDS
Mar 21	Margery the wyfe of John BYLLINGSLEY

Births & Baptismes ao 1658

- Apr 20 — Ann d of Henry KNIGHT & Jane his wyfe born 20 March 1657
- Apr 20 — Margrett d of Thomas CORBYN Esqr & Margrett his wyfe born 6th April
- Apr 24 — John s of Norman YORKE & Margaret his wyfe born 14 April
- Jun 19 — Thomas s of Michell SPARRY & Abbygayle his wyfe born 9th May
- May 21 — Thomas s of Thomas COMBER & Dorothie his wyfe born 12th May
- Jul 22 — William s of William TALBOTT gent & Mary his wyfe born 7th July
- Jun 27 — Richard s of Richard BYRDE & Allice his wife born 18th June
- May 8 — John s of John REA & Mary his wyfe
- Jun 20 — William s of Roger DAVIS & Prissilla his wyfe born 17th June
- Jun 20 — Roger s of Roger CADSALL & Jane his wyfe born 10th June
- Jul 27 — Abygayle d of Richard SMYTH & Jane his wyfe born 17th July
- Aug 15 — Thomas s of Richard BARKER & Ellinor his wyfe
- Sep 17 — John s of John JOHNES & Margrett his wyfe born 6th September
- Oct 27 — Richard s of Richard GARRETT & Ellinor his wyfe born 22nd October
- Nov 2 — Thomas s of Thomas SMYTH & Mary his wyfe was born the 8th October
- Nov 2 — Abigayle d of John HUBBALD born 7th October

[It appears that there has been an attempt to erase the next entry, the only decipherable portion remaining:]

- 27 Dec — s of John MOSELEY & Margery born 16th December
- Feb 7 — William s of Humphrey PERRY & Ellinor his wyfe born 4th February
- Feb 23 — Thomas s of Thomas PYXELL & Ellyner his wyfe born 11th February
- Mar 12 — William & John MOSELEY twynes the sonnes of Thomas MOSELEY & Elizabeth his wyfe were born 26 February
- Dec 31 — John s of John BRYSCOAD & Jane his wyfe born 25th December
- Dec 31 — Humphrey s of John MOSELEY & Margery his wyfe born 17th December

Anno 1658 Marriages

- Jun 5 — Thomas HITCHENS & Margrett MOSELEY
- Jun 29 — Joseph MYATT & Margrett DOVERDALE
- Jul 1 — Henry ELCOCK & Isabell BANNISTER
- [blank] — [blank] BANNISTER & Ann GARRETT
- Oct 12 — William WESSON & Ann GARRETT of Kinvar
- Oct 28 — Thomas GOOLDE [BT's: "GOULD"] & Elizabeth KETTLEY
- Oct 27 — Edward CHAMBERLAYNE & Abigayle COOKE

[The next two entries seem to have a large "X" through them, but note they are repeated again later:]

- Feb 28 — William CRUNDALL & Theodosia HACKETT
- Feb 28 — Thomas LYNE & Ellinor HILL

Anno 1658 Births & Baptismes

[The next two entries have large "X"'s through them with a comment at the side "was forgot":]

Feb 23   Thomas s of Thomas PIXELL & Ellinor his wife was born 11th February

Feb 12[sic]   William & John sonns of Thomas MOSELEY & Elizabeth his wyfe being twynes were borne 26th February[sic]

Burialls Anno 1658

Apr 28   Thomas LONGMOR s of Henry LONGMOR of Stourton & Elizabeth his wyfe
May 1   John WATKYS of Compton
May 20   William WHEELDEN
Jun 8   Susanna POWELL wyfe of Robert POWELL
Jun 10   Joyce BACHE of Whittington
Jun 29   Joyce DUNN wyfe of Will. DUNN
Jul 16   Richard KETTLEY the younger
Jul 24   Will: DUNN
Aug 18   Margrett HITCHENS
Aug 21   Joane AURDEN of Whittington wyddow
Aug 2   Isabell d of Richard BRYNLEY & Hester his wyfe
Sep 28   Roger KYMBERLEY Mynnister of this place
Oct 10   Elizabeth BAKER
Nov 2   Edward s of Edmund HURST
Nov 7   Bridgett BACHE of Stourton wyddow
Nov 11   Hannah d of Humphrey KETTLEY & Susan his wyfe
Dec 1   Ann the wyfe of George WHITE
Dec 10   Ann the wyddow of Will: HILL
Dec 12   Ann BACHE d of the Wyddow Bridgett BACHE
Dec 14   Richard WESSONN Clarke of this psh
Dec 21   William VINCENT of the Hyde
Jan 21   William PAGETT
Jan 25   Thomas JOHNSON Church Warden
Feb 19   Jane the wyfe of John HUBBALL

Births & Baptismes a 1659

Apr 6   Richard s of Richard SERIDEN & Francis his wyfe
Apr 6   [blank] the s of Henry HUTT & his wyfe
Apr 6   Ann d of Joseph MYATT & Margrett his wyfe

Burials 1658

Feb 22   Mrs Francis WASHBURN
Mar 23   Edward GROVE of Compton

Marriages ao 1658

[These entries also appear previously]

Feb 28   William CRUNDALL & Theodosea HACKETT
Feb 28   Thomas LYNE & Ellinor HILL

Burialles 1659

Apr 5	John s of Thomas MOSELEY & Elizabeth his wyfe
Apr 11	John SELVESTER
Apr 21	Jonas HOLLOWAY
Apr 27	Katherine the wyfe of Will. KETTLE
	Marie d of John NURTHILL & Ann his wyfe was borne & baptised the 28th of April but was buried the 29th of the same
May 4	John CORBITT of Haffcoat
May 11	Elizabeth WEBB wyddow
May 13	[BT's:15th] Ann the wyddow of Wil: TAYLOR
May 14	Elizabeth d of William KETTLE
May 21	John s of John REA
May 23	Addam STOAKES
May 24	Frances COOKE
May 25	Norman YORKE
Jun 27	Elizabeth d of John TEARNE
Jul 14	Ann the wyfe of George COMBER
Aug 10	Jerome LOWE
Oct 3	Elizabeth the wyfe of Humphrey LYNE
Oct 8	Jane the wyfe of George GARNER [B T's: "GARNOUR"]

Births & Baptismes ao 1659

May 29	Jane d of Richard BROOKE & Jane his wyfe born 18th May
May 23	Mary d of Henry LONGMOR & Elizabeth his wyfe born 25th April
Aug 21	Amye [BT's: "Amie"] d of John HILLMAN [BT's: "HYLLMAN"] & Meriall his wyfe born 30th July
Aug 4	Elizabeth d of Will. WOOD & [blank] his wyfe born 24 July

Marriages ao 1659

Jun 13	Thomas PEARSE & Mary BYRDE
Nov 17	Niccolas COMBSON & Ann MOSELEY
Dec 5	Thomas GYBS & Mary JOHNSON
Mar 5	John RAYBOLDE & Mary HOPE

Births & Baptismes ao 1659

Aug 30	Hannah d of Allexander LAWDER Schoolemaster & Ann his wyfe born 22th August
Sep 19	Marie d of Edward HALE & Issabell his wyfe born 1st September
Sep 27	John s of John JOHNSON & Ann his wyfe born 21 September
Nov 5	Margery d of Will. TAYLOR & Margery his wyfe
Nov 13	Mary ["Marie" in BT's], d of Will. KETTLEY & Marye his wyfe born 4 November
Nov 28	William s of John DUNN & Ellinor his wyfe born 13th November
Dec 6	John s of Will. BANNISTER & Ann his wyfe born 21st November
Dec 10	Elizabeth d of Will. COWPER & his wyfe

Dec 9	Marye ["Marie" in BT's] d of Edward HARVEY & Margrett his wyfe born 4th December
Jan 7	Hannah d of Will: GREAVES & Ann his wyfe born 25 December
Jan 8	Charles s of John PURSLOWE & Margery his wyfe born 25 December
Jan 8	William s of Will. CRUNDALL the younger & Theodocea his wyfe born 1st January

Burialls ao 1659

Dec 15	Roger OLDNALL
Dec 23	George s of Richard SMYTH
Dec 24	John GARRETT
Jan 11	William s of Roger DAVIS & Priscilla
Jan 18	John BILLINGSLEY
Feb 2	Allice SYTCHE wyddow
Feb 10	Theodocea the wyfe of Will: CRUNDALL the younger
Feb 25	John DAVIES
Mar 8	John s of Will: BANNISTER & Ann his wyfe

Births & Baptismes ao 1659

Feb 26	An d of Richard GARRETT & Elliner his wyfe born 16th February
Feb 26	Thomas s of Thomas MOSELEY & Collibra his wyfe born 25th February
Mar 11	Mary d of Roger DAVIS & Prissilla his wyfe
Mar 14	Mary d of Henry HACKETT & Mary his wyfe
Mar 17	John s of Oliver HILL & Anne his wyfe

Anno 1660 Births & Baptismes

Apr 16	John s of Anthony BATE & Mary his wyfe was born 31st March
May 20	Mary d of John PEN & Elizabeth his wyfe
Jul 1	Elizabeth d of Will: FEILD & Margery his wyfe
Aug 14	Joseph s of Thomas SMYTH & Marye his wyfe
Jul 28	Thomas s of John HILLMAN & Meriall his wyfe [Charles is also written underneath Thomas]
Feb 22	Frauncis s of Richard SMYTH baptized the 22th February being [.... to ....before ....?]
Jan 29	John s of John RAYBOULD born 17th January

Burialls Anno 1660

Apr 11	Abygaile the wyfe of Mychell SPARRIE [BT's: SPARRY"]
Apr 16	Thomas TAYLOR
Jun 12	Humphrey HACKETT
Jun 26	Joane PHILLIPS a poore woman dyed in the Church porche
May 15	Allice the wyfe of Richard BYRDE
Jul 11	Margery the wyddow of John LONGMORE
Aug 19	Frauncis WOLDRIGE
Aug 21	Dorothie the wyfe of Thomas COMBER
Sep 5	Mary the wyfe of Anthony BATE

Nov 3	Richard OVERLEY ["NURTHALL" in BT's]
Nov 20	Richard MOLE s of Richard MOLE
Nov 22	[blank] the wyfe of John SUTHALL
Jan 14	Talbott s of Allexander LAWDER & Ann his wyfe
Feb 12	William s of John PEN & Elizabeth his wyfe

Baptisms 1660

Sep 2	William s of William WARREN & Jane his wyfe
Sep 1	Abigayle d of Edward YORK & Abigayle his wyfe
Oct 9	Thomas s of Thomas NORRIS & Bridgett his wyfe
Nov 6	Talbott s of Mr Allexander LAWDER & Ann his wyfe born 28th October
Dec 5	Edward s of John SMYTH & Jane his wyfe
Dec 23	Allyce d of John MOSELEY & Margery his wyfe
May 10	1661 Elizabeth d of Edward HALE & Isabell his wyfe

Weddings Anno 1660

Jul 3	George COMBER & Elizabeth PAVIE
Jun 9	John ANDREWES & Ann WHEELDON

Baptisms 1661

[The following baptisms appear in the BT's but not in the OR's]

~~Mar~~ Feb 10	Jane d of Edward HALE
May 24	Elizabeth d of Gylbert PENN
Jun 23	Ann d of Thomas TEARNE
Jun 23	Thomas s of Humphrey CLARK
Aug 18	William s of Will FEILD

[Entries are now the same in OR and BT's]

Nov 12	Christian d of Humphrey PERRIE & Elliner his wyfe
Nov 17	Elizabeth d of John LOWE & Ann his wyfe
Dec 10	Ann d of William KETTLEY & Mary his wyfe
Feb 18	Joane d of Henry LONGMOR & Elizabeth his wyfe
Feb 8	William s of Raphe POWELL & Sarah his wyfe
Feb 12	Elizabeth d of John HYLLMAN & Elizabeth his wyfe

Burialls Anno 1661

Apr 2	Mary the wyddow of Sherrington TALBOTT Esq
Nov 26	Elizabeth the wyfe of Thomas CLARKE
Jun 20	William SYTCHE
Jul 11	Richard WARRALL of Checkhill
Jul 21	Jane the wyfe of John BAKER
Sep 4	Robert COOKE
Sep 23	Richard WYTHE alies Nick KNACK
Oct 9	Humphrey LYNE

Baptismes Anno 1662

[blank]	Robert s of Richard BYRD & Eliner his wyfe
Dec 22	William s of John RAYBOLD & Marie his wyfe
Dec 26	Elizabeth d of Thomas PIXELL & Ellinor his wyfe
Dec 28	Margrett d of Humphrey PERRY & Elliner his wyfe

Jan 6	Frauncis s of Frauncis BRETTELL & Jane his wyfe
Dec 27	Samuell s of Thomas RAYBOULD & Betteridge his wyfe
May 29	Sarah d of William EM & Maudlen his wyfe
Jun 14	Judeth d of Mychell SPARRY & Elizabeth his wyfe
Jun 15	Katherine d of Thomas HORTON & Margrett his wyfe
Jul 3	Ouswald s of John PEN & Elizabeth his wyfe
Jul 13	Samuell s of Thomas SMYTH & Mary his wyfe
Apr 25	John s of William NYCCOLES & Judeth his wyfe
Apr 25	Samuell s of John PURSLOW & Margery his wyfe
Apr 12	Ann d of Roger DAVIES & Prissilla his wyfe
May 24	Elizabeth d of Gilbert PEN & Margery his wyfe
Jun 23	Thomas s of Humphrey CLARKE
Jul 28	Lancelott s of Mr Allexander LAWDER Schoolemaster & Ann his wyfe
Aug 10	James s of Richard HARRIES & Elizabeth his wyfe
Feb 8	John s of Humphrey CLARKE & Ellinor his wyfe
Feb 22	Marie d of Richard FERIDEA & Frances his wyfe
Mar 22	Elizabeth d of Edward HARVIE & Margrett his wyfe
Apr 28	John s of William NYCHOLAS & Judith his wyfe

Weddings Anno 1662

May 26	Thomas BARBER & Ann HARRISON
Sep 4	Randle BORE & Elizabeth CLARKE
Jan 6	Henry SUTHALL & Theodocea LOWE
Feb 2	Edward DUNN & Sarah HYLLMAN
Feb 2	William STANLEY & Marie DUNN
Feb 22	Thomas LEE & Joane WEDGE

Burialles Anno 1662

Apr 7	Maurice NEWNAM
Aug 6	Richard LUCE
Aug 6	Joyce BACHE
Dec 18	Isabell the wyfe of Mr George BRYNLEY

[At the start of the next column, an entry has been erased, which seems to read (but note the next entry):]

[?]	Elizabeth the wyfe of Richard BANNISTER was buried
Feb 2	Margrett the wyfe of Richard BANNISTER
Feb 21	Ann MOSELEY of Halfcoatt
Mar 1	Margery BRISDOW wyddowe
Mar 21	Ellinor the wyfe of Richard EVANS
1663	
Mar 28	Ann the wyddowe of Jerome LOWE
Apr 4	Frauncis LYNES
Apr 20	Margery the wyfe of Will FEILD
May 1	Ryce TAYLOR

Baptismes Anno 1662

[The first entry has been crossed out]:

[?]	Margaret d of Richard [?] & Elizabeth his wyfe
Mar 3 1663[sic]	William s of Henry HUTT & Mar....[?] his wyfe

1662
Dec 22   William s of John RAYBOLD & Mary his wyfe
Dec 26   Elizabeth d of Thomas PIXELL & Elinor his wyfe
Dec 27   Samuell s of Thomas RAYBOLD & Betteridge his wyfe
Dec 2[?] Margret d of Humphrey PEN & Elinor his wyfe
Jan 6   Francis s of Francis BRETTLE & Jane[?] his wyfe
Feb 8   John s of Humphrey CLARKE & Elliner his wyfe
Feb 22   Jane d of Richard FEREDAY & Frances his wyfe
Mar 22   [?]rah d of Edward HARVIE & Margaret his wyfe
1663
Apr 20   Marie d of Richard LINES & Sarah his wyfe
Apr 25   Marjorie d of Richard WARREN & Anne his wyfe
Apr 26   [?]beth d of Thomas MORRICE & Elizabeth his wyfe
May 9   William s of Will: EM & Magd. his wyfe
May 15   Humphrey s of Will: WARREN
May 16   John s of Tho: MOSELEY jun & Collibro his wyfe
Jun 25   [?]ester d of John CLARKE & Mary his wyfe
Jul 20   Elizabeth d of Robert WHITE & Margarett his wyfe
Jul 26   Thomas s of John TROWE & Elinor his wyfe
[The writting for the remaining entries in this section is extremely small]
Oct 10   Alice d of William GREEVES & Emme his wyfe
Oct 17   Theodocia d of Thomas MOSELEY & Elizabeth his wyfe
Oct 17   John[?] s of Jos POWELL & Eliz. his wyfe
Dec 26   William s of Wm KETTLE & Elizab his wyfe
Dec 28   [?]abeth d of Nicholas COMPTON & Anne his wyfe
Jan 1   Edward s of John JOHNSON & Ann his wyfe
Jan 10   [?]rah d of John PENNE & Mary HOBBY illeg.
Jan 11   [?]beth d of John MOSELEY & Marjorie his wyfe
Jan 30   [Michael] s of Michael SPARRY & Elizab. his wyfe
Feb 8   [?   ] s of John HILLMAN & Elizab. his wyfe
Feb 8   [?   ] of Robt POWELL by Frances his wyfe
Mar 6   [?   ] d of Bartholomew KETTLE
            [Writing returns to normal size]

Weddings Anno 1663
May 13   Joseph LOW & Judith BROOKES
Jun 15   William CRANDIGE & Elizabeth MOSELEY
Jun 15   William PUE & Anne RUSSELL
Jun 16   Ralph WEBBE & Alice SAUEAKER[?]
Nov 21   Andrew SUCH & Ann NEWNAM
Dec 26   John BANNISTER & Isabell BROOK
Feb 1   Edward ADDENBROOKE & Hester BODNAM

Burialls Anno 1662/3
Dec 18   Isabell the wyfe of George BRINLEY Esq
Jan 19   Ann d of Robert POWELL & Frances his wyfe
Jan 30   Margarett the wyfe of Richard BANNISTER
Feb 21   Ann MOSELEY
Mar 1   Marjorie BRISCOE
Mar 3   An infant child of Randle BORE

Mar 24	Eliner the wyfe of Richard JEAVANS	
Mar 8	Anne ROW Widdow	

1663

Apr 4	Frances LYNES
Apr 20	Margery the wyfe of William FIELD
May 1	Rich. TAYLOR
May 9	Nicholas WHEELER
May 19	Thomas s of Edward HALE & Isabell his wyfe
May 6	Margerie RICE
May--	Thomas HOBBY
Jun 1	John BROOK
Jun 21	Anne d of Will. BANNISTER
Jul 8	Mary d of Joseph MYETT & Margrett his wyfe

Burialls Anno 1663

Jun 29	Joseph s of John SMITH & Margrett & his wife
Jul 13	Samuell FOORD
Jul 24	Rebecca d of Peeter SMITH & Jane his wife
Jul 25	Marie d of Roger DAVIES & Driseilla his wife
Aug 4	Adam CLARKE
Aug 6	Felice BANNISTER
Aug 21	John s of John HENLEY & Margerit his wife
Aug 24	Elizabeth d of Nicholas BARDEN a stranger
Dec 4	Thomas CRANDIGE
Dec 9	John s of Richard BANNISTER & Margorie his wife
Jan 3	William s of William KETTLE
Jan 26	Elizabeth d of George COMBER & Elizabeth his wife
Feb 20	Ann PRETTY Widdow
Feb 21	Thomas DARLESTON
Mar 22	Joyce PATCHET widow
Mar 7	Isabell d of Roger BROWNE & Isabell his wife
Mar 23	Elizabeth d of Bartholomew KETTLE
	[It appears that there has been an attempt to erase the next two entries. But see Burials 1664 below]
Apr 1	Thomas s of John [?] & Margret his wife
Apr 24	Anne d of John PERKES

Baptismes 1664

Mar 26	Thomas s of Thomas NORTON
Apr 4	Humfrey s of Humfrey MOSELEY
Apr 12	Elizabeth d of W^m PUE & Anne his wife
Apr 23	Amie d of Wm TAYLER & Margerie his wife
Dec 27	1664 John s of Mr Jonathan NEWEY & Mary his wife was born 4th inst.

Burials 1664

Apr 1	Thomas s of Thomas HORTON & Margrett his wife
Apr 24	Amie d John PERKES
May 6	Margret d of Humphrey PERRY & Elizabeth his wife

May 22	John TEARNE
Jun	John s of George BAKER & Elien[r] his wife
Jul 11	Thom. s of Mr Richard WILLETTS & Jane his wife
Jul 17	John TANNER
Jul 30	Jane JOHNSON
Sep 10	Thomas s of W[m] CRANDIGE
Nov 28	Widdow DAVIES
Nov 29	An Infant of Humfrey CLARKE
Nov 30	Sam[el] s of John PURSLOW & Margery his wife
Dec 17	John COOK
Dec 28	Old goodman STANLEY
Jan 2	John ANDREWS
Jan 19	Elizabeth d of John COMBER & Mary his wife
Jan 20	Edmond KETTLE
Feb 6	An infant child of John PURSLOW
Feb 8th 5[th][sic]	Joyce RICE widdow
Feb 13	Mary d of Andrew SUCH
Feb 25	Widdow ROBBINSON
Mar 13	George BRINDLEY Esq[r]

Weddings 1664

Jun 2	Mr Tho JUKES & Mrs Elizabeth MOSELEY
Jun 27	Edward JOHNSON & Margrett WESTON
Nov 1	Edward HILLMAN & Elien[r] GOODMAN
Nov 1	Henry SHAXPER & Anne HYDE
Dec 6	W[m] KIDSON & Mary HILL
Dec 26	Henry TAYLOR & Margery SUTHWELL
Jan 4	Humfrey GARRETT & Mary LUCE

More Baptismes 1664

(The writing in this section is extremely small and cramped)

May 20	Jane d of Roger DAVIES by Priscilla his wife
	[An entry which appears to have been erased]
Jun 24	Thom. s of Falk GRIFFITH & Isabell his wife
Jul 4	Alice d of John SMITH by Jane his wife
Aug 2	Gilbert s of Gilbert PENNE
Sep 27	Thom. s of John BRISCOE by Jane his wife
[?] 27	Elizabeth d of Henry SUTHWELL by Theodosia his wife
Oct 6	Elizab d of John OLDNALL by Anne his wife
Oct 28	Sebright s of Edw YORK by Abigail his wife
Nov 8	Rich. s of John LEREGO
Nov 19	John s of Peter SMITH & Jane his wife
Nov 19	Barbara d of Will. WESTON by Ann his wife
Nov 29	Edward s of Edw. [?] by Sarah his wife
Nov 26	Elizabeth d of John COMBER & Mary
Nov 28	Elizab. d of John WHERRIT & Elizab. his wife
Nov 30	Mary d of Joseph LOW & Judith his wife
Dec	Anne d of Henry LONGMOR & Elizab. his wife
Dec 17	Edward s of Edw. TROMAN[?] & Elizab. his wife
Jan 3	Francis d of W[m] COX by Mary his wife

Dec 25 Mary d of Joseph MYATT & Margrett his wife
Dec 26 Elizab. d of Rich. SMALMAN
[?]   Thomas[?] s of John[?] DAVIES
Jan 6   Elizabeth d of Randolph BORE
Jan 15 Susanna d of William KETTLEY
        Mary[?] d of Andrew[?] SUCH[?] by Anne his wife
[?]

Baptismes 1665

Mar 25 Mary d of John HILLMAN & Elizabeth his wife
Apr 3   Elizabeth d of Robt BROWNE & Isabel his wife
Apr 9   Richard s of John RAYBOULD & Mary his wife
Apr 27 Thomas s of Thomas BARBER & Anne his wife
Jun 9   Elin^r d of Edward HILLMAN & Elin^r his wife
Jun 11 Elizabeth being a child that was found upon Ively Heath
Jun [?] [blank] s of Wm NICHOLAS
Jul 13 Edward s of Richard LYNE & Sarah his wife
Aug 12 Theodocia d of Wm CRANDIGE & Elizabeth his wife
Sep 2   Mary d of Wm KIDSON & [blank] his wife
Sep 10 Wm s of John PENNE & Elizabeth his wife
Oct 7   Anne d of John HAYES & Anne his wife
Nov 7   Charles s of Richard CARLESSE & Mary his wife
Nov 11 Anne d of John WYER & Anne his wife
Nov 18 Humfrey s of Humfrey CLARK & Elian^r his wife
Nov 19 Edward s of Edward JOHNSON & Margret his wife
Dec 18 W^m s of Ralph WEBB & Alice his wife
Dec 20 Mary d of Henry HUTT & Margerie his wife
Jan 5   William s of John POWEL & Alice his wife
Jan 20 Mary d of Thomas MOSELEY & Collebra his wife
Jan 29 John & Thomas sonnes of Richard WARREN & Anne his wife
Jan 31 Anne d of John ATKIS & [blank] his wife
Feb 3   Anne d of Wm RICE alias PUE & Anne his wife
Feb 27 Mary d of Thomas SMITH & Mary his wife
Mar 13 Mary d of Frances BRITTLE & [blank] his wife
Mar 17 Richard s of Thomas MORRICE & Elizabeth his wife

Weddings 1665

Apr 11 Thomas EGGINTON & Mary WATKIES
Jul 1   Edward HILLMAN & Mary COOK
Sep 29 James HILLMAN & Elizabeth LEVER
Oct 3   Robt WEBB & Elizabeth TEARNE
Jan 16 Richard KETTLEY & Joanne TAYLOR

Burials 1665

Mar 25 John LONGMORE of Romsley
Apr 2   Elizabeth d of John PUE & Ann his wife
Apr 3   Richard BACH
Apr 6   Elizabeth d of Thomas MORRICE & Joyce his wife
Apr 13 Mrs HAMMERTON wife of Mr. John HAMMERTON was lay^d
        in ye earth

Apr 18   Elizabeth the wife of Edward HILLMAN
Apr 27   Joane the wife of John WESTON
Apr 27   Alice d of John SMITH
May 18   Margret HARRISON widow
Jun 2   William s of John RAYBOULD & Mary his wife
Jun 29   Elin^r. d of Edward HILLMAN & Elizabeth his wife
Jul 26   Katherine the wife of Richard GROVE
Sep 12   An infant Child of John COMBER & Mary his wife was layd in ye Earth
Sep 13   Dorothy[?] another child of John COMBER & Mary his wife
Sep 21   [blank] s of John CLARK & his wife
Sep 23   John s of William IMMS & Magdelin his wife
Oct 27   Edward TRAVELLER alias GREEN
Nov 17   Richard CARELESS [BT's: "CARLISTE"]
Dec 5   Magdeline the wife of William BOWYER
Dec 23   A Chrisom Child of Henry LONGMORE
Jan 14   Mary the wife of William CRANDALE [BT's: "CRAUNDALL"]
Jan [BT's: "15"]   Eliner HILL of Check Hill
Jan 26   Elizabeth PUTTERFIELD
         John HOWE [BT's: "HOYER"]   John WARREL   Churchwardens

Baptismes Anno 1666
Apr 9   Edward s of John PURSLOW & Margarie his wife
Apr 16   Thomas s of John HILLMAN & Elizabeth his wife
Apr 17   Thomas s of Wm WOOD & Sarah his wife
May 2   Dorothy d of Rich: FEREDAY & Frances his wife
May 18   John s of John MOSELEY & Margerie his wife
Jul 16   Margaret d of Andrew SUCH & Margaret his wife
Aug 5   William s of Henry SUTHWELL & Theodosia his wife
Aug 11   William s of William GARRITT & his wife
Aug 11   Abigail d of John TROW & Elinor his wife
Aug 18   Thomas s of John SMITH & Jane his wife
Sep 9   Barbara d of Wm TYRER & his wife
Oct 6   Mary d of John COMBER & Mary his wife
Nov 1   Edward s of Thomas LYNE & his wife
Nov 10   Mary d of John OLDNALL & his wife
Jan 16   William s of William SARBETT & Mary his wife
Jan 19   Anne d of Wm IMMS & Magdelen his wife
Jan 22   Elizabeth d of Mr Jonathan NEWEY & Mary his wife
Jan 28   Elizabeth d of John CLARK & Mary his wife
Feb 5   Elizabeth d of Richard BIRD & Elienor his wife
Feb 10   Margaritt d of James HILLMAN & Elizabeth his wife
Feb 11   Thomas s of Thomas BARBER & Anne his wife
Feb 24   Thomas s of Edward DUNNE & Sarah his wife
Mar 3   Anne d of John RAYBOULD & Mary his wife
May 23   Elizabeth d of Mr George NURTHALL & his wife

Weddings Anno 1666
Jul 9   Rich. OLIVER & Mary BANNISTER
Nov 29   Rich. HACKIT & Isabel HALE [BT's: Elizab"]

Dec 19   Mr Gualter LITTLETON & Mrs Katherine TALBOTT
Feb 16   Wm STOKES & Rebecca BAYLIS

Burials Anno 1666

Apr 7   Francis BENNETT
May 19   An infant child of Edw. TRANTER & Elizabeth his wife was layd in ye earth
May 28   Richard HALL
Jun 6   Abigail d of Anthony BATE
Jun 16   Ann d of Thomas TEARNE
Jun 16   Alice ye wife of Thomas TEARNE
Jun 28   Theodocia d of Thomas MOSELEY & Elizabeth his wife
Aug 7   Anne d of John HAYES & his wife
Aug 14   John GARRET [BT's: GARRITT"]
Sep 15   Anne d of Joseph ATKIES & Mary his wife
Sep 16   Joan the wife of Richard SMITH
Dec 10   Thomas s of Thomas BARBER & Anne his wife
Dec 18   Francis s of Thomas BROWNE & Jane his wife
Dec 19   Anthony BATE
Jan 5   Anne the wife of William SARBETT
Jan 6   [blank] the wife of Mr William BAGLEY
Jan 18   A son [BT's: "William"] of William SARBETT & Mary his wife
Jan 23   An. GARRITT widow
Feb 19   A poor Cripple Boy y^t came wth a passe to ^{ye} Constable
Feb 27   An. [BT's: "Amii"] d of Wm TAYLER & Margerie his wife
Mar 1   Henry HACKET
Mar 14   Edward WINDLE
Mar 18   Margery the wife of Humfrey HOPE
         [Entered in the BT's for this year:]
         "Persons standing Excommunicated
         Mary HOBBY over four years
         John BRISCOE over three years
         Richard HALL & Elizabeth LYNES about two years
         Thomas LLOYD about one year"

Baptisms Anno 1667

Apr 8   Elizabeth d of Edward ADDENBROOKE & Hester his wife
Apr 9   Susannah d of Henry LONGMOR & Elizabeth his wife
May 19   Hester d of Richard SMALMAN & his wife
May 7   Anne d of Randolph BOARE & his wife
May 13   Anne d of Edward [BT's: "Richard"] WIDGEN
May 13   John s of Richard GARRETT
Jun 8   Elizabeth d of Edward TRAUNTER & Elizabeth
Jun 8   Anne d of Richard HARRICE & Elizabeth his wife
Jun 30   Richard.s of Richard OLIVER & his wife
Jul 7   Elizabeth.d of William CRANDIGE & Elizabeth his wife
Aug 16   Jane d of Foulk GRIFFITHS & Isabel his wife
Aug 24   William s of John HAYES & his wife
Sep 23   Nicholas s of Edward LUCE & his wife
Oct 6   Elizabeth d of Robt BROWN & his wife

Oct 14	Barbara d of Richard HACKET & Isabel his wife
Oct 15	Margrett d of Edward HARRICE & Margret his wife
Oct 26	[?] [BT's: "Alice"] d of John HORTON & Joan his wife
Nov 19	Sarah d of William KETTLEY & his wife
Nov 24	Anne d of John LEONARD & his wife
Jan 1	Elizabeth d of Wm STOKES & his wife
Jan 6	William s of Humfrey CLARKE & his wife
Feb 9	Jane d of Bartholomew KETTLE & his wife
[blank]	[blank] of Ralph POWEL & [blank]
Mar 2	Margrett d of William PUI alias RICE
Mar 1	Mary d of John HAYCOCK & Mary his wife
Mar 3	Richard s of Francis BRETTLE & his wife
Mar 7	Anne d of Joseph MYATT & Margrett his wife
Mar 23	Jane d of Robt POWELL & Frances his wife

Weddings Anno 1667

May 16	John DARBY & Anne DAUNCER [BT's: "DANCER"]
Mar 23	Edward BIRD & Elizabeth BATE

Burialls Anno 1667

Apr 1	Steven OLDNAL s of ye wid. OLDNAL
Apr 2	Edward s of Rob. POWELL
Apr 3	Elizabeth d of Robt BROWN & his wife [BT's: "Isabel his wife"]
Apr 16	Margrett the wife of old HUST [BT's: "wife of Edmond HUST"]
May 6	William s of Tho. MOSELEY & Elizab. his wife
May 10	Hester d of Randolph BOARE [BT's: BORR"] & Elizabeth his wife
May 12	[BT's: "19th"] Elianor HARRISON
May 17	Mr Richard KETTLEBY
May 19	Christian d of Humfrey PERRY & Elienor his wife
Jun 11	John s of John MOSELEY & Margery his wife
Jul 8	Edward s of Edward TRAUNTER & Elizabeth his wife
Jul 8	Mary d of Mr Jonathan NEWEY [BT's: "& Mary his wife"]
Jul 9	Elienor ye wife of Tho. LYNE
Aug 22	Sarah ye wife of Wm WOOD
Aug 26	Emme ye wife of William GREENES
Sep 4	Edward JORDEN Gentleman
Sep 14	John BANNISTER
Sep 16	Humfrey HACKET [BT's: Humfrey ye son of ye widdow HACKETT]
Nov 21	Tho. LYNE
Dec 16	Elizabeth d of John POWEL & Elienor his wife
Dec 19	Elizabeth MOSELEY Widdow
	Elizab. the wife of John LYNE & her young child were buried y^e [blank]
	[The entries in the BT's for the above entry are:]
	Elizabeth ye wife of John LYNE was buried
	Edwards son of Jho LYNE & Elian^r his wife was buried March 10"

Feb 12   An infant child of Henry ELCOCK & Margrett his wife was layd in ye earth
Mar 10   Edward s of Tho. LYNE
         Rich. HILL George LOW Churchwardens

Baptisms 1668

Apr 6   Thomas s of Edward JOHNSON & Margrett his wife
Apr 13   John s of John OLDNALL & Anne his wife
May 11   Margery d of John CROW
May 14   Humfrey s of Humfrey SARBETT & Mary his wife
May 24   Anne d of Henry SUTHWELL & Theodocea his wife
May 26   John s of Wm TYRER & Mary his wife
Jun 7   Mary d of John MOSELEY & Margery his wife
Jun 16   Anne d of William EGGINTON & Hannah his wife
Jul 30   John s of Richard WILLET & Jane his wife
Aug 6   Thomas s of Thomas JUKES & Elizabeth his wife
Aug 15   John s of Humfrey HOPE & Mary his wife
Aug 16   Isabel d of John POWELL & Isabell his wife
Aug 18   Mary d of John WHITE by Elizabeth TRISTRAM illegitimate
Sep 20   Dorothy d of Edward TRAUNTER & Elizabeth [BT's: "Isabell"] his wife
Sep 24   Sarah d of George NURTHALL & his wife
Sep 28   Theodosia & Elizabeth daughters of Thom. MOSELEY & Collibra his wife
Oct 5   Edward s of John HILLMAN & Elizab. his wife
Nov 9   Isabell d of Will. WESTON & Anne his wife
Nov 21   John ye s of Joseph LOW & [blank] his wife
Nov 22   Anne d of James HILLMAN & Elizabeth his wife
Dec 4   Jane d of Mr Jonathan NEWEY & Mary his wife
Dec 5   Mary d of Richard WARREN & Anne his wife
Dec 1   Humfrey & Margery son & daughter of Richard HOPE
Dec 26   Mary d of William IMME & Magdelen his wife
Dec 29   Elizabeth d of John RICHARDS & Mary his wife
[blank] Elizab. d of Thom. BARBER & Anne his wife
Jan 15   John the Sonne of John COMBER & Mary his wife
Jan 21   Richard s of John TROW & Elienor his wife
[blank] [blank] of Edward DUNN & Sarah his wife
Feb 3   Elizabeth d of Thom. SMITH & Mary his wife
Feb 20   Frances d of Wm AUDEN & Mary his wife
Feb 24   Jane d of John HORTON & Jone his wife
Feb [blank]   [?] [BT's: "John"] s of John CLARK & Mary his wife

Weddings 1668

Jun 23   Richard WEBB & Sarah TEARNE
Jun 24   John SMALMAN & Elizabeth DUDLEY
Jun 27   George HILL & Anne NEWMAN
Aug 6   Thomas WINDLE & Frances BOWERS
Oct 29   William WILLMOTT & Alice WILCOX
Dec 26   Saml TAYLER & Mary HOBBEY [BT's: "HOBBY"]
Jan 3   John WOOLEY & Katherine MILLARD

Feb 24   William ONLEY & Dorothy TRAUNTER

Burials Anno Dm. 1668

Mar 30   Richard GROVE
Apr 6   Frances d of Mr Thomas TALBOTT
Apr 13   Isabel d of John POWELL & Alice his wife
Apr 27   Mary POWELL widdow
May 29   Jane the wife of Bartholomew KETTELL   [This entry is marked by two "X"'s – see later entry below]
Apr 29   A young child of Randolph BORE was layd in ye Earth   [BT's "A chrysome child …"]
May 12   John WORRALL
May 29   Jane the wife of Bartholomew KETTELL   [see entry above]
Jun 3   Richard s of Richard LYNE & Sarah his wife
Apr 25   Thom. s of Humfrey CLARK & Elienor his wife
Sep 10   Sarah wife of Richard LYNE
Sep 11   Margery ye wife of John MOSELEY
Sep 28   Dorothy the Widdow of Edward TRAUNTER
Oct 26   [blank] KETTLEY of Compton Widdow
Nov 11   Elizabeth d of Henry SHAXPER & Anne his wife
Nov 12   Joane HUMFREYS widow
Dec 4   William CORBETT was buried in Kinfare church yard
Dec 6   Margery d of Richard HOPE & Joan his wife
Dec 8   Humfrey s of Richard HOPE & Joan his wife
Dec 26   Agnes WOOLVERLEY [BT's: "WOLVERLEY"] widow
Jan 18   John s of John COMBER & Mary his wife
Jan 21   Barbara ye wife of John HACKETT
Feb 9   Alexander s of John LYNE
Feb 10   Elizabeth SISSON widow
Mar 6   Emma the wife of William OAKE

Baptismes Anno Dom. 1669

Apr 3   Anne d of George HILL & Anne his wife
May 23   Hannah d of Wm STOKES & Rebecca his wife
Jun 2   Priscilla d of John RAYBOULD Senr & Jane his wife
Jun 2   Margrett d of William GARRETT & Sisilia his wife
Sep 9   Margrett d of John PURSLOW & Margery his wife
Sep 20   Sarah d of Thomas BRETTLE & Anne his wife
Oct 4   Thomas s of Henry ELCOCK & Margret his wife
Oct 13   Richard s of Edward TRAUNTER & Elizab. his wife
Nov 1   William s of William TYRER & Mary his wife
Nov 1   Anne d of Richard SMALMAN & Anne his wife
Dec 5   Gerard s of Richard WARREN & [blank] his wife
Jan 6   Richard s of Richard HARRICE & Elizab. his wife
Jan 6   Katherine d of Richard FEREDAY & Frances his wife
Jan 12   Eleanor d of John HILLMAN & Elizab. his wife
Jan 25   Edward s of Thomas FLOYD & Frances his wife
Feb 13   Edward s of Ralph WEBB & Alise his wife
Feb 17   Mary d of W^m PUE alias RICE & Anne his wife

© Staffordhire Parish Registers Society

Feb 20	Elizabeth d of John SMITH & Jane his wife
Feb 24	John s of George NURTHALL & [blank] his wife
Mar 7	Richard s of Richard HOPE & Joan his wife
Mar 8	Isabel d of Richard BIRD & Elien[r] his wife
May 9	Joseph s of John BRISCOE bapt. at Kinfare
Mar 14	Elizabeth d of Edward KNOWLEY & Grace his wife

Weddinges An° Dom 1669

Sep 21	John SHAXPER & Elizabeth LLOYD
Oct 17	John SITCH & Francis GOODYER
Oct 17	John BARNFIELD & Rebecca BRADLEY
Nov 30	John SLATER & Joyce HARTELL
Feb 2	Rich PURSLOW & Katherine POTTER
Feb 2	Hugh DAVIES & Anne WHITMORE

Burialls Anno Dom. 1669

Apr 20	Alice WINDLE Widow was buried in Kinfare
Apr 29	Thomas s of John RAYBOULD & Mary his wife
May 2	A young child of John CLARKE & Mary his wife
Jun 2	Samuel SMITH was buried in Kinvar Churchyard
Jun 25	John MOSELEY was buried in Kinvar Churchyard
Jun 27	Hugh JONES was buried in Kinvar Churchyard
Jul 5	Elizabeth d of John HILLMAN & Elizabeth his wife
Jul 28	William s of Henry SUTHWELL & Theodocia his wife
Aug 18	Thomas LLOYD was buried in Kinvar Churchyard
Aug 29	Elizabeth BOWYER d of William BOWYER
Sep 14	Mary NEWNAM widow
Sep 22	M[r] John WHORWOOD Esq[r] was buried in Kinvar Chancill
Sep 23	Elienor the wife of Edward HILLMAN
Sep 24	Richard BANNISTER was buried in Kinfare Churchyard
Nov 5	Mrs HULKES widdow
Nov 24	John CORBET
Nov 23	Thomas GEORGE of Ashwood was buried in Kinvar
Jan 5	Francis TALBOTT Gent was buried in Kinfare Chancel
Jan 9	Alice the wife of John POWEL
Jan 12	Magdelin BATE Spinster
Jan 12	Jane the wife of Richard BROOK
Feb 10	John DOVEY a blind man
Feb 15	[blank] the wife of Rob[t] PITT Schoolm[r]
Feb 27	Abigail the wife of Edward YORK
Mar 9	[?n] the wife of John BRISCOE
Mar 17	William BOWYER was buried in Kinver Churchyard
Mar 22	Theodosia d of Thom. MOSELEY & Callibra his wife

Baptismes Anno Dom. 1670

Apr 4	[blank] daughter of Humfrey CLARK & Eleanor his wife
Apr 5	Elianor d of Richard KETTLEY & Joan his wife
Apr 5	Mary d of John RAYBOULD & Mary his wife
Apr 16	Henry s of Henry SUTHWELL & Theodocia his wife
Apr 25	Phebe d of John COMBER & Mary his wife

May 1	Job[?] & Alice s & d of Robt POWEL & Frances his wife
May 16	Mary d of Richard HACKETT & Isabel his wife
May 23	Ann[?] d of John HAYES & Anne his wife
May 24	George s of Sam^{el} TAYLER & Mary his wife
Jul 31	Katherine d of Sam^{el}SAVAKER
Jul 31	John & Richard sonnes of Hugh DAVIES & Anne his wife
Aug 14	Isabel d of William WESTON & Anne his wife
Aug 15	Anne d of Humfrey SARBETT & Mary his wife
Sep 11	Roger s of Richard OLDNALL
Oct 1	Jonathan s of John CLARK & Mary his wife
Oct 3	George s of George HILL & Anne his wife
Oct 17	John s of William TAYLER & Margery his wife
Jan 8	Hannah d of William KETTLEY & Mary his wife
Jan 23	Rich. s of John RAYBOLD Senr & Jane his wife
Jan 23	Elizabeth d of Francis KETTLEY & Martha his wife
Jan 31	Abigail d of Humfrey HOPE & Mary his wife
Feb 2	Elizabeth d of John HORTON & Jone his wife
Feb 15	Richard s of Mary REYNOLDS a stranger
Feb 27	Elizabeth d of Edward YARNSHAW & Elizab. his wife
Feb 28	John s of John RICHARDS & Mary his wife
Mar 21	Francis s of Richard GARRETT & Elien^r his wife
Mar 23	Deanes d of Mr Jonathan NEWEY Rect^r

Weddings An° 1670

Apr 10	Francis KETTLEY & Martha OLDNALL
Nov 1	John JORDAN & Judeth HILLMAN
Nov 12	Richard BROOK & Elizabeth MORRICE
Nov 19	John MOSELEY & Anne BELLINGHAM
Feb 23	Thomas LYE & Mary WILDEN

Burialls Anno Dom 1670

Apr 25	Humfrey MOSELEY was buried at Kinfare
May 2	Thomas HORTON was buried in Kinfare Churchyard
May 16	Francis HILL of Hafcote was buried at Oldswinford
May 23	Elizabeth d of John SMITH & Jane his wife
Jun 2	Jane d of John PURSLOW & Margery his wife
Jun 6	Thomas MOSELEY
Jun 15	Mary d of Richard HACKETT & Isabel his wife
Jul 17	Elizabeth HILLMAN
Jul 29	Richard s of Hugh DAVIES & Anne his wife
Aug 28	Richard KETTLEY the young^r
Sep 22	Richard KETTLEY the elder
Sep 24	Anne the wife of the deceased Richard KETTLEY the Elder
Oct 20	Randolph BORE was buried in Kinfare
Nov 25	Anne the wife of Wm WESTON
Nov 7	Jane d of Mr Jonathan NEWEY
Jan 26	Mary the wife of Humfrey LOW
Feb 7	Richard JUKES was buried in Kinfare Chancel
Feb 9	John LYNES

Feb 16   Anne SUTHWELL
Feb 24   Humfrey LOW
Feb 28   Anne the wife of William HALL
Mar 5   John GROVE
Mar 6   Thomas CANTRELL
Mar 11   Hester d of John RAYBOLD Sen[r]
         Thomas BRETTELL   John LYE   Churchw.

Baptismes Anno Dom 1671

Apr 28   Anne d of Edward JOHNSON & Margrett his wife
May 11   William s of William AUDEN & his wife
May 15   Richard s of John SMITH & Jane his wife
May 21   William s of Thomas MORRICE & his wife
May 23   Elizabeth d of Edw[d] BIRD & El[?] his wife
Jun 29   Joyce d of Edward DUNNE & Sarah his wife
Aug 8   Dorothy d of S[r] William KEYT K[t] & Baronett & Dame Elizabeth his wife
Aug 25   Joseph s of Joseph MYATT & Margrett his wife
Sep 2   Constance d of Thomas BENNET & Elien his wife
Sep 8   John s of Phillip SPENCER & Mary his wife
Sep 12   James s of Thomas SMITH & Mary his wife
Sep 29   James s of Richard BROOK & Elizab. his wife
Nov 18   Jane d of John JORDAN & Judith his wife
Nov 19   Mary d of W[m] SIMMES & Anne his wife
Feb 2   George s of Sam[l] TAYLER & Mary his wife
Feb 2   Margrett d of John HOLLOWAY & Dorothy his wife
Mar 5   Elizabeth d of John MOSELEY & Anne his wife
Mar 10   [?]hn s of John DAW & Ann his wife

Marriages Anno Dom 1671

May 31   John DAY & Dorothy COMBER
Jun 3   John HALLOWAY & Dorothy HORTON
Jun 12   Edward HILLMAN & Katherine SMITH
Jul 3   Edward LYNALL & Elizabeth CANTRELL
Jul 15   Roger BRADLEY & Joanne KETTLEY
Sep 30   Joseph SMITH & Elizabeth HILLMAN
Jan 30   George HARRENS[?] & Mary DOVEY

Burials Anno 1671

May 23   Humfrey s of Humfrey SARBETT & Mary his wife
Jun 23   Isabel the wife of Edward HALE
Jun 29   Mary the wife of George NURTHALL
Jul 25   John s of William AUDEN & his wife
Aug 15   Henry s of Henry SOUTHWELL & Theodosia his wife
Aug 18   Thomas s of John SMITH & Jane his wife
Aug 21   Elien[r] the wife of George BAKER
Sep 25   John s of William TAYLER & Margery his wife
Sep 28   William VINCENT was buried in Kinver
Oct 2   Jane POWELL was buried in Kinfare churchyard
Oct --   Deanes d of M[r] Jonathan NEWEY Rect[r]

Nov 2	Widdow HIGGINS of Iverley
Nov 12	Constance d of Thomas BENNETT & Elienor his wife
Nov 23	Elizabeth d of Humfrey CLARKE & Elienor his wife
Dec 9	Henry HUTT was buried in Kinver church yard
Dec 17	Elizabeth JONES Widdow
Feb 14	Thomas GYBBS was buried in Kinfare
Mar 24	Elizabeth PAYTON widdow

Baptismes Anno Dom 1672

Apr 1	Richard s of Rich. HACKET & Isabel his wife
Apr 2	Sarah d of Wm EGGINTON & [blank] his wife
Apr 8	Joyce d of Wm PUGH & Anne his wife
Apr 27	Elizab d of Humfrey CLARK & Elizabeth his wife
May 27	Ralph & Mary s & d of Ralph WEBB & Alice his wife
Jun 29	Margarett d of [blank] WEATHERHILL & Margret his wife
Jul 20	Samuel s of John TROW & Elienor his wife
Jul 26	Mary d of Henry ELCOCK & Margret his wife
Aug 24	Thomas s of Sir William KITE & Lady Elizabeth his wife
Aug 31	William s of William STOKES & Rebecca his wife
Sep 1	Thomas s of Roger BRADLEY & Joane his wife
Sep 22	Anne d of Mr Jonathan NEWEY & Mary his wife
Oct 1	Jonathan s of John HILLMAN & Elizabeth his wife
Oct 5	Roger LAMB s of Rog^r & [blank] his wife
Oct 11	John s of Thomas LYE & Mary his wife
Oct 28	Hester d of George HILL & Anne his wife
Oct 29	John s of Edward BIRD & Elizab. his wife
Nov 3	Wm s of Wm CRANDIDGE & Elizabeth his wife
Nov 10	Richard s of Richard SMALEMAN the yonger & Mary his wife
Nov 25	Joseph s of Richard SMALLMAN the Senr & [blank] his wife
Nov 8	William s of Will: SIMMES & Anne his wife
Nov 9	Sarah d of Robt POWEL & Frances his wife
Dec 26	John s of William IMMS & Magdelin his wife
Dec 27	William s of John HORTON & Joane his wife
Jan 1	Walter s of Thomas PENN & Susannah his wife
Jan 3	[blank] d of Francis BRETTELL & Jane his wife
Jan 19	Mary d of Will DUNNE & Mary his wife
Jan 21	Margery d of Humfrey HOPE & Mary his wife
Jan 28	John s of John RAYBOLD Senr & Jane his wife
Feb 8	Theodocia d of John RICHARDS & [M?] his wife
Feb 14	Anne d of Thom. BENNETT & Elien^r his wife
Feb 16	[blank] of Richard GLADWAY & [blank] his wife
Mar 6	Thomas s of Thom. LLOYD & Frances his wife
Mar 8	Margarett d of Richard YORK & his wife
Mar 11	Ann d of Will. NICHOLS & his wife

Marriages Anno 1672

Apr 8	Hugh PUGH & Frances FARMER
Apr 14	Henry HOLT & Mary HOLLY
Apr 9	William DUN & Sarah BENBOW
Apr 20	Richard BRADLEY & Mary MOSELEY

Apr 20	Richard FRANCIS & Anne KETTLEY
Apr 25	William COOK & Jane MASON
May 6	Thomas HOPKINS & Elizabeth BORE
May 7	Thomas GYBBES & Isabell JONES
May 27	John WHITEHOUSE & Mary ASHBEY
Jul 25	Mr John WOWEN & Elizabeth BARTON
Jul 29	Richard PARKHOUSE & Constance BENNETT
Aug 27	Maurice CALLOW & Anne MOLE
Sep 16	John HILLMAN & Bridgett PAGETT

Burials Anno 1672

Mar 28	Dorothy the wife of Nicholas LUCE
Mar 31	William OAKE
Mar 31	Hannah d of William HAWKES a stranger
May 16	Mary d of Tho: CARTWRIGHT & his wife
May 24	Margarett APSLEY of Stowerton Widow
May 29	Widdow YORK of Checkhill
Jun 20	Margarett HORTON widdow
Jun 27	Hannah d of William STOKES & Rebecca his wife
Jun 30	Katherine d of Rich. FEREDAY & Frances^r his wife
Jul 7	Edward s of Richard GARRETT & Elien^r his wife
Jul 24	Henry GARRETT of Stowerton
Aug 7	Alice d of William GREAVES
Aug 16	Thomas TAYLOR
Nov 4	Margarett d of Tho: & Margarett HORTON
Nov 28	Anne[?] the wife of John WILLFORD
Dec 19	Edward s of William VEAL & Anne his wife
Jan 5	Jane[?] d of Frances BRETTELL & Jane his wife
Jan 7	Edward GARRETT
Jan 7	Elienor LYNE
Jan 14	John s of James HILLMAN & Elizabeth his wife
Jan 19	Mary GROVE Widdow
Jan 21	Anne d of Henry SUTHWELL & Theodocia his wife
Feb 12	Thomas s of John RAYBOULD Senr & Jane his wife
Mar 1	John WESTON
Mar 3	Richard GARRETT
Mar 6	John JORDAN was buryed at Kinfare
Mar 8	Margery TIMMINGS
Mar 9	George POWELL
Mar 12	Anne d of Wm NICHOLLS & his wife

Baptismes Anno 1673

Mar 31	John s of Judith JORDAN widdow
Apr 2	Anne d of Richard FRANCIS & Anne his wife
Apr 16	Thomas s of Thomas HOPKINS & Elizabeth his wife
Apr 28	Anne d of George BATE & [blank] his wife
May 20	George s of Edward DUNNE & Sarah
Jun 23	Margarett d of Saml SAVEAKER & Anne his wife
Aug 1	Humfrey s of Humfrey BATE & Jane his wife
Aug 9	Jane Jane[sic] d of Thom. GIBBS & Isabel his wife

Aug 24	Joseph s of Joseph PARTRIDGE & Elizabeth his wife
Sep 7	Isabel d of Richard BOOTH & Jane his wife
Sep 8	[blank] of John HALLOWAY & [blank] his wife
Oct 3	Elizabeth d of Edward HILLMAN & Elizabeth his wife
Oct 25	William s of Edward JOHNSON & Margarett his wife
Oct 28	Jerome s of Joseph LOW & Judith his wife
Oct 9[?]	Margrett d of Edward WALTERS[?] & Elizabeth his wife
[blank]	Margrett d of Thomas RUSSELL & [blank] his wife
Dec [blank]	[Blank] of Francis KETTLEY & Martha his wife
Dec [blank]	William s of Hugh PUGH & Frances his wife
Dec 21	Jane d of Thomas MIARICE[?] & his wife
Dec 26	William s of Edward BRADELY & Mary his wife
Jan 27	Charles s of Richard GARRETT & Elian^r his wife
Feb 17	Thomas s of Thomas LYE & Mary his wife
Feb 19	John s of James HILLMAN & Elizabeth his wife
Feb 23	Mary d of John SITCH & Frances his wife
Feb 27	Edward s of Edward BIRD & Elizabeth his wife
Mar 2	Elien^r d of Thomas BENNETT & Elien^r his wife
Mar 6	Nicholas s of Roger BRADELEY & Jane his wife

Weddings Anno 1673

Nov 11	Richard BIBBE & Mary COOKE

Burials Anno Diem 1673

Mar 30	Richard s of Richard HACKETT & Isabel his wife
Apr 1	Roger s of Richard OLDNALL & Ann his wife
Apr 4	Ann d of Thomas BENNETT & Elien^r his wife
Apr 8	Joseph s of Humfrey SARBETT & Mary his wife
Apr 13	Mary HACKETT widdow
Apr 16	Thomas s of Thomas HOPKINS & Elizabeth his wife
Apr 20	Joan HACKETT widdow being aged
Apr 22	Anne d of Mr. Jonathan NEWEY & Mrs Mary his wife
Apr 24	William GREAVES was buryed at Kinfare
Apr 26	Elizabeth d of Tho. SMITH & Mary his wife
May 20	John HACKETT buryed at Kinfare
Jun 11	Joyce WALKER was buryed at Kinfare
Jun 27	William ASTON was buryed at Kinfare
Nov 7	William GARRETT
Dec 24	William s of Hugh PUGH & Frances his wife
Jan 6	Elizabeth BARRET
Feb 3	George LOW
Feb 28	Saml s of Samuel TAYE
Feb 5	Thomas PITT a poor Souldier
Feb 7	Margrett the wife of Mr Edward MOSELEY & Elien^r his wife
Feb 9	Edward MOSELEY Gent was buryed at Kinfare
Mar 4	Elizabeth the wife of James HILLMAN
Mar 6	Elizabeth the wife of Francis DEE buried at Enfield
Mar 15	Henry DUNNE

Weddings Anno 1674

May 1   John COMPTON & Margaret BEST
May 12   John BROWNE & Mary SUTHWELL
May 27   Robt PITT Schoolm^r & Mrs Elizabeth KETTLEBY
Jul 13   Francis DEE & Mary KETTLEBY
Jul 30   Simon DEGGE Esqr & Mrs Mary MOOR
Oct 24   John DUNN & Alice COLERICK
Dec 1   Thomas HUST & Elizabeth HOPKINS
Nov 30   Thomas MASON & Mary HUST
Jan 27   William PRICE & Judith MASON

Baptismes Anno 1674

Apr 7   Sarah d of Mr Jonathan NEWEY & Mary his wife
Apr 10   Elizabeth d of Humfrey JOHNSON & Dorothy his wife
Apr 12   [?lliam] s of John TROW & Elien^r his wife
Apr 14   [?   ] d of William PEUGH alias RICE & Anne his wife
Apr 20   Elizabeth d of Edward TRAUNTER & Elizab. his wife
Apr 24   Jane d of Richard HOPE & his wife
Apr 25   Elizabeth of Richard GLADWAY & Anne his wife
[blank]   Rachel d of   }
Apr 27   Rebecca d of   } John HILLMAN & Bridget his wife
May 10   John s of Will. KETTLEY & Mary his wife
Jun 3   Samuel s of Francis BRETTELL & Jane his wife
Jun 9   John s of Richard SMALMAN & Mary his wife
Jun 27   William s of Rog^r CRINBER[?] & his wife
Jul 19   Elizabeth d of John POWEL & Miriam his wife
Aug 16   Phillip s of Ralph WEBB & Alice his wife
Aug 30   Mary d of John PAGETT & Mary his wife
Sep 21   Wm s of Wm DUNNE & Sarah his wife
Sep 24   John s of Robt NURTHAL & Hannah his wife
Oct 13   John s of Richard HACKETT & Isabell his wife
Oct 25   Daniel s of William ROWLEY & Anne his wife
Oct 25   David s of Tho. SMITH & Mary his wife
Oct 26   Elizabeth d of John DAW & Ann his wife
Nov 6   Thomas s of John WINFORD & Margery his wife
Nov [blank]   Edward s of Humfrey SARBETT & Mary his wife
Dec 12   John s of John HORTON & Joan his wife
Dec 31   William s of William COLLINS & [blank] his wife
       [There appears to have been a partial entry deleted at this point.]
Jan 20   John s of Humfrey BATE & Anne his wife
Jan 31   Samuel s of Samuel TAYLER & Mary his wife
Feb 9   Henry ELCOCK s of Henry & Margarett his wife
Feb 16   Joseph s of John HILLMAN & Elizabeth his wife
Feb 18   Elien^r d of John MOSELEY Gent & Mary his wife
Mar 16   John s of Thomas GOODYER & [blank] his wife
Mar 17   Susanna d of Richard YORK & Susanna his wife

Burials Anno Dom 1674

Mar 27   John s of James HILLMAN & Elizabeth his wife (deceased)
May 3   Ralph s of Ralph WEBB & Alice his wife

Jun 17	Richard WEDGE buryed at Kinvar
Jun 29	Elizabeth d of Edward TRAUNTER & Elizab. his wife
Jul 14	David DAW was Buryed at Kinfare
Jul 23	Sarah d of William KETTLEY & Mary his wife
Aug 20	Richard HILL of Whittington
Sep 3	Mary the wife of John PAGETT
Sep 10	Joane SITCH widow was buryed at Kinver
Oct 1	Anne PAINE was burued at Kinfare
Oct 2	[blank] d of Phillip FOLEY Esqr & Lady [blank] his wife
Oct 17	John s of Richard HACKETT & Isabel his wife
Oct 13	A still born child of Thomas HOPKINS & Elizib. his wife
Nov 6	Rich. s of Richard HARRICE & Elizabeth his wife laid in Earth
Nov 21	John LYE killed by a fall from his Horse
Dec 23	Mary d of Robt BROWN
Dec 9	William WISHAM
Jan 15	Oliver HILL churchwarden
Jan 17	Edward JOHNSON Mason
Jan 29	Mary d of John POWELL Junr
Feb 13	Henry s of Henry ELCOCK & Margaret his wife
Feb 12	Katherine wife of Edward EVANS
Feb 15	John JONES s of Margarett stabbed to death
Mar 1	Thomas s of John WINFORD & Margery his wife
Mar 8	Elizabeth the wife of John PENNE

Wedddings Anno 1675

Jul 22	Sr Edward WILLIAMS s of Sr Thomas WILLIAMS Baronet & Lady Elizabeth WILLIAMS of Bentley Hall were married by vertue of a Licence from Ld. Archbp^s Court
Apr 25	George BAKER & Sarah ROBBINS
Apr 25	Will. LYNE & Mary BAKER were marryed the same day
May 13	John MANOX & Anne HUTT
May 31	John WORRALL & Margrett DARLASTON
Jul 1	Wm SOUTHALL & Margrett BROWNE
Jan 17	Richard BATE & Mary WALDEN

Baptismes 1675

Mar 28	Mary d of John BROWN & Elizab. his wife
Apr 4	Mary d of Will. SPENCER & Elizab. his wife
Apr 6	Elizabeth d of Rich. BRADLY & Mary his wife
Apr 26	Elizabeth d of George HILL & Anne his wife
May 6	Rachel d of John HAYES & Elizabeth his wife
May 29	[?] s of Henry SOUTHWELL & Dorcas his wife
May 29	[?] d of Wm & IMMS & Magdelen his wife
May 31	Humfrey s of George BATE & Joyce his wife
Jun 12	Sarah d of Henry LONGMORE & Elien^r his wife
Jun 20	Samuel & John sons of Sam^{el} SAVEAKER & Anne his wife
Jun 4	Katherine d of Humfrey CLARK & Elien^r his wife
Jul 11	[Jane] d of Hugh DAVIES & Anne his wife
Jul 31	Francis d of Rich: OLIVER & Mary his wife
Aug 1	Phillip s of Mr Robt PITT & Elizabeth his wife

Sep 12 John s of Humfrey HILLMAN & Sarah his wife
Aug 15 Thomas s of Wm VEAL & Elizab. his wife
Sep 19 John s of John CAMBER & Mary his wife
Oct 6 Alice d of Rich: GLADWAY & Anne his wife
Oct 10 [?]iel s of Joseph MAYETT & Margrett his wife
Oct 15 [?]nry s of Joseph PARTRIDGE & Elizabeth his wife
Oct 24 Joan d of Will: EARNSHAW & Elizab. his wife
Oct 26 John s of John LOW & Anne his wife
Nov 1 [?]ary d of Will. LYNE & Mary his wife
Nov 5 William s of Tho. HUST & Elizabeth his wife
Nov 8 Mary d of Richard & FRANCES & Anne his wife
Nov 11 Thomas s of Tho: PENNE & Susannah his wife
Dec 2 John s of John WINFORD & Margery his wife
Dec 21 Elizabeth d of Roger BRADELY & Joan his wife
Dec 17 [?]ary d of Wm PRICE & Judith his wife
Jan 16 Hannah d of John POWEL & Hannah his wife
Jan 16 Andrew s of Hugh PUE & Frances his wife
Feb 6 John s of Thomas MERRYHURST & Betteridge his wife
Feb 6 Elizabeth d of John LEONARD & Bridgitt his wife
Feb 7 Theodocia d of Edw. BIRD & Elizabeth his wife
Feb 7 Elizabeth d of John HOPE & Lyddia his wife
Feb 13 Wm s of John HALLOWAY & Dorothy his wife
Feb 20 Will. s of John MOSELEY & Anne his wife
Mar 4 Thomas s of Richard HOPE & Joan his wife
Mar 9 Ann d of George BAKER & Sarah his wife
Mar 12 Mary d of John WORRALL & Margrett his wife
Mar 17 Mary d of John RICHARDS & Mary his wife

Burialls Anno Dom 1675

May 27 Elizabeth TRAUNTER
May 30 John HILLMAN Clark
Jun 25 Margrett HILL
Jun 26 Mr John BARTON was Buryed in ye Middle Chancel [The name is entered in large italic writing]
Oct 4 George HILL
Oct 21 Elizabeth d of Mr Jonath. NEWEY
Oct 23 Alice d of Ralph WEBB
Nov 3 Mary the wife of Sam^{el} TAYLER
Dec 5 Mary d of Wm FIELD baptised
Dec 10 Tho: FFORD
Dec 10 Edward PIKE the Husband of Ann
Dec 24 Ann wife of Will BANNISTER
Jan 1 Elizabeth d of Wm EGGINTON
Feb 4 Elizabeth wife of Tho. HOPKINS
Mar 5 Francis husband of [blank] WORRALL
Mar 7 John DAVIES s of Mrs DAVIES of Beaudley

Weddings Anno 1676

May 1 Thomas HOPKINS & Anne HAYLEY
May 1 John PAGETT & Amie HILL were married likewise

May 14	Samuel DAVIES & Elizabeth HARRICE
Aug 13	William PERRINS & Anne BANNISTER
Sep 21	William PIKE & Elizabeth WILLETS
Oct 30	John HUNT Gent & Mrs Mary NEWBROUGH
Nov 18	Edward GROVE & Joan BRODFIELD

Baptismes 1676

Apr 12	John s of Henry ELCOCK & Margrett his wife
Apr 13	Hester d of Rob[t] NURTHALL & Hanna his wife
Apr 20	Thomas s of Tho. MASON & Mary his wife
May 7	Henry s of Edward DUNN & Sarah his wife
May 14	Margrett d of Thomas LLOYD & Mary [crossed through] Frances his wife
Jun 1	William s of William FRENCH & Elizabeth his wife
Jun 2	Mary d of Thomas LYE & Mary his wife
Jun 8	William s of William DERRICK & Joan his wife
Jul 20	Daniel s of William DUNN & Sarah his wife
Jul 29	Richard s of Richard BRADILY & Mary his wife
Aug 17	Katherine d of M[r] Jonathan NEWEY & Mary his wife
Sep 29	Thomas s of Thomas GIBBS & Isabel his wife
Oct 28	Richard s of William CRANDIGE & Elizabeth his wife
Nov 4	Anne d of Joseph LOW & Judith his wife
Nov 16	Margret d of Thomas BENNET & Elien[r] his wife
Nov 19	Thomas s of Francis KETLEY & Martha his wife
Dec 12	James s of John HILLMAN & Elisabeth his wife
Nov 25	Joseph s of Joseph MORRICE & Marg..[?] his wife
Jan 1	Mary d of William STOKES & Rebecca his wife
Jan 7	Anne d of John WINFORD & Margery his wife
Jan 13	Edward s of Rich. BATE & Martha his wife
Feb 11	Edward s of Richard HACKET & Isabel his wife
Feb 12	Thomas s of Thomas HUST & Elizabeth his wife
Feb 10	Phillip s of Phillip SPENCER & Mary his wife
Mar 1	Mary d of John HORTON & Joan his wife
Mar 5	Mary d of Sam[el] DAVIES & Elizabeth his wife
Mar 7	Elizabeth d of John GEARING & Margery his wife
Mar 18	Joseph s of John DAW & Mary his wife
Mar 18	Sarah d of Edward WARD & Joan his wife

Burialls 1676

Apr 3	Alice LYE was buried in Kinfare Churchyard
Apr 14	Edward MOSELEY Gent: was Buried in Mr GRAYs Chancel
May 13	[blank] MOAL widow was buried in Kinfare
May 21	Elizabeth BACH was buried in Kinfare
Aug 14	Edward BIRD was buried in Kinfare
Sep 14	Elizabeth WHITE widow of John WHITE
Sep 18	Sarah WATKINS
Nov 1	Thomas HICHINS
Nov 14	Richard BANNISTER
Nov 29	Thomas BENNET
Dec 5	Abigail CHAMBERLAIN

Dec 23 John SALE was buried in Kinfare
Dec 24 A chrisom son of William IMMS
Dec 25 Richard EVANS was buried at Kinfare
Jan 23 John BROOK was buried in Kinfare
Feb 23 Richard PURSLOE Sen[r]
Mar 16 Mrs Margret BRADELY

Weddings Anno 1677
May 11 Henry HUTT & Mary SHAW
May 26 Henry COOK & Mary BROOK [BT's: BROOKE"]
Jun 24 William TAYLER & Joan WYER
Nov 5   William LYE & Margerie BATE
Nov 18 Sam[l] TAYLER & Margrett JOHNSONS
Nov 29 Francis SIMMS & Margrett BUTTERFIELD
Feb 4   Jeremiah BENNET & Elizabeth GREAVES

Baptismes 1677
Mar 26 Richard s of Thomas HILLMAN & Anne his wife
Mar 27 Anne d of Sam[el] SAUEAKER [BT's: SAUATRE"] & Anne his wife
Apr 3   Sarah d of Thomas HOPKINS & Anne his wife
Apr 16 Elizabeth d of Humfrey BATE & Elizabeth his wife
Apr 16 James s of John BROWN & Elizabeth his wife
Apr 23 Ann d of William PERRINS & Anne his wife
May 7   Maximilian s of Robert PITT Schoolmaster & Elizabeth his wife
May 25 Mary d of Humfrey JOHNSONS & Dorothy his wife
Jun 3   Richard s of Richard YORK & Susannah his wife
Jun 6   Frances d of Sam[el] RENSHAW & Mary his wife
Jun 18 Elizabeth d of William BANNISTER & Elizabeth his wife
Jun 25 William s of William HATTON & Mary his wife
Jul 26 Henry s of Henry ELCOCKE & Margret his wife
Aug 26 George s of Thomas RUSSELL & Mary his wife
Aug 27 Sam[el] s of Robert NURTHALL & Hannah his wife
Oct 3   George s of George BAKER & Sarah his wife
Oct 10 Judith s of William PRICE & Judith his wife
Oct 22 John s of Ralph WEBB & Alice his wife
Oct 30 Elienor d of George BATE & Joyce his wife
Nov 8   Humfrey s of Humfrey HOPE & Mary his wife
Dec 14 Rich. s of Rich. BRADELEY Gent & Anne his wife
Jan 4   Mary d of Joseph PARTRIDGE & Elizabeth his wife
Jan 18 Dorothy d of John COMBER & Mary his wife
Feb 16 Sarah d of Thomas JONES & Jane his wife
Feb 24 Robert s of John TROW & Elianor his wife
Mar 9   John s of Thomas JOHNSONS & Sarah his wife

Burialls Anno 1677
Mar 7   John JOHNSONS
Apr 26 Joseph MAYOTT s of Joseph MAYOTT [BT's: HYATT?]

Apr 3	John DARLESTON was layd in ye Earth wthout Chistian Buryall
Apr 28	Isabel BERRY was buried at Kinfare
May 18	Charles s of Thomas BARBER & Anne his wife
May 20	Elienor HILLMAN was Buried at Kinfare
May 24	George COMBER was buried at Kinfare
Jun 2	Mary TAYLER
Jun 25	John PENNE was buried at Kinfare
Jul 7	Margery BRADELEY was buried at Kinfare
Jul 25	Isabel BIRD
Aug 3	Joyce DUNNE [BT's: "DONNE"] was buried at Kinfare
Aug 6	Henry DUNNE [BT's: "DONNE"] was Buryed at Kinfare
Oct 4	William ROBBINSON
Oct 11	Richard SMITH
Oct 21	William FIELD was buried at Kinfare
Dec 8	Thomas NEWMAN
Jan 3	John BRADELEY Gent
Jan 28	Joanne BATE
Feb 27	Humfrey CLARKE

Weddings Anno 1678

May 16	William EGGINTON & Elizabeth ROWLEY
Sep 29	Thomas KNIGHT & Isabel BANNISTER

Baptismes Anno 1678

Mar 26	Richard s of George LOW & Elienor his wife
Apr 2	Thomas s of William IMMS & Magdelin [BT's: Maudlin"] his wife
Apr 16	Martha d of Richard BATE & Martha his wife
Apr 18	Sarah d of John RICHARDS & Mary his wife
Apr 20	Edward s of Edward YEARNSHAW & Elizab. his wife
Apr 30	Thomas s of Humfrey HILLMAN & Sarah his wife
May 24	Thomas s of Edward GROVE & Joan his wife
May 30	Samuel d of John WINFORD & Margery his wife
Jun 14	John s of Roger BRADELEY & Joan his wife
Jun 17	John s of Joseph HILLMAN & Hannah his wife
Jun 20	Frances d of Mr Jonathan NEWEY Min^r & Mary his wife
Jun 27	Isabel d of Richard HACKETT & Isabel his wife
Jun 30	Elizabeth d of Roger LAMBETH & Elizabeth his wife
Jul 4	Elizabeth d of Edward DUNNE & Sarah his wife
Jul 6	Margret d of John HALE & Mary his wife
Jul 12	Samuel s of Joshua MORRICE & Mary [BT's: "Margaret"] his wife
Jul 18	Edmond s of Thomas MASON & Mary his wife
Aug 23	John s of John WARROLL [BT's: "WARRALL"] & Margrett his wife
Sep 13	William s of Thomas LYE & Mary his wife
Aug 24	Benjamin s of John PAGET & Amie his wife. This should have been written next before Will: son of Tho: LYE er.
Oct 8	Mary d of Samuel TAYLOR & Margrett his wife

Oct 13	Dorothy d of William PEW
Oct 14	David s of John DAW & Anne his wife
Oct 19	Mary d of Edward WARD & Mary his wife
Dec 17	Elizabeth d of Henry ELCOCK & Margret his wife

[The next two entries are in the BT's but not in the OR:]

Dec 23	John, s of William BANNISTER & Elizabeth his wife
Dec 26	Elizabeth d of Thomas HURST & Elizabeth his wife
Feb 10	Richard s of John HORTON & Joan his wife
Feb 11	Mary d of Mr Richard BRADELEY & Anne his wife
Feb 16	John s of Henry COOK & Mary his wife
Feb 25	Mary d of John POWEL & Jane his wife
Mar 3	Katharine d of Humfrey BATE & Elizabeth his wife
Mar 11	Merriall d of John POWEL & Merrial his wife
Mar 11	Susannah d of Humfrey SARBITT & Mary his wife
Mar 17	Mary d of James HILLMAN & Mary his wife
Mar 24	Hannah d of Robert NURTHALL & Hannah his wife
Feb 1	Mary d of Tho: MERRYHUST & Betterige his wife

Burials Anno 1678

Apr 8	John SMITH was buried at Kinfare
May 20	Anne FRANCIS was buried in Kinfare Churchyard
Jul 7	Thomas SMITH was buried at Kinfare
Jul 14	Norman MILNER was buried at Kinfare
Aug 20	Edward BRADELEY was the first that was buryed in linnen after the Woollen Act took force & therefore there was 50 shillings forfeited & paid to ye poor of the parish & no more because his Executors made the first discovery to ye Justices
Sep 4	Elizabeth TRAUNTER [BT's: "TRANTER"] was buryed but not in woolen, & being poor she left nothing that could be distrained.
Sep 11	Mrs Mary KETTLESBY widdow was buryed in Wolen wth an Affidavit had according to ye Act. [This entry has a considerable amount apparently crossed out and unreadable]
Sep 13	Phillip s of Mr Phillip FOLEY was buryed in the FOLEY's Chancel, by & wth an Affidavit had according to law as may app^r upon the file
Sep 16	Joan the wife of Richard HOPE was buryed wth an Affidavit had according to Law
Oct 17	Jane GIBBS widow was buryed wth an Affidavit had according to Law
Oct 20	Mr Ambrose GRAY was buryed wth an Affidavit had according to Law as may app^r upon the file
Oct 20	A Chrisome child of John MOUNTSTEVENS was layed in the Earth wrapped in woolen but no Affidavit had tho the Min^r signified it to ye officers wth in Eight dayes
Nov 24	Jane SPENCER was buryed wth an Affidavit had according to Law
Dec 1	Richard HOPE was buryed wth an Affid. according to Law
Jan 21	Mrs Margrett JORDEN Junr was buryed in woolen wth an Affid. had according to Law as may app^r on the file

Jan 30   William JOHNSON was buryed & an Affid. had as may app[ers] upon the file
Feb 15   A Chrisom Child of William BANNISTERs was Layd in the Earth wth an Affidavit had   [BT's: "John s of"]
Feb 28   Sarah LOW wife of George LOW was buryed. Affid. had according to Law
Mar 11   Widow LLOYD was buryed wth an Affid. had in the case

Weddings Anno 1679
Let it be Registered that not one wedding was Solemnized in the Church of Kinfare the year 1679

Baptismes 1679
Mar 25   Richard s of Richard GLADWAY & Anne his wife
Mar 25   Grizwald d of John GEARING & his wife
Apr 9   Thomas s of Thomas HOPKINS & Anne his wife
Jun 1   Elizabeth d of Hugh DAVIES [BT's: "DAVIS"] & Ann his wife
Jul 20   Mary d of Thomas KNIGHT & Isabel his wife
Aug 31   John s of Thomas HILLMAN & Anne his wife
Sep 4   Ann d of Rob[t] PITT Schoolm[r] & Elizab. his wife
Sep 20   Abraham s of William CRANDIGE [BT's: CRANIGE"] & Elizabeth his wife
Sep 29   Joseph s of John HILLMAN & Elizabeth his wife
Oct 25   Susannah d of Sam[l] LEONARD [BT's: "LENART"] & Hannah his wife
Oct 27   Thomas s of John WINFORD & M...[?] his wife
Dec 4   Margret d of John HOPE & Lydia his wife
Dec 29   Sarah d of John BROWN & Elizabeth his wife
Jan 11   Thomas s of John WARRELL & Margaret his wife
Jan 12   John s of John DAVIES
Jan 19   Mary d of William MARTYN [BT's "MARSON"] & Anne his wife
Jan 27   Richard s of Richard BATE & Martha his wife
Feb 2   John s of William HARRICE [BT's: "PRICE"] & Judith his wife
Feb 8   Anne d of John HALLOWAY & Dorothy his wife
Feb 12   Charles s of M[r] Sam[el] JUKES & Frances his wife
Feb 17   Mary d of Edward HILLMAN & Joan [BT's: "Jane"] his wife

Burialls 1679
Apr 14   A chrisom child of William LYNE & his wife was buryed wth Affidavit had accordingly as may app[r] on this file
Apr 17   John WITHURST buried and Affidavit had in the case
Apr 23   A chrisom child of Frances KETTLEY & Martha his wife was laid in the earth and Addidavit had accordingly
May 5   [?] ANDREWS widow was buried & Affidavit had according to Law
Apr 20   Thomas LONGMORE was buryed with Affidavit had according to Law
May 14   Thomas WILLETTS buryed & Affidavit had according to Law as may app[r] on the file

Jun 5	Mary LYE the wife of Thomas LYE was buryed & Affidavit had according to Law
Jun 14	Henry PENN of Stapenhill was buryed & Affidavit had according to Law as may app[r]
Jul 26	Richard BATE Husband of Martha BATE was buryed & Affidavit had according to Law
Aug 13	Elizabeth WHERRIT was buryed & Affidavit had according to Law in that behalf
Sep 29	Joseph HILLMAN was buryed wth Affidavit had according to Law in that behalf
Oct 13	Mary DEE d of M[r] John KETTLEBY & wife of Francis DEE was buried in M[r] Henry GRAY's Chancell leave being first obtained of the Said Henry GRAY wth Affidavit had according to Law
Oct 13	William DERICK was buryed & Affidavit had in the case from M[r] Sam[l] HUNT p[tt][?] in y[e] Chancel
Oct 14	Edward HARVIE s of Edw HARVIE was buryed & wth Affidavit had according to Law
Oct 20	Humfrey KETTLEY buryed with Affidavit had according to Law as may app[r] upon the file
Oct 21	William SARBITT was buryed & Affidavit had as may app[r] upon the file
Oct 28	[BT's: "23rd"] A chrisom child of Edw WARD's was laid in the Earth & Affidavit had in the case
Oct 25	A child of Humfrey SARBITT was buryed and Affid. had
Oct 25	A child of John MOUNTSTEVEN's buryed & Querie whether an Affidavit was had according to Law
Nov 10	Thomas SMITH Jun[r] was buryed & Affidavit had according to Law
Dec 9	Thomas s of Phillip FOLEY Esq[r] was buryed & w[th] Affidavit had according to Law and brought to the Min[r] w[th]in eight dayes but in the keeping of the sayd Phillip
Dec 19	[blank] HILL Widow who dyed at Elizabeth COMBERS & was buryed in Woollen with Affidavit had according to Law
Jan 3	Edmond HUST [BT's: "HURST"] was buryed & Affidavit had in the case as doth app[r] on the file
Jan 4	John SOUTHALL [BT's: "SOUTHWALL"] buryed & Affidavit had in the case as may app[r] on the file
Mar 10	Thomas BARBER Gent was buryed & Affidavit had according to LAW as may app[r] on the file

Weddings 1680

May 11	Humfrey HOPE & Eliz: CHAMBERS
Jun 24	John SMITH & Elizabeth BACH
Jan 19	Tho GROVE & Isabel GUEST
	John HOPE Richard WARREN Church Wardens

Baptismes 1680

Mar 13	Elizabeth d of Fra: BIRDWHISTLE & Rachel his wife [BT's: "of Francis BIRD"]

Apr 8   Elizabeth d of Ja: HALE & Mary his wife
Apr 12   Hester d of Mr Tho: BRINDLEY & [blank] his wife
Apr 19 [BT's: "13"]   Mary d of Wm BANNISTER & his wife
Apr 25   John s of Edward HATTON & his wife
May 8   James s of Sam^{el} RENSHAW & his wife
May 13   Margret d of Joseph LOW & Judith his wife
May 16   Anne d of Roger LAMBETH [BT's: "LAMBERT"] & his wife
Jul 23   Amie d of Tho. LYE & his wife
Sep 6   Samuel s of Edward WARD & his wife
Oct 28   Tho: s of Richard MOSELEY & Mary his wife
Nov 1   Richard s of Francis KETTLEY & Martha his wife
Nov 4   Henry s of Jo. RICHARDS & Mary his wife
Nov 8   Elizabeth d of Edw. GROVE & Jone his wife
Nov 13   John s of Tho. LLOYD & Katherine his wife
Dec 14   Lydia d of Jo. COMBER & his wife
Dec 28   Margret d of Wm WHITTAKER
Jan 7   Joseph s of John PAGETT & Amy his wife
Feb 15   Jane d of Humphry BATE
Feb 24   Joseph s of Edward DUN & Sarah his wife
Mar 1   Anne d of Humfrey HILLMAN & Sarah his wife
Mar 13   John s of Sam^{el} TAYLER & his wife
Mar 20   Mary d of Tho. BARNSTONE

Burials 1680

Apr 24   John COMBER   wth Affidavit according to Law
May 27   Elizabeth WOOD   wth Affidavit according to Law
Jun 24   John MASON   wth Affidavit according to Law
Jul 3   Margret MYATT   wth Affidavit according to Law
Nov 11   John JONES   wth Affidavit according to Law
Nov 30   Anne HILLMAN   Affid. according to Law
Dec 25   Tho. HOPE   wth Affid. according to Law
Dec 29   Alice HIGGINS   wth Affid.
Jan 5   Humfrey LYNE   Affid. according to Law
Jan 5   Widow BACH [BT's: BATCH]   wth Affid. according to Law
Jan 13   Alice WEBB   wth Affid.
Jan 18   Mary HOPE the wife of Humpfrey HOPE   Affid.
Jan 25   John WHERRET   wth Affid.
Feb 4   Elizab. HARRICE the wife of Richard HARRICE [BT's: "HARRIS"] wth Affid.
Feb 5   Edward BENNET   wth Affid.
Feb 7   Elizabeth SPARRY the wife of Michael SPARRY   wth Affid.
Feb 17   Roger BRADELY   wth Affid. according e.c
Feb 15   William KETTLE [BT's: "KETTLEY"]   wth Affid. according   e.c.
Feb [blank; BT's: "19"]   Robert NURTHALL   wth Affid. according   e.c.
Feb 24   Joseph LOW   wth Affid. according   e.c.
Mar 15   Joan HENSHAW   wth Affid. according to Law
Mar 24   Mrs Margaret JORDEN relict of Mr Edward JORDEN   wth Affidavit according to Law

Weddings Anno 1681

Jun 9	Richard [BT's: "Nicholas"] FRANCIS & Judith BROMFIELD
Jun 11	Henry HACKET & Amy HILLMAN
Jun 25	Francis OVERS & Abigail YORK
Jul 15	William NORTON & Anne PEN [BT's: "PENN"]

Baptismes Anno 1681

Mar 28	John s of Humfrey SARBET
Mar 31	Richard s of John POWEL
Apr 4	[? ; BT's: "Thomas"] s of John SMITH
Apr 5	Elizabeth d of Edward COMBER
Apr 11	Thomas s of Mr Richard BRADELY & Anne his wife
Apr 17	George s of John POWEL
Apr 23	Elizabeth d of Richard HACKET & Isabel his wife
Jun 19	Humfrey s of John WORRALL
Jun 29	Elizabeth d of Thomas DARLESTON [BT's: "DARLASON"] & Judith his wife
Jun 30	Samuel s of Mr Jonath: NEWEY & Mary his wife
Sep 18	John s of James HILLMAN
Sep 22	Sherington s of Mr Sam: JUKES & Mrs Frances his wife
Oct 19	Elizabeth d of Nicholas WHITE
Oct 31	Anne d of John DAWS
Nov 24	John s of Rog^r LAMBETH [BT's: "LAMBERT"]
Dec 15	Elizabeth d of Edward HILLMAN
Dec 15	John [BT's: "Richard"] s of Richard PRICE
Dec 21	John [BT's: "Thomas"] s of Mr Tho. BRINDLEY
Dec 26	Elizabeth d of John NORRICE
Dec 27	Miriam [BT's: "Merriall"] d of Thomas HILLMAN
Jan 10	John s of Jo: ATHERSITCH [BT's: "ATHERSICH"]
Feb 13	Thomas s of Will: STOKES
Feb 15	Anne d of John MOLE & Dorothy his wife
Feb 24	Mary d of Francis KETLEY & Martha his wife
Feb 27	Miriam [BT's: "Merriall"] d of Joseph HILLMAN
Feb 27	William s of Henry COOK
Feb 28	Jonathan s of John YORK
Mar 12	Humphrey s of Hugh ap PUE [BT's: "Hugh PEW"]
Mar 20	Charles s of Henry WHITWICK [BT's: WHITEWICK"]

Burials 1681

Apr 4	Elizabeth HILLMAN wth Affidavit according to Law
Apr 6	A child of William BANNISTER with Affid.
Apr 7	[blank; BT's: "A child"] of Samuel TAYLOR & Margrit his wife with Affid.
Apr 8	Mr Wm HAMERTON was interred wth Affid. according to Law
Apr 10	[blank; BT's: "A child"] of William ap PUGH [BT's: "PEW"] wth Affid.
May 25	John s of Jo: DAW [BT's: "DAVYES"] wth Affid. e.c.
May 19	Charles HILLMAN wth Affid. e.c.t
May 23	Mr Richard BRADELEY wth Affid. e.c.
May 27	Margery TAYLER wth Affid. e.c.

May 28 William PATCH [BT's: BATCH"] wth Affid. e.c.
May 29 Abigail SMITH wth Affid. e.c.
May 30 Robert WEBB wth Affid. e.c.
Jun 1 [blank] a forge man was buryed wth Affid. e.c.
Sep 18 [blank, B T's: "A Child"] of Hugh DAVIES wth Affid.
Oct 12 Mary d [BT's: "A child"] of Mr Richard BRADELEY & Anne his wife wth Affid.
Nov 13 George BAKER Senr wth Affid. e.c.
Mar 3 George BAKER jun^r wth Affid. e.c.
Mar 3 Elizabeth PHEZIE [BT's: "PHESEY"] wth Affid. e.c.
Mar 4 John PURSLOW wth Affidavit according to Law
Mar 30 1682 [BT's: "Mar 19"] Judith WILLETS

Weddings Anno 1682

Jun 6 Cornelius DEACON & Mary KNOWLS
Feb 20 John John[sic] MOSELEY & Barbara HACKET

Baptisms 1682

Mar 28 Elizabeth d of William & Judith PR[?]
Apr 18 Elizabeth d of Saml & Margaret TAYLER
May 12 John s of Henry & Amie HACKET
May 23 Frances d of Mr Henry GROVE
May 30 Winnifred d of John & Miriam POWEL
Jun 11 Edward s of John & Mary HALE
Jul 18 Margret d of Henry & Margret ELCOCK
Aug 8 Lydia d of John & Lydia HOPE
Nov 6 Henry s of Edward & Joan WARD[?]
Nov 7 Mary d of John & Mary BRISCOE
Dec 5 Samuel s of Mr Samuel & Madam Frances JUKES
Jan 28 Edward s of Francis & Elizabeth WORRAL
Feb 3 William s of Thomas & Judith DARLISTON
Feb 12 William s of William & Elienor DUNCALF
Feb 23 Samuel s of Edward & Sarah DUNN
Mar 11 Amie d of John & Margret WARROL
Mar 12 Henry[?] s of Richard & Mary MOSELEY

Burials Anno 1682

Mar 19 [Judith] WILLETS of Stepenhil
May 17 Jane BATE the wife of Humfrey BATE
May 27 John WORRAL of Sturton
May 30 Abigail TAYLER both deaf & dumb
Sep 7 John SMITH Aleman
Sep 15 Mr George BRINLEY s of Mr Richard BRINLEY
Sep 23 Thomas BROOK wth Affid. according to Law
Nov 7 Widow BUTTERFIELD very old buryed
Nov 10 William HAYES wth Affid.
Dec 21 William CRANDIDGE Husband to Eliz. CRANDIGE
Jan 15 Humfrey JOHNSONS without a Note
Feb 3 John BATT of Whittington Forge
Feb 12 Elizabeth LYNE Widow buryed but not wth Christian buryall

All these buried wth Affidavit according to Law
John GROVE   ) Churchwardens 1683:1684
Joseph SMITH for Jos: MAURICE)

Weddings Anno 1683
Apr 10   John BACH & Elizabeth COMBER
Dec 9   Thomas NEWMAN & Margret HARRICE

Baptisms 1683
Apr 17   John s of William HATTON
Apr 30   Joyce d of George BATE & Joyce his wife
May 22   Mary d of Humfrey BATE & his wife
May 26   William s of John DAW
Jun 2   Robt s of Richard YORK [BT's: "& Susannah"]
Jun 11   Sarah d of William PERINS
Jul 7   Ann d of Wm CRANDIGE & Elizab. his wife
Jul 28   Elizabeth d of Will: MONAX
Oct 2   George s of Mr Tho: BRINDLEY
Oct 14   Elienor d of John POWELL
Oct 22   Henry s of Mr Henry GROVE
Nov 25   Mary d of Tho. MASON & Mary his wife
Nov 25   Sarah d of James LAVEND^r [BT's: "LAVENDER"]
Nov 26   Sarah d of Henry HACKET & Amie his wife
Nov 28   Henry s of John WINFORD
Nov 28   Mary d of Wm SMITH & Anne his wife
Dec 23   Joseph s of Roger LAMBETH
Feb 25   Henry s of John BROWN
Feb 26   John s of John & Barbary MOSELEY
Mar 10   William s of William WHITTAKER
Mar 11   John s of Thomas LYNE

Buryalls 1683
Mar 29   Anne wife of John MOSELEY
Apr 20   John WHITBROOK of Sturton
Apr 23   William ELICE [BT's: "ELLIS"] of Hyde
May 30   Margrit SMITH [BT's: "of ye Towne"]
Jun 8   Richard s of Richard HOPE
Jun 23   [blank, BT's: "Elizabeth"] daughter of Mrs TURNER
Jul 2   Mr Edmond PETTY [BT's: "of ye Towne"]
Jul 20   John s of Thomas HILLMAN
Aug 27   Joseph MYATT [BT's: "Taylor of Kinfare"]
Aug 30   Elien^r the wife of Tho: HILLMAN
Sep 12   John BACH [BT's: "of Whittington"]
Oct 9   Thomas HILLMAN of Dunsley
Oct 24   William HARRICE [BT's: "of ye parish of Kinfare"]
Oct 28   Mary d of Tho: SMITH Butcher deceased [BT's: "Mary d of ye Widow SMITH"]
Nov 29   Thomas JOHNSONE [BT's: "of Kinfare Town"]
Dec 12   Thomas CLARK [BT's: "of Halfcott"]

Jan 31 [BT's: "Mr"] John s of [BT's: "Mr"] John NEWEY of Darhill in Chadesley Parish
Feb 24 Elizabeth d of Richard GARRIT [BT's: "GARRETT"]
All had Affidavits according to Law
John GROVE   Joseph SMITH   Wardens

Weddings Anno 1684
Apr 14 John PARKES [BT's: "PERKES"] & Margret BROWN
May 1 Richard KETTLEY & Elizabeth BORE
May 4 Robert DANIEL & Anne ELIOTS
Jun 1 William BECKLEY & Anne ASLEY [BT's: "ASTLEY"]

Baptisms 1684
Mar 27 James s of James HILMAN & Mary his wife
Apr 1 Mary d of John HALE & Mary his wife
Apr 5 Rebecca d of John HOPE & Lydia his wife
Apr 7 Hannah d of Edw. HILLMAN & Joan his wife
Apr 30 Mary d of Tho: KNIGHT & Isabel his wife
Jun 22 Mary d of Nicholas WOOD
Jun 24 Marg. [BT's: "Margery"] d of Jo: GEARING & Mary his wife
Jul 18 Richard s of Tho: LYNE & Amie his wife
Jul 26 Anne d of John HUTT & his wife
Jul 27 Elizabeth d of Francis OVERS & Abigail his wife
Jul 28 Jane [BT's: "Joan"] d of John HORTON & Joan his wife
Sep 1 Thomas s of Tho: HILLMAN & Anne his wife
Sep 4 Hannah d of Henry ELCOCK & Margret his wife
Sep 7 Susannah d of Tho: JOHNSONS
Oct 22 Thomas s of Tho: NEWMAN & Margret his wife
Oct 29 John s of Andrew FRIEND
Nov 2 Thomas s of John NORRICE & Abbigail his wife
Dec 26 Elizabeth d of John TROW
Jan 12 John s of William BECKLEY & Anne his wife
Jan 25 Thomas s of James LAVENDER
Jan 31 Samuel s of John DAW & Anne his wife
Feb 20 Mary d of Henry HACKET & Amie his wife
Feb 17 Jeremiah [BT's: "Jeremie"] s of Humfrey BATE
Mar 22 John s of Edw. WARD & Joan his wife

Burialls 1684
Apr 18 Thomas s Tho REYBOULD [BT's: "RAYBOULD of Compton"]
Apr 22 Richard LOW of Kinfare Town
May 18 John WOOD s of Robt WOOD [BT's: "of Sturton"]
May 11 Bridget BAYLYES of Hafcote
Jul 20 George RUSSEL an old man
Aug 20 Elizabeth BATE of Hafcote widow
Sep 11 Mary the wife of John CLARK
Oct 19 Mrs Margaret VINCENT wonderfull old
Oct 26 Thomas MOSELEY Senr of ye Town
Nov 9 Jane the wife of William HOWLES
Nov 13 Elizabeth WHISTONs Mayd

Dec 14	Charles s of Mr John HAMERTON
Jan 1	The wife of Richard LYNES
Jan 29	Edward s of Edward COMBER & Elizab: his wife
Jan 30	William s of Henry COOK
Jan 31	John s of Henry COOK
Feb 18	William TAYLER late Servt at Hyde [BT's: "of Kinfare"]
Feb 10	Edward HALE of Kinfare Clothier
Feb 15	George LOW Tayler
Feb 16	Lydia PURSLOW widow
Mar 2	Widow KETTLEY of Sturton
May 3	Frances the wife of Thomas WINDLE
Mar 18	Humfrey PERRY Turner
Mar 21	George HACKET s of Old John
Mar 21	Isabell the wife of Richard HACKET
	All had affidavits according to Law

Weddings Anno 1685

Sep 17	William [blank, BT's: "PHILLIP"] & Mary [blank, BT's: "DENSICK"]
Nov 3	John HAYWARD & Isabell WORRALL
Feb 14	John LOW & Sarah WOOD

Baptismes 1685

Mar 28	Margaret d of Jo. & Elizab SMITH
Apr 7	Thomas s of Mr Fra. JORDEN & Sarah his wife
May 2	Katherine d of Mr Henry GROVE
May 3	Hugh s of Hugh ap PUE & Fra. [BT's: "Francis"] his wife
May 11	Richard s of William LYNE & Elien^r
May 12	Edward s of Will. SMITH & Anne his wife
May 18	Mary d of Edward YERNSHAW & Elizabeth his wife
Jun 25	Anne d of Richard MOSELEY & Mary his wife
Sep 28	Thomas s of Francis TAGG & Elien^r his wife
Oct 20	Sarah d of Humfrey HILLMAN & Sarah his wife
Oct 23	John s of John HUTT & Anne his wife
Nov 20	Luke s of John POWELL & Anne his wife
Jan 4	William s of Charles JONES & Elizab his wife
Jan 30	Charles s of Wm SIMMS & Anne his wife
Mar 4	Susannah d of Edw: DUNN & Sarah his wife
Mar 19	James s of Jn: RICHARDS & Mary his wife
Mar 2	[blank] son of John PENN & [blank] his wife

Buryals 1685

Mar 27	[BT's: "Mr"] Jo. NEWEY Senr with Affid. according to Law
Apr 27	[BT's: "Mr"] Richard COOK Senr wth Such[?] Affid.
Apr 9	Will: HOWLES wth Such[?] Affid.
Apr 15	Bridget PRICE d of Will: PRICE wth Affid.
Apr 26	Ralph THACKER wth Affid. according to law
May 10	Elizab. d of Rich. HACKET wth Such Affid.
May 17	Richard BARKER wth Affid.
May 19	Charles s of Henry WHITWICK wth Such Affid.

May 31   Anne JOHNSONS wid   wth Such Affid.
Jul[sic] 4 Tho. BARNSTONE   wth Such Affid.
May 15   Elizab. d of Tho: BARNSTONE   wth Such Affid.
Aug 16   Anne d of Tho. HOPKINS   wth Such Affid.
Dec 10   [blank] son of Mr Richard WHEELER   wth Such Affid.
Dec 12   Tho. HOPKINS   wth Such Affid.
Oct 31   Richard HARRICE [BT's: "HARRIS"]   wth Affid.
Nov 3   William BACH   wth Such Affid.
Nov 20   Hugh DAVIES   wth Such Affid.
Nov 29   Sam^{el} s of James LAVENDER
Dec 28   Roger LAMBERT   wth affid. according to Law
Jan 7   Mrs Susannah PENN   wth Affid.
Feb 1   Richard HILLMAN   wth Such Affid.
Mar 4   Anne COOK wid   wth Such Affid.
Mar 4   [blank] Son of John PENN   wth Affid.
Mar 12   Mary d of Richard HACKET   wth Such Affid.
Mar 19   Mrs Anne NURTHALL wife of M^r Jo. [BT's: "Jn"] NURTHALL wth Such Affid.
Mar 24   Mary d of Jo. [BT's: "Jn"] GEARING   wth Affid.
    Fra: [BT's: "Francis"] DEE   Humphrey BATE   Churchwardens

Weddings Anno Dom 1686
[There are no entries under this heading in the OR, although there are some signs that there may have been entries but which had faded. But see below for BT entries]

Baptisms 1686
[The only entry on this page is:]
Aug 10   Samuel s of Mr Thomas BRINDLEY & Martha his wife was born Ju[ly] 21 & Baptized August 10 1686
[Again there are some signs that there may have been entries but which had faded.   But see below for BT entries]

Baptisms 1686   [As recorded in the BT's]
Apr 6   Jane d of Tho & Elizabeth ROGERS
Apr 10   Will s of John & Mary HALE
Apr 19   Daniel s of Daniel & Mary ROWLEY
May 25   Richard s of Richd & Mary BROWN
Jul 10   Mary d of Willm & Mary IYMMANS [or TIMMENS"]
Sep 19   Daniel s of Roger LAMBETH
Oct 16   Eliener d of Tho. & Mary DARLISSON
Oct 17   Richard s of Jn & Margaret WORRALL
Nov 1   Richard s of Willm & Judeth PRICE
Nov 2   Alice d of Tho & Amy LYE
Nov 17   Anne d of Jn & Anne DAW
Nov 18   Samuel s of Mr Tho BRINDLEY
Dec 13   Elizabeth d of James & Mary HILLMAN
Feb 20   John s of Willm & Margaret WHITTAKER
Mar 14   Mary d of John & Elizabeth SMITH
Mar 18   Mary d of Edwd & Anne LINES

Marriages 1686   [As recorded in the BT's]

Apr 12   Edward SICH & Ann WHITBROOK
Apr 12   William CHAMBERS & Anne GARRAT
May 5   John BOLLORD & Alice PAITEN
May 25   William BOLIS & Hester MYSULL [or MYHUT]
Sep 23   John BATE & Anne COOK
Oct 21   Humphrey MOSELEY & Mary HUTTON
Nov 4   Richard HACKET & Amy BARNSTON
Nov 19   William DERRICK & Joyce BAKER
Dec 21   Michael SPARRY & Elizabeth YORK
Feb 12   Adam ROUND & Anne PRICE

Burials 1686   [As recorded in the BT's]

May 12   Anne DERRICK
May 24   John BAKER
May 28   Hannah BRITEN
Jun 24   Humfphrey HOPE
Jun 26   John HAYES
Jul 20   Alice BOLLARD
Jul 24   John SOUTHALL
Aug 19   Thomas HILLMAN
Sep 30   John MOSELEY
Oct 17   Henry BAYLIS
Oct 23   Humphrey SIMMS
Nov 9   Jane BATE
Nov 12   Mrs Sarah NEWEY
Nov 17   Henry ELLCOCK
Nov 3   Mr Richard COOK
Jan 1   Thomas HILL
Dec 26   Mary REA
Dec 29   John REA
Feb 18   William WOOD

All these buried with Affid^t according to Law
Frances DEE   Humphrey BATE   Churchwardens

[The entries in the OR now resume
although the writing style changes at this point]

Weddings 1687

Jun 23   Richard WARREN & Margery TOY
Oct 10   Edward THOMASON & Phebe STEADMAN
Nov 5   Nathaniel BROOK & Mary LYNE [BT's: "LINE"]
Feb 28   Edward LAMBATH & Jane HOPE

Baptismes Anno Dom 1687

Apr 5   Elizabeth d of John HUTT & Elizabeth his wife
Apr 5   Anne d of Wm SMITH & Anne his wife
Jul 16   Margret d of John NORRICE [BT's: "NORRIS"] & Abigail his wife
Aug 5   Mary d of Richard CLARK & Mary his wife

Aug 14   Richard s of Edward WARD & Joan his wife
Aug 16   John s of Humfrey MOSELEY & Mary his wife
Sep 17   Francis s of Francis OVERS & Abigail his wife
Oct 2   Abel s of Thomas JOHNSONS & Mary his wife
Oct 5   Thomas s of Thomas WANNERTON & Abigail his wife
Oct 14   Elizabeth d of Tho: ROGERS & Elizab. his wife
Oct 24   Henry s of Edward DUNN & Sarah his wife
Oct 28   Michael s of Michael SPARRY & Elizab: his wife
Nov 5   Mary d of Wm CRANDIGE & Elizabeth his wife
Dec 27   John s of John BATE & Anne his wife
Jan 6   Elizabeth d of Rich: & Mary MOSELEY
Jan 29   Robert s of Robt DALE & [blank] his wife
Feb 18   Margret s of Humphrey BATE & Jane his wife
Feb 2   Rachel d of Daniel ROWLEY & Rachel his wife
Feb 26   John s of John BRISCOE
Mar 6   Wm s of Francis TAGG & Elien^r his wife
Mar 7   Hannah d of John GROVE & Hannah his wife
Mar 9   Sarah d of Sam^{el} RICE & Sarah his wife
Mar 19   Sarah d of Andrew FRIEND & Susannah his wife

Burials Anno Dom 1687

Apr 2   Mrs PETTY aged 80 years   wth Affidavit
May 15   Henry MOSELEY son of Tho: MOSELEY   wth Affidavit
May 25   A child of Francis WARREL [BT's: "WORRALL"]   wth Affid.
May 28   Robert POWEL   wth Affifidavit
Jun 17   Margery BANNISTER Widow   wth Affid.
Jun 23   Margret BRINLEY [BT's: "BRINDLEY"]   wth Affid.
Aug 3   Mary KETTLEY [BT's: "KETLEY"] widow   wth Affid.
Sep 26   Isabel BACH wife of Tho: BACH   wth Affid.
Nov 21   Mary LOW d Judith LOW   wth Affid.
Nov 29   Francis s of Francis PAGET   wth Affid.
Jan 3   Elizabeth WEBB widow   wth Affid.
Jan 8   A child of Francis PAGET Still born
Jan 21   A child of William LYNE   wth Affid.
Feb 10   A child of Thomas BATE & his wife   wth Affid.
Feb 21   A child of Rich: PRICE   wth Affid.
Mar 12   Jana WATKINS Virgin   wth Affid.
Apr 9   Anne PIKE Widow wth Affid. [This entry is crossed out in the BT's]

Weddings 1688

[None recorded]

Baptismes 1688

Mar 29   Sarah d of James HILMAN & Mary his wife
Mar 29   Elizabeth d of Henry HACKET & Amie his wife
Apr 1   Margret d of Wm SIMMES
Apr 9   Edward s of John BROOK
Apr 14   Edward s of Edward HUTT & Jane his wife
Apr 16   William s of John RICHARDS & Mary his wife

Apr 19　Elizabeth d of Mr Francis JORDEN & [BT's: "Sarah"] his wife
May 16　James s of James MARTIN
May 17　Hannah d of Nicholas WHITE & Elien^r his wife
Jun 19　Frances d of the Honble Jo. [BT's: "Jn"] GRAY Esqr
Jul 13　Mary d of Edward THOMASON & Phebe his wife
Jul 22　Margret d of John MOSELEY & Barbara his wife
Sep 23　William s of Tho: LYNE & Mary his wife
Oct 16　Martha d of Mr Tho: BRINLEY
Oct 16　William s of Thomas COOKSEY & Margret his wife
Oct 23　Elizabeth d of Joseph BROWN & Magdelin his wife but illegit.
Nov [BT's: "Sep"] 17　John s of Nathaniel BROOK & Mary his wife
Nov 27　Nazareth d of Edward COMBER & Elizab. his wife
Dec 18　Elizabeth d of Wm SMALLMAN & Elizab: his wife
Dec 27　William s of Jo. [BT's: "John"] HUTT & Elizabeth his wife
Jan 13　John s of Tho. DUNN & his wife
Feb 15　Thomas s of Wm SIMS [BT's: "SIMMS"] & Elizab. his wife
Feb 25　Jane d of Michael SPARRY & Elizab. his wife
Mar 10　Thomas s of Edward WALDRON & Hannah his wife
Mar 10　John s of Richard WARROL & Mary his wife

Buryalls 1688

Apr 9　Anne PIKE widow　wth Affidavit
May 4　Jane BROWN　wth Affid.
Jun 12　John TROW　wth Affid.
Jun 12　Margret COOK the Relict of Richard COOK was buryed in Linen but paid ye forfeiture
Sep 9　Mary BRADLEY　wth Affid.
Sep 22　Joan HILLMAN the wife of Edw. HILMAN　wth Affid.
Sep 29　A child of William TAYLERS　wth Affid.
Oct 27　A child of John PRITCHARDS
Oct 28　A child of Richard BECKLEYES　wth Affid.
Nov 18　Francis KETTLEY [BT's: "KETLEY"]　wth Affid.
Dec 16　A child of John RICHARDS　wth Affid.
Dec 27　A child of John WILFORDS　wth Affid.
Dec 31　A child of James HARRICES　wth Affid.
Jan 12　Thomas LONGMORE　wth Affid.
Jan 13　A child of Edward LAMBERTS　wth Affid.
Jan 16　A child of Jo. [BT's: "Jn"] HUTT
Jan 21　Joan PRITCHARD　wth Affid.
Jan 28　A child of William CHAMBERS　wth Affid.
Feb 20　Edward YEARNSHAW　wth Affid.
Mar 14　Tho. ASPLEY　wth Affid.
　　　　　John PENN & John HALE Churchw.

Weddings Anno 1689

Sep 30　Edward HILLMAN & Elien^{er} SIMMS
Oct 7　Thomas NORRICE & Anne HUNT
Oct 8　Richard DIXON & Mary BRETTEL
Nov 7　Thomas WALDRON & Anne BRADLEY
Nov 16　John GARRET & Ursula HOLLOWAY

Dec 1	William ROBINSON & Mary MYATT
Jan 15	Henry BARRET & Margret SPENSER

Baptismes Anno 1689

Apr 24	Mary d Francis WARREL [BT's: "WARROL"] & Elizabeth his wife
May 6	Hannah d Robt & Hannah GRIFFITH
May 7	John s of Robt & Susannah DALE
Jul 14	John s of John & Elizabeth COOK
Jul 21	Edward s of Edward & Marcy DUNN
Jul 22	Sarah d of William & Sarah BAYLIS
Sep 22	Joseph s of Richard & Mary BROWN
Sep 26	Anne d of Richard & Mary CLARK
Oct 6	William s of William & Rose SMITH
Nov 5	Jane d of John & Margery GEARING
Dec 2	Thomas s of Humfrey & Jan [BT's: "Jane"] BATE
Dec 26	Elienor d of Adam & Anne ROUND
Jan 22	Hannah d of William & Anne SIMS
Jan 24	Humfrey s of Henry & Amy HACKET
Feb 28	Anne d of Robert & Anne HARRINGTON
Mar 10	Richard s of John & Elienor WORRAL
Mar 12	Mary d of Thomas & Sarah [BT's: "Mary"] JOHNSON

Buryalls An° 1689

Mar 31	Mary WORRAL [BT's: "WARROL"] wth Affid.
Apr 18	Anne HOPE Wid. wth Affid.
Apr 26	Anne WARREN wth Affid.
Apr 29	Charles JONES wth Affid.
Apr 17	Elizabeth BLOWER wth Affid.
Apr 22	[blank] Daughter of James MARTIN wth Affid.
May 5	Elizabeth MOSELEY wth Affid.
May 7	Edward TUNCKS [BT's: "JUNKS"] wth Affid.
Jun 7	William TAYLER wth Affid.
Jul 10	Serjeant LAMBETH in his March to Ireland was buryed wth Affid.
Jul 18	Sarah POWEL
Jul 19	Sarah GEARING
Jul 28	Elizabeth KETLEY wth Affid.
Aug 22	Jonathan YORK wth Affid.
Oct 6	Priscilla SPENCER wth Affid.
Oct 13	Elizabeth d of Mr Fran: JORDEN wth Affid.
Oct 15	Lewis SPICER [BT's: "SPENCER"] alias DEVOURS wth Affid.
Nov 11	Anne ASPLEY wth Affid.
Dec 14	Mary PIECE [BT's: "PEIRCE"] wth Affid.
Dec 15	John HUTT wth Affid.
Dec 16	Margery PAGETT wth Affid.
Jan 10	Elienor WORRALL [BT's: "WARROLL"] wid. wth Affid.
Jan 25	William s of John WORRALL [BT's: "WARROLL"] wth Affid.
Feb 4	John NURTHAL wth Affid.
Feb 10	Sarah d of Mr Fra. JORDEN wth Affid.

[Blank; BT's: "All were Buried with Affidavt according to Law John COOK, John WOOD"]   Churchwardens

Weddings Anno 1690
Dec 27   John JANNES & Anne GROVE
Feb 24   Roger LAMBETH & Mary JOHNSON

Baptismes Ano 1690
Apr 5   Edward s of Edward & Phœbe THOMASSON
Apr 21   Williams s of William & Anne PERINS
Apr 22   John s of Francis & Abigail OVERS
May 23   Mary d of Edward & Jane HUTT
May 27   Anne d of Daniel & Rachel ROWLEY
Jun 10   Samuel s of Thomas & Anne LYE
Jun 20   Richard s of Rich. & Mary BROOK
Jun 30   Richard s of Richard & Mary MOSELEY
Jul 7   Mary d of Richard & Mary DICKSON alias THAX [BT's: "THICKS"]
Jul 30   Sarah d of Edward & Anne LYNES [BT's: "LINES"]
Aug 28   John s of Thomas & Ann WALDRON
Sep 17   Hannah d of William & Hannah PERREY
Sep 19   William s of Tho. & Elizabeth RUTTER
Sep 22   Elizabeth d of John & Ursula GARRETT
Sep 29   Sam^{el} s of John & Barbara MOSELEY
Oct 4   Elizabeth d of James LAVENDER
Oct 10   Anne d of John & Mary HALE
Oct 21   John s of John & Elizabeth CRUTCHLEY
Oct 28   Margarit d of Tho. & Elizabeth WHITEHART [BT's: "WHITEHEART"]
Nov 10   Margarit d of John & Margret WARROL [BT's: "WARRALL"]
Dec 14   Joseph s of Edward & Jane WARD
Jan 12   John s of John & Hannah GROVE
Nov 10   Anne d of Thomas & Margrit NEWMAN
Jan 19   Daniel s of John & Anne DAW was baptized
Jan 19   Martha d of Edward & Hannah WALDRON
Jan 20   Benjamin s of Saml & Mary RENSHAW
Jan 22   Ann d of Edward & Ann TAYLOR
Jan 26   Elizabeth d of George & Elizab. DOREY
Feb 5   Thomas s of Tho. & Margery DUNN
Feb 30   John s of Thomas & Jane LYNE
Mar 3   William s of Thomas BRINLEY [BT's: "Mr Tho. BRINDLEY"] & his wife
Mar 11   John s of the Honble John GRAY Esq'e

Burials Anno 1690
Apr 17   Elizabeth BLOWER spinster
Apr 22   Mary d of James MARTIN
May 5   Elizabeth d of Rich MOSELEY
May 24   John RAYBOULD Senr
Jul 20   William PRICE

Aug 11   Richard & Jane MOUNSTEVEN Twins
Sep 2   Margret ye wife of John MOUNSTEVEN
Sep 10   Robt EVANS
Sep 17   John HUTT Carpenter
Sep 28   John WHITE Carpenter
Oct 4   Mary LAVENDER wife of James LAVDENDER
Nov 2   Elienor HILMAN
Nov 18   Thomas BERREY [BT's: "BERRY"] Usher
Dec 17   Thomas MORRICE of Compton
Dec 21   Elizabeth YEARNSHAW [BT's: "LEAVER"]
Dec 21   Thomas BACH alias LEAVES
Jan 7   Thomas HACKET of the Heath
Feb 1   Margery HUTT
Mar 23   Mary d of Mary WYLEY illegitimate of Old swinford
         All these had Affidavits according to Law
  Churchwardens   [no signatures, BT's: "John COOK, John WOOD"]

Weddings 1691

Jun 7   Thomas WINDLE & Jane RAYBOULD widow
Jun 18   William BURTON & Mary TIMINGS [BT's: "TIMMINS"]
Nov 16   George NICHOLS & Mary BLAKEMORE
Jan 14   William HUTT & Mary DAW

Baptisms Anno 1691

Apr 27   William s of John & Margaret WOOD
May 25   John s of William & Mary TIMMINGS
May 25   Mary d of Richard & Mary MORRICE
Apr 9   Mary & Elizabeth d of Nathaniel & Mary BROOK
Jul 12   Mary d of James & Mary MARTIN
Jul 21   Elizabeth d of James & Mary HILMAN
Oct 5   William s of John & Abigail NORRICE
Oct 8   Edward s of John & Ann JONES
Oct 19   Mary d of Richard & Mary CLARK
Nov 3   John s of John & Elizabeth CLARK
Nov 5   Richard s of John & Rose SMITH
Nov 8   Richard s of John & Elizabeth COOK
Dec 3   Edward s of James & Dorothy HARRICE
Dec 7   Jane d of John & Mary OWEN
Dec 11   Sarah d of John & Eliz^h WORRAL
[no date; BT's: "Dec 14"]   Sarah LAMBERT d of Edward & Jane
         LAMBETH[sic]
Dec 16   Penelope d of Richard & Penelope WARREN
Jan 17   Mary d of Abraham & Priscilla CHAMBERLAIN
Feb 2   Mary d of William & Mary BAYLIS
Feb 15   Thomas s of Saml & Mary SMITH
Feb 16   William s of William & Anne SMITH
Feb 16   Samuel s of Rowland & Joyce WHITE [BT's: "WHYTE"]
Mar 2   Richard s of Richard & Mary WORRAL
Mar 9   Humfrey s of Humfrey & Mary MOSELEY
Mar 13   Jane d of Roger & Mary LAW

Mar 17 Sarah d of William & Mary BURTON
Mar 17 Elizabeth d of Henry & Elizabeth BARRET

Burials 1691
May 23 Sarah d of James HILLMAN & Mary his wife
Jun 20 Jane HACKET   with Affidavit
Jul 24 Nazareth a poor man was buryed   wth Affidavit
Aug 9   Anne MOSELEY wth Affidavit
Aug 14 William MOSELEY Glover   wth Affid.
Oct 2   Anne TRAUNTER   wth Affid.
Oct 19 Nicholas LUCE   wth Affid.
Nov 26 The Widow HOPKINS of Sturton
Dec 24 Humfrey HOPE s of Tho: HOPE
Jan 9   Margrit JONES Widow
Jan 24 Thomas BROWN widower
Feb 5   John KINGSON   with Affid.
Mar 2   Edward s of Wm & Ann CHAMBERS   wth Affid.
Mar 4   Dorothy the wife of John WHITE
Mar 17 Mary BURTON   wth Affid.
Mar 24 Thomas DEACON   wth Affid.
         All these buryed wth Affid. according to Law
         John NORRICE   Tho: WALDRON   Church Wardens

Weddings Anno 1692
Jun 2   Humfrey CLARK & Mary ELCOCK
Jun 26 Jeffrey JOLLEY [BT's: "JOLLY] & Sarah BENNIT [BT's: "BENNETT]
Jul 31 Thomas BROWN & Mary LANE
Oct 13 Richard MOOR & Sarah MULLINER
Nov 5   William SALE & Mary EGGINTON
Jan 14 James LAVENDER & Sarah BAKER
Jan 14 Samuel TALBOT & Elizabeth CROFT
Feb 2   Robert PARKES & Anne IMMS
Feb 2   John WIGGAN & Anne BROWN

Baptismes Anno 1692
Apr 6   John s of John & Margery GEARING
Apr 6   Humfrey s of John & Margery GEARING   twins
Apr 12 Jane d of Edward & Jane HUTT
Apr 23 John s of Rob[t] & Elizabeth GRIFFIN
May 12 Thomas s of Thomas WHITEHART
May 24 William s of Edward & Phœbe THOMASON
Jun 1   Thomas s of Thomas & Anne WALDRON
Jun 2   Harry s of Thomas & Elizabeth ROGERS
Jun 8   Samuel s of Michael & Elizab SPARRY
Jun 27 Mary d of Henry & Amie HACKET
Jul 4   Edward s of Thomas & Isabel GROVE
Jul 11 Elizabeth d of Edw. & Elizabeth YEARNSHAW
Jul 21 Anne d of William & Hannah PERRY
Jul 24 Mary d of William & Mary WHITAKER

Aug 12 Thomas s of Mr Thomas & Elizabeth JUKES
Aug 19 George s of Richard & Mary BROWN
Aug 10 Sarah d of John & Anne DAW
Sep 27 Richard of Richard & Anne WHITE
Oct 17 John s of Richard DIXON alias THICK
Oct 25 Mary d of Richard & Mary BROOK
Nov 22 Edward s of Edward & Hannah WALDRON
Dec 21 Margret d of John & Margret BROOK
Jan 29 Thomas s Thomas & Elizabeth BATE
Feb 2   John s of Edward & Jane LAMBERT
Feb 21 John s of Thomas & Hester BRINLEY
Feb 27 Hester d of Richard & Mary CLARKE
Mar 11 Anne d of Thomas & Sarah JONSONS

Burials Anno 1692

Apr 9   John s of John & Margery GEARING
Apr 7   Richard SMITH wth Affid. according to Law
Apr 16 Humfrey s of John GEARING & Margery his wife
Apr 23 Humfrey BATE [BT's: "sen^r"] of the Bank wth Affid.
Apr 24 Elizabeth CLARK wth Affidavit
Apr 25 Richard SENIER wth Affid. According to the Law
Apr 28 Margret YORK daughter of ye Wid YORK
May 13 Thomas s of Thomas WHITEHART
May 20 Richard BIRD of Dunsley wth Affid.
May 24 Mary wife of Richard MORRICE
Jun 3   Richard NEWNAM wth Affidavit according to Law
Jul 14 Judith SPAREY d of Michael SPAREY [BT's: "SPARREY"]
Jul 20 Judith KNOWLES virgin wth Affid:
Aug 21 Anne ye wife of John WYER wth Affid
Sep 18 Amy the wife of John PAGET of Enfield
Sep 25 Thomas TALBOTT Gent wth Affid
Nov 13 John WYER [BT's: "WYRE"] wth Affid according to Law
Dec 4   John BRISCO alias CAVALIER
Dec 10 William HUTT Carpenter at ye Forge
Dec 19 William ROWLEY wth Affid according to Law
Jan 1   Thomas BRETTEL of Whitnalls End
Jan 28 Elienor the wife of honest Robt WOOD
Jan 26 John POWEL [BT's: "senr"] Anthony's Father
Feb 7   Thomas CLARK wth Affid according to Law
Feb 27 Edward DUNN Starved in ye great Snow
        John NORRICE   Thomas WALDRON   Church Wardens

Baptisms Ann Dom 1693

Apr 7   Elizabeth d of Edward & Anne LYNES
Apr 18 John s of Rich: & Mary MOSELEY
Apr 30 James s of Wm & Anne BECKLEY
May 9   William s of Walter & Mary ELIOTS
May 12 Sarah d of Nicholas & Elianr^r WHITE
May 16 Mary d of Wm & Mary TIMMINGS [BT's: "TIMMINS"]
May 30 Richard s of Rich: & Penelope WARROL [BT's: "WARRALL"]

Jun 24	Anne d of John & Margery GEARING
Jul 2	John s of Wm & Anne CHAMBERS
Jul 27	Sarah d of John & Sarah BATE
Aug 6	Margret d of Wm & Mary ROBBINSON
Aug 6	Margret d of John & Barbara MOSELEY
Sep 13	George s of Tho: & Margret DUNN
Sep 17	Elizabeth d of Jo: & Elizabeth CRUTCHLEY
Oct 29	Richard s of Tho: & Margret NEWMAN
Nov 14	Samuel s of John & Hannah GROVE
Nov 20	John s of John & Elien^r WARROL [BT's: "WORRALL"]
Nov 20	Elizabeth d of Francis & Susannah HATCHET
Nov 21	Sarah d of Rich: & Mary WARROL
Nov 22	Sarah d of Rich: OLIVER illegit.
Nov 30	Hannah d of Henry & Margret BARRET
Dec 14	William s of Tho: & Anne WALDRON
Dec 24	Elizabeth d of Robt & Anne PARKES
Jan 4	Thomas s of James & Mary HILMAN
Jan 6	Amie [BT's: "Amy"] d of Thomas & Amie HILMAN
Jan 13	Henry s of Henry & Amie HACKETT
Jan 23	John s of John & Margret WOOD
Mar 13	Susannah d of Mr. Tho: & Elizabeth JUKES
Mar 18	Mary d of W^m & Hannah PERRY
Mar 23	Edward s of W^m & Mary[crossed out] Jane WEBB

Burials 1693

Apr 7	Joseph GREAVES wth Affid.
Apr 15	Edward HUTT s of Edw. HUTT wth Affid. [BT's: "of the Bank"]
Apr 27	Humfrey BATE Senr wth Affid.
Aug 1	Sarah d of John BATE wth Affid.
Aug 14	Ann LOW Spinster wth Affid.
Sep 4	Humfrey DAVIES Thatcher
Nov 22	Mary d of Elien^r POWEL wth Affid.
[no date]	Sarah OLIVER bas^d d of Hannah THACKER wth Affid. [BT's: "Novem^{ber} last day" and "Sarah base d of OLIVER jun^r"]
Nov 29	Mary WARRAL [BT's: "WORRAL"] wth Affid
Dec 5	Dionese HILLMAN a widower wth Affid. [BT's: "Day labour"]
Dec 16	Humfrey HOPE s of Tho: HOPE wth Affid.
Dec 17	Joyce WATKIS [BT's: "WATKINS"] widow wth Affid.
Dec 21	Katherine WORROLL wife of Rich: WORROL [BT's: "WORRALL"] wth Affid.
Jan 1	Sarah WHITTEN wth Affid.
Jan 4	Martha COX wth Affid.
Feb 6	Elizabeth MOSELEY Spinster wth Affid.
Mar 8	Robt YORK s of Margret YORK Wid wth Affid.

Marriages 1693

May 24	Rich. OLiVER & Anne WILLIT
May 26	Tho. HUITT & Elizabeth STEWART [BT's: "HUIT" & "STEWARD"]
Jul 6 [BT's: "2nd"]	Joseph PHILLIPS & Jane WEBB

Oct 12 John POWEL & Anne PARKS
Dec 26 Saml BATE & Jane BRADELY
Dec 31 Edward KNOWLES & Elizabeth BRADLEY [BT's "BRADELY"]
Jan 24 Joseph [blank] & Mary BESE [BT's: "BOAS"]
Jan 31 John [blank] & Elizabeth [blank]

Marriages 1694

Apr 12 John [blank] & Mary [blank]
Jul 1   James SMITH & Abigail BIRD
Aug 16 [BT's: "15th"] Isack PRIER [BT's: "PRIOR"] & Anne BATE
Sep 8   Francis [blank] & Elienor [blank]
Feb 2   William WALLINS & Hannah OWLES

Baptisms 1694

Apr 10 Elizabeth d of John & Elizabeth COOK
Apr 25 Phœbe d of Edward & Phœbe THOMAS
May 6   Hannah d of William & Anne ROWLEY
May 14 John s of Humfrey & Mary CLARK
May 25 Elizabeth & Margret daughters of John & Anne JONES
Jun 11 Ruth d of Tho: & Elizabeth HALL
Jul 5   John s of Tho. & Dorothy HILMAN
Jul 12 Samuel s of John & Katherine BRISCOE
Sep 5   Humfrey s of John & Anne BATE
Sep 17 John s of John & Anne POWEL
Sep 18 John s of Abraham & Priscilla CHAMBERLAIN
Dec 10 Thomas s of Rowland & Joyce WHITE
[The next entry would appear to have been squeezed in at a later date:]
        John BAYLIS was baptized ye same day son of Willm B...[?]
Dec 11 Samuel s of John & Mary OWEN
Jan 13 Samuel s of Francis & Abigail OVERS
Feb 10 Samuel s of Rich: & Anne WHITE
Mar 4   Samuel s of Samuel & Mary SMITH
Mar 5   Joseph s of Tho. & Amy LYE
Mar 20 Mary d of John & Margret BROOK

Burials 1694

Mar 30 Susannah BAKER widow wth Affid.
Apr 12 Mrs Sarah JORDEN wife of Mr Fra: JORDEN wth Affid.
Apr 17 Daniel ROWLEY Senr wth Affid.
Apr 23 Anne OLDNALL [BT's: "wife of John"] & Affid. was made 1694
May 4   Phœbe THOMASON the wife of Edward THOMASON
May 4   Phœbe THOMASON d of Edw. THOMASON & Phœbe his wife
May 13 Thomas HIGGINS Batchler wth Affid.
Jun 12 Thomas HILMAN [BT's: "of the Hill" crossed out] wth Affid.
May 30 Sarah HACKET wth Affid.
Oct 23 Mrs Hester BRINDLEY Relict of Mr Rich wth Affid.
Nov 21 Anne d of Rich. WARREN Senr
Jan 17 Elienor POWEL widow aged about 100 years
Jan 20 Elizabeth BACH widow

Jan 20   Joyce DERICK [BT's: "relict of William DERRICK"]   wth Affid.
Jan 29   William DERICK [BT's: "himself"]   wth Affid.
Mar 22   Thomas BALLARD [BT's: "clothworker"]   wth Affid.
         All these had Affid. according to Law
         Thomas HURST   Thomas LYE   Church Wardens

Births & Baptismes for Anno 1695

Mar 26   Mary d of Isaak FRYER & Anne his wife was born [blank; BT's: "March 1"] & Bap^t March 26
Apr 1   Sarah d of John BATE & Sarah his wife was born [blank; BT's: "Feb 26"] & Bap^t Apr 1
Apr 30   Joseph s of Joseph PHILLIPS & Jane his wife
         Penelope d of Daniel ROWLEY & Rachel his wife born before May day but Bapt May 6   [BT's: "born April 30"]
May 13   Anne d of Rich WARREN & Parnel his wife   born May 12
May 19   Rebecca d of Rich WARREN & Parnel his wife   born May 12
May 26   William s of Robt DALE & Susannah his wife   born [blank]
May 30   Henry s of Mr Tho. JUKES & Elizabeth his wife   born May [blank]
Jun 16   Elizabeth d of Rich. BROWN & Mary his wife   born [blank]
Jun 23   William s of Wm TOLLEY & Mary his supposed wife   Mr. EGGINTON's Sev^t
Jun 28   Catherine d of Francis WORRAL & Elizab   born June 17
Oct 10   Elizabeth d of Rich CLARK & Mary his wife   born Sep 24
Oct 4   Amie d of Henry HACKET & Amie his wife   born Sep 18
Oct 25[?]   James s of James SMITH & Isabel his wife   born Oct 24 [BT's: "born Oct 2 & bapt Oct 27"]
Oct 22   Mary d of Rich. OLIVER jun^r & Anne his wife   born Oct 2
Nov 11   Charles s of Wm WELLINS [BT's: "WALLINS"] & [blank] his wife
Nov 29   John s of Edw WALDRON & Hannah his wife   born Nov 16
Dec 10   Daniel s of Tho. DUNN & Margret his wife
Dec 27   Rich. s of Rich. KETLEY & Elizab. his wife   born [blank]
Jan 17   William s of Tho. SPARRY & Margret his wife   born & bapt Jan 17
Feb 3   Mary d of Will. WEBB & Jane his wife
Feb 10   Edward s of Edw LAMBERT & Jane his wife   born & bapt. Feb 10
Feb 13   Edward s of William BECKLEY & Anne his wife   born [blank]
Mar 10   Sarah d of Wm TIMMINGS & Mary his wife   born Mar 6
Jul 1 1695 [BT's: "July 7th"] Susannah d of Wm PARDOE & Anne his wife   but misplaced

Burials 1695

Apr 9   William s of Tho: WALDRON & Anne
Apr 13   Mrs Hester BRINDLEY Wid.   wth Affid. according to Law
Apr 25   Martha d of Martha BATE wid.   wth Affid.
May 2   Mary d of James HARRICE & Dorothy his wife   wth Affid.
May 7   William s of William VEALE & Hanna his wife but dwelt in Alveley   wth Affid.

May 14   Edward s of Jane SMITH wid   wth Affid.
May 14   Joseph s of Joseph PHILLIPS & Jane his wife   wth Affid.
May 23   Ralph CRADDOCK Servt to Tho: BRINDLEY   wth Affid.
Jun 19   Mary d of Roger LAMBERT & Mary his wife   wth Affid.
Jun 18   A dead [BT's: "still borne"] Child of Simon BRETTEL & Anne his wife   wth Affid.
Jun 22   Elizabeth PENN widow   wth Affid.
Jul 1   Joseph GIBBS husband of Susannah GIBBS   wth Affid.
Jul 2   A child baseley born [BT's: "still borne child"] at Wm EGGINTON's of ye Park ye Mo^r fled
Nov 1   Hannah wife of Jo. [BT's: "John"] GROVE was buryed on All Sts day   wth Affid.
Dec 1   Charles s of William WELLINS [BT's: "WALLENS"]   wth Affid.
Dec 21   Sarah d of Sarah POWEL illeg.   wth Affid.
Dec 22   Margret BACH wid [BT's: "aged 90 years"]   wth Affid.
Dec 30   Mary d of Jo: [BT's: "John"] POWEL & Hannah his wife   wth Affid.
Jan 20   Elienor d of Jo: POWEL & Hanna his wife   wth Affid.
Jan 21   A stil born Child of Tho: HATCHET was layd in ye Earth
Mar 8   Thomas TEARN [BT's: "a batchelor"]   wth Affid.
Mar 17   Joyce wife of George BATE [BT's: "butcher"]   wth Affid.

Marriages 1695

Jul 13   Richard HARTLE & Mary LAWLEY
Jul 14   Richard PERRY & Mary ap PUE alias RICE
Jul 19   Wm HARVEY [BT's: "HARFORD"] & Elizabeth PIXEL
Jul 18   Richard AINSWORTH & Elizabeth BANNISTER
Dec 19   Benjamin PLANT & Elizabeth BRADELY
Dec 22   Richard HADLEY & Sarah WARD
Dec 26   George RICHARDS & Anne COLLIT [BT's: "COLLET"]
Dec 30   Daniel HANCOX & Mary LOW
Jan 5   John TRUMAN & Sarah CLARK
Jan 20   John BLYKE & Abigail MEBRAY
Feb 29   1696[sic] [BT's: "1695"]   Richard CORFIELD & Dorothy FEREDAY

Marriages 1696

Jul 14   John BANKES [BT's: "BANCKES"] & Anne PITTS
Jan 27   Jonathan HAND & Elienor BLAKEWAY
Feb 2   William MARSH of Womborn & Jane BROWN
Feb 16   Francis WIGGON [BT's: "WYGGAN"] & Elizabeth PAGET
Mar 23   John PAYTON & Susannah GIBBS

Christenings 1696

Mar 27   Anne d of Richard & Mary MOSELEY   born March March[sic] 24
Mar 29   Joseph s of Joseph & Barbara MOSELEY   born March 26
Apr 13   Samuel s of Wm PENNS [BT's: "PENN"] & Anne his wife   born March 22
Jun 22   Dorothy d of Tho. & Dorothy HILMAN   born June 7

Apr 13   Joseph s of Anne READ illegit.   born April 6
Jul 14   Anne d of Robt PARKS & Anne his wife   born June 19
Jul 28   Wm s of John & Elizabeth CLARK   born July 27
         Anne d of Edw & Anne LYNES   born & bapt. Aug 11
Sep 29   Joseph s of Henry & Margret BARRET   born Sep 17
Sep 30   Isaak s of Isaak & Elizab. FRYER   born Sep 25
Sep 14   Jane d of Joseph & Jane PHILLIPS   born Sep 4
Nov 17   Margret d of Humfrey & Mary CLARK   born Nov 3
Dec 1   Mary d of John & Catherine TRUMAN   born Nov 9
Nov 18   Mary d of Richard & Sarah HADLEY   born Nov 15
Nov 24   Abraham s of Abr. & Priscilla CHAMBERLAIN   born Nov 4
Nov 19   Elizabeth d of Michael & Elizabeth SPARRY   born & bapt. Nov 19
Dec 10   John s of John JONES & his wife   born & bapt. Dec 10
[Looks like Dec & Nov overwritten] 26 [BT's: "Dec 26"] Joseph s of
         Tho. & Anne HILMAN   born Nov 20
Dec 9   Roger s of Roger NORMCOTE & Elizab. his wife   born Dec 8
         [BT's for above give: born "Dec 8" & baptised "Nov 9[sic]"]
Feb 2   Anne d of Jo. & Elizabeth TAYLER   born Dec 5
Jan 14   Sarah d of Richard & Mary WATKENS [BT's: "WATKINS"]
         born Jan 12
Jan 27   Elizabeth d of Richard & Dorothy CORFIELD   born & bapt. Jan 27
Feb 18   Anne d of Richard & Anne WHITE   born Jan 31
Jan 8[sic]   Tho: s of Francis & Susanna HATCHIT   born Feb 4[sic]
[BT's: "Feb 28"]   Mary d of Wm & Anne BECKLEY   born Feb 7 & bapt.
Feb 21   Richard s of James & Dorothy HARRIS   born Feb 20
Feb 25   Rich. s of Thomas & Joan NORMCOTT   born Feb 19
Feb 25   Bridget d of Wm & Hannah PERRY   born Feb 21
Mar 31   Wm s of Wm & Hannah ROWLEY   born Mar 16

Burials Anno 1696

Mar 28   Margret YORK Wid   wth Affid.
Mar 29   Hannah d of Robt & Hannah GRIFFITH
Mar 31   Mary d of Lewis SPENCER & Elizabeth his wife   wth Affid.
Jul 20   John PERKES of Hafcote Husb of Collibra   wth Affid.
Jul 29   Elizabeth the wife of Benjamin PLANT
Aug 25   Wm BANNISTER of Sturton   wth Affid.
Aug 29   Wm LYNES of Sturton   wth Affid.
Aug 31   Richard WILLETS   wth Affid.
Sep 26   Joseph s of Henry BARRET & Margret his wife
Sep 28   Widow DAW of Kinfare
         Francis CLARK of Compton dyed here Sep but buried at
         Powick   [BT's: "buried at Powick Sep 18"]
Apr [sic] 25   The wife of Ralph WEBB   wth Affid.
Apr [sic] 1   Anne d of Jo. & Margery WINFORD
Oct 25   Henry TAYLER [BT's: "Crier of Kinfare"]   wth Affid.
Nov 8   Nathaniel BROOK [BT's: "Sythsmith"]   wth Affid.
Nov 20   Anne OLIVER the wife of Rich. OLIVER junr
Nov 22   A Stil born Child of Wm HARFIELD

Dec 8   Joseph s of Wm TOLLEY
Dec 10   Elizabeth the wife of John JONES
Dec 12   John DAW of Sturton Forge [BT's: "Forgeman"]   wth Affid.
Dec 15   Isabel WARROL [BT's: "WARRAL"] Widow   wth Affid.
Jan 7   Edward s of Edward HUTT
Jan 19   Thomas s of Tho. COOKSEY   wth Affid.
Feb 8   John s of Wm BECKLEY
Feb 13   Anne d of Edward & Anne LYNES
Feb 14   John MOSELEY Sythgrinder   wth Affid.
Feb 18   Edward HILMAN ye eldest Tayler   wth Affid.
Feb 18   A stil born Child of Simon BRETTELS
Feb 21   Ursulah GARRET wife of Jo: GARRET
Feb 28   A Stil born child of Wm PARDOES
Mar 4   William PIKE Weaver
Mar 9   Hannah NURTHAL Widow
Mar 9   Wm MONOX [BT's: "MONAX"] of Sturton Tayler
Mar 17   Mary d of Wm BECKLEY
             [The next entry has been crossed through; see later entry:]
             ~~John WIGGEN Scribbler was bur~~
Mar 24   Frances FEREDAY widow
May 9[sic]   Rich BROOK of Kinfare
May 19   Margret wife of Tho. SPARRY
May 19   A Child of Wm & Hannah WELLINGS [BT's: "WALLINS"]
Aug 7   John MOLE Glover   wth Affid.
Sep 20   Elienor GARRET wife of Rich GARRET
             [One illegible entry]

Marriages 1697
[The next three marriage entries are obscured to various degrees]
[BT's: "Apr 10"]   Richard PRITCHARD & Mary PERINS
[BT's: "May"] 27   Thomas SPARRY & Joyce SMITH
Dec 27   John RICHARDS & Rebeccah HINCKS

Baptisms 1697
Apr 6   Elizabeth d of James & Isabel SMITH born Apr 6 & bapt. ye same day
Apr 11   Edward s of Tho: & NEWMAN & Margret his wife   born Apr 10
Apr 20   Elizabeth d of John & Elizabeth BOWERS   born Apr 3
May 14   Joseph s of Rowland & Joyce WHITE   born May 11
Jun 13   William s of Wm WALLENS [BT's: "WALLINS"] & Hannah his wife   born Jun 2
             John s of Lewis & Elizabeth SPENCER   born & bapt Aug 26
[blank; BT's: "Sep"]   Rachel d of Edward & Anne TAYLER   born Aug 23 & baptized
Sep 7   Tho: s of W^m & Margrett WHITTAKER [BT's: "WHITTACRE"] born Aug
Sep 24   Sarah d of Edward & Mercy DUNN   born Sep 23
Sep 29   Sarah d of Edward & Jane HUTT   born Sep 26
Oct 18   Mary d of W^m & Mary ROBINSON   born Oct 1

Oct 19	Humfrey s of John & Sarah BATE born Oct 3
Oct 20	Richard s of John & Elizabeth POWEL born Oct 19
	Abigail d of [blank] BLYKE & Abigail his wife born Nov 6 & baptized
Dec 14	Joseph s of Tho: COOKSEY & Margret his wife born Nov 18
Dec 27	Mary d of Samuel & Mary SMITH born Dec 16
Dec 28	Bridget d of Richard & Bridget HUMFREYS born Dec 18
Jan 11	Francis s of Francis & Anne PAGET born Jan 7
	Mary d of Tho: & Mary BROWN born Jan 11 & baptized
[BT's: "bap Jan 21"]	Elizabeth d of W^m & Jane WEBB born Jan 12 & baptized
Jan 18	Elizabeth d of W^m & Sarah BAYLIS born Jan 13
	Sarah d of Edward PARDOE & Mary his wife born Jan 16 & baptized [BT's: "born Jan 10, bapt Jan 26"]
Feb 2	Elizabeth d of Edward & Hannah WALDRON born Jan 24
Mar 16	Elizabeth d of William & Ann BECKLEY born Feb 8
Mar 8	Ithiel s of Thos & Mary HALE born Mar 5

Burials 1697

Apr 7	Anne d of John & Mary HALE
Apr 21	Mary SOUTHALL widow
Apr 20	Widow ROBINSON of Sturton
Apr 11	John WIGGON [see crossed out entry in 1696] [BT's: "Clothworker"]
Apr 30	John WHITE Junr
May 1	John WORRALL of Sturton [BT's: ""buryed in ye prime of his time"]
May 4	Thomas HILMAN [BT's: "Day laborour"]
May 8	William s of John & Margret WOOD his wife
May 30	Mary d of John PITT & Alice his wife
Jun 1	John WHITE Senr & Milner
Jun 8	Tho s of Tho WALDRON & Anne his wife
Jun 1	Bridget d of Wm & Hannah PERRY
Jun 10	Hannah the wife of William PERRY
Jul 5	Dorothy HILMAN d of Tho HILMAN [BT's: "& Mary his wife"
Aug 10	Elizabeth PIKE Widow [BT's: "the Relict of William PIKE"]
Sep 2	Elizabeth the wife of Roger NORMCOTE
Nov 15	Elizabeth KETTLE Widow
Nov [22]	Widow JONES widow mother in law to Tho GIBBS
Dec 18	Joane HADEN wife of [blank] HADEN [BT's: "of Kingswinford"]
Feb 13	Anne BAKER [BT's: "junr"] said to dye for Loue
Feb 26	Elizabeth d of Edward & Hannah WALDRON
Jun 21	John HOLLOWAY Wheelwrite
	All wth Affidavit

Marriages An° Dom 1698

Apr 25	John KETLEY & Jane POWEL
Jul 11	Joseph TUNNERTON & Elizabeth HURST
Feb 6	Thomas DAVIES & Anne LOVEL

Baptismes Anno Dom 1698

	Thomas s of Rich. & Anne WORRAL born March 2 1698
Apr 13	John[?] the illegitimate son of Rich. HILMAN & Margret HOLLOWAY was born April 6
Apr 26	Margret d of John & Margret WOOD born April 11
May 18	Richard s of Richard & Mary CLARK born May 3
May 20	Anne d of Adam & Anne ROUND born May 5
May 9	Edward s of Edward & Anne LYNES born May 7
May 29	Mary d of Rich. & Mary PRITCHARD born May 16
Jun 3	Sarah d of Edw THOMASSON & his wife born May 28
Jul 7	William s of William CARTWRIGHT a strang illegitimate child was born 26th of June of one Mary JONES
Jul 10	John s of Jo & Elizabeth ROBBINS born July 10 & baptized ye same day
Jul 15	Saml s of Daniel HANCOX & Mary his wife born July 12
Aug 8	Jane d of Joseph BROWN & Magdelen his wife born 29 July
Aug 25	Mary d of Thomas DUNN & Margret his wife born Aug 24
Sep 26	John s of William & Mary HICKMAN born Aug 30
Sep 25	Margret d of John & Margret BROOK born September 5
Sep 27	Thomas s of Robert & Anne PARKES born Sep 3
Sep 11	Elizabeth d of Rich. HADLEY & Sarah his wife born September 10
Oct 17	Sarah d of John & Rebecca RICHARDS born October 15
Nov 4	Thomas s of Isaak & Anne FRYER born Oct 19
Nov 2	Thomas s of William HARFORD & Elizabeth his wife born October 22
Nov 9	William s of Alice POWEL illegimate born November 3
Nov 16	William s of Edward & Hannah WALDRON born Nov 16 & baptized ye same day
	William s of Rich. & Elizabeth KETTLEY born Nov 28 & baptized
Jan 3	John s of Rich. & Petronella WARREN born Dec 4
Jan 3	Thomas s of Robert DALE & his wife born Dec 22
Jan 28[? date has been altered]	John s of John & Elizabeth ROBBINS born Jan 16
Jan 27	Mary d of John & Jane KETTLEY born Jan 23
Feb 20	Joseph s of Henry BARRET & Margret his wife born Feb 7
Apr 6	William s of Edward & Mercy DUNN born March 22

Burials An° 1698

Mar 30	Edward ADDENBROOKE of Winsor Lane
Apr 12	Richard GARRET jun^r of Kinfare batchler
Apr 13	Humfrey SARBETT of Sturton
Apr 28	[blank] d of Widow VEAL at Acres Stile
May 6	Martha KETTLEY widow of Kinfare Town
Jun 21	Anne BANNISTER of Sturton Widow
Jun 21	John GARRET s of Richard GARRET Glover
Jul 10	Benjamine FRY a journey man Clothyer
Jul 15	John HEATH of Checkhil Walk-mill
Jul 20	John BRADLEY s of Roger BRADLEY deceased

Sep 10	Lewis SPENCER Forgeman of Whittington
Sep 12	Catherine the wife of John NEW
	Honest Anthony. POWEL Innocent was buryed in a short time after he was from the Widow DAVIES
Nov 24	Elienor WORRAL the Relict of John WORREL Senr
Nov 26	Mary d of Abraham CHAMBERLAIN
Dec 7	William s of Edward WALDRON & Hannah his wife
Dec 11	Phillip BOSTOCK Servt in Tho: LYE
Jan 18	Thomas DARLASTON of Kinfare
Jan 3	Wm CLARE an Anabaptist from Bewdley was buried by their preacher
Jan 4	[blank] TIMMINGS Widow from the Hafcote
Jan 8	Edward s of William WEBB & Jane his wife was drowned & buryed Jan 8
Jan 13	William s of Alice POWEL illegitimate
Jan 26	John GROVE Clothier w^o left 20^{ff} to ye poor of Kinfare
Jan 25	John s of John & Elizabeth ROBBINS
Feb 6	Mary the wife of Sam^{el} RENSHAW
Feb 9	Jane the wife of Edward LAMBERT
Feb 22	Margret WEATHERHIL Widow of Kinver
Apr 2	A strang Woman from Sturton named ye Widow BRASIER
	John HORTON John BROWN Churchwardens

Marriages Anno Dom 1699

May 14	Richard [blank; BT's: "COATS"] & Mary SITCH botp were marryed May 14th & Kings pay rec'd
[BT's: "May"] 28	Alexander ROBBINSON & Anne HOLLOWAY botp were marryed
May 29	Richard FEREDAY & Mary PROUDLEY [BT's: "PROUDLY"]
Oct 2	John COMBER & Elien^r [BT's: "Elizab."] GREEN of Trescott
Nov 14	John WALLIS & Mary BROOK
Dec 2	William LAMBERT & Susannah JOLLIT [BT's: "JOLLISS"]
Dec 29	James COMSON [BT's: "COMPSON"] of Old Swinford & Lucie NEWAN [BT's: "NEWNAM"] otp
Dec 19	Francis HUGHS & Mary HOLLOWAY
Jan 1	[Blank] AUDEN & [Blank] [BT's: "Frances AUDEN otp & Elizabeth COX[?]"]
Jan 7	William PERRY & Anne PAIN [BT's: "botp"]
Feb 11	George BATE & Ann GARRET [BT's: "botp"]

Baptisms Anno 1699

Apr 14	Sarah d of Richard OLIVER & Lydia his wife born Apr 14
Apr 29	Mary d of John BIRD & [blank] his wife born Apr 13
Apr 22	John s of John BATE & Sarah his wife born Apr 17
Apr 23	Jonathan s of Thomas & Mary SMALMAN born Mar 26
Jun 21	Elienor d of Rich. & Anne WHITE born Jun 4
Jul 18	Elizabeth d of William & Hannah WELLINS born Jun 24
Aug 15	Hannah d of Henry & Amy HACKET born Jul 28
Aug 13	Elizabeth d of William & Sarah JOHNSON born Aug 7
Aug 30	Samuel s of Roger & Mary LAMBERT born Aug 10

Sep 9   Margret d of Thomas & Margret NEW   born Sep 2
           Edward s of James & Isabel SMITH born Sep 13 baptized Sep
Sep [blank]   Edward s of Tho: HILMAN & Dorothy his wife born Sep 14
Sep [blank]   Joseph s of Joseph & Elizabeth TUNNERTON born Sep
           14, bapt by a Nonconf.
Oct 7   Anne d of Francis & Anne PAGET   born Oct 1
Oct 10   Elizabeth d of Alexander & Anne ROBBINSON   born Oct 6
Nov [blank, BT's: "18th"]   Nehemiah s of John & Elizabeth POWEL
           born Oct 26
Dec 3   Mary d of Will: & Anne BRADLEY   born Nov 11
Jan [blank, BT's: "1st"] [blank, BT's: "John"] s of Edward & Margret
           SEVERN   born Novr 30
Dec [blank, BT's: "27th"]   John s of Tho: & Katherine POWEL   born
           Dec 11
Jan 1   Gilbert s of Gilbert & Mary DIXON   born Dec 25
Jan 1   Blower DAVIES s of Tho: DAVIES & Anne his wife   born Dec
           26
Jan 3   Elizabeth d of Will: & Elizabeth HART   born Jan 3 & bapt the
           same day
Jan 9   Joseph s of Joseph & Jane PHILLIPS   born Jan 1
Feb 26   Elizabeth d of Richard COATES & Mary his wife   born Feb 8
[BT's: "Feb"]   John s of John & Jane KETTLEY   born Feb 8 bapt.
Apr 2   Mary d of Edward & Abigail LAMBERT   born Mar 4
Mar 14   John s of Sam¹ & Elizabeth GARDINER   born Mar 3
           James s of Tho: NEWMAN & Margret his wife   born Mar 10
Mar 15   John s of Richard & Mary FEREDAY   born Mar 11
Mar 23   Edward s of William & Jane WEBB   born Mar 17

Burials Anno 1699
Apr 2   Widow BRAZIER a Stranger from Sturton
Apr 10   Edward YEARSHAW [BT's: "YEARNSHAW"] of Stapenhill
Apr 15   Sarah d of Rich & Lydia OLIVER # [Entry missing; see below]
Apr 30   Jane d of John & Jane KETTLEY ** [Entry missing; see below]
May 21   Elizabeth MOSELEY Widow & midwife
Jun 3   Margret d of Thomas BROWN
Aug 16   Mr. John HAMERTON
Sep 23   Joan the wife of Edward GROVE
Sep 30   Anne BRETTLE Widow of Compton
Oct 3   Richard WHITE of the Towns End
Nov 4   John HOPE Maltman was buryed at Kinfare [BT's: "of Kinfare
           Hill"
Nov 11   Sarah DUNN Widow
Apr 18   Thomas COOKSEY was buried dying of a Consumption
** May 10 John GEARING
[Comment in register:] These two last should be placed as you see the
           marks
Nov 17   William s of John & Elizabeth CLARK
Dec 17   Thomas GROVE junr Cloth worker
Dec 2   Mary d of William PERRY
Dec 16   Margret d of Humfrey CLARK

Feb 1	Eleanor the wife of John TYSOME
Feb 19	Samuel s of Samuel & Eliz. GARDINER
Feb 20	Samuel s of Daniel & Mary HANCOX
Mar 21	Tho: COOK head workman of Sturton Slitting mill
	Thomas HILMAN Richard PURSLOW Church wardens

An° 1700 Marriages

Jul 30	John HILMAN & Lydia COMBER botp
Nov 17	Charles COWEL & Mary JONES
Mar 4	Lawrence KNOXEN & Elizabeth LAMBERT

Baptisms Anno 1700

Mar 27	Mary d of William & Margret [BT's: "Mary"] TOLLEY born Mar 25
(	Joseph s of W^m & Hannah ROWLEY born & baptized Mar 27)
(	Mary d of William & Hannah ROWLEY born Mar 25[sic] &)
(	bapt 27 of the same, Twins [BT's: "born & bapt Mar 27"])
Apr 11	Hannah d of W^m & Elizabeth HARFORD born Mar 25
Apr 12	Sarah d of Rowland & Joyce WHITE born Apr 8
Apr 20	Samuel s of W^m & Anne PARDOE born Apr 19 [BT's: "born & bapt Apr 20"]
Apr 29	Francis s of Francis & Susannah HATCHET born Apr 26
May 1	Mary d of John & Elizabeth TAYLER born Apr 27
May 7	William s of William & Mary ALDEN born Apr 30
May 24	Elizabeth d of Henry & Mary SPARRY born Apr 23
Jun 21	Elizabeth d of Richard & Ann WARROL [BT's: "WORRALL"] born May 24
Jun 17	Mary d of Joseph & Mary BENHALL born Jun 7 [BT's: "Born Jun 7 & bapt."]
Jun 24	Mary d of Rich: & Dorothy CORFIELD born Jun 21
Jun 28	Elizabeth d of Edward & Elizab. ALLEN born Jun 25
Jun 27	Elizab d of George & Anne BATE born Jun 27 & baptized ye same day
Aug 15	John s of John & Elien^r COMBER born Jul 30
Aug 18	Mary d of James & Dorothy HARRIS born Aug 13
Oct 16	Mary d of Rich. & Anne HILMAN born Oct 15
Sep [?, BT's: "9th"]	Mary d of Wm & Susanna LAMBERT born Sep 9
Nov [?]	Elizabeth d of Saml & Mary SMITH born Oct 30 [BT's: "born Oct 30 & bapt."]
Nov 6	Thomas s of Wm & Anne PERRY born Nov 4
Nov 25	Anne d of Isaak & Anne FRYER born Nov 21
Dec 13	Henry d of John & Mary COLE born Dec 6
Jan 14	Tho: s of Richard WARREN & Petronella his wife born Dec 13
Jan 31	Jonathan s of Jonath: & Jane JONES [BT's: "cobler"] born Jan 8
	Benson s of Edward & Hannah WALDRON born Jan 9 & bapt
Feb 1	William [BT's: "John"] s of John & Margret BROOK born Jan 9 [BT's: "born Jan 9 & bapt Jan 18"]

	Joseph s of Joseph CHILLINGWORTH [BT's: "& Elizabeth"] born Jan 14 & bapt.
Feb 19	Thomas s of Joseph BROWN & Elizabeth his wife born Feb 16
Feb 23	John s of Rich & Mary HADLEY born Feb 18
Feb 23	Mary d of Joseph & Elizabeth BRASIER born Feb 19
	Margret d of Guilbert & Margret DIXON born 23 Feb & baptized
Feb 28	Elizabeth d of Joseph & Mary HANCOX born Feb 26
Mar [?]	Mary d of Robert & Anne PARKS born Mar 1
Mar 31	William s of Tho: & Margret DUNN born Mar 2
Mar 12	John s of Edward & Sarah SARBET born Mar 12 & bapt^d ye same day
Mar 30	[BT's: "John"] s of Alexander ROBINSON & Ann his wife born Mar 23

(Sevayd by me   E.C.)

[The BT's have the following three burial entries for 1700 which are not in the OR's]
"Mar 30 1700   Hannah ye wife of William ROWLEY
Apr 11 1700 Mary d of William ROWLEY & Hannah his wife
Apr 8   1700   Joseph s of Barbary MOSELEY"

Buryalls An. Dom 1700

Apr 11	Margret d of Barbara MOSELEY Wid.
Apr 19	John s of Edward & Mercy DUNN
Apr 28	Jane d of Joseph & Magdelene BROWN
May 5	Henry HACKET Mason
May 6	Richard s of Thomas LYE
May 15	Joshua MORRICE Junr [BT's: "of Sturton"]
May 27	Wm JONES Clark of Whittington Forge
May 29	Mary d of Thomas HURST Senr
Jun 7	Margret the daughter of the said Tho: HURST Senr
Jun 8	Elizabeth COX Spinster [BT's: "dyed of a malignant Fevor"]
Jul 9	Hester ADDENBROOK widow
Aug 11	Widow TAYLOR was buryed on a Lords day
Aug 15	Elien^r the wife of John COMBER
Sep 4	Elien^r HILL Aunt to ye Widow WHITE Aged 86 years
Sep 11	William PRICE of Hafcote
Oct 5	Joan ye Relict of Joshua MORRICE Junr
Oct 19	Elienor widow of Humfrey CLARK Carpent^r
Dec 4	Margery TAYLER dyed as is thought thro' excessive drinking of Brandy [BT's: "as was thought thro intemperance"]
Dec 8	Abigail WHITE widow
Jan 3	Elien^r PERREY widow
Feb 24	Anne BAKER ye great Snush-taker

Sveyd by me E.C.

Oct 31	Jane DAVIES widow	) but here misplaced
Nov 1	John s of John & Jane KETTLEY	) tho' both in this year
	All wth Affid. according to Law	

Marriages Anno Dom 1701

Jun 29 John HAYWOOD & Elizabeth RAYBOULD
Jun 29 Edward BANNISTER & Jane BARNSLEY were marryed ye same day
Sep 6   William STOKES & Mary SYLVESTER
                                          Sevayd by me   E.C.
Oct 17 Esdras POOL of Kingswinford & Anne POWEL of this parish

[Entry in BT's: "Marriages 1701 From Michaelmus this yeare we find no marriages in the Book except Esdras POOL & Anne POWEL married Oct 17th]

Baptismes Anno Dom 1701
[Entries down to Sep 20 are not in the BT's]
        Jane s of John & Sarah BATE was born Apr^{ll} & bapt^d then
Apr 4   John s of Alexander & Anne ROBINSON   born Mar 30
Apr 27 Mary d of John & Elizab. FORREST   born Apr 27 & bapt^d ye same
May 27 Hannah d of Abraham CHAMBERLAIN & his wife born May 1
May 26 William s of William HART   born May 4
Jun 22 Thomas s of William & Sarah BAYLIS   born Jun [?]
Jun 9   ~~Elizabeth~~ Elienor d of ~~William~~ Edwd & Anne LYNES   born 7 Jun [Names altered]
Jun 22 Hannah d of Tho: & Jane SPARRY   born Jun 4
Jun 22 Elizabeth d of Willm & Anne PARDO   born Jun 21
Jun 22 Thomas s of John RICHARDS & Rebecca his wife born Jun 2^d
Jul 21 Edmund s of Oliver & Anne DIXON   born Jun 30
Jul 27 John s of Tho: & Joan NORMCOTE   born Jul 20
Jul 28 Anne d of Richard & Mary BROWN   born Jul 18
Sep 3   John s of Edward & Mary PARDO   born Aug 26
Sep 3   Hannah d of Charles & Mary COWEL   born Aug 27
Sep 20 John s of John HILMAN Glazier & Lydia his wife   born Sepr 9
                                          Survd by me E.C.
Oct 27 Richard s of Rich: OLIVER Junr & Lydia his wife   born Oct 3
Oct 5   Benjamin s of John HILMAN Senr & Susanna his wife   born Oct 5 & bapt ye same day
Nov 11 Hester d of William & Mary TIMMINGS   born Oct 24
Nov 21 Joseph s of Joseph & Mary RAWLEY   born Oct 27
Nov 5   John s of William & Mary ALDEN   born Oct 23
Nov 21 William s of Edward & Abigail [BT's: "Mary"] LAMBERT   born Nov 20
Nov 21 [BT's: "Dec 3"] Martha d of Nicholas & Elien^r WHITE
        Elizabeth d of Tho: & Jane BRADLEY [BT's: "BRADELY" & "bapt Dec 6"]   born Nov 22 bapt.
Nov 30 James s of Roger & Mary LAMBERT   born Nov 30 bap^t on ye same
Dec 2   Saml s of Saml & Elizab. GARDNER   born Nov 26
Dec 3   Mary d of William WALLENS & Hannah his wife   born Nov 28
Dec 7   Ruth d of Tho: & Margret NEW   born Nov 3
Dec 21 Michael s of John & Elizab POWEL   born Dec 19

Jan 2	Anne d of Tho. & Mary SMALEMAN born Dec 31
Feb 2	William s of William & Anne BURTON born Jan 1
	Sarah d of Henry & Mary SPARRY born Jan 22 [BT's: "bapt. Feb 10"]
	Thomas s of Mr Clement ACTON & Mary his wife born Feb Baptized [BT's: "bapt. Feb"]
	John s of Edward & Jane HUTT born 27 Bapt [BT's: "bapt. Mar 10"]
Mar 12	William s of William & Jane WEBB born Mar 6
Mar 20	Thomas s of Tho: POWEL & Catherine his wife born March

Buryals Anno 1701

Mar 28	John OLDMAN alias OLDNAL [BT's: "smith"]
Apr 1	Walter A son of Walter KIDSONS
Apr 28	William KETLEY Weaver
May 2	Mary HILMAN widow mother to Margaret MOSELEY
May 19	Maurice CALLOW Mole Ketcher
May 20	Hannah the wife of Joseph HILMAN Clark
Apr 27	Mary d of Jo: & Elizabeth FORREST
Jun 1	Elizabeth ye wife of Joseph BRAZIER
Jun 23	Elizabeth d of William & Anne PARDO
Jun 23	Martha BATE Widow was decently buried

Surveyed by me E.C.

Oct 6	Benjamin s of John [BT's: "John Senr"] & Susannah HILMAN
Oct 9	Joan REA Widow Mother in Law to Jo: [BT's: "John"] CLARK
Oct [?] [BT's: "1^{sb}"]	Joseph HILMAN parish Clark of Kinfare
Oct 17	William s of Thomas & Margret DUNN
Oct 26	William NEW of Whittington
Oct 31	Jane DAVIES widow aged abt 80 years
Nov 1	John s of John KETTLEY & Jane his wife
Nov 22	Anne KETTLEY of Sturton Widow aged abt 100 years
Dec 7	Mrs GEORGE Soe called, but wife to Clem^t [BT's: "Clement"] HOLLOWAY
Jan 4	Richard CRANDIGE Weaver
Jan 17	William BAYLIS a very poor but honest man of Hafcote
Jan 22	Sam [BT's: "Samuel"] s of Roger LAMBERT & Mary his wife with Affidavit according to Law
Mar 2	Anne the wife of Edward TAYLER of Enfield
Mar 14	Thomas s of the Widow VEAL [BT's: "Ms VEAL of Compton"] wth Affid.

Surveyed p^r me   Edward CORBETT

Marriages Ano Dom 1702

Apr 19	George BATE & Jane BRIAN of the parish of Enfield
May 4	John SARBETT & Mary DAVIES both of this parish
Jun 28	John GREEN [BT's: "of Kingswinford"] & Isabel BIRD [BT's: "otp"] were married at Kinfare Church
Jul 27	Saml COOPER of Asley & Elizabeth RICE of this parish
Apr 19	George BATE & Jane BRIAN both of this parish

Jan 5   John COMBER & Anne NORRIS both of this parish

Baptismes 1702

Apr 20 John s of Rich WARROL & [blank] his wife   born Mar 26
        Mary d of Francis OVERS & Abigail his wife   born Apr 20 &
        Bapt^d [BT's: "bapt. Apr 30"]
        Thomas s of Joseph & Eliz: TUNNERTON   born Apr 5 &
        baptised by a Nonconf.
        Anne d of William BECKLEY & his wife   born Apr 24 & bapt.
        [BT's: "bapt. May 2"]
        Thomas s of Tho. SANDERS base son   born 18th of May
        [BT's: "bapt. May 31"]
May 27 Anne d of William HADLINGTON   born May 21
Jun 24 Richard s of Humfrey & Mary CLARK   born Jun 6
        A Child of Edward KEMMS born April 1702 [BT's: "born Apr 29"]
Jul 15 Benjamine s of Benjamine & Joyce PLANT   born Jun 30
Aug 16 Elizabeth d of John DUNNE & Susannah his wife born Aug 10
Aug 15 Humfrey s of Isaak FRYER & Anne his wife born & bap Aug 15
Aug 26 Daniel s of John HILMAN [BT's: "sen^r"] & Susannah his wife
        born Aug 22
Aug 16 William s of Esdras & Anne POOL   born Aug 15
Sep 29 Sarah s of John & Elizab. FORREST   born Sep 22
Oct 7   [blank] of Phillip WEB & his wife   born Oct 5
Nov 16 Gillians s of Gilbert DIXON & Margret his wife   born Nov 4
        Jonathan [BT's: "John"] s of John HILMAN Clark & Judith his
        wife   born Nov 6 & bapt
Nov 23 Richard s of Richard MORRICE & Mary his wife   born Nov 17
        Anne d of Rich HILMAN & Margret his wife   born Nov 20 &
        bapt. [BT's: "bapt. Nov 20"]
Dec 7   Elienor d of Sam^{el} PLASTER & Anne his wife   born Nov 24
        Sam^{el} s of Tho: DAVIES & Anne his wife   born Dec 20 &
        bapt. [BT's: "bapt. Jan 6"]
        Humfrey s of William & Anne PERRY   born Jan 3 & bapt^d
        [BT's: "Jan 14"]
Jan 24 William s of Rich HADLEY & Sarah his wife   born Jan 22
Feb 9   Richard s of John KETTLEY & his wife   born Jan 24
Feb 11 Samuel s of John & Mary SARBETT   born Feb 7
        John s of Edward LYTHAL & Sarah his wife   born Feb 7 &
        bapt [BT's: "bapt. Feb 17"]
Feb 15 Mary d of John & Sarah BATE   born Feb 9
        Elizabeth d of William & Mary STOKES   born Feb 15 & bapt
        [BT's: "bapt. 25th"]
Mar 5   Thomas s of Will. RADFORD & Mary his wife   born Mar 4
        [The next entry has been crossed out:]
        The son of Will. & Alice BRISCO born Nov 5
        William s of Walther [BT's: "Walter"] KIDSON & Rachel his
        wife   born Mar 11 & bapt. [BT's: "bapt Mar 21"]

Martha d of Benjam. & Joyce PLANT   born Mar 5   [BT's: "bapt. Mar 15"]

Buryals 1702

Apr 28   John PITT of Compton
Jul 28   Anne d of Elizabeth HAGLINGTON illegitimate
Aug 4   Theodocia the wife of Henry SUTHALL
Aug 6   Thomas s of Joseph CHILLINGWORTH clericus & Eliz. his wife
Aug 31   Edward s of Will: & Jane WEBB
Jul 1[sic] Richard HADLEY a worker at ye clothing trade
Sep 10   Francis s of Rich: OLIVER & Mary his wife
Oct 14   Rachel the wife of Daniel ROWLEY
Nov 6   Margery PURSLOW Widow
Nov 19   Elizabeth the wife of Will: TIMINGS Senr
Dec 11   Elizabeth BIRDWHISTLE Spinster
Dec 13   William EGGINTON of ye park
Dec 29   Nicholas BRADLEY [BT: "BRADELY"] of Stowerton Batchelor
           Edw. WALDRON & Nich. WHITE   Churchw.

Weddings Anno Dom. 1703

Mar 30   Tho: HOPKINS & Anne HOUSMAN both of this parish
Dec 27   John TISAM [BT's: "TYSEHAM"] & Anne DARLASTON both of this parish
Jan 23   Henry MOSELEY & Miriam POWEL both of this parish
Jan 26   Daniel ROWLEY & [BT's: "Grace"] ye relict of Francis DEE
Feb 1   George DODSON & Margret TIMINGS both of this parish
Feb 3   Henry RICHARDS & Elizabeth KING both of this parish
           [The next entry appears to have been inserted later:]
Aug 29[sic]   Wm FORREST & Anne WIGGAN

Baptismes Anno 1703

Mar 29   Mary d of Edward & Sarah SARBETT   born Mar 25
Mar 29   Elizabeth d of Sam^{el} Son in Law to Sam^{el} RICE   )
           born Mar 29 & baptized ye same day   )
           Sarah d of the said Sam^{el} was born March 29   )
           & baptized ye same day   ) twins

[The entry in the BT's for above two baptisms is:
"Mar 29   Elizabeth d of Samuel COOPER & his wife bapt. March 29
Mar 29   Sarah d of Samuel COOPER & his wife, these last two being twins"]

           Anne d of John & Margret BROOK   born May 30 & bapt.
               [BT's: "bapt. Jun 6"]
Jul 23   Thomas s of Tho: & Hannah COOPER   born Jul 18
           Isaak s of Abraham & Priscilla CHAMBERLAIN   born Apr 11
               [BT's: "bapt. Apr 21"]
Apr 18   Joseph s of Edward & Abigail LAMBERT   born Apr 17

	William s of Samuel & Mary SMITH born [?] 16 & bapt [BT's: "bapt. Apr 26"]
Apr 25	Thomas s of Tho: & Elizabeth SEAVERN born & baptized Apr 25
	Jane d of William HART & Elizabeth his wife born Apr 25 & bapt. [BT's: "bapt. May 6"]
	William s of William & Mary JOHNSON born May 2 & bapt. [BT's: "bapt.May 22"]
Apr 25	Thomas s of Alexander & Anne ROBBINSON born May 2 & bapt. [BT's: "bapt. May 13"]
Jun 2	Humfrey s of Sam^{el} & Elizabeth GARDNER born May 21
Aug 17	Mary d of John PERRY & his wife born Jul 15
Aug 19	Elizabeth d of John HILMAN & Susannah his wife born Aug 14
	Walter s of John BUTTON & Alice his wife born Oct 15 & bapt. [BT's: "bapt. Oct 25"]
	Mary d of John & Mary SPENCER born Nov 14 & bapt. by a Nonconf. [BT's: "born Oct 15"]
Dec 27	Edward s of Thomas & Margret NEW born Dec 13
Jan 19	John s of William & Anne BECKLEY born Dec 20
	Edward s of Richard & Lydia OLIVER born Dec 30 & bapt. [BT's: "bapt. Jan 20"]
Jan 19	John s of William & Anne BURTON born Jan 1
Feb 2	John s of Robert & Ann PARKES born Jan 1
	Eliz. d of Jo. & Eliz. TAYLOR born Jan 5
	[The above entry appears to have been squeezed in. The entry in the BT's is: "Feb 3 Elizabeth d of John & Elizab TAYLOR"]
	Margret d of Edward & Jane BANNISTER born Jan 28 & bapt. [BT's: "bapt. Feb 10"]
	Elizabeth d of Rich: & Eliz: KETTLEY born Jan 29 & bapt. [BT's: "bapt. Feb 22"]
	Anne d of John & Sarah LOW born Jan 17 & bapt. [BT's: "Feb 24"]
	William s of Francis & Mary FIDDLER born & bapt. Jan 17 [BT's: "bapt. Jan 27"]
Mar 28	Mary d of Charles & Mary COWEL born Mar 1
	John s of Edw & Eliz. ALLIN born Feb 18 [BT's: "bap Feb 23"]

Buryals Anno 1703

Apr 10	William LYE of Compton
Apr 20	Theodocia the wife of Valentine BINGE [BT's: "BING"]
May 17	Norman s of Rich: & Susannah YORK, w^m God p'served wonderfully from being stiffled or starved in ye snow was unfortunately drowned at Mans state & buryed.
Jul 13	John HALE Clothier was buryed decently at Kinfare
Aug 8	Wm TIMMINGS [then some words crossed out] buryed Aug 8 [BT's: "Aug 1 William TIMMINGS Father of Wm TIMMINGS buried"]
	[The next entry appears to have been squeezed in]
	[blank] son of Edw LAMBERT buryed Sept 3
Oct 18	Elizabeth d of John & Susannah HILMAN

Dec 19   Jane d of James & Isabel [BT's: "Isabeth"] SMITH
Dec 26   Mother in Law of Thomas HUST Sen[r] [Possibly altered to HURST; BT's: "HURST"]
Jan 14   William s of Francis & Mary FIELDER
Jan 20   John s of William & Anne BURTON
Feb 2   William SPITTLE a Strang[r] Servant to Guilbert DIXON
Feb 16   Anne the wife Richard HACKETT
Mar 15   Margret SITCH wife of Humfrey
Jun[sic] 5   Jane the wife of Old Jo: POWEL [BT's: "Jane the wife of old John POWEL bapt. June 5 but misplaced"]
         All these wth Affidavits

Marriages Anno 1704

May 4   Joseph BATE & Elizabeth COX both of y[e] parish of Wolverley
Jun 28   Edw. GROVE & Margery y[e] relict of W[m] LYE
Jun 29   William LYE & Hannah GROVE
Jun 6   John LLOYD of Wolverley & Elizabeth SIMS of this parish
Jun 6   Richard HEMMING of Bromsgrove & Margrett PITT were married also June 6
Apr 16   George ROGERS & Mary SIMS
Apr 17   Jeremiah PAYTON & Elizabeth TERVY [BT's: "TURVY"]
Jul 27   Edward WARROL & Mary MOOR
Jul 30   Thomas BAYLIS & Hannah NURTHALL
Nov 3   Samuel TALBUTT & Mary HOOPER
Nov 5   Rich. BAYLIS & Marry PRICE
Jan 6   John MOSELEY & Anne MOLE
Feb 5   Tho. KIDSON & Sarah DAVIES
Feb 19   Thomas GIBBS & Abigail BIBB

Baptisms 1704

         Edward s of Edward SCHELDING & Hester his wife   born 26 Mar & bapt. [BT's: "bapt. Mar 30"]
Apr 20   Elizabeth d of Richard & Petronella WARREN   born Mar 30
Apr --   Tho. s of Tho. & Jane BRADELY [BT's: "BRADLEY"] born Mar 28
Apr 18   Tho. s of William & Mary AUDEN [BT's: "ALDEN"] born Apr 13
Apr 14   Susannah d of Edward & Anne LYNES   born Apr 12
May 25   Richard s of Richard & Anne WARROL   born May 2
May 8   John s of William & Hannah WALLINS   born Apr 3
May 10   Elizabeth d of Tho: & Elizabeth BROWN   born May 7
May 11   Margret d of Rich. & Mary HILMAN   born May 11 Bapt ye same day
Jun 19   Jonathan s of Humfrey & Mary CLARK   born Jun 16
May 22   Humfrey s of John TRUMAN & his wife   born May 22 & baptized on ye same
         Josiah s of Joseph & Mary RAWLEY was [sic] Jun 17th & Bapt. [BT's: "bapt. Jun 30"]
Jun 24   Thomas s of Henry MOSELEY & Miriam his wife   born Jun 2
Jun 30   Richard s of Rich. & Mary FEREDAY   born Jun 25
Jul 21   John s of John & Rebecca RICHARDS   born Jul 17

© Staffordhire Parish Registers Society   144

Jul 25	Samuel s of Roger & Mary LAMBERT born Jul 7
	Samuel s of John HILMAN Sen[r] & Susanna his wife born Sep. [?] & bapt. [BT's: "bapt. Sep 4"]
Sep 19	Nicholas s of W[m] & Mary RADFORD born Sep 1
Sep 21	Anne d of Edward KEMM & Anne his wife born Aug 19
Oct 10	John s of W[m] & Margret CRUNDAL born Sep 29
Oct 26	John s of Richard & Elizab. HOPE born Sep 30
Oct 12	William s of Isaak & Anne FRYER born Sep 1
Oct 17	John s of John TYSAM & Anne his wife born Oct 5
Oct 29	John s of John OLDNAL & Mary his wife born Oct 28
Oct 30	Mary d of John & Anne COMBER born 23[?] Oct
Oct 10[sic; BT's: "Nov 12"]	James s of Alexander ROBINSON & Anne his wife born 5.
	Edward s of John & Elizabeth LOW born Jan the [blank] [BT's: "was bapt at Compton Nov."]
Nov 5	John s of Edw. & Sarah LYTHAL born Oct 27
Nov 23	Frances d of Rich. & Dorothy CORFIELD born 20 Nov
Dec 7	Edw. s of Edward & Abigail LAMBERT born Dec 6
Dec 24	Francis s of Gilbert & Mary [BT's: "Margaret"] DIXON born Dec 12
Dec 20	John s of John & Judith HILMAN born 10th
Jan 6	Mary d of Edward & Mary WORRAL [BT's: "WARROLL"] born 20 Dec
Jan 6	Tho. s of John PERRY & his wife born Dec 3
Jan 15	Benjamine s of Rowland & Joyce WHITE born Jan 7
Jan 16	Mary d of Esdras & Anne POOL born Dec 25
Jan 31	William s of W[m] & Anne PERRY born Jan 8
Feb 4	Simon s of Thomas NORMCOTE & Hannah his wife born 21 Jan
Feb 5	Paul s of Sam[el] GARDNER & his wife born Jan 25
Feb 12	Anne d of John BOWERS Jun[r] & Eliz. his wife born Feb 4
Feb 13	Anne d of Tho. & Anne VEAL born 17 Jan
Feb 14	Mary d of George DODSON & Margret his wife born Jan 23
Feb 16	Mary d of George & Mary ROGERS born Jan 26
Mar 24	William s of Richard & Mary COTES born 16 Feb
	Sarah d of John & Alice BUTTON born Mar 23 Bapt. [BT's: "born & bapt. Mar 24"]
	Elizabeth d of Robert & Sarah JOHNSON born))
	Oct 10 Bapt. y[e] same Day) twins
	Mary d of Rob[t] & Sarah JOHNSON born Oct 10)
	Bapt. y[e] same Day)
	) misplaced
	Edw. & Eliz. s & d of John WOOD born

Burials 1704

Apr 17	Alice y[e] wife of William BRISCOE
Apr 17	Tho. s of Thomas COOPER & Hannah his wife
May 2	Anne the wife of Richard OLDNAL [BT's: "OLDMAN alias OLDNAL"]
Jun 25	Sam[el] s of Rob[t] NURTHAL [BT's: "long since deceased"]

Aug 1	Francis CLARK of Compton Hall
Sep 9	Samuel s of John HILMAN Senr [BT's: "& Susannah his wife"]
Oct 30	Anne KESTER ye wife of Richard KESTER
Nov 2	Sarah d of Robt & Sarah JOHNSON
Nov 24	Old Widow BANNISTER of Stowerton
Jan 9	Anne ROWLEY the Relict of Wm ROWLAND [BT's: "relict of William ROWLEY"]
Jan 15	Hannah ye wife of Thomas COOPER [BT's: "clothworker"]
Jan 25	John s of Samuel & Sarah RICE [BT's: "dyed of a Fever"]
Mar 8	John JONES of Whittington [BT's: "dyed of a Feav^r"]
Mar 24	Anne d of Thomas & Anne VEAL

Surveyed by me Ed. CORBETT

                    John OWEN   Tho. HURST jun^r Churchw

Weddings Anno Dom 1705

Jun 12	Mr Joseph PALMER & Mrs Hannah GROVE
Jun 21	Thomas POSTERNS & Hannah ELCOCK
Jul 25	Wm TAYLER & Elizabeth BATE

                                    surveyed by me E. CORBETT

Aug 25	John GROVE & Joan HORTON both of ye Town
Sep 8	Richard LAVENDER & Anne HUTT
Nov 30	Richard MORRICE & Mary ROADS
Dec 26	John COOK & Mary GLADWAY
Jan 16	John GUEST & Elizabeth GREEN

Births & Baptisms 1705

Mar 28	John s of Joseph & Elizabeth SPITTLE born Mar 20
Mar 30	Sarah d of John BUTTON born Mar 25 [BT's: "of Jo. & Alice"]
Apr 4	Sarah d of John & Mary SARBET born Mar 28
May 28	John s of Tho: & Hannah BAYLIS born 18 [BT's: "18th May"]
May 28	John s of John & Elizabeth FORREST born 20 [BT's: "20th May"]
Jun 2	Richard s of John NEW & his wife [BT's: "20th May"]
Jun 13	Thomas s of Tho: & Elizabeth JOHNSON born 1st [BT's: "1st June"]
Jun 27	Mary d of Francis & Elizabeth FIELDER born & Bapt. Jun 27
Aug 9	Mary d of Richard & Alice LOW born July 30

                                      by me Ed. CORBETT

Aug 27	Elizabeth d of George & Elizabeth POWEL born Aug 20
Sep 1	Sarah d of John & Margret BROOK [BT's: "born & bapt Sep 1"]
	Susannah d of Thomas & Margret DUNN born Sep 8th & bapt. [BT's: "Born Sept 8, bap Sep 17"]
Sep 19	Thomas s of Richard & Mary BAILIS born & bapt. Sep. 19th [BT's: "BAYLIS, born & bap Sep 25"]
Sep 25	Thomas s of Tho: & Ann HOPKINS born 20th
Sep 30	Susannah d of Edward & Elizabeth SARBETT [BT's: "SARBET"]
Oct 14	Elienor d of John & Susannah HILMAN
Oct 26	Richard s of Phillip & Mary WEBB born Oct [BT's: "born 5th"]

Oct 12	Joseph [in the OR there is some indication that another name had been rubbed out; BT's: "John"] of John & Anne MOSELEY born Sep 28th BT's: "born Sep 28, bap Oct 12"]
Oct 22	Susannah d of Richard & Mary CLARK born 13th Anne d of John & Mary SPENCER born Oct 22 bapt by a Noncon. 12th
Nov 28	Henry s of Henry & Miriam MOSELEY born & baptized Nov 28
Dec 3	Mary d of Wm & Mary STOKES
Dec 12	Anne d of Edward & Bridget HUMPHRYES born 7th
Jan 14	Sarah d of Samuel & Anne PLASTER born 7th
Feb 18	Mary d of Tho: & Sarah KIDSON born Jan 24th
Feb 18	John s of John & Elizabeth TAYLER born Jan 27
Jan 21	Joseph s of James & Isabel [BT's: "Elizab."] SMITH
Mar 16	Thomas s of Tho: & Elizabeth BROWN born Mar 8th

Burials Anno Dom 1705

Apr 10	Robert JOHNSONS Tayler
Apr 13	Dorothy JOHNSONS buryed at Kinfare
Apr 17	Mary HUTT wide of Edward HUTT
Apr 21	Edward WARD day Labourer
Apr 24	Mary NEW of Whittington
Jun 12	Humfrey NEWTON [29th altered to 12th]
Jun 28	Mary d of Francis FIELDER & Elizab his wife
Jul 28	Elienor LOW wife of George LOW
Aug 5	John s of John WOOD of Compton
Aug 22	Mrs Elizab. JUKES wife of Mr Tho: JUKES
Aug 31	Hannah ye wife of [blank; BT's: "William"] LYE
Oct 25	Priscilla CHAMBERLAIN wife of Abr. CHAMBERLAIN
Sep 12	Samuel s of Rowland WHITE
Oct 22	Lidia HILMAN the wife of John HILMAN Glazier
Oct 25	Richard s of Philip WEBB of Stowerton
Nov 15	Fulk GRIFFITH Servt to Mr BRINDLEY [BT's: "BRINLEY"]
Nov 16	Widow BAYLIS of Hafcote
Nov 22	Mr COX Schoolmaster [BT's: "Schoolmaster of Kinfare"]
Dec 11	Anne d of Edward HUMFRYES
Dec 22	Sarah HIGGINSON of this parish
Jan 14	William SITCH of Kinfare
Feb 16	Mary COMBER Widow & Mor of John COMBER
Mar 9	Edward WALDRON Cloth worker [The BT's indicate that all were buried with Affidavits]

Weddings 1706

Mar 26	Joseph RICE & Mary TAYLER
May 23	Henry FINNEY & Hester NURTHAL
Jun 8	William SMALMAN [BT's: "SMALEMAN"] & Mary AINGER
Aug 22	George GROVE & Margret WHITTAKER
Nov 10	William BRISCO & Katherine EDGLEY
Feb 10	Samuel GRIFFIN & Hannah TILLER

Baptismes 1706

	Elizabeth d of William & Anne BRADELY born Apr 2 [BT's: "born April 2 & bap"]
Apr 14	Susannah d of Francis & Susannah HATCHET
Apr 15	Hannah d of Jo: [BT's: "John"] & Sarah LOW
Apr 28	Hannah d of Joseph & Jane PHILLIPS [BT's: "born & bap Apr 28"]
	Mary d of William & Elizab: TAYLER born Apr 23 [BT's: "bap May 1"]
Apr 30	Anne d of Mr Richard WARROL
Jun 28	Elien^r d of George & Mary ROGERS
	James s of Jo: [BT's: "John"] & Rebecca RICHARDS born Jun 30 [BT's: "born Jun 30 & baptized after"]
	Abigail d of Tho: & Abigail GIBBS born in July [BT's: "Born in July & baptized by a nonconformist"]
Jul 21	Jane d of Edward & Abigail LAMBERT
Aug 2	Joan d of Jo: [BT's: "John"] & Joan GROVE
Aug 15	Jane d of Edw. & Jane BANNISTER
Sep 5	Sarah d of William WEB [BT's: "WEBB"] & his wife
Sep 15	John s of Edward & Mary WARROL
Oct 6	Mary d of Jo. & Dorothy JOHNSON
Oct 5 [BT's: "Oct 7"]	Elizabeth d of Francis FIELDER
Oct 15	[blank] s of John LOW [BT's: "& his wife"]
Oct 24	Elizabeth d of John & Mary COOK [BT's: "shoemaker"]
Nov 15	John s of John & Mary RICE
Dec 2	Hannah d of Humphry CLARK & Mary his wife
Dec 5	Richard s of Rich. COTES
Jan 13	Edward s of John & Elizabeth LLOYD)
Jan 13	Elizabeth d of Jo: & Elizab LLOYD [not in BT's]) Twins
Jan 20	Elizabeth d of Isaak & Anne FRYAR
Jan 20	John s of Tho & Jane BRADLEY
	A child of HATTENS was baptized [An attempt appears to have been made to erase "was baptized"; not in BT's]
Feb 25	Elizabeth d of Rich HILMAN

Burials 1706

Apr 15	Mr Francis JORDAN Lawyer [BT's: "Attorney"]
Apr 15	John POWEL of Compton
Apr 22	Jane HUTT wife of Edward HUTT was buryed April 22^d month
Apr 24	John SCOTT of Stowerton [BT's: "husband man"]
May 1	Hannah d of Joseph & Jane PHILLIPS
May 15	Robert GRIFFITH of ye Town
May 20	John COOK Mercer Exemplarily good
May 20	Thomas s of Joseph & Isabel [BT's: "Elizab."] COCKS
May 25	Judeth CHAPMAN [BT's: "CHAMPMAN"] widow
May 23	Elienor d of Sam: PLASTER
May 23 [BT's: "30"]	John s of John & Elizab FORREST
Jun 1	John HILMAN Carpenter
Jun 8	Mary BROOK Widow
Jun 10	Joseph s of Sarah WARD

Jun 18   Catherine ROUND [BT's: "widow"]
Jun 30   Sam^{el} BEST & his wife of Iverley Excommunicated [BT's only name Samuel as being buried"]
Jul 28   Anne d of Robert BROOK
Jul 30   Isaak s of Abraham CHAMBERLAIN
Aug 9   Elizabeth d of Edw LAMBERT
Sep 8   Mary HACKET [BT's: "spinster"]
Oct 15   Margret MOSELEY Widow ["widow" is crossed through] [BT's: "wife of Tho."]
Nov 7   John s of John HILMAN & Judith his wife
Nov 21   Thomas DAVIS Mason
Jan 10   Anne CALLOWAY Widow
Jan 16   Edward s of John LLOYD   )
Jan 16   Elizabeth d [blank, BT's: "John"] LLOYD   ) twins
Feb 2   Elizabeth d of Isaak FRYAR
Feb 13   Mary d of John RICHARD Senr
Feb 17   Catherine the wife of Rich. PURSLOW
Feb 19   Mary SMITH Widow [BT's: "relict of Thos SMITH"]
Mar 16   William PERRINS of Stowerton
Mar 19   Richard GREEN uncle to John WOOD
Mar 24   Mrs Mary HALE Widow [BT's: "relict of Mr. John HALE"]
             Jo: COMBER   Wm SUTHWEL   Churchwardens

Weddings Anno Dom 1707
May 1   John & Mary MASON [BT's: "John HORTON & Mary MASON"]
May 12   Will: TIMMINGS [BT's: "TIMMINS"] & Elizabeth CRANE
Jun 1   George WINFORD & Anne HARTLE
Jun 4   Henry GOSLING [BT's: "GOSLIN"] & Jane FRECLETON
Jan 19   John BLOWER & Mary COWPER [BT's: "COOPER"]

Christenings 1707
Apr 14   Elizabeth d of John FORREST [BT's: "& Elizab. his wife"]
Apr 14   Hannah d of Henry & Hester FINNY
Apr 17   John s of Edward & Sarah LYTHALL
Apr 25   Mary d of Guilbert & Margret DIXON
May 13   Hannah d of Thos & Hannah BAYLIS
May 30   Richard s of Thomas NEW [BT's: "& his wife"]
Jul 13   Susannah d of Charles & Mary COWEL
Jul 17   Richard s of John PERREY [BT's: "PERRY & his wife"]
Jul 8   Tho: s of Tho: SMALMAN
Jul 8   Henry s of Esdras & Mary POOL
Sep 2   Mary d of George & Margret GROVE
Aug 30   Mary d of Richard WARREN
Sep 22   Giles s of Mr Tho: TOMKINS [BT's: "& Mary his wife"]
Sep 14   Mary d of Edward SARBETT
Sep 25   Hester d of W^m & Hester LYNE
Sep 30   Mary d of Henry & Eliz: RICHARDS
Oct 6   Jeremiah s of John & Catherine TRUMAN
Oct 14   Mary d of John & Mary SARBET

Oct 14	Richard s of Rich: & Dorothy CORFIELD
Dec 1	Phebe d of Edw. & Anne LYNES
Dec 7	Mary d of Rich. & Mary BAYLIS
Dec 15	Herbert s of John GROVE & Anne [BT's: "Jane"] his wife
Dec 16	Phebe d of Tho. & Anne HOPKINS
Dec 11	William s of John NEW [BT's: "& his wife"]
Dec 26	Margret d of John & Anne COMBER
Jan 2	Elizab. d of George POWEL
Jan 6	Elizab. d of Miriam & Henry MOSELEY
Jan 19	Jane d of Edw. & Mary BIRD
Jan 21	Mary d of Will: & Elizabeth TIMMINGS [BT's: "TIMENS"]
Jan 31	Tho. s of Mr Rich: BATE [BT's: "Scoolmaster"]
Feb 11	Wm s of Thomas JOHNSON
Feb 20	Anne d of Rich: & Ann LAVENDER
Mar 15	Thomas s of John & Susannah HILMAN
Mar 21	Tho. s of George & Anne WINFORD
Mar 24	Isabel d of Isaak & Ann FRYER
Oct 24	Margret d of George DODSON [Entry is in the correct location in the BT's]

Burials Ano 1707

Apr 12	Richard YORK Senr [BT's: "carpenter"]
Apr 24	Joane BRADELY
May 2	William RICE day Labourer [BT's: "of Kinfare near ye mill"]
Jun 15	Elizabeth SMITH
Jul 8	Thomas HILMAN
Jul 20	Robert WEBB
Jul 20	Mary PURSLOW
Aug 29	Joane NORMCOTE [BT's: "wife of Tho."]
Oct 8	Jane BATE d of Humphry BATE Senr
Nov 23	Richard GARRAT [BT's: "GLOVER"]
Dec 21	Old good wife SPARRY aged 109 years
Dec 21	Sarah CHAMBERLAIN [BT's: "d of Abr"]
Dec 25	Edward HILMAN [BT's: "of Church Hill"]
Dec 25	Andrew SITCH of Stourton
Feb 1	John LYNE an Old Man [BT's: "aged 93 years"]
Feb 1 [BT's: "18"]	Thomas s of John TISAM [BT's: "TYSOM"]
Feb 8 [BT's: "18"]	Richard s of Richard [crossed out] Phillip HAINES

Marriages Anno 1708

Aug 24	Tho. NEWMAN & Joan NORMCOTE
Sep 13	William GREEN & Elizab. MONAX
Feb 9	William MATHEWS & Sarah STAMP

Christenings 1708

Mar 26	William s of Tho. KIDSON
Apr 5	Mary d of Richard MORRICE
Apr 8	Henry s of Edward LAMBERT
Apr 7	Sarah d of William STOKES
May 3	Mary d of John COOKE & Mary his wife

May 19	Tho. s of William PERRINS
May 26	Mary d of Sam^{el} GRIFFITH
Jun 16	Joseph s of Joseph BELL
Jul 13	Mary d of Rowland & Joyce WHITE
Aug 5	Mary d of Francis AMES
Aug 6	Edward s of Edw. & Mary WORRAL
Aug 13	Margret d of William TAYLER
Oct 25	John s of Rich: & Lydia OLIFER
Oct 28	Mary d of Mr. Rich: WARROL
Nov 5	Elienor d of Sam^{el} PLASTER
Nov 7	Tho. s of Alexander ROBINSON
Jan 20	Mary d of Rich: LUCKETT
Feb 2	Mary d of Henry & Hester FINNY
Mar 7	Mary d of W^m & Mary ALDEN
Mar 16	Tho. s of Tho. & Elizabeth HANCOX
Mar 20	Mary d of John RICHARDS
Mar 30	Rich. s of James SMITH

Burials 1708

Mar 26	Frances POWEL [BT's: "widow"]
Apr 3	Thomas BUTTERIS [BT's: "of Sturton"]
Apr 9	Richard HOPE of Sturton
Apr 9	Sarah HADLEY d of [blank] HADLEY [BT's: "grandchild to Widow WARD"]
May 25	Hierom DODSON s of George DODSON
Jun 22	Widow SITCH [BT's: "of the Town"]
Jul 26	A child of John & Ann MOSELEY was layed in ye ground
Jul 29	Good wife MEBREY
Sep 9	Samuel RENSHAW Senr
Sep 27	Margret the wife of Wm SOUTHWEL
Sep 30	Jonathan HILMAN Clothier
Oct 11	Margret MAURICE [BT's: "MORRICE"]
Oct 20	William VEAL of Compton
Oct 30	John s of John BROOKE & Marg^t his wife
Dec 5	A travelling woman was buryed
Dec 5	Rachel HILMAN a poor Cripple [BT's: "a crippled twin"]
Dec 14	Hester PITT [BT's: "d of Widow PITT"]
Dec 21	Elizabeth d of John NORRIS
Dec 31	Dorothy NEWMAN Widow
Jan 29	Magdelin IMME
Jan 17	The Widow HOWPER [BT's: "HOOPER"]
Feb 5	Thomas PERRINS of Sturton
Mar 17	Thomas PIXEL an old man [BT's: "a very old man"]
Mar 19	John HILMAN Father of the HILMANS
Mar 27	Richard OLDNAL [BT's: "brother to John"]
Apr 5 1708	Mary GRIFFITH d of the widow GRIFFITH

Weddings 1709

May 12	Richard PURSLOW [no other details given]
Jan 3	Esau PENSON & Mary KNIGHT

Jan 31　William MARTYN & Abigail COOPER

Baptisms 1709

Mar 30　Rich: s of James & Isabel SMITH
Feb 21　Elienor d of Humfrey & Mary [no surname given, BT's: "CLARK"]
Mar 1　Samuel s of John & Elizabeth LLOYD
Mar 8　Thos s of Thos & Joan NEWMAN
Apr 6　Elizabeth d of Mr KITCHINMAN an Oficer of Excise
Jun 26　Jonath: [BT's: "Jonathan"] s of John & Anne MOSELEY
Jul 23　Jane d of Tho: & Anne HOPKINS
Jun [sic] 26　Charles s of John & Anne TISOME
Jul 27　Jane d of Tho. & Anne BRADLEY
Aug 2　Elizabeth d of W^m & Eliz. TIMINGS
Jul 26　Joseph s of Saml & Eliz. GARDNER
Aug 8　Charles s of John & Jane HILMAN
Sep 13　William s of John & Joan GROVE
Oct 28　John s of Edward & Mary BIRD
Nov 1　Elizabeth d of Richard & Alice LOW
Nov 8　Elizabeth d of Mr Rich: & Mrs Eliz. BRADELY
Nov 18　Mary d of Sam^{el} RENSHAW & [?] RADFORD illegit.
Nov 23　Anne d of Esdras & Anne POOL
Jan 2　Richard s of John & Isabel GREEN
Jan 17　Sarah d of John & Mary COOKE
Jan 18　Elizabeth d of Mr Richard & Mrs Eliz. BATE
Feb 2　Mary d of Henry & Miriam MOSELEY
Feb 5　Edward s of Edw. & Mary SARBETT

Buryalls An° 1709

Mar 1　George s of George DODSON
Mar 1　Sarah d of John FORREST & his wife
Mar [blank; BT's: "3"]　A child of Tho. GIBBS & Abigail his wife was layd in ye earth

　　　　　　　　　　　These misplaced
Mar 25　Richard OLDNALD [BT's: "OLDNAL"]
Apr 4　Tho: WINDLE of the Town
Apr 19　Tho: s of Mr Rich & Mrs Eliz. BATE
Apr 21　Alexander ROBINSON
May 1　John IMMS s of old W^m
May 8　Edward RUEBOTTOM Clothier [BT's: "RUBOTTOM"]
May 10　John SMITH
May 12　Mr William TROTMAN unfortunately killed wth a pistol
May 16　Elienor LYNE was decently buried
Jun 13　John [BT's: "Joan"] WORRAL of Compton
Jun 18　William ALDEN of Hafcote
Jun 26　Humfrey COOPER of Sturton
Jun 26　John TISOME mason
May 16　William WHITTACRE Smith
Jul 13　Elizabeth HADLEY grandaughter to Joan WARD
Jul 15　Richard s of John HORTON

Jul 21	John HILMAN ye Parish Clark
Sep 10	Elizabeth TYRER d of Widow TYRER
Sep 30	A Child of Edmond MASON lay^d in ye Ground
Oct 22	Mrs Susannah ye wife of Mr Francis HATCHET
Oct 28	A son of Phillip HEYNS [BT's: "HAYNES"]
Nov 10	Mrs COOK of the Slitting Mill
Dec 30	Richard NEWNAM [BT's: "NEWMAN"] of Compton
Jan 21	Mary d of Saml RENSHAW illegit.

Rich: OLIVER & Tho. NEW   Church Wardens

Weddings An° Dom. 1710

Apr 13	John SALE & Mary PARKS now his wife were marryed
Dec 16	Edward VEAL & Mary his wife
Dec 24	John SMALMAN & Mary his wife
Dec 26	William SMITH & Elizab. his wife
Dec 27	Benjamin RENSHAW & Dorothy his wife
Feb 9	Doctor HALLYFAX & Mrs [BT's: "Madam"] Mary DAVENPORT his now wife

Baptisms Anno Dom 1710

May 5	Susanna d of Susanna HILMAN
May 24	Elizabeth d of George ROGERS & Mary his wife
May 29	Elizabeth d of Edward LAMBETH & Abigail his wife
Jul 3	John s of Isaak PENSON & Mary his wife
Jun 13	Thomas s of Joseph BELL & Anne his wife
Jun 26	Elizabeth d of Will: MATHEWS & Sarah his wife
Jul 2	Anne d of James BROWN & Mary his wife
Jul 2	Elizabeth d of Rich. BAYLIS & Mary his wife
Jul 9	Richard s of Rich: HOPE & [blank]
Jul 9	Elizabeth d of Edward LYTHAL & Sarah his wife
Jul 11	Richard s of Edward OLIVER & Sarah his wife
Jul 11	Elizabeth d of William PARR & Elizab. his wife
Jul 30	Elizabeth d of Richard MORRICE [BT's: "d of Sam^{el} MORRIS"] & his wife
Aug 13	Anne d of George WINFORD & Anne his wife
Sep 13	Caleb s of Sam^{el} SMITH & Mary his wife
Sep 14	Josiah s of John NEW & Anne his wife
Sep 24	Elizabeth d of Rich: LAVENDER & Anne his wife
Sep 29	Edward s of Edward ALLEN & Elizab his wife
Oct 12	Joshua s of Sam^{el} MORRIS & Mary his wife
Oct 13	Phillip s of Phillip HAINES [BT's: "HAYNES"] & Margret his wife
Nov 1	Margret d of Will. CRUNDAL & Margret his wife
Nov 7	Sarah d of John SARBET & Mary his wife
Nov 12	Richard s of Mr. Rich. BRADLEY & Elizabeth his wife
Dec 26	John s of Thomas HANCOX & Elizabeth his wife
Dec 26	Edmund s of Edmund MASON & Elizab. his wife
Dec 28	Elizabeth d of Henry RICHARDS & Elizab. his wife
Dec 31	Richard s of Widow PURSLOW
Jan 8	Sarah d of Rich. HILMAN & Mary his wife

[The next entry appears only in the BT's:
Feb 18   Sarah, d of Edw. & Mary BANISTER
Feb 27   Lydiah d of Rich OLIVER & Lydia his wife
Mar 9   Salomon s of Will: WALLENS & Hannah his wife
Mar 16   Esther d of Will: TIMMINS jun[r] & Elizabeth his wife

Burials Anno 1710

Apr 16   James MARTIN
Apr 18   Michael SPARRY Sen[r]
Apr 23   Anne SIMKIS [BT's: "wife of Jo:"]
May 6   James s of James SMITH [BT's: "& Isabel"]
Jun 1   Mary SITCH Widow
Jun [?, BT's: "19"]   Samuel s of James LENOWARD
Jul 11   John s of Isaak PENSON [BT's: "s of Esau & Mary his wife"]
Jul 15   Tho: s of Robert DALE
Jul 18   Sarah d of John BATE
[?, BT's: "31"]   Elizabeth d of Tho: SHELDING
Jul 31   Richard HOPE Weaver
Aug 7   Richard s of George LOW
Aug 19   Ralph WEBB [BT's: "Killed by a waggon"]
Sep [?; Bt's: "5"]   Richard PURSLOW Glazier & Astronom[r]
Sep 11   John s of Rich: HILMAN
Sep 15   Jane WINDLE Widow
Sep 17   Sarah d of Rowland WHITE
Oct 13   Edward TRAUNTER verger
Nov 18   John HORTON Sen[r]
Sep 21   Margret d of W[m] CRUNDEL
Dec 30   Richard BRADLEY of Compton
Jan 5   Edmund MASON Jun[r]
Jan 17   John GIBBS [BT's: "of Herrings Yate"]
Feb 1   John s of W[m] HALE
Feb 19   Anne ROBINSON Widow
Feb 25   Anne WHITE jun[r]
Mar 2   Margret WARROL Widow
Mar 13   Widow WHITEHOUSE

[On the flysheet:]
Mr Paul FOLEY son of Philip FOLEY Esq[r] & Madam Penelope his wife was born June 7th 1684/ baptized June 9th 1684
[which is then repeated in copper plate style writing]

[On back cover[?] various scribblings plus the following, the first two lines of which were then repeated in copper plate style writing:]
Ralph LITTLE-HALFE of y[e] parish of Dawley
Enquired after a bastard
child born June 26
1698

© Staffordhire Parish Registers Society

Kinver Parish Register, 1711-1775

[on the fly-leaf:]
"Commences April 1711 and ends Dec[r] 31 – 1775"

Baptizmes Anno Dom 1711

Apr 11   Sarah d of John TAYLOR [BT's: "& Mary"]
Apr 12   John HACKET alis GRIFIS
Apr 16   Margret d of Sam[el] MOESLEY [BT's: "& Mary"]
May 20   Mary d of Benjamin RENSHA [BT's: "RENSHAW & Dorothy"]
Jun 16   Ruth of James LENARD [BT's: "& Ann"]
Jun 28 [BT's: "12th"] Joseph DERICK alis BISHOP
Jun 27   Martha d of M[r] [BT's: "Richard"] BATE Clerk [BT's: "& Elizabeth"]
Jul 21   Tho[s] son of Richard FERIDAY [BT's: "FERIDE"]
Aug 12   Joseph s of Danil EDERDS [BT's: "& Mary"]
Aug 27   Joseph & Benjamin sons of John GROVE
Sep 5   Francis s of Esau PENSON [BT's: "& Mary his wife"]
Sep 7   Jane & Mary daughters of Georg POWEL [BT's: "& Elizabeth his wife"]
Sep 13   John s of Henry FINNY [BT's: "& Ester his wife"]
Oct 1   Ester d of Georg DODSON [BT's: "& Margaret his wife"]
Oct 11   Mary d of Mr HOLINS [BT's: "HOLLENS & Ann his wife"] of the Castle
Oct 21   William s of Charles COWEL [BT's: "& Mary"]
Oct 23   John s of John DAVIS [BT's: "& Mary"]
Nov 5   Thomas s of Richard MORRIS [BT's: "& Mary"]
Dec 11   Will[m] s of Mr Thom[s] NORIS [BT's: "NORRIS & Elizabeth"]
Dec 11   Mary d of Edward BIRD [BT's: "& Mary"]
Dec 12   Mary d of Edward VEAL [BT's: "& Mary"]
Dec 17   Joseph s of Henri PERINS [BT's: "& Eliner"]
Feb 2   Jane d of Sam[l] GRIFIS [BT's: "& Hannah"]
Feb 3   Jane d of John RICE [BT's: "& Mary"]
Feb 23   James s of Tho[s] NEWMAN [BT's: "& Jane"]
Mar 5   John s of John COOCK [BT's: "& Mary"]

Weddings Anno Dom: ..11:38

Jun 5   Edward and Elizabeth PIDDOCK
Nov 6   John & Mary DAVIS

Burials Anno Dom: 1711

Mar 30   Mary d of Rob[t] PARKS
Apr 7   Georg s of Gamely BELY
Apr 14   Tho[s] BATE Limedon
Apr 17   Jane SMITH widow
Apr 23   Sarah the wife of Humphry HILLMAN
May 3   Sam[l] MATHUS [BT's: "the brother of Will[mn]"]
May 7   Humphry SICH
May 12   Elisabeth BRITTAN
May 12   Beterig RAYBOULD [BT's: "wife of Thomas"]

May 28 John JONES
Jul 7 Ruth d of James LENARD
Aug 16 Elizabeth the wife of Mr Tho JUKES
Aug 17 David BRANSTON
[?; BT's: Aug"] 30   John BLOWE [BT's: "BLOWER"]
Oct 11 Elizabeth HUTT
Nov 1 Francis OVERS
Nov 8 Elizabeth wife of John SICH
Nov 17 Edwd s of Mr [BT's: "John"] WOOD
Dec 29 Anne d of John BROOK
Jan 1 John JAMES
Jan 12 Elizabeth FLOYD [BT's: "wife of John"]
Jan 16 William FRIER [BT's: "son of Izaak & Ann"]
Feb 10 John OLLIVER [BT's: "son of Richard OLIVER"]
Feb 17 Elizabeth HILLMAN [BT's: "d of Richard"]
Feb 25 Ann FLOYD [BT's: "d of John"]
Mar 2 Samuel OVERS
Mar 3 Mary BATE [BT's: "d of" but the name lost due to a hole]
Mar 7 Edward HILLMAN

Baptismes 1712

Apr 13 Patiencs d of Mr KEELING Aterny
May 11 Sarah d of Thos KIDSON [BT's: "& Sara"]
Jun 23 Richard s of Richard BRADLY [BT's: "s of Willm & Ann"]
Jun 22 Elizabeth d of Mickel RAYBOULD [BT's: "& Mary"]
Jul 1 Willm s of HORTON [BT's: "of John HORTON & Mary"]
Jul 7 Willm s of John CORREDINE [BT's: "& Ann"]
Jul 9 Sarah d of Benjamin MATHUS [BT's: "& Sarah his wife"]
Jul 13 Joseph s of Willm SMALMAN [BT's: "& Ann"]
Jul 13 Shuesana d of Esderas POOLE [BT's: "Shusannah d of Esdrus POOL & Ann"]
Jul 15 Thom^s PLASTER s of Saml PLASTER [BT's: "& Ann"]
Jul 20 Ann d of Georg ROGERS [BT's: "& Mary"]
Jul 20 Hanah d of Francis NEW [BT's: "& Sarah"]
Jul 25 Willm s of John MOESLEY [BT's: "& Ann"]
Jul 28 James s of James SMITH [BT's: "& Isbil"]
Aug 5 Katherine d of Willm MILLES [BT's: "& Elizabeth"]
Aug 10 Ann d of Mr BRADLEY [BT's: "Aug 15" & "of Mr Richard & Elizabeth"]
Sep 26 Mary d of Huphry CLARK [BT's: "Sep 18" & "of Mary"]
Oct 4 John s of Willm HARWOOD [BT's: "& Elizabeth"]
Oct 14 John s of John WORRAL [BT's: "& Elizabeth"]
Oct 16 Willm s of Will TIMINS [BT's: "& Elizabeth"]
Oct 21 Thomas s of Rachel ROWLEY Illegittimat
Nov 5 Humphry s of Edrd SARBIT [BT's: "& Sarah"]
Nov [?, BT's: "27"]   Richard s of Mr Richard BATE Clerk & Elizabeth his wife
Jan 2 Elizabeth d of Mr COMBER [BT's: "& Ann"]
Jan 6 Edward s of Edrd OLLIVER [BT's: "OLIVER & Ann"]

Jan 25   Daniel s of John JOHNSONS [BT's: "John s of John
         JOHNSON & Dorothy his wife"]
Feb 2   William s of Willm PAR
Feb 3   Ann d of Edman MASON
Mar 19   Frances d of Richard COLTS

Weddings: 1712
Jul 22   Edward BROOK and Milisent his wife
Oct 21   Mr Thomas WELLES and Elizabeth his wife

Burials: 1712
Mar 25   Ann d of ye widdow BATE
Mar 28   Rich^d s of ye Widdow LOW
Apr 14   Phœbe d of Thomas HOPKINS & Ann his wife
Apr 8   James s of Widdow BENNET [BT's: "BENIT"]
Apr 12   Mr John WILLIT
Apr 23   Will s of ye Widdow LAMBETH
Apr 25   Eliz d of [BT's: "Mr"] Richd WORRAL Senr
Apr 29   John HACKETT alias GRIFFIS
May 3   Jane the wife of Joseph PHILIPS
May 26   Eleanor BARKER Widdow
Jun 30   Judith [BT's: "Jude"] DARLISON wife [blank] [BT's: "wi^d"]
Jul 9   John BOWERS
Jul 18   Ann d of Tho: BRADLEY & Jane his wife
Jul 30   Ann d of Willm PERRY
Aug 2   Eliz wife of Tho HURST
Aug 5   Charles s of the Wid TISOW [BT's: "TISO"]
Sep 5   Eliz SHEERWOOD
Sep 7   Mary d of Wid HUMPHRIS
Sep 28   Mary d of Humphry CLARK and Mary his wife
Sep 29   Eliz wife of Tho BATE
Oct 3   Eliz d of the Wid JOHNSONS
Oct 4   Will BURTON
Oct 8   James RICH
Oct 14   Ann d of John PERRY and Ann his wife
Oct 15   Tho COOPER
Oct 19 [BT's: "16th"] Richard KIDSON
Nov 3   Joshua MORRIS
Nov 7   Robert STOKES
Nov 12   Tho: HURST
Nov 13   John BATE
Nov 15   Edw s of Edwd WORRAL
Nov 24   Tho RAYBOLD [BT's: "RAYBOULD"]
Nov 25   John POWEL of Wittington
Dec 14   Adam ROUND
Dec 23   John WORRAL
Jan 11   Eliz wife of Francis WORRAL
Jan 21 [BT's: "12th"] Tho s of Rachel ROWLEY
Jan 25   Will s of Will PERRY

[The BT's have at this point a number of entries which are out of date sequence and are not in the OR's]
"Aug 2 1712   Mary wife of Rich[d] BAYLIS
Aug 30 1712   Shusannah YORK
Sep 27 1712   Ann d of Tho BATE
Oct 10 1712   Willm s of W[m] MATHUS"

Jan 30   John s of Mr NORRIS
Feb 10   Mrs BIRD
Feb 12   Joseph s of John GROVE
Mar 10   John SIMKIS
Mar 18   John s of Richd FEREDAY   [BT's: "FERIDE"]

Baptisms 1713

Mar [?; BT's :"25th"] Daniel s of John PERRY & Ann his wife
Apr 28   Sarah d of Tho: BRADLEY & Jane his wife
May 3   Humphry s of Edward LYTHAL & Sarah his wife
May 4 [BT's: "June 13"]   Tho: s of Rich HILLMANS & Margarett his wife
Jun 13   Eliz d of Francis OLIVER & Mary his wife
Jun [?, BT's: "27th"]   Richd son of Henry MOSELY & Merial his wife
Jul [?, BT's: "1st"]   Ann daughter of Philip HAYNS & Margaret his wife
Jul 10   Michael s of Michael ALLIN & Dorothy his wife
Jul 12   Thomas s of John TAYLOR & Mary his wife
Jul 27   Hannah d of Richd BAYLIS & Mary his wife
Aug 6   Samuel s of Sam: MORRIS & Mary his wife
Aug 11   Mary d of William CARDES & Rose his wife
Aug 12   Joseph s of Thomas SALE & Eliz his wife
Aug 22   Sarah d of John DAVIS & Mary his wife
Sep 5   Mary d of Edward BROOK & Milisent his wife

[Then following entries are in the BT's but not in the OR's:]
"Sep 28   Elizabeth d of Mr Tho[s] BROWN & Febe his wife
Sep 30   Elizabeth d of Ed[rd] BANISTER & Jane his wife
Oct 4   Will[m] s of Will[m] & MATHUS
Aug 25   John s of John INCHMORE & Elizabeth
Oct 28   Sarah d of Will[m] CRUNDALL & Margret his wife
Oct 13   John s of Georg WINFORD & Ann his wife
Nov 5   Richard s of Izack FRIER & Ann his wife
Nov 16   John s of John GROVE & Jone his wife
Dec 3   Ann d of Ed[rd] BIRD & Mary his wife
Dec 14   Elisabeth d of James BUXTON & Rose his wife
Jan 8   Hester d of Sam[el] LYE & Elizabeth his wife
Jan 30   John s of Danil ROWLY & Mary his wife
Jan 25   Ann d of John COOCK & Mary his wife
Feb 9   Elinor d of Henry PERINIS & Eliner PERINS

Wedings for the Year 1713

Jul 16   William WHITTICKER & Ann his wife
Aug 1   John HILLMAN & Mary his wife"

Marriages 1713
[No entries in the OR's]

Burials 1713

Mar 31 [BT's: "13"] Jane the wife of Humphry BATE
Apr 30 Tho LYE
May 21 Ann d of Richd CLARK [BT's: "CLARCK"]
Jul 29 Michael s of Michael ALLIN & Dorothy his wife
Aug 2 Mary wife of Richd BAYLIS
Aug 4 Tho BRISCOW [BT's: "BRISKO"]
Aug 30 Susannah YORK Widdow
Sep 27 Ann d of Tho: BATE
Oct 10 Will s of Will MATTHEWS [BT's: "MATHUS"]
Oct 15 Richd HACKETT
Nov 14 Richd s of Isaac FRIAR
Dec 2 Eleanor PIESEL Widdow
Dec 6 Eliz d of Mr Tho BROWN of Wolverhampton
Dec 7 Jane WARD widdow
Dec 30 Mary wife of John WHERET
Jan 2 Nathan JINKS [BT's: "GINKES"]
Feb 2 Dorothy wife of Benjn RENSHAW
Feb 8 John NEW
Mar 15 Rebeccah HILLMAN
Mar 17 Mary COOKE [BT's: "COCK"]

Baptisms 1714

Apr 18 Sam, s of Henry & Esther FINNY
Apr 27 Mary d of Tho DOOLITTLE & Eliz his wife
May 12 Will s of Benjamin MATTHEWS & Sarah his wife
May 16 Daniel s of Samuel GRIFFIS & Hannah his wife
May 18 Eliz d of Tho NORRIS & Eliz his wife
May 25 Phebe d of Tho HOPKINS & Ann his wife
Jun 21 Hannah d of Richd MORRIS & Mary his wife bap
Jun 25 Ann d of Edward SMALLMAN & Abigal his wife
Jul 8 Joseph s of Tho WHITE & Mary his wife
Jul 24 Jone d of Tho FINNEY & Jone his wife
Aug 4 John s of Mr Richd BATE & Eliz his wife
Aug 11 Ann d of John TURNER & Ann his wife
Aug 27 James s of James SMITH & Isabell his wife
Sep 26 John s of Tho KIDSON & Sarah his wife
Oct 5 Will s of Tho HOLLOWAY & Sarah his wife
Oct 12 Tho s of Richd OLIVER & Lydia his wife
Oct 21 Joseph s of Joseph OWEN & Sarah his wife
Nov 11 George s of Ann GEARING illegitimate
Dec 5 William s of William MATTHEWS & Sarah his wife
Dec 27 Eliz d of Will SMALLMAN
Dec 30 Will s of Will WITTAKER & Ann his wife
Jan 14 Rebeccah d of a traveling woman
Jan 22 Eliz [BT's: "Betty"] d of Isack FRIAR & Ann his wife
Jan 30 Joseph s of Jane SPARRY

Feb 19 Sarah d of Will [?] & Mary his wife
Feb 28 Martha d of Edward DUN & Sarah his wife
Mar 12 Tho: s of John & DERICK & Eliz his wife
Mar 23 Martha d of Esdras[?] POOL[?] & Ann his wife
 [The next entry would appear to have been added later; not in BT's.]
Jan 23 Ann d of Zacharia BRIDGENS & Allis his wife

Marriages 1714

Mar   Tho: NORMCOTT [BT's: "NORCOT"] & Eliz his wife
Apr 10   John DERICK & Eliz his wife
May 15 [BT's: "16"] Edward DUNN & Sarah his wife
May 17   Edward KNOLES [BT's: "KNOALS"] & Eliz his wife
May 23   Thos EVANS & Eliz his wife
Aug 31   John MOSELEY & Eliz his wife
Oct 16   Rich DUNN & Allis his wife
Oct 19   John SICH & Mary his wife
Oct 26   Will TURNER & Mary his wife
Nov 16   Humphrey PEW & Ann his wife
Dec 8   Richd DOLPHIN & Ann his wife
Dec 27   Henry WARD & Eliz his wife
Dec 27   Will WARD & Sarah his wife
Dec 27   John TIMMINS & Mary his wife
Dec 30   John MOUNTSTEPHEN & Jane his wife
Jan 1   [Entry may have been erased]

Burials 1714

Mar 28 [BT's: "29"] The Widow SCOTT
Apr 3 [BT's: "11"] Jonathan s of Widow PERRINS
Apr 16   Rob [BT's: "Sam"] TAYLOR pauper
May 9   Robert WOOD
May 23   Will s of Charles COWEL & Mary his wife
May 26   Mrs Eliz COOK Wid
May 26   John ye [?] of Jno [BT's: "John"] WELLS & Eliz his wife
Jun 9   Sarah RICE wid
Jun 14   Richard LAVENDER
Aug 23   Ester wife of John PENN
Nov 9   Tho: s of Robert PARKES
Nov 17   Philip s of Paul FOLEY Esq
Dec 3   John HACKETT
Dec 6   Jane BOWERS
Dec 30   Mary d of John COOK & Mary his wife
Jan 14   Tho: s of Henry PERINS
Jan 10   John ROBINSON
Jan 14   Ann wife of John TURNER
Feb 11   Mary HOLLINS
Feb 13   Tho [remainder blank; BT's: "EVANS"]
Mar 4   George LOW pauper
Mar 9   Will WEBB

Baptisms 1715

Apr 9	Winifred d of Henry MOSELEY & Meriel his wife
Apr 21	John s of John HILLMAN & Mary his wife
Apr 21	Richd s of John HORTON & Mary his wife
Apr 30	Martha d of George ROGERS & Mary his wife
May 15	Phillis d of John JOHNSON & Dorothy his wife
May 16	Mary d of Peter TOY [BT's: "TAY"] & Eliz his wife
Jun 6	John s of John WOOLEY & Eliz his wife
Jun 13	Daniel s of John ROSE & Agnis his wife
Jul 2	Eliz d of John MOSELEY & Eliz his wife

[The next three entries have been obscured but no entries in BT's.]

Jul 4	Mary d of John SICH & Mary his wife
Jul 4	Michael s of John RAYBOLD & Mary his wife
Jul 5	Will s of John RICE & Mary his wife
Aug 5	Esther d of Thomas ROGERS & Esther his wife
Aug 8	Edward s of Edward BROOK & Milisent his wife
Aug 10	Margaret d of John MOSELEY & Ann his wife
Aug 14	Mary d of Will TURNER & Mercy his wife [Entered twice in the BT's, once on August 14 and once on August 21]
Aug 22	Francis s of Francis AMIS & Ann his wife
Sep 7	Mary d of John TIMMINS & Mary his wife
Sep 15	Ann d of Richd FEREDEY & Eliz his wife

[An entry only in the BT's: "Sep 18 James BUXTON bap"]

Sep 18	Will s of James ROWLEY & Rose his wife [Entry not in BT's.]
Oct 11	Mary d of Henry WARD & Eliz his wife
Oct 16	Sarah d of Mr Richd BRADLEY & Eliz his wife
Oct 17	Zacharias s of Joseph TONKS & Sarah his wife
Oct 17	Sam: s of Sam LYE & Eliz his wife
Oct 19	Ann d of Mr John MITCHIL & Jane his wife
Oct 24	Sam: s of John DAVIS & Mary his wife
Oct 25	Esther d of Will TIMMINS & Eliz his wife
Oct 27	Edwd s of Will WARD & Sarah his wife
Oct 28	Jane d of John HILLMAN & Jane his wife
Nov 2	Phœbe d of Mr John COMBER & Ann his wife
Nov 8	Aaron s of Thomas HAER [BT's: "HARE"] & Ann his wife
Nov 13	Eleanor & Eliz daughters of Edward BIRD & Mary his wife
Dec 3	Tho s of Tho SIMMES & Mary his wife
Dec 26	Mary d of Edward OLIVER & Sarah his wife
Dec 31	Tho s of John GROVE & Jane his wife
Jan 7	Ann d of Richd DOLPHIN & Ann his wife
Feb 4	Richd s of John INCHMORE & Eliz his wife
Feb 11	Mary d of William CHAMBERS & Eliz his wife
Feb 13	Eliz d of Tho SALE & Eliz his wife

[This entry appears only in the BT's: "Feb 14 Richd ASHWOOD"]

Feb 11	Edward s of Abraham HILLMAN[?] & Mary wife [Entry not in BT's.]
Feb 2 [BT's: "23"]	Will s of Mr Jno COLLEY & Martha his wife
Feb 26	Mary d of John COOK & Mary his wife
Mar 2	Edward s of the Reverend Mr BATE & Eliz: his wife
Mar 15	Tho s of Tho DOLITTLE & Eliz his wife

Mar 17   Sam s of Philip HAYNS [BT's: "HAYNES"] & Margaret his wife
Mar 21   Edward s of George POWEL & Eliz his wife

Marriages 1715

Apr 23   Mr John COLLEY & Martha his wife
Apr 23   John HINTON & Ann his wife
May 1   Abel JOHNSONS & Ann his wife
May 7   Christopher BROWN & Martha his wife
Jun 11   Mr Francis DAVIS & Eliz his wife
Jun 13   Richd WILCOX [BT's: "WILLCOCKS"] & Katharine his wife
Jun 25   Richd WORRAL & Eliz his wife
Dec 25   Tho SMITH & Mary his wife
Jan 7   John TILEY & Catharine his wife

Burials 1715

Apr 3   Sarah wife of Tho KIDSON
May 2   John s of Edward SARBITT
May 29   Will s of Sam: PLASTER
Jun 3   The Rev^d Mr Will BRINDLY
Jun 4   Richd s of Rich. DUNN
Jun 19   George s of George GROVE
Jun 19   Eliz wife of Tho IFENS [BT's: "EVANS"]
Jun 24   Hannah s of Richd BAYLIS
Aug 19   Mary d of Edward BROOK
Oct 11   Will ROWLEY
Oct 28   Ann d of Mr John MITCHIL
Oct 31   Will JONES [BT's: "JANNES"[?]]
Nov 7   Tho s of Edward SMALLMAN
Nov 15   Sarah d of Edw. SMALLMAN
Nov 28   Sarah RICE
Nov 30   Jane d of Tho LYNE [BT's: "LINE"]
Dec 11   Sam s of Henry FINNY
Dec 11   Tho WORRAL
Dec 21   Grace wife of Daniel ROWLEY
Dec 23   Eliz d of Edwd BIRD
Dec 29   Edward s of James HARRIS
Dec 29   Will s of James LEANARD
Dec 31   Robert HEAVENS
Jan 8   Daniel GLOVER
Jan [?; BT's: "25"]   Zacharias s of Joseph TONKS
Feb 4   Edward s of Will WARD
Feb 19   Margaret WORAL
Feb 28 [BT's: "29"]   Eliz wife of John INCHMORE
Mar 9   Margery CRANE
Mar 15   Mr George BRINDLEY

Baptisms 1716

Mar 27   Tho s of Tho NORMCOTT [BT's: "NORCOT"]
Apr 2   Eliz d of Christopher BROWN
Apr 3   Mary d of John CRANE

Apr 5   Hurst s of Oliver DIXON
Apr 8   Tho WEBB illegitimate
Apr 15   Tho s of Ann CRANAGE illegitimate
Apr 18   Richd s of Saml MOSELEY
Apr 22   Sarah d of Sarah d of Mr John WHITE
May 29   John s of Rich WORRAL junior
Jun 4   Will s of Richd DUNN
Jun 5   Mary d of Randle SEVERN
Jun 10   Richd s of Richard EVERLY
Jun 16   Ann d of John PERRY
Jul 4   Joseph s of Henry PERRINS
Jul 14   George s of John TAYLOR
Jul 19   John s of Tho SMITH
Jul 28   George s of George DODSON
Jul 29   Mary d of John LINE
Aug 11   Jeremiah s of Eliz LINE
Aug 14   Sarah d of Richd VEALE [BT's: "VEAL"]
Aug 18   Eliz d of Richd PRICE
Aug 19   Jane d of Tho. WHITE
Aug 19   Mary d of John WEBB
May 20   Daniel s of Daniel ROWLEY
Sep 8   John s of James BROWN & Mary his wife
Sep 15   John s of Edward HUTT
Oct 13   Will s of Edward LINE
Oct 28   Joseph s of [blank] WILLIAMS
Nov 3   Eliz d of John KETLEY & Eliz his wife
Nov 10   John s of Will WITTAKER & Ann his wife
Dec 16   Thomas s of Will MILLS
Dec 19   Ann d of Tho: NEWMAN
Dec 22   Mary d of Edward MASON [BT's: "MASN & Ann"]
Dec 23   Will s of John TILLY
Dec 23   Eliz d of Ellin LEWIS a travelling woman
Jan 5 [BT's: "17th"]   Ann d of Sam: PLASTER
Jan 10 [BT's: "20th"] Sarah d of Edwd LYTHAL & Sarah his wife
Jan 24   Sarah d of John TIMMINS
Jan 24   John s of John MOSELEY Mason
Jan 27   Tho s of Edwd HILL
Feb 2   Thos: Will & Edward sons of John POPE & Mary his wife
Feb 14   Sarah d of Tho NORRIS
Feb 16   Francis s of Tho SIMMES
Feb 15 [BT's: "17th"]   Eliz d of John TURNER
Feb 19   Eliz d of Thomas ORAM
Mar 3 [BT's: "2nd"]   Tho s of Will TURNER
Mar 4   Eliz d of Esau PENSON & Mary his wife
Mar 24   Mary d of Eliz DERICK

Marriages 1716

Apr 30   Richd YORK & Margaret his wife
May 6   Will TAYLOR & Eliz his wife
Jun 7   Jos FONSBROOK [BT's: "FOSBROOK"] & Hannah his wife

Oct 24   John CHAMBERS & Hannah his wife
Feb 14   Humphry BATE & Ann his wife
Feb 28   Rich BROOK & Margaret his wife

Burials 1716

Mar 25   Catharine HILLMAN
Mar 29   Margaret BATE Widdow
Apr 17   Mary wife of John BROWN
Jun 11   Ann d of Rich DOLPHIN
Jul 7   William SUTHAL
Jul 13   Tho DOLITTLE
Aug 24   John s of Mr Rich WORRAL
Aug 27   The Revd Mr Jonathan NEWEY
Aug 30   Tho ROGERS
Sep 18   Mary PEW
Nov 16   Sarah wife of James LAVENDER
Nov 30   The Worshipful Philip FOLEY Esq
Dec 11   Margaret TAYLOR
Dec 28   John s of John TAYLOR
Jan 5   David s of Sam: GRIFFIS
Jan 7   John RICHARDS
Jan 10   William WARD
Jan 12 [BT's: "21st"] John CLIMER
Jan 23   Tho POPE
Feb 15   Dr WHEELER
Feb 27   Tho HILLMAN
Mar 22   John s of Abraham ASHWOOD
Mar 23   William LAMBETH

Baptisms 1717

Mar 26   Mary d of Joseph OWEN & Sarah his wife
Mar 26   Eliz d of John CRANE
Mar 30   Eliz d of John HILLMAN
May 5   Eliz d of James GRIFFIS
May 25   Richd s of Richd DOLPHIN
May 12   John s of Mr John WHITE
May 13   Eliz d of Willm EGGINTON
Jun 22   Tho. s of of Francis NEW
Jun 22   Mary d of George WILFORD
Jul 8   Tho s of Edward BROOK
Jul 24   Mary d of Edwd DUN
Jul 27   John s of James LEONARD Junior
Aug 6   Sam: s of Peter TOY
Sep 4   Jos s of ye Revd Mr Mr Richd BATE
Sep 11   Tho s of Richd WORRAL Junior
Sep 21   Richd s of Richd HILLMAN
Sep 29   Edwd s of Will HARWOOD
Oct 5   Mary d of Will PARR
Oct 10   Eldred s of Mr John MITCHIL
Oct 12   Sarah d of Isach FRIER

Oct 14	Will s of John SICH
Oct 19	John s of George ROGERS
Oct 22	Margaret d of Will TIMMINS
Oct 27	John s of Mr SELL Excise man
Nov 9	Hannah d of Will STOKES
Nov 16	Eliz d of Benj RENSHAW
Nov 20	Martha d of Mr John COLLEY
Nov 30	Jane d of John LINES
Dec 21	Tho s of Tho SALE
Dec 3	Esther d of Ezdras POOL
Jan 13	Henry s of John RICHARDS
Jan 24	Jane d of Humphry BATE
Jan 26	Richd s of J HARRIS
Jan 25	Mary d of Richd BROOK
Jan 30	Hannah d of John GROVE
Feb 8	Gilbert s of John JOHNSON
Feb 14	Susannah SMART

Marriages 1717

Apr 22	Edward GROVE & & Margaret his wife
May 2	Richd HILL & Gathrick his wife
May 4	William ROBINSON & Eliz his wife
Sep 12	Abraham CRANE & Mary his wife
Nov 10	Sam: DERICK & Eliz his wife

Burials 1717

Apr 2	Daniel s of Daniel ROWLEY
Apr 6	Galibira PARKS
Apr 7	Eliz CLIMER [BT's: "CLIMAR"]
Apr 8	Eli DARLISON
Apr 13	John a child yt was found [BT's: "A child left in Kinfare"]
May 6	Eliz d of Tho SALE
May 13	Tho s of [blank] POPE
May 19 [BT's: "13th"]	Ann wife of Will PERRY
May 22	Eliz WHITE
May 22	Ann d of Tho HOPKINS
May 28	Eliz BIRD Widdow
May 28	Mary d of ye Widd NEW
May 29	Martha d of Edmund MASON
Jun 3	Joseph s of Sam: MORRIS
Jun 7	Simon CRANE
Jun 12	Mary WORRAL
Jun 17	Margaret d of Sam MORRIS
Jul 7	Sarah d of Wm TAYLOR
Jul 24	John s of Michael RAYBOLD [BT's: "RABOLD"]
Jul 24	Mary of John HILLMAN
Jul 16	Abigail [BT's: "Ann"] wife of Mr NORRIS Senior
Jul 25	Eliz NOXON
Aug 22	Joyce NEWNAM
Sep 15	Francis GARRET

Oct 8; 3   John WINFORD   [Two dates appear to have been entered in the OR; BT's: "3rd"]
Oct 10   George BATE
Oct 26   Edwd s of Mr SKELDING of Asley
Nov 1   Eldred s of Mr John MITCHIL
Dec 3   Dorothy MOSELEY
Dec 16   John s of Mr John WHITE
Jan 27   Luke POWEL
Feb 16   Widd HAYES
Feb 16   Martha d of John SPENCER
Feb 19   Hanah d of John GROVE
Mar 3   Will H[?]
Mar 3   Will NORMICOTT
          [The two entries above are not in the BT's.
          However, there is an extra entry in the BT's:
          "Mar 21   Will NXLEY[?] was buried"

Baptisms 1718
          [The BT's for this year only start with the July 20 entry.]
Mar 31   Margaret d of Oliver DIXON
Apr 14   Will s of Will TAYLOR
Apr 25   Sarah d of Henry MOSELEY by Merial his wife
May 2   Eliz d of William ROBINSON
May 20   John s of Sam LYE
May 22   Hannah d of Rose BUXTON
Jun 7   [blank] d of John HILLMAN
Jun 8   Edward s of Edward BIRD
Jun 14   John s of John MOSELEY
Jul 20   Ann WEAD an adult
Jul 16   Joseph s of John TAYLOR & Eliz
Jul 6   Richd s of John COOK
Aug 6   Tho s of Tho VEAL
Aug 1   Edward s of Thomas SMITH & Mary his wife
Aug 22   George s of John & RICE
Aug 23   Ann d of Richard DOLPHIN
Aug 30   Sarah d of William MATTHEWS & Sarah his wife
Sep 6   Samson s of Saml: SMITH
         [The next entry appears to have been inserted later]
Sep 7   Mary d of John BISHOP & Hannah his wife
Sep 9   Ann d of Francis AMIS
Sep 9   Thos s of William HICKMANS
Sep 21   Mary d of Benjamin POTTER & Mary his wife
Sep 28   Judith d of Rich: PRICE & Margaret his wife
Sep 20   Benjamin s of Henry PERINS & Eleanor his wife
         [The remaining baptismal entries for this year
         are badly stained on the right-hand side]
Oct 5   Ann d of Mr John COMBER & Ann his wife
Oct 8   John s of Edward OLIVERS [BT's: "OLIVER"] & Sarah his wife
Oct 14   John s of John CRANE & Mary his wife
Oct 25   Ellen d of Edward LINE & Mary his wife

Oct 30	Benj s of Joseph OWEN & Sarah his wife
Nov 1	Francis s of William WITTAKER & Ann his wife
Nov 1	Edward s of John POWEL & Mary his wife
Nov 14	Elizabeth d of Thomas & Mary HILL
Nov 30	Henry s of Sarah WARD
Dec 3	Nicholas s of Mr John WHITE & Sarah his wife
Dec 20	Hannah d of Thos & Mary KIDSON
Jan 12	Sarah d of Joseph ACRY & Elianor his wife
Jan 23	Edward s of Edward WALDRON & Sarah his wife
Jan 24	Sarah d of Michael RAYBOLD & Mary his wife
Jan 27	Mary d of John DAVIS & [?]
	Tho: s of [?] & Mary [BT's: Thos s of Christopher BROWN bap Feb 2"]
Mar 5	Samuel & Mary s & d of Samuel MOSELEY & Mary his wife
Mar 10	Mary d of John TOWNSEND

Marriages 1718

Apr 23	Jos: PARKER & Lydia his wife
May 1	Richd NEWMAN & Sarah his wife
May 10	Lawrence NOXON & Merial his wife
May 10	John TOWNSEND & Ann his wife
Jul 27	John POWELL & Mary his wife
Oct 4	Joseph ACRY & Eleanor his wife
Oct 6	James BECKLEY & Catharine his wife
Nov 5	Richard WORRAL & Elizabeth his wife
Dec 27	Edwd GROVE & Margrett his wife
Dec 29	James RICHARD [BT's: "RICHARDS"] & Anne his wife
Mar 30	John DAVIS & Ann his wife

Burials 1718

Apr 4	Paul FOLEY Esq
Apr 5	Tho HOPKINS
Apr 20	Humphry s of Edward LYTHAL
Apr 22	Eliz d of John LOW
Apr 23	Margaret wife of Edward GROVE
Apr 29	Margery wife of Edward GROVE
May 8	Mrs OWEN Widdow
May 9	Eliz wife of Edward MASON
May 14	Mary MASON Widdow
May 16	William STOKES Senior
May 22	Ann HILLMAN
Jun 13	Mary CRANE
Jun 17	Ann LYE widdow
Jun 22	Will s of Will WALINS [BT's: "WALLINS"]
Jul 16	Ann wife of John MANOX
Aug 9	Thomas the s of Tho VEAL
Sep 15	Isabel HACKET
Sep 30	Elizabeth SICH [BT's: "SUCH"]
Oct 1	Dorothy MOLE
Oct 13	Mr John SPENCER

Nov 11   Francis CLIMER
Dec 5 [BT's:7"]   Will LYE of Enfield psh
Dec 26 [BT's: "24"]   Will AUDIN
Dec 26   Mr JUKES Senior
Dec 26   Hugh PEWS wife
Jan 8   Michael BAILIS
Jan 14   A son of Tho GIBBS of the psh of Auvley
Jan 15   Judith LOW Widd
Feb 2   Mr John WHERRET
Feb 2   Ann DAVIS Widd
Feb 21   John PENN

Burials 1719
Mar 11 [BT's: "4th"]   Ann wife of Sampson SPENCER
Mar 19   John WILLIAMS
Mar 24   Eleanor d of Edward BIRD & Mary his wife
Mar 29 1719   Sam & Mary s & d of Sam MOSELEY & Mary his wife
Apr 11   Mary wife of John HAYWOOD sen^r
May 13   [blank] the wife of Gilburt FOENS [BT's: "FONES"]
May 19   Mary d of Georg WINFORD
May 22   Thos BATE
May 22   Mary d of John COOK & Mary his wife
May 24   AURLDEN widow [BT's: " widow AUDIN"] buried
May 28   Joseph s of Easau [BT's: "Esau"] & Mary PENSON
Jul 16   Mary JONES
Aug 14   Edward JONES the son of Edrd JONES
Sep 5   Sarah the wife of John BATE
Sep 18   Lousy [BT's: "Lucia"] COMSON wid:
Nov 1   Thomas DOLITTLE
Nov 28   Mary the wife of Willm TIMINS Senr
Dec 5   Dorothy HOLLY widow
Dec 10   Richard LINE [BT's: "LYNE"]
Dec 11   Richard s of Edward SMALLMAN

Baptisms 1719
Mar 14   Humphrey s of Humphrey BATE & [blank] his wife
Mar 13   Benjamin s of Edward BROOK & Millescent his wife
Mar 16   A bastard Child of Amis [BT's: "Amy"] HILLMAN of Stourton
Mar 17   Sarah d of the Rev^d Mr Jos: COLLIER & Sarah his wife
Mar 29   Sarah d of Will WHITE & Ann his wife
Mar 31   William s of Jos. PARKER & Lydia his wife
Mar 31   Mary d of Richd PROSSER & Amey his wife
Apr 6   Sarah d of Will TURNER & Mary his wife
Apr 1   Sarah d of Richard NEWMAN & Sarah his wife
May 17   Ann d of Edrd & Sarah LITHAL [BT's: "LYTHALL"]
May 19   Joseph s of Easaw [BT's: "Esau"] and [sic] PENSON
May 25   Jes [BT's: "Jesse"] s of John & Jane GROVE
Jun 9   Sarah d of John COLLY & Martha his wife
Jun 20   Willm s of Willm CHAMBERS & Elizabeth his wife

Jul 18	John s of John KETLEY [BT's: "KETTLEY"] & Elizabeth his wife
Jul 18	Thomas s of Thomas NORRIS & Sarah his wife
Jul 26	Mary d of James BECKLY [BT's: "BECKLEY"] & Katern his wife
Aug 8	Elizabath d of Georg WINFORD & Ann his wife
Aug 11	John s of John TERNER [BT's: "TURNER"] & Katern his wife
Aug 16	Nickols s of Elisabeth GROVE Elegitimat
Sep 15	Jane d of Benjamin RENSHAW & Jane his wife (Par)
	[The next entry appears to have been squeezed in possibly at a later date]
Sep 20	Joseph s of Willm & Sarah his wife [No surname given; BT's: "PARR"]
Sep 26	John s of James RICHARDS & Ann his wife
Sep 27	John s of Danil LUN
Oct 1	Daniel of Samuel GRIFFIS & Hannah his wife
Oct 3	John s of John TILLY & Catherine his wife
Sep 18	Sarah d of Richard WORRAL & Elizth his wife was bap being misplaced
Oct 4	Henry s of the Reverend Mr Richard BATE & Elisabeth his wife
Oct 18	Francis s of Mr Thos WALDRON & Mrs Ann=Elin his wife
Oct 24	Thom^s s of John LYNE & [blank] his wife
Oct 24	Sarah d of Willm ROBISON and Elizabeth his wife
Nov 3	Ester d of John TIMINS & Mary his wife
Nov 3	Mary d of Thos HARE & Ann his wife
Nov 5	James s of Peeter TOYEY [BT's: "Peter TOY"] & Elisabeth his wife
Nov 4	Richard s of Richard DUNN & Ales his wife

[There are no more baptisms listed in the OR, but the following are given in the BT's:]

"Dec 30 John s of Richard WORRALL jun
Dec 31 Edward s of John HILLMAN Grinder
Jan 6   Mary d of John HAYS
Jan 9   Joseph s of Laurence NOXON
Jan 24 Sarah BECKLEY an illegitimate
Jan 27 William s of William PERRINS
Jan 28 Thomas s of Walter EGGINTON
Feb 6   [blank] the s of Roger LAMBETH
Feb 9   John s of John DAVIS
Feb 7   Nathaniel s of [blank]
Feb 15 Sarah d of John SUCH
Feb 28 Hannah d of John BAYLIS
Mar 3   Edward s of Edward GROVE
Mar 6   Hannah d of William VEAL

Burials 1719

Dec 16	Margret CHAPMAN was buried
Jan 24	Joseph s of Joseph OWIN
Jan 25	John SANBY the Gran Son of Richard WORREN buried

Jan 30	Willm s of John & Mary SICH
Jan 31	Mr GEEARY
Mar 12	William WALINS Senr

Burials 1720

Apr 9	Edward s of Thos SMITH & Mary his wife
May 3 [BT's: "1st"]	Thos s of James LENARD [BT's: "LEONARD"] Junr & Elizabeth his wife
May 16	Saml s of the widow DAVIS
Jun 4	Edward GROVE of Comton
Jun 13	John s of Thos NEW Talor [BT's: "Taylor"] being misplaced. [Note at side in a different hand "With Aff"]
Jun 12	Ester FINNY [BT's: "FINNEY"] the wife of Harry FINNY
Jun 12	Elner d of Harry PERINS [BT's: "Eleanor d of Henry"]
Jun 20	Elisabeth d of the Widow BROOK
Jul 2	Lidia the wife of Richd: OLIFER
Jul 9	Mr Richard BRINDLEY
Jul 30	Willm DODSON
Aug 5	Mary HUTT
Aug 19	Richard FERIDAY
Dec 30	John s of Richard WARALL Jun & Elisath his wife
Dec 31	Edward s of John HILLMAN Grinder
Jan 6	Mary d of John HAYES
Jan 19	Joseph s of Larans NOXSON & Meryale his wife [The next entry has been squeezed in]
Jan 24	Sarah BECKLY illegitimate
Jan 27	William s of Willm PERINS & Elisabeth his wife
Jan 28	Thomas s of Water EGINTON and [blank] his wife
Feb 6	[blank] the son of Rodger LAMBETH & [blank] his wife
Feb 9	John s of John DAVIS & Ann his wife
Feb 17	Nathaniel s of [no further details given]
Feb 15	Sarah d of John & Mary SICH
Feb 28	Hanah d of John BAYLIS & Sarah his wife
Mar 6	Hanah d of Willm VEALL & Ann his wife
Mar 3	Edward s of Edward GROVE & Margret his wife being mis placed

Marriages 1719

Nov 19	Daniel DUN & Sarah his wife
Nov 30	Samson SPENCER & Mary his wife
Feb 8	John DODSON & Joyce his wife

Baptisms 1720

Apr 3	Thom^s s of Robert DALE & Frances his wife
Apr 18	Antony s of Thom^s SALE & Elisabeth his wife
Apr 19	Thomas s of James LENARD [BT's: "LEONARD"] & Elisabeth his wife
Apr 30	Edward s of Edward DUN [BT's: "DUNN"] & Sarah his wife
Apr 30	Thomas s of Georg & Mary ROGERS
Apr 26	Joseph s of John & Mary CRANE

Apr 29	John s of John & Ruth GREEN
Jun 5	Thos s of Thos & Mary SMITH
Jun 11	Richard s of Richard & Ame PROSER
Jun 27	Richard s of Richard & Margret BROOK
Jul 14	Willm s of John COLE & Elisabeth his wife
Aug 28	Sarah d of Richd NEWMAN & Sarah his wife
	Margret d of Mr Tawlbut [BT's: "Talbot"] JUKES Esq & Frances his wife born July 20 and baptized August 30 1720
Sep 4	Mary d of Mr John WHITE & Sarah his wife ["Mr" & "Sarah his wife" inserted later]
Sep 11	William s of Willm TAYLER & Elisabeth his wife
Sep 27	Thomas s of John HILLMAN & Jane his wife
Sep 16	Shuesanah d of Mr John BACH & Shuesanah his wife (bein mis placed)
Oct 13	Phebe d of Benjamin POTTER & Mary his wife
Oct 14	Elisabeth d of John & Mary DAVIS
Oct 24	Mary d of Samson SPENCER & Mary his wife
Nov 7	William s of Sam^{ll} LYE & Elisabeth his wife
Nov 19	Mary d of Sam^{ll} & Elisabeth SMITH
Nov 22	Elisabeth d of Richard COOK & Margaret his wife
Dec 4	Thomas s of John & Mary COOK
Dec 20	Thomas s of Joseph OWEN & Sarah his wife
Dec 30	Edward a bastard child of Mary ROBINSON
Jan 2	Sarah & Mary ds of Edward & Marjery LINES
Jan 6	Richard s of Thomas & Mary KIDSON
Jan 6	Samuel s of Samuel & Mary MOSELEY

Burials 1720

Sep 2	Hannah d of Edrd JONES with Affid
Sep 11	[BT's: "1st"] Sam^{ll} BATE with affid
Sep 12	Shusanah d of Mr John BACH with Affidavit [Mr being inserted]
Sep 22	Darothy [BT's: "Dorothy"] the wife of Richard CORFIELD
Sep 24	Shusanah ye wife of Mr John BACH with Affid [Mr being inserted]
Oct 11	Richard MORIS with Affidavit
Oct 12	Elnor DARLISON
Oct 15	Elizabeth d of John & Mary DAVIS
Nov 2	Ales DAVIS with Affidavit
Nov 2	Richard BIB [BT's: "BIBB"] came from Ould=Swinford
Nov 9	Sarah GIBBS widow with Affid
Nov 9	Margret WHITICKER widow with affid
Nov 28	Samuel BRINDLEY
	[Entries partially overwritten with comment "With Affidavit"]
Dec 1	Mr Richard COLLEY with Affidavit
Jan 29	William BULLOCK with Affidavit
Feb 3	Henry RICHARDS with Affidavit
Feb 17	Anne LEA with Affidavit
Feb 23	Mary wife of Samuel SMITH with Affidavit
Mar 1	Mr John NORRIS with Affidavit

Mar 4   Sarah d of Richard & Sarah NEWMAN with Affidavit
Mar 11   Sarah d of Edward Marjery LINES with Affidavit

Baptisms 1720

Jan 24   Mary d of William HICKMANS & Catherine his wife
Jan 25   Joseph & Mary s & d of Joseph & Mary FOXHOLE
Jan 31   Anne d of Humphrey BATE &Anne his wife
Feb 21   Mary d of Joseph PARKER & Lydia his wife
Mar 6   Susanna d of Gray CHRISTOPHER & Mary his wife
Mar 8   Mary d of John TURNER & Katharine his unlawful wife
Mar 12   John s of John COLLEY & Martha his wife

Burials 1720

Mar 12   Thomas WOOLLEY with affidavit
Mar 12   Winifred d of Henry MOSELEY & Merial his wife with no Affid which was signified by the Church Wardens by a note under mine own hand
Mar 14   Richard s of Richard KETTLEY with affidavit
Mar 23   Francis COOK with Affidavit
Mar 23   Edward ROBINSON an illegitimate son of Mary ROBINSON with Affidavit
Mar 23   Elizabeth wife of William CHAMBERS with Affidavit
Oct 21   John BROOK with Affid. Misplaced

Marriages 1720

Apr 21   Edmund MASON & Ann his wife
May 3   John INCHMORE & Mary his wife
May 26   Edward WILLIAMS & Elisabeth his wife
Oct 20   John CHAMBERLAIN and Sarah his wife
Feb 16   Charles JONES & Mary his wife
Feb 16   John JINKES & Elizabeth his wife

Baptisms 1721

Apr 10   Elisabeth d of Francis AMIS & Anne his wife
Apr 12   Mary d of John DODSON & Joyce his wife
May 16   John s of John WHITESIDES & Anne his wife
May 18   Mary d of Henry HACKETT & Barbara his wife
May 21   William s of John & Anne TOWNSEND
May 22   Eleanor d of William & Mercy TURNER
May 29   Edward s of John & Anne DAVIS
May 29   John s of Edward & Elizabeth BENNISON
Jun 18   Hannah d of John & Mary SARBET
Jun 24   Mary d of Henry & Sarah SMITH
Jul 22   Richard s of John & Mary RICE
Aug 1   Thomas s of John & Mary CRANE
Aug 7   Zacharias s of Edward & Margaret GROVE
Aug 16   Milicent d of Edward & Milicent BROOK
Aug 19   Elisabeth d of John & Sarah CHAMBERLAIN
Aug 27   Sarah d of Edward & Sarah OLIVER
Sep 18   William s of John & Mary DAVIS

Sep 24	Bridgett d of Richard & Margaret PRICE
Oct 7	John s of John & Jane ALLEN
Oct 7	Thomas s of Richard & Jane HOLLINS
Oct 8	Anne d of James & Anne RICHARDS
Nov 15	William s of Charles & Mary JONES
Nov 21	Anne d of Benjamin & Jane RENSHAW
Nov 29	Sarah d of Edward & Sarah WALDRON
Dec 7	Samuel s of Talbot JUKES [BT's: "JEWKES"] Esqr & Frances his wife
Dec 8	James s of Christopher & Mary BROWN
Dec 16	Anne d of Michael & Mary RAYBOLD
Jan 1	Elisabetha Maria d of John & Jane BROOK
Jan 10	John s of Samuel & Eleanor WHITE
Jan 13	Joseph s of Joseph & Hannah FOSBROOK
Jan 14	William s of Thomas & Jane NEWMAN
Jan 18	William s of James & Elisabeth LENNARD [BT's: "LEONARD"]
Jan 25	Paul s of Jane PEARSALL
Jan 30	Mary d of John HILLMAN & Mary his wife
Feb 6	Samuel s of John & Catharine TILLEY
Feb 12	Mary d of John & Elizabeth SWINFEN
Feb 18	Elisabeth d of John & Mary INCHMORE
Feb 21	Mary d of Richard & Margaret COOK
Mar 10	Mary d of William & Elisabeth ROBINSON
Feb 27	Elisabeth d of John & Mary TIMMINS

Burials 1721

Mar 26	Thomas SPARY [BT's: "SPARRY"] with affidavit
Mar 31	Humphrey MOSELEY with affidavit
Mar 31	Mary d of John & Katherine TURNER with affidavit
Apr 3	Elisha BRISSELL with affidavit
Apr 4	Mary d of Jane SPARRY Wid. with affidavit
Apr 5	Mr John WOOD with affidavit
Apr 6	Thomas GIBBS with affidavit
Apr 8	Sarah d of William & Elisabeth ROBINSON with affidavit
Apr 14	Hugh PEW with affidavit
May 7	Mary d of Peter TOYE with affidavit
May 15	Penelope Relict of Philip FOLEY Esq with affidavit
May 19	Mary d of Henry & Barbara HACKETT with affidavit
May 21	Mary the wife of Henry COOK with affid.
May 22	William BOWEN
May 29	Thomas s of Thomas & Jane BRADLEY with affidavit
Jun 10	Martha d of Mr John COLLEY & Martha his wife with affidavit
Jun 26	John HILLMAN of Stourton with affidavit
Jul 12	Mary GUEST with affidavit
Jul 19	Bridget HILLMAN with affidavit
Jul 20	Elisabeth the wife of Edward WILLIAMS with affidavit
Jul 21	Elisabeth OKE with affidavit
Aug 15	James LAVENDER with affidavit
Sep 4	Thomas s of Edward & Abigail SMALLMAN

Sep 17	Elisabeth HACKETT with affidavit
Sep 17	Joseph s of Abigail GIBBS with affidavit
Oct 1	Elisabeth d of John & Sarah CHAMBERLAIN with aff.
Oct 4	Elisabeth wife of Thomas FREYAR [BT's: FRYER"] with affidavit
Oct 13	Thomas GIBBS with affidavit
Oct 28	Sarah NEW with affidavit
Nov 5	Elisabeth the wife of Samuel DAVIES with affidavit
Dec 1	William BECKLEY
Dec 3	Elisabeth d of George & Margaret GROVE with affidavit
Dec 10	George s of John & Mary RICE
Dec 17	Sarah BENNET with affidavit
Dec 22	James s of Christopher & Mary BROWN with aff
Jan 6	Sarah d of Thomas & Mary BROWN with affid
Jan 6	Anne LOW widow with Affidavit
Jan 6	Margaret d of William & Elizabeth TIMMINS with affidavit
Jan 10	Elisabeth d of Francis & Anne AMIS with affid
Jan 11	Sarah d of William & Anne WHITE with affidavit
Jan 17	Eleanor d of George & Mary ROGERS
Jan 27	John s of Samuel & Eleanor WHITE with affidavit
Jan 28	George s of Edward & Winifred JONES with Affidavit
Feb 2	William KETLEY [BT's: "KETTLEY"] with Affid
Feb 4	John MOSELEY
Feb 8	Elisabeth CRANDIGE Widow with Affidavit
Feb 9	Nicholas s of John WHITE with Affidavit
Mar 5	Elisabeth d of John INCHMORE with affidavit
Mar 7	Mary BRADLEY with Affidavit
Mar 8	Jonathan s of Thomas HARE with affidavit
Mar 11	Thomas JOHNSON with affidavit

Marriages 1721

Jun 3	Henry FINNEY & Judith HILLMAN
Aug 1	Joseph ALDEN & Anne MOSELEY
Aug 3	Richard BATE & Mary JOHNSONS
Sep 7	Timothy SUTCLIFF & Anne PARKS
Sep 10	Samuel WHITE & Eleanor DREW
Oct 27	Humphrey BATE & Mary TOWNSEND
Dec 10	William DAVIES & Alice MALPUS
Dec 21	Thomas WORRALL & Catharine COX
Feb 1	John JOYCE & Hannah HARVEY

Marriages 1722

May 14	William BRICE & Hannah HACKETT
Jun 26	William POOL & Margaret SMALLMAN
Jul 3	Thomas FRYAR & Elizabeth MARTEN
Sep 25	John NORMECOTT & Elizabeth BECKLEY
Nov 4	William ONIONS & Mary ROBERTSON
Dec 26	Thomas IDDINS & Margaret ROBERTSON
Jan 5 [BT's: "3rd"]	Thomas BATE & Anne WEBB
Feb 2	Richard DAVIES & Susanna PARDO

Baptisms 1722

Mar 28	Mary & Elizabeth daughters of Alexander & Isabel STEVENS
Apr 8	Mary d of John & Jane GROVE
Apr 10	Elisabeth d of Henry & Barbara HACKETT
Apr 14	Mary d of Lawrence & Merial NOXON
Apr 15	Mary d of Edward & Sarah LYTHALL
Apr 22	John s of James & Catharine BECKLEY
Apr 22	Samuel s of William & Elisabeth TAYLER
Apr 28	William s of John & Elizabeth JINKES
May 1	John s of William PARR
May 13	Mary d of Richard & Mary BATE
May 14	Thomas s of Daniel & Sarah DUNN
May 16	John s of Richard & Margaret BROOK
May 19	Judith d of Henry & Judith PHINEY
May 26	Elisabeth d of John & Anne LINES
Jun 4	Matthew an illegitimate child of Mary TAYLER
Jun 13	Anne d of Richard & Alice DUNN
Jun 17	William s of Thomas & Mary RICHARDS
Jun 24	Anne d of Samson & Mary SPENCER
Jun 24	John s of Timothy & Anne SUTCLIFF
Jun 27	Thomas s of Peter & Elisabeth TOY
Jul 5	Edward s of Edward & Mary VEAL
Jul 12	Susannah d of Thomas & Mary WHITE
Jul 22	John s of John & Elisabeth COLE
Jul 29	John s of Sebastion & Mary JONES
Aug 2	Zacharias s of Zacharias & Alice BRIDGENS
Aug 19	Richard s of Joseph & Ann AUDEN
Sep 1	William s of William & Mary KIDSON
Sep 8	Nanny d of Samuel & Elisabeth SMITH
Sep 11	Hannah d of Mr John & Sarah WHITE
Sep 18	Hannah d of John & Hannah JOYCE
Sep 23	James s of John & Mary BAYLIS
Sep 30	Joseph s of William & Elisabeth HARRIS
Sep 30	George s of Richard & Amy PROSER
Oct 6	William s of John & Elisabeth KETTLEY
Oct 14	William s of William & Ann WHITE
Oct 20	William s of Robert & Frances DALE
Oct 23	Jane d of William & Margaret WEBB
Nov 5	Jane an illegitimate child of John & Catherine TURNER
Nov 11	Jane d of Benjamin & Mary POTTER
Nov 24	Sarah d of Richard & Sarah NEWMAN
Dec 5	John s of Christopher & Mary BROWN
Dec 9	Anne d of Joseph & Eleanor EYEERY [BT's: "EYERY"]
Dec 11	Richard s of Mr John COLLEY & Martha his wife
Dec 11	Mary d of John & Sarah CHAMBERLAIN
Dec 24	Mary d of Samuel & Mary WICKWARD
Dec 26	George s of Shadrach & Jane CRUMP
Dec 27	John s of Thomas & Sarah NORRIS
Dec 28	William s of William & Catharine HICKMANS
Jan 20	John s of Gray & Mary CHRISTOPHER

Jan 21   John s of Humphry & Anne BATE
Feb 19   Elisabeth & Hannah the daughters of John & Mary SUCH
Mar 2   George s of Edward & Elisabeth BARTHOLOMEW
Mar 3   William s of John & Mary INCHMORE
Mar 16   Mary d of Samuel & Eleanor WHITE

Burials 1722

Mar 30   Mary DONAWAY with affidavit
Mar 30   John s of Thomas & Martha COOK   with Affidavit
Apr 1   Edward LINES   with Affidavit
Apr 3   Richard B[hole]Y [BT's: "BRADLEY"]   with Affidavit
Apr 5   Mary & Elisabeth the daughters of Alexander STEVENS
Apr 12   Elisabeth d of Henry & Barbara HACKETT
Apr 15   Elizabeth the wife of John TAYLOR   with affid.
Apr 16   Elizabeth d of James BUXTON [BT's: "BUCKSTON"]
Apr 19   Elisabeth d of John TURNER   with Affid.
Apr 21   Martha d of Mr John BRINDLY [BT's: "BRINDLEY"] with Affidavit
May 12   Jesse s of Mr John GROVE   with affidavit
May 24   Mrs Mary CARELESS   with Affidavit
May 27   Elisabeth d of John & Mary TIMMINS   with Affid.
May 27   Anne the wife of William BRADLEY with Affid.
Jun 19   John HAYWOOD with Affidavit
Jun 21   John s of Richard & Margaret BROOK with Affid.
Jun 21   Hannah d of John & Mary SARBET   with Aff.
Jun 22   John ACTON   with affidavit
Jul 3   John s of John & Martha COLLEY with Affidavit
Jul 6   Phebe d of John & Anne COMBER   with Aff.
Jul 6   Isabell GIBBS   with aff.
Jul 7   Mary d of William & Mary LIE   with Affid.
Jul 9   Sarah an illegitimate child of Elizabeth BECKLEY   with Affid.
Jul 10   John s of Timothy & Anne SUTCLIFFE   with Affid.
Jul 12   Mary KNOTT   with Affidavit
Jul 17   Mary LAVENDER
Jul 21   Humphrey HILLMAN   with Affididavit
Jul 26   Mary d of Edward & Sarah DUNN   with Affid.
Jul 27   Mary wid. of William STOKES   with Affid.
Aug 7   Elisabeth d of John & Anne COMBER with Aff.
Aug 9   James s of Thomas FRYAR   with Affidavit
Aug 16   Mary BROWN   with Affid.
Aug 19   Dorothy the wife of Edward HILLMAN with Aff.
Aug 24   Anne HILLMAN widow   with Affidavit
Aug 28   Samuel SMITH   with Affidavit
Sep 7   Thomas s of Daniel DUNN
Sep 7   Sarah the wife of Daniel DUNN
Aug 18   Jane the wife of Samuel BRYAN being misplaced   with Affid.
Sep 20   Sampson s of Samuel & Elizabeth SMITH   with Affid.
Sep 20   John s of John & Hannah JOYCE   with Affid.
Sep 24   John HILLMAN   with Affidavit
Sep 25   Samuel s of John & Catharine TILLEY   with Affidavit

Sep 29	Dorothy WHEATCROFT	
Oct 20	Essex FOLEY d of Robert FOLEY Esqr	with Affidavit
Oct 21	Richard WEBB with Affid.	
Nov 9	Martha the wife of Thomas COOK	with Affid.
Dec 25	Margaret WILLETTS with Affid	
Dec 28	William PERRY with Affid.	
Jan 12	Sarah d of Michael RAYBOLD with Affid.	
Jan 13	Mary d of John CHAMBERLAIN	
Jan 31	Jane the wife of John SUMMERS	with Affid.
Feb 3	Mary d of Mary HILLMAN [Widow]	with Affid.
Feb 8	William s of William TAYLOR with Affid.	
Feb 13	Thomas s of Richard HOLLINS	with Affid.
Feb 21	Sarah BARRETT with Affidavit	
Mar 8	John BROWN an infant with Aff.	
Mar 13	Anne MARTIN with Affid.	
Mar 19	Susannah WHITE an infant with Affid.	
Mar 19	Margery BEELY with Affid.	
Mar 21	John NORRIS an infant with Affid.	

Marriages 1722

Feb 4	William DUNN & Sarah SMITH
Feb 17	Nicholas LEECH & Margery HILLMAN

Baptisms 1723

Mar 31	John s of Thomas & Anne Ellen WALDRON
Apr 27	William s of Thomas & Elisabeth FRYAR
May 19	Elisabeth d of William & Elisabeth PERINS
May 26	William s of John & Elisabeth NORCOTT
Jun 11	Mary d of Samuel & Mary MOSELEY
Jun 20	Dalton s of John & Ruth GREEN
Jun 21	Elisabeth d of Mr Thomas JUKES & Margaret his wife
Jul 15	Joseph s of William & TUMBLINS
Jul 18	John an illegitimate child of Sarah WARREN
Jul 21	Samuel s of John & Mary CRANE
Aug 7	John s of Walter & Elisabeth EGINGTON
Aug 9	William s of Edward & Sarah DUNN
Aug 10	Anne d of Edward & Milicent BROOK
Aug 20	William s of William & Margaret POOL
Aug 23	Betty d of Thomas & Elisabeth SALE
Sep 8	Mary d of Timothy & Anne SUTCLIFFE
Sep 14	Mary d of Samuel & Elisabeth LYE
Sep 16	John s of Richard & Margaret COOK
Sep 21	Thomas s of Thomas & Margaret IDDINS
Sep 25	John s of William & Elisabeth TIMMINS
Sep 29	Elisabeth d of William & Hannah BRICE
Oct 4	Lightfoot s of Mr John BACH & Elisabeth his wife
Oct 4	James s of Philip & Sarah HELY
Oct 27	Margaret d of John & Mary COOK
Oct 29	John & Richard sons of Richard & Margaret PRICE
Nov 12	Hannah d of Edward & Margaret GROVE

Dec 27	Anne d of Joseph & Lydia PARKER
Dec 30	Humphry s of Richard & Margaret BROOK
Jan 8	George s of George & Elisabeth JORDEN
Jan 14	John s of William & Elisabeth TAYLER
Nov 18	Elisabeth d of John & Mary TIMMINS
Dec 2	Edward s of Nicholas & Margery LEECH
Dec 8	Joseph s of John & Anne TOWNSEND
Dec 14	Elisabeth d of Charles & Mary JONES
Jan 30	Joseph s of Christopher & Mary BROWN
Feb 1	John s of Richard & Jane HOLLINS
Feb 2	Sarah d of John & Sarah CHAMBERLAIN
Feb 4	Susannah d of Mr John HODGETS
Feb 11	Jane d of John & Jane BROOK
Feb 12	John s of Joseph & Hannah POOL
Feb 17	George & Martha s & d of Mr John and Mrs Mary BRINDLY
Feb 22	Phebe d of Jonathan & Elisabeth GIBBINS
Feb 22	Hannah d of Thomas & Sarah NORRIS
Mar 10	Paul s of Mr John WHITE & Sarah his wife

Burials 1723

Apr 26	Margery WINFORD with affid.
May 6	Isabel KNIGHT with affid.
May 18	Owen PRICE
Jun 8	Martha wife of Edward CHAMBERLAIN with affid.
Jun 13	Anne BANNISTER with affid.
Jul 4	Mary JOHNSONS with affid.
Jul 9	John LOW with affid.
Aug 4	Thomas NORCOTT with affid.
Aug 11	William DUNN with affid.
Aug 26	Elisabeth EGINGTON with affid
Oct 1	Joseph TUMBLINS an infant with affid.
Oct 2	Elisabeth KETTLEY with affid.
Oct 11	Thomas SARBETT with affid.
Oct 12	Francis NEW with affid.
Oct 20	Judith PRICE with affid.
Oct 22	John MONAX with affid.
Nov 1	Richard s of Richard OLIVER
Nov 30	Thomas EVANS with affid.
Dec 24	Joseph s of John & Anne TOWNSEND
Jan 8	Richard s of Richard PRICE with affid.
Jan 15	Mary d of John DAVIES
Jan 17	John s of William TAYLOR with affid.
Jan 23	Anne the wife of Mr Thomas WALDRON with affid.
Feb 12	Clement HOLLOWAY with affid.
Feb 29	Martha d of Mr John BRINDLEY with affid.
Feb 29	Mary wife of Mr John BRINDLEY with affid.
Mar 1	Joseph s of Christopher BROWN with affid.
Mar 3	Joseph PARKER with affid.
Mar 21	Thomas s of Thomas & Margaret IDDINS with affid.

Marriages 1723

Apr 15	Thomas MASON & Mary DUNN
Apr 25	Richard OLIVER & Elizabeth DOOLITTLE
May 19	Richard LONGFORD & Jane ROBINSON
Jun 2	Humphry YOLDEN & Anne YOLDEN [BT's: "Humphrey YOLDEN & Anne his wife"]
Jun 26	William HADLEY & Elizabeth COATES
Aug 1	Thomas HATCHETT & Sarah WHITE
Sep 9	John CLERK & Mary TREWMAN [BT's: "TRUEMAN"]
Nov 10	John ENGLISH & Anne GEARING
Nov 17	John OSBONE & Mary WIGESBY
Dec 26	George BAKER & Mary HANDY
Jan 1	Edward WILLIAMS & Amy HILLMAN
Feb 17	Luke MECHAM & Elizabeth WORRALL

Marriages 1724

Apr 16	Blower DAVIES & Mary FRYAR
May 24	John WALL & Mary HICKMANS
Jun 28	Robert WITTEN & Hannah PERRY
Oct 12	Benjamin PLANT & Susannah CROUTHER
Dec 21	James TAYLOR & Elisabeth BROWN
Jan 1	Joseph PATCHETT & Mary MOSELEY

Baptisms 1724

Apr 10	Thomas s of Thomas & Mary MASON
Apr 14	Mary d of John & Catharine TILLEY
Apr 16	George s of William & Sarah DUNN
Apr 25	Edward s of Edward & Margery LINES
Apr 25	Margaret d of Henry & Mary CLARKE
Jun 23	William s of William & Elisabeth HADLEY
Jun 27	Sarah d of Lawrence & Merial NOXON
Jul 11	James s of John & Mary DAVIES
Jul 17	Mary d of John TURNER
Jul 21	Elizabeth illegitimate d of Mary TAYLER
Jul 20	Mary d of Thomas & Mary SMITH
Jul 28	Elisabeth d of Edward & Sarah OLIVER
Aug 2	John s of John & Elisabeth JENKES
Aug 10	Katharine d of John & Mary CLERKE
Aug 10	John s of John & Anne LINES
Aug 29	Mary d of James & Elisabeth LENNARD
Sep 5	Lavender s of James & Mary BROWN
Sep 13	Elisabeth d of Richard & Amy PROSER
Sep 16	Joshua s of Timothy & Anne SUTTCLIFF
Sep 22	Sarah d of John & Katharine TURNER
Sep 25	Edward s of Edward HARRIS & Mary his wife
Oct 6	Joseph s of Joseph & Sarah OWEN
Oct 7	Sarah d of Richard & Mary BATE
Oct 17	Anne d of William & Elisabeth ROBINSON
Oct 17	Anne d of Jonathan & Margaret DASH
Oct 25	John s of Edward & Sarah WALDRON

Nov 5	James s of Edward & Jane SMALLMAN
Nov 8	Sarah d of Henry & Barbara HACKETT
Nov 9	Elisabeth d of Anne HANLEY
Nov 14	Anne d of George & Mary BAKER
Nov 24	Humfrey s of Mr John BACH & Elisabeth his wife
Dec 6	Anne d of Edward & Susanah LINES
Dec 10	John s of Edward & Amy WILLIAMS
Dec 12	John s of Richard & Alice LEWIS
Dec 12	Samuel s of Edward & Sarah DUNN
Dec 13	Abigail d of Thomas & Elisabeth FRYAR
Dec 13	Mary d of James & Anne RICHARDS
Dec 25	Joan d of Benjamin & Mary POTTER
Jan 4	Humphrey s of Samuel & Mary MOSELEY
Jan 6	Margarett d of William & Elisabeth TAYLER
Jan 9	Joseph s of James & Katharine BECKLEY
Jan 19	Elizabeth d of John & Mary INCHMORE
Jan 25	Edward s of Thomas & Dorothy HUGHES
Feb 2	Samuel s of Robert & Frances DALE
Feb 13	Samuel and John sons of John & Mary WEBB
Feb 26	Sarah d of Henry & Sarah SMITH
Feb 28	Anne d of Mr Thomas WALDRON & Anne=Ellen his wife
Mar 6	Peregrine an illegitimate son of Eleanor LINES
Mar 10	Roger s of John & Elisabeth COLE
Mar 14	Anne d of John & Jane GROVE

Burials 1724

Apr 4	Joan HORTON with Affidavit
May 1	Anne d of Samson & Mary SPENCER with Affid.
May 19	Mary LEA with Affidavit
Jul 6	William s of William HADLEY with Affid.
Jul 28	Mary RICHARDS with Affidavit
Aug 7	Susannah COWELL with Affidavit
Aug 17	Parnel WARREN with Affidavit
Aug 17	John SUCH
Aug 18	Thomas DUNN with Affidavit
Sep 15	Henry COOK with Affidavit
Oct 8	Margaret DUNN with Affidavit
Oct 14	Anne RICE with Affidavit
Oct 18	Daniel ROWLEY with Affidavit
Nov 18	Sarah wife of Thomas NORRIS with Affidavit
Nov 22	James HILLMAN with Affidavit
Dec 1	Anne d of George & Mary BAKER
Dec 13	Jane the wife of Joseph TUMBLINS with Affid.
Dec 21	George ROGERS with Affid.
Jan 5	Francis WORRALL with Affidavit
Jan 19	Anne d of Penelope SANDYLAND
Feb 10	Thomas GRYFFITH with Affidavit
Feb 20	Mary the wife of Joseph PADGETT with Affidavit
Feb 24	Humphry BATE with Affidavit
Mar 17	Mary the wife of Thomas WHITE with Affidavit

Marriages 1725

May 18	Edward DIXON & Jane GROVE
Oct 31	Timothy PRICE & Mary OVERS
Nov 11	Thomas LAVENDER & Sarah RICHARDS

Baptisms 1725

Mar 27	John s of Samuel & Mary WICKWARD
Mar 30	William s of Christopher & Mary BROWN
Apr 3	Rachel d of William & Sarah KIDSON
Apr 11	Sarah d of John & Sarah BAYLIS
Apr 14	Sarah d of Benjamin & Jane RENSHAW
May 2	Thomas ARKELUS an illegitimate child
May 8	Anne d of Blower & Mary DAVIES
May 22	Richard s of Richard & Margaret COOK
May 26	Mary d of William TUMBLINS
May 31	James s of Thomas & Mary KIDSON
Jun 30	John s of William & Anne WHITE
Jul 2	Mary d of John & Eleanor RAWLEY
Jul 19	William s of William & Mercy TURNER
Jul 24	Mary d of William & Elisabeth THOMAS
Aug 28	Thomas s of Humphrey & Anne BATE
Sep 12	John s of Timothy & Anne SUTCLIFF
Sep 15	Anne d of Samuel & Eleanor WHITE
Sep 20	John s of Zacharias & Alice BRIDGENS
Sep 26	Phebe d of Richard & Mary WOOD
Sep 26	Anne d of James & Elisabeth TAYLOR
Sep 29	Hannah d of John & Anne MOSELEY
Oct 3	Mary d of William & Hannah BRICE
Oct 9	Betty d of Henry & Mary CLERKE
Oct 10	Sarah d of George & Elizabeth JORDEN
Oct 11	Margaret d of Mr Thomas JUKES & Margaret his wife
Oct 20	Martha d of Thomas & Anne BATE
Oct 27	John s of John & Mary SUCH
Oct 30	Elisabeth d of Thomas & Margaret IDDINS
Nov 1	John s of Joseph & Anne MORRIS
Nov 1	Elisabeth d of Gamaliel & Elisabeth BAYLIE
Nov 5	Henry s of John & Elisabeth KEYTLEY
Nov 6	Richard s of John & Elisabeth KETLEY
Nov 14	Benjamin s of Humphry & Elisabeth GARDINER
Dec 10	Mary d of George & Mary BAKER
Dec 12	Mary d of Benjamin & Susannah PLANT
Dec 12	Mary d of Richard & Margaret PRICE
Dec 12	Thomas s of John & Mary HADLEY
Dec 17	William s of Robert & Hannah WITTEN
Jan 7	Elisabeth d of Mr John WHITE & Sarah his wife
Jan 19	Mary d of William & Elisabeth HADLEY
Jan 23	John s of John & Hannah JOYCE
Feb 6	Edmund s of Thomas & Mary MASON
Feb 20	Richard s of Thomas & Dorothy HUGHES

Feb 27   John s of John & Jane BROOK
Feb 8   Humphry s of John & Mary CLERK
Mar 13   Joseph s of Samuel & [blank] RAWLEY
Mar 19   Anne an illegitimate child of Mary ROBINSON
Mar 21   William s of Benjamin & [blank] HARRIS
Mar 22   Oliver s of Edward & Jane DIXON

Burials 1725

Apr 14   Mary wife of James BROWN   with Affidavit
May 18   Margaret wife of Richard BROOK   with Affidavit
May 22   Elizabeth d of Richard PROSER   with Affidavit
May 27   Richard PROSER   with Affidavit
Jun 9   Joseph LAMBERT   with Affidavit
Jun 9   Eleanor LINES   with affidavit
Jun 14   George s of Mr John BRINDLEY   with Affidavit
Jun 17   Jane w of Thomas LYNE   with Affidavit
Jun 21   William ROBINSON   with Affidavit
Jun 20   Margery GEARING   with Affidavit
Jun 27   Margaret TOLLEY   with Affidavit
Jun 30   William s of Christopher & Mary BROWN   with Affid.
Jul 3   Edward s of Thomas & Dorothy HUGHES   with Affidavit
Jul 5   Anne RICHARDS   with Affidavit
Jul 18   Elizabeth TAYLER   with Affidavit
Jul 25   Thomas COOK   with Affidavit
Jul 26   Mary LENNARD   with Affidavit
Sep 6   Sarah d of Richard & Mary BATE   with Aff.
Sep 11   James s of John DAVIS
Oct 29   Anne TAYLER   with Aff.
Nov 24   John BRITTON   with Aff.
Nov 27   John DUNN   with Aff.
Dec 17   Mary wife of Edward WORRALL   with Aff.
Dec 17   Susannah HILLMAN   with Aff.
Dec 21   Grizell FRANKLYN   with Aff.
Dec 22   Thomas NORMCOTT   with Affid.
Jan 17   John TURNER   with Affid.
Jan 20   Sarah wife of Mr Thomas HATCHET   with Affid.
Jan 21   Anne LINES
Feb 3   Edward VEAL   with Affid.
Feb 4   Philip HAYNES   with Affidavit
Feb 8   John COOK   with Affid.
Feb 10   Hannah NORRIS with Affidavit
Feb 12   Alice wife of Thomas EVANS   with Aff.
Mar 13   John TAYLER   with Affid.
Mar 19   Katherine wife of John BRISCOE   with Aff.

Baptisms 1726

Apr 3   Newton s of Mary ASTON illeg.
Apr 15   Richard s of Richard & Dorothy CULSHETH
Apr 18   Major s of John & Jane GROVE
May 1   William s of Richard & Mary KIDSON

May 8	Elizabeth d of Shadrach & Jane CRUMP	
May 21	John s of William & Sarah DUNN	
Jun 2	Jonathan s of Jonathan & Hannah FLUID	
Jun 11	Letitia d of William & Margaret WEBB	
Jun 19	Simon s of John & Mary CRANE	
Jul 1	Richard s of Catharine TURNER widow	
Jul 10	John s of Mr John BACH & Elizabeth his wife	
Aug 18	Catharine d of William & Catharine HICKMANS	
Sep 2	Mary d of Blower DAVIES & Mary his wife	
Sep 7	Samuel s of Richard & Jane HOLLINS	
Sep 8	Esdras s of Richard & Margaret POOL	
Sep 18	Henry s of Christopher & Mary BROWN	
Sep 26	Timothy s of Timothy & Anne SUTCLIFF	
Sep 28	John s of John & Mary TIMMINS	
Sep 30	Martha d of Thomas & Eleanor NORMCOTT	
Oct 29	Catharine d of Robert & Frances DALE	
Oct 30	William s of William & Alice AUDIN	
Oct 30	Anne d of Thomas & Elizabeth SALE	
Nov 5	Priscilla d of John & Sarah CHAMBERLAIN	
Nov 12	James s of James & Elizabeth LENNARD	
Nov 29	Mary d of Edward & Amy WILLIAMS	
Nov 30	Elizabeth d of James & Elizabeth TAYLER	
Dec 5	Margaret d of William & Elizabeth ROBINSON	
Dec 24	Mary d of William & Jane BROOK	
Jan 1	Anne d of John & Mary HODGETS	
Jan 7	John s of Thomas & Mary DUTTON	
Jan 11	Hannah d of Sarah FIELDUS	
Jan 15	William s of William & Elizabeth TAYLER	
Jan 18	Dinah d of John & Elizabeth ROBERTS	
Feb 2	Anne d of Samuel & Sarah PARDOE	
Feb 25	Joseph s of James & Elizabeth NEWMAN	
Mar 17	Margery d of Humphry & Martha BROOK	
Mar 18	Harry s of Edward & Jane DIXON	

Burials 1726

Apr 3	Anne DAVIES	with aff.
Apr 3	Bridget DAWS	with aff.
Apr 4	Humfry PEW	with aff.
Apr 22	Joseph TUMBLINS	with aff.
May 10	Melicent wife of Edward BROOK	with aff.
May 14	Richard BROOK	with affid.
May 16	Thomas BROWN	with affid.
Jun 2	Elisabeth WHERRET	with affid.
Jul 1	William DODSON	with affid.
Jul 2	Margaret BROOK	with affidavit
Aug 29	William BENNISON	with affidavit
Aug 29	Humphry s of John & Mary CLARKE	with no affid.
Sep 1	Esther MOSELEY	with affid.
Sep 1	Rebecca MORRIS	with affid.
Sep 2	Simon s of John & Mary CRANE	with affid.

Sep 29   Elizabeth MOP   with affid.
Oct 15   Peter TOYE   with affid.
Oct 21   Anne wife of James RICHARDS   with affid.
Nov 4   Sarah WEBB   with affidavit
Dec 19   Martha d of Thomas & Eleanor NORMCOTT with affidavit
Dec 21   Mary BATEMAN   with affidavit
Dec 24   Sarah wife of Joseph OWEN   with affid.
Dec 25   Sarah d of William BENNISON with affid.
Dec 26   Mary d of William & Jane BROOK   with affid.
Dec 26   Barbara MOSELEY   with aff.
Dec 30   Thomas BRADLEY   with aff.
Jan 5   Jane d of William BROOK   with aff.
Jan 24   Samuel s of Mr John BRINDLEY   with aff.
Feb 5   Edward SMALLMAN   with aff.
Feb 21   Cornelius DEACON   with aff.
Mar 1   Anne wife of Richard PRICE   with aff.
Mar 7   Joseph s of James & Elisabeth NEWMAN   with aff.
Mar 10   Edward SMALLMAN   with aff.
Mar 16   Richard NEWMAN   with aff.

Marriages 1726

May 29   James NEWMAN & Elisabeth JOHNSONS
Jun 4   Thomas EVANS & Sarah LEA
Jul 7   William PARDOE & Sarah LOWE
Aug 28   William SHELDON & Mary WEABURROW
Sep 24   Edward BROOK & Elisabeth WEBB
Oct 2   Anthony SMITH & Hannah TWICROSS
Oct 27   Benjamin BIRD & Sarah WEBB
Nov 6   Anthony RUSSEL & Elisabeth KETTLEY [BT's: "KETLEY"]
Jan 7   Thomas NOKE & Esther TIMMINS
Jan 25   Walter SWAIN & Elisabeth HOLLIS

Marriages 1727

May 8   Joseph HILLMAN & Elisabeth HANCOKS
Jun 4   John TYSOE & Anne GOUGH
Nov 6   John HOPE & Mary WALLINS
Dec 13   George HARDWICK & Margaret TAYLER
Jan 13   Thomas GITTINS & Elizabeth WALLINS

Baptisms 1727

Mar 25   Elisabeth d of Edward & Margery LINES
Apr 4   John s of Richard & Mary BATE
Apr 5   John s of Richard & Mary WOOD
Apr 9   John s of William & Joyce BOWATER
Apr 26   Arthur s of Richard & [blank] HEYDEN
May 6   Richard s of John & Anne LYNES
May 6   Thomas s of Richard & Alice LEWIS
May 7   Mary d of John & Mary INCHMORE
May 13   John s of Samuel & Abigail LAMBERT
Jun 19   Jane d of John & Anne FOWNES

Jun 19	Thomas s of William & Elisabeth TIMMINS
Jun 10	William s of William & Dorothy TUMBLINS
Jun 15	Joseph s of John & Martha TUNKES
Aug 6	Anne d of Joseph & Jane AUDIN
Aug 13	John s of William & Hannah BRICE
Aug 29	Thomas s of George & Margaret DODSON
Sep 2	Bowers s of John & Mary HADLEY
Sep 14	Sarah d of Benjamin & Mary POTTER
Sep 19	Thomas s of Samuel & Elisabeth LYE
Sep 23	Robert s of Edward & Sarah DUNN
Sep 28	Margaret d of Richard & Margaret COOK
Oct 3	Sarah d of George & Mary BAKER
Oct 9	Sarah d of John & Mary CLARK
Oct 11	Walter s of William & Sarah KIDSON
Oct 12	Betty d of John & Elizabeth COLE
Oct 13	Susannah d of Mr Thomas JUKES & Margaret his wife
Oct 16	Joseph s of Samuel & Sarah BRISCOE
Oct 18	Richard s of Richard & Margaret PRICE
Oct 23	Mary d of John & Mary WALL
Oct 29	Richard s of William FOXALL & Sarah his wife
Nov 5	John s of John & Sarah BAYLIS
Nov 5	Edward s of Thomas & Dorothy HUGHES
Nov 6	Mary d of Benjamin & Sarah WEBB
Nov 18	Betty d of Samuel & Mary WICKWARD
Nov 20	Betty d of Thomas & Anne BATE
Dec 10	John s of Samson & Mary SPENCER
Dec 26	Mary d of Thomas & Eleanor NORMCOTT
Dec 27	Mary d of Susannah LINES illeg.
Dec 27	Mary d of William & Mary SHELDON
Dec 28	Mary d of Gamaliel & Elizabeth BEELY
Jan 7	John s of Stephen & Sarah BACH
Jan 27	Susannah d of John & Mary SUCH
Jan 28	Sarah d of Richard & Sarah BROOK
Jan 29	Arthur, s of Richard & Mary KIDSON
Feb 10	Mary d of Charles & Mary JONES
Mar 14	Eleanor d of Mr John WHITE & Sarah his wife
Mar 16	Thomas s of Thomas & Ester NOKE
Mar 17	Jane & Mary daughters of Jacob & Margrett BUTTON

Burials 1727

Mar 30	Isaac FRYAR with aff.	
May 10	Anne wife of Mr Humphry BATE	with aff.
May 22	Thomas WORRALL with aff.	
Jul 4	John GALLEY with aff.	
Jul 10	Susannah YORK with aff.	
Jul 20	William s of William & Dorothy TUMBLIN	with aff.
Jul 24	Mary SARBETT widow with aff.	
Jul 31	Mary d of William & Elisabeth HADLEY	with
Jul 31	Edward HILLMAN with aff.	
Aug 1	John BATE with aff.	

Aug 5	John WATSON s of John & Mary WATSON	with aff.
Aug 5	Margaret d of John & Mary WATSON	with aff.
Aug 6	Jane ROWLEY	with aff.
Aug 11	William HART	with aff.
Aug 11	Thomas WORRAL	with aff.
Aug 17	Margaret IMMS	with aff.
Aug 19	Elisabeth WILLIAMS	with aff.
Aug 31	Mary KIDSON	with aff.
Sep 4	William EGINGTON	with aff.
Sep 13	Elisabeth d of John TIMMINS	with aff.
Sep 23	James KIDSON	with aff.
Sep 27	Sarah d of Thomas NORRIS	with aff.
Sep 28	Thomas WHITE	with aff.
Sep 27	Elisabeth wife of John KETTLEY misplaced	with aff.
Oct 5	Elisabeth d of Mr John WHITE	with aff.
Oct 9	Robert DALE	with aff.
Oct 13	Mary the wife of James CASWELL	with aff.
Oct 14	John HAYES	with aff.
Oct 19	Margaret wife of Richard PRICE	with aff.
Oct 21	Mary MORRIS	with aff.
Oct 24	Mary d of John NEW	with aff.
Oct 25	Joseph s of Samuel BRISCOE	with aff.
Oct 28	Richard KETLEY	with aff.
Oct 29	William FAUCYTH	with aff.
Nov 12	Richard CLARK	with aff.
Nov 22	Eleanor BIRD	with aff.
Dec 3	Joseph s of John & Martha TUNKES	with aff.
Jan 2	John s of William & Sarah DUNN	with aff.
Jan 3	Katherine BOWERS	with aff.
Jan 3	Jane MILNER	with aff.
Jan 9	John s of Richard & Mary BATE	with aff.
Jan 24	Nicholas WHITE	with aff.
Feb 8	Eleanor WHITE	with aff.
Feb 12	Roger LAMBERT	with aff.
Feb 14	Thomas HARVEY	with aff.
Feb 14	Richard PRICE	with aff.
Feb 16	Edward s of Edward DUNN	with aff.
Feb 24	Samuel s of Edward DUNN	with aff.
Feb 25	Joseph HILLMAN	with aff.
Mar 3	Mary d of Rich PRICE	with aff.
Mar 12	Elisabeth wife of Thomas JOHNSON	with aff.
Mar 13	Timothy s of Timothy & Anne SUTCLIFF	with aff.
Mar 18	Elizabeth PITT widow	with aff.
Mar 20	John RICHARDS with aff.	
Mar 20	Jane & Mary daughters of Jacob & Margaret BUTTON	
Mar 22	William DUNN	with aff.
Mar 10	Richard MOSELEY	with aff.

Marriages 1728

May 23	John LOW & Catherine DAVIS
Jun 1	Henry LAMBERT & Mary TAYLOR
Jul 10	Joseph CHAMBERLAIN & Elisabeth BRADLEY
Sep 6	George GROVE & Alice LYE
Oct 15	Thomas RAYBOULD & Mary COMBER
Feb 6	Humphrey BROWN & Hannah GALLEY
Feb 10	William WARTON & Elizabeth JONES
Feb 16	John PARKS & Elizabeth CORFIELD
Feb 17	John EVERARD & Jane LAMBERTH

Burials 1728

Apr 4	Abigail LAMBERT with aff.
Apr 13	Robert BUTLER with aff.
Apr 15	Joseph EYEERY [BT's: "EYECRY"] with aff.
May 1	Anne wife of John LYNE with aff.
May 15	Thomas s of Joseph OWEN with aff.
May 18	Sarah DONAWAY with affid.
May 21	Mary SMITH widow with aff.
May 26	Elisabeth wife of Edward ALLEN with aff.
May 26	John COOK without Affidavit which was signified to the Church Wardens by a note under my hand Aug 20
Jun 1	Mary BACH with affid.
Jun 9	Mary BROOK with aff.
Jul 1	Merial POOL without Affidavit which was signified to the Church Wardens by a note under my hand Aug 20
Jul 6	Mr Thomas BRINDLEY with aff.
Jul 27	John WALDRON with aff.
Jul 30	Mary DUNN with aff.
Aug 5	Mary CLARKE with aff.
Aug 10	Elizabeth d of William & Elisabeth TOMASON buried without Affidavit which was signified to the Church Wardens by a note under my hand Aug 20
Aug 12	Charles JONES with aff.
Aug 14	Sarah ROGERS with aff.
Aug 16	Margaret GROOBY with aff.
Aug 18	Joseph ROWLEY with aff.
Aug 18	Dorothy GLOVER with aff.
Sep 3	Elizabeth BANNISTER with aff.
Sep 3	Bowers HADLEY with aff.
Oct 9	John s of John NEW with aff.
Oct 10	Mary wife of Richard OLIVER with aff.
Oct 10	Thomas COATES with aff.
Oct 13	Jane wife of Gamaliel BEELEY with aff.
Oct 20	Mary w of John NEW with aff.
Oct 27	Elizabeth KIDSON with aff.
Oct 29	John YORK with aff.
Nov 2	John s of William WHITTAKER with aff.
Nov 5	Thomas LINE with aff.
Nov 25	Susannah wife of Robert DALE with aff.

Nov 26	Thomas JOHNSON with aff.
Nov 30	Richard s of Richard PRICE with aff.
Dec 1	Isabel wife of James SMITH with aff.
Dec 1	Richard s of Samuel & Eleanor WHITE without affidavit which was signified to the Church Wardens Dec 21
Dec 12	Anne DAW with aff.
Dec 13	Elizabeth d of George & Margaret HARDWICK with aff.
Dec 15	Mary LINES with aff.
Dec 29	Laurence NOXON with aff.
Dec 29	Mary wife of John HADLEY with aff.
Dec 24	Eleanor HILLMAN with aff.
Jan 1	Francis BEECH with aff.
Jan 4	William DENT with aff.
Jan 7	William s of William BACH with aff.
Jan 10	George HARRIS with aff.
Jan 11	Edward BANNISTER with aff.
Jan 25	Roger s of John & Elizabeth COLE with aff.
Feb 1	Humphrey CLARKE with aff.
Feb 7	Elizabeth wife of John FORREST with aff.
Feb 10	Mary d of Mr John WHITE with aff.
Feb 19	John FORREST with aff.
Feb 20	Elizabeth wife of George POWEL with aff.
Feb 27	Richard OLIVER with aff.
Feb 27	Anne PERRINS with aff.
Feb 27	Samuel s of William & Joyce BOWATER with aff.
Mar 8	Mary wife of Richard BATE with aff.
Mar 11	Anne wife of Joseph HARRISON with aff.

Baptisms 1728

Apr 17	Frances Eleanor d of Anthony DEAN Esq[r] & Susannah his wife
Apr 22	Thomas s of George & Catherine DUNN
Apr 23	Nathaniel s of John & Jane BROOK
May 12	Susannah d of Benjamin & Jane RENSHAW
May 12	Samuel s of Samuel & Elizabeth RAWLEY
Jun 30	James s of Mary COOK illegitimate
Jul 14	[BT's: "11[thm]"] Sarah d of Edward & Elisabeth BENNISON
Jul 14	Mary d of James & Elizabeth NEWMAN
Jul 19	Margaret d of Thomas & Mary HORAM
Jul 28	Elizabeth d of Benjamin & Susannah PLANT
Sep 22	Elizabeth d of George & Margaret HARDWICK
Sep 28	Richard s of Samuel & Eleanor WHITE
Oct 7	John s of John & Mary NEW
Dec 1	Mary d of John & Mary INSALL
Dec 11	Anne d of Edward & Jane DIXEN
Dec 13	Thomas s of Richard & Sarah BROOK
Dec 19	Martha d of Joseph & Mary COLLEY
Dec 22	Hannah d of Thomas & Elizabeth GITTINS
Jan 15	William s of John & Mary CRANE
Jan 19	Thomas s of John & Katharine TILLEY

Feb 15   Hannah d of Henry & Sarah SMITH
Feb 17   Hannah d of Thomas & Margaret IDDINS
Feb 23   Samuel s of William & Joyce BOWATER
Mar 2   Helene d of Edward & Margery LINES
Mar 9   Mary d of Samuel & Sarah PARDOE
Mar 13   Martha d of William THOMAS & Elisabeth his wife
Mar [?; Bt's: "19th"]   Thomas s of John & Esther CARDALE
Mar 22   Sarah d of Joseph & Elisabeth HILLMAN
           [The following two entries are in the BT's only:]
           "Mar 23   Mary d of Jonathan & Margaret BUTTON
           Mar 24   Elisabeth d of John & Elisabeth JINKES"

Burials 1728

Mar 11   Anne BATE   with aff.
Mar 18   Amy HACKETT   with aff.
Mar 19   Joseph OWEN   with aff.
Mar 20   Richard YORK   with aff.

Baptisms 1728

Mar 23   Mary d of Jonathan & Margaret BURTON
Mar 24   Elisabeth d of John & Elisabeth JINKES

Burials 1729

Mar 30   Thomas COMBRIDGE   with aff.
Mar 31   Hannah d of Thomas & Margaret IDDINS   with aff.
Apr 5   Mary CHAMBERS   with aff.
Apr 12   James REYNOLDS   with aff.
Apr 13   Isabel APPERLY with aff.
Apr 17   Abigail OVERS   with aff.
Apr 19   Elisabeth d of John & Elisabeth JINKES   with aff.
Apr 25   Betty d of Samuel & Mary WICKWARD   with aff.
Apr 28   Elisabeth wife of Edward BENNISON with aff.
May 6   Sarah wife of John LOW   with aff.
May 8   Ann d of Mr Thomas WORRAL   with aff.
May 15   Thomas s of William TAYLER   with aff.
May 18   Thomas NORMCOTT   with aff.
May 18   Margaret d of Mr Richard COOK   with aff.
May 17   Robert s of Edward DUNN   with aff.
Jun 1   John LOW   with aff.
Jun 15   James HARRIS without Affd. which was signified to the
         Officers by a note under my hand July 1
Jun 18   William CHANCE without Affidavit which was signified to the
         Officers by a note under my hand July 1
Jun 18   Mary OLDNALL   without Affidavit which was signified to the
         Officers by a note under my hand July 1
Jul 11   John CLARKE   with aff.
Jul 23   Catharine the wife of Thomas POWELL   with aff.
Aug 18   Margaret wife of Francis WARNER   with aff.
Sep 7   Esau PENSON   with aff.
Sep 14   Esther BRINDLEY   with aff.

Sep 16 John PERRY with aff.
Sep 17 Rowland WHITE with aff.
Sep 29 Richard DOLPHIN with aff.
Oct 4 Joseph HARRISON with aff.
Oct 9 Hannah GRIFFITH with aff.
Oct 12 Hannah MORRIS with aff.
Oct 16 Ann the wife of William CHAMBERS with aff.
Oct 26 Gamaliel BEELEY with aff.
Oct 31 Benson WALDRON with aff.
Nov 3 Eleanor the wife of Henry PERINS with aff.
Nov 6 Ann BECKLEY with aff.
Nov 15 Mary CLARKE with aff.
Dec 10 Dorothy HARRIS with aff.
Dec 17 Mary the wife of Josua MORRIS with aff.
Jan 8 Ann d of William & Mary ONIONS with aff.
Jan 20 Elizabeth MARTIN with aff.
Jan 21 Henry TURNER without aff.
Jan 29 John WARREN with aff.
Feb 5 Thomas PARKS with aff.
Feb 7 Mary RADFORD without aff.
Feb 13 Ann WHITE without Aff. which was signified to John LYE churchwarden by a note under my hand March 16
Feb 14 Jane RENSHAW with aff.
Memorandum that I signified to John LYE Churchwarden that Henry TURNER and Mary RADFORD were buried without any Affidavit by a note under my hand February 19
Feb 21 Margaret d of Thomas & Mary HORAM
Feb 22 Hannah WITTEN without Aff. which was signified to John LYE Church Warden by a note under my hand March 16
Feb 25 Mary ROBINSON with aff.
Feb 26 John s of William WHITE without Aff. which was signified to John LYE church warden by a note under my hand March 16
Feb 27 Hannah d of William WHITE without Aff. which was signified to John LYE church warden by a note under my hand March 16

Baptisms 1729

Apr 13 Anne d of William & Mary ONIONS
May 12 Thomas s of William & Elizabeth TAYLER
May 25 Mary d of John & Sarah CHAMBERLAIN
Jun 13 Arthur s of Thomas & Mary KIDSON
Jul 4 Martha d of Joseph & Esther PLANT
Aug 19 Thomas s of Gabriel & Elisabeth MOYL
Aug 31 William s of Margaret WALLINS illegitimate
Sep 5 Nancy d of Mr John GROVE & Hannah his wife
Oct 7 Anthony s of Anthony DEAN Esqre & Susannah his wife
Oct 12 Sarah d of Samuel & Abigail LAMBERT
Oct 19 William s of William & Hannah BRICE
Oct 22 Elisabeth d of Samuel & Sarah BRISCOE
Nov 1 Mary d of Christopher & Elisabeth TOLLEY
Nov 5 William s of Richard & Mary COOK

Dec 4	Hannah d of William & Elisabeth ROBINSON
Dec 9	Hannah d of John & Mary CLARKE
Jan 2	Margaret d of Richard & Mary WOOD
Jan 17	Joseph s of Thomas & Mary MASON
Jan 17	Mary of Thomas & Mary MASON
Jan 18	Caleb s of Benjamin & Mary POTTER
Jan 17	John s of Thomas & Susanna WARREN
Jan 26	Thomas s of John & Elisabeth PARKS
Jan 31	Paul s of William & Joyce BOWATER
Feb 7	Mary d of Edward & Hannah BROWN
Feb 8	Samson & Bishop sons of Samuel & Elisabeth SMITH
Feb 15	Mary d of Richard & Mary HARRIS
Feb 24	John s of Edward & Sarah OLIVER
Feb 21	Thomas s of Edward & Amy WILLIAMS
Mar 21	Samuel s of Samuel & Mary WICKWARD

Marriages 1729

May 4	William JEVONS & Hannah MORGAN
Jun 24	Christopher TOLLEY & Elisabeth STOKES
Jul 13	Richard JONES & Margaret NEW
Aug 3	Thomas WARREN & Susanna WITTEN
Aug 10	Joseph CROMPTON & Susannah PYM
Oct 31	Moses DILWORTH & Sarah BOWEN
Nov 4	Joseph MOLE & Hannah POWEL
Nov 11	John POWEL & Elisabeth HANCOX
Dec 9	Thomas DARBY & Sarah TIMMINS
Dec 26	John BATE & Anne GOULD
Jan 1	Isaac FRYAR & Elisabeth SMITH
Jan 29	Edward BOWIN & Nan ALLSOP
Feb 10	Humphry FRYAR & Mary HILLMAN

Burials 1729

Mar 2	John s of Edward OLIVER with aff.
Mar 10	Joseph s of Thomas & Mary MASON with aff.
Mar 18	William s of William & Hannah BRICE without Aff. which was signified to Edward OLIVER by a note under my hand Apr 18
Mar 24	Martha d of Joseph & Esther PLANT without Aff. which was signified to Edward OLIVER by a note under my hand Apr 18

Baptisms 1730

Mar 25	Susanna d of John & Elisabeth COLE
Mar 30	John s of John & Hannah DAVIS
Apr 13	George s of George & Mary BAKER
Apr 22	John s of John & Katharine LOW
Apr 22	John s of George & Margaret HARDWICK
May 2	William s of William & Elisabeth HADLEY
May 27	James s of William & Mary HALE
Jul 12	Thomas s of Thomas & Mary DUDTON
Jul 12	Samuel s of James & Elisabeth LENNARD

Jul 26	Sarah d of Moses & Sarah DILWORTH
Aug 23	Mary d of William & Sarah FOXALL
Aug 29	Mary d of Joseph & Susanna CROMPTON
Sep 9	Elisabeth d of Humphrey & Jane DOOLITTLE
Sep 13	George s of John & Ann BATE
Sep 13	Margaret d of Joseph & Hannah MOLE
Sep 18	George s of Daniel & Catharine DUNN
Sep 19	Joseph s of Benjamin & Sarah BIRD
Oct 11	John s of John & Elizabeth POWEL
Oct 16	Thomas s of John & Jane KETLEY
Oct 25	Mary d of Thomas & Esther KNOCK
Oct 31	Mary d of Humphry & Mary FRYAR
Nov 1	Richard s of James & Elisabeth NEWMAN
Nov 5	George s of Christopher & Mary BROWN
Nov 9	Bernard s of Edward & Jane DIXEN
Nov 21	John s of William & Sarah KIDSON
Nov 24	Richard s of Richard & Jane HOLLINS
Nov 29	Ann d of John & Ann TOWNSEND
Dec 6	John s of John & Ann NORTHCOT
Dec 24	Jane d of Edward & Mary LINES
Dec 30	Sarah d of Richard & Margaret COOK
Jan 6	Thomas s of William & Mary SHELDEN
Jan 13	Hannah d of Samuel & Joyce WHITE
Jan 22	Richard s of Thomas & Susanna WARREN
Jan 23	John s of Benjamin & Susannah PLANT
Jan 26	William s of William & Elisabeth SEAGER
Jan 30	Ann d of Margaret HILLMAN illegitimate

Burials 1730

Mar 26	Esther the wife of Joseph PLANT	without Aff. whereof notice was given to Mr John BRINDLY by note under my hand
Mar 31	Sarah d of James & Mary RICHARDS	without Aff. whereof notice was given to Mr John BRINDLY by note under my hand
Mar 31	Mary DODSON with aff.	
Apr 2	Benjamin BECKLEY with aff.	
Apr 5	John s of John & Jane BROOK with aff.	
Apr 9	Elisabeth d of Walter LITTLETON Esqr with aff.	
Apr 15	Nancy d of Mr John GROVE with aff.	
Apr 19	Betty d of Henry & Mary CLERKE with aff.	
Apr 28	Ann HAYNES with aff.	
May 16	Richard LINES with aff.	
May 21	William ONIONS with aff.	
Jul 7	William TIMMINS with aff.	
Jul 10	Mary RUSSELL with aff.	
Sep 30	Jane WEBB with aff.	
Nov 2	Thomas EVANS with aff.	
Nov 6	Richard HOLLINS with aff.	
Dec 28	Jane d of Edward & Mary LINES with aff.	

Dec 30 Sarah d of Richard & Margaret COOK   with aff.
Jan 3   Margaret BARRETT   with aff.
Jan 6   Ann BURTON .
Jan 18 George DUNN
Jan 28 Richard s of John & Mary RICE   with aff.
Feb 3   Ann d of Margarett HILLMAN
Feb 14 Benjamin PLANT with affidavit
Feb 18 George s of Christopher & Mary BROWN   with aff.
Mar 4   Mary GRANGER of the City of London
Mar 6   Mary d of James & Katharine BECKLEY   with aff.
Mar 7   Susanna d of Daniel DUNN

Baptisms 1730
Feb 21 Sarah d of William & Hannah BRICE
Feb 24 Ann d of John & Martha TUNKES [BT's: "TUNKS"]
Mar 10 William s of Samuel & Sarah PARDOE

Marriages 1730
Apr 16 John THOMAS & Susanna YORK
May 17 Thomas RICHARDS & Mary DODSON
May 19 Joseph AUDIN & Ann BROOK
May 20 Richard LINE & Mary OLIVER
Jul 29 Thomas KIDSON & Elisabeth RENOLES
Sep 14 John PADGET & Elizabeth BARNET
Oct 12 John RICHARDS & Mary BAXTER
Nov 8   Richard BATE & Ann CHANCE
Nov 10 Humfrey BATE & Jane MOUNSTEVEN
Nov 12 Thomas BROWN & Sarah PARKS
Dec 8   Samuel CARELESS & Sarah GREEN
Dec 26 Thomas BAYLIS & Ann ENGLISH
Jan 19 John PARRY & Margaret BANNISTER
Jan 28 William COATES & Jane BANNISTER
Feb 4   Edward BLUN & Elisabeth SMITH
Feb 6   Thomas BAYLIS & Ann FRYAR

Burials 1731
Mar 28 Edward CHAMBERLAIN   with aff.
Apr 6   Ann PARDOW [BT's: "PARDEN"]   with aff.
Apr 8   Sarah d of William & Hannah BRICE
May 8   Isabel the wife of Thomas GROVE   with aff.
May 12 The Rev^d Mr James HILLMAN Master of the free school of Brood
May 26 Elisabeth the wife of Thomas GITTINS   with aff.
May 26 John NORMCOTT   with aff.
Jun 6   Elisabeth the wife of Walter LITTLETON Esqr with aff.
Jul 1   Mr John BRINDLEY   with aff.
Jul 5   Arthur KIDSON   with aff.
Jul 21 Thomas s of Timothy & Ann SUTCLIFF.
Jul 23 Moses s of Ann MASON
Jul 26 Mary the wife of Edward BIRD   with aff.

Jul 27	Edward BENNISON	with aff.
Jul 28	Harry s of Christopher & Mary BROWN	with aff.
Jul 30	Nathaniel s of John & Jane BROOK	with aff.
Jul 31	William s of William & Hannah BROOK	with aff.
Jul 31	John s of Timothy & Ann SUTCLIFF	with aff.
Aug 9	Elisabeth d of William & Hannah BRICE	with aff.
Aug 14	John s of John & Mary RICHARDS	with aff.
Aug 17	Letitia d of William & Margaret WEBB	with aff.
Aug 17	Hannah d of John & Ann MOSELEY	with aff.
Aug 19	Benjamin GARDINER	with aff.
Aug 25	Ann POWELL	with aff.
Sep 1	Robert ROBERTS	
Sep 12	John s of Richard & Margaret COOK	with aff.
Sep 21	Mary d of Richard & Margaret COOK	with aff.
Sep 21	Richard s of Richard & Margaret COOK	with aff.
Oct 4	John s of the Rev^d Mr William YATE & Martha his wife	with aff.
Oct 9	Thomas MOSELEY	with aff.
Sep[sic] 30	Thomas JOHNSON [BT's: say "misplaced"]	with aff.
Oct 9	Barnett DIXON	with aff.
Oct 20	Joseph AUDIN	with aff.
Oct 23	Ann ROBINSON	with aff.
Oct 24	Harry DIXON	with aff.

Baptisms 1731

Apr 24	John s of William & Alice AUDEN
Apr 29	John s of Thomas & Mary RICHARDS
May 29	Mary d of Thomas & Mary KNOWLES
Jun 13	Thomas s of John & Jane BROOK
Jun 17	Mary d of Richard & Mary LINE
May 16	Thomas s of John & Hannah GROVE misplaced
Jul 4	William s of William & Hannah BROOK
Jul 9	Thomas s of Timothy & Ann SUTCLIFF
Jul 21	Moses s of Ann MASON illegitimate
Aug 1	Joseph s of Joseph & Ann AUDIN
Aug 8	Josias s of Samuel & Elisabeth RAWLEY [BT's: "RAWLY"]
Aug 17	John s of the reverend^d Mr William YATE & Martha his wife
Aug 21	Elisabeth d of William & Elisabeth TAYLER
Aug 29	Jane d of Humfrey & Jane DOOLITTLE
Oct 12	Margery d of James & Elisabeth TAYLER
Oct 15	Mary d of John & Mary STOCKIN
Oct 16	Sarah d of Christopher & Elisabeth TOLLEY
Nov 14	John s of Benjamin & Sarah HARRIS
Nov 18	James s of John & Mary RICHARDS
Nov 18	Rebekkah d of John & Mary RICHARDS
Dec 5	Joseph s of William & Sarah LYE
Dec 28	Sarah d of William & Mary HEMMIN
Jan 9	Mary d of James & Mary BARRETT
Jan 16	Ann d of William & Sarah ROBINSON
Jan 22	Jane d of John & Sarah BAYLIS

Jan 23	Jane d of John & Mary INCHMORE
Feb 5	Elisabeth d of Joseph & Mary SHAW
Feb 12	Mary d of Richard & Mary WOOD
Feb 26	Betty d of George & Elisabeth JORDAN
Mar 4	Sarah d of John & Katharine LOW
Mar 5	Martha d of John & Sarah CHAMBERLAIN
Mar 10	Elisabeth d of Thomas & Margaret COOK
Mar 11	William s of Humphrey & Hannah BROWN
Mar 23	Jane d of Edward & Margery LINE
Mar 23	Mary d of John & Ann HAMMERS

Marriages 1731

Apr 25	Richard EILLBEACK [BT's: "EILBEACK"] & Ann HAWKES
May 9	William ROBINSON & Sarah HUTT
Jun 14	William WHITE & Sarah DUNN
Jul 1	Thomas COOK & Margaret HILLMAN
Jul 20	John SHINTON & Sarah TRUEMAN
Oct 17	Jeremy TRUEMAN & Mary BIVAN
Nov 30	William BRYON & Mary RUSSEL
Dec 25	Robert MILLS & Elisabeth ROSE
Jan 23	The Rev^d Mr John BIRCH & Mrs Elizabeth WOOD
Jan 27	John MATHER & Mary BEELEY
Feb 21	William CHAMBERS & Elizabeth NORMCOTT

Burials 1731

Oct 27	Hannah ROBINSON with aff.
	Memorandum that I signified to Mr John GREEN Church Warden that the Rev^d Mr James HILLMAN, Mr John BRINDLEY, Thomas SUTCLIFFE, Moses MASON, Robert ROBERTS, were buried without Affidavits of their being buried in woollen By a note under my Hand November 2
Nov 4	Sushannah HATCHET with aff.
Nov 7	Mary d of John & Mary STOCKIN with aff.
Nov 12	Richard COATES with aff.
Nov 27	Rebeckkah d of John & Mary RICHARDS with aff.
Dec 2	Matthew MASON with aff.
Dec 6	Elizabeth JONES with aff.
Dec 26	Mary MASON with aff.
Jan 2	Margaret the wife of George HARDWICK with aff.
Jan 12	Mr Richard WORRALL with aff.
Jan 14	Elizabeth YEARNSHAW with aff.
Jan 21	Hannah the wife of William BROOK with aff.
Jan 30	Thomas s of Richard & Alice LEWIS with aff.
Feb 6	Hannah the wife of Joseph POOL with aff.

Baptisms 1732

Mar 27	Elijah s of Benjamin & Mary GROVE
Mar 27	Richard s of John & Mary TIMMINS
Apr 16	Edward s of Gabriel & Elisabeth MOILE
Apr 16	Joan d of William & Elisabeth ROBINSON

Apr 23	John s of John & Mary TILLEY
Apr 23	Mary d of Thomas & Ann BAYLIS
May 12	Mary d of Edward & Sarah DUNN
May 12	Roger s of John & Elisabeth COLE
May 30	Mary d of James & Catharine BECKLEY
Jun 9	Elisabeth d of Richard & Alice LEWIS
Jun 11	Mary d of John & Ann BATE
Jun 24	Betty d of Isaac & Elisabeth FRYAR
Jul 12	Mary d of Simon & Jane WALKER
Jul 19	Ann d of John & Mary SUCH
Jul 22	Catherine d of John & Elisabeth POWEL
Jul 23	Joseph s of Joseph & Sarah GUEST
Jul 30	John s of Moses & Sarah DILWORTH
Aug 3	Mary d of John & Elisabeth PARKS
Aug 5	John s of John & Mary CLARKE
Aug 19	Harry s of Harry & Mary CLARKE
Sep 24	William s of John & Mary STOCKIN
Sep 27	Elisabeth d of Edward & Jane DIXON
Oct 8	Thomas s of William & Hannah BRICE
Oct 13	Samuel s of Timothy & Ann SUTCLIFF
Oct 14	Thomas s of Thomas & Mary RICHARDS
Oct 15	Hannah d of Mr [BT's: "Master"] John GROVE & Hannah his wife
Nov 6[sic]	William s of Samuel & Mary WICKWARD
Oct 19	Martha d of Thomas & Mary MASON
Oct 29	Humfry s of John & Eleanor COLEBORN
Nov 16	Thomas s of Edward & Elisabeth HOPKINS
Dec 2	Richard s of John & Sarah SHINTON
Dec 5	Joseph s of Joseph & Ann AUDIN
Dec 9	William s of Robert & Elisabeth MILLS
Dec 27	John s of John & Mary INSALL
Dec 27	Mary d of James & Elisabeth TAYLER
Dec 28	Martha d of Christopher & Elisabeth TOLLY
Jan 6	John s of Young & Elisabeth LAMBERT
Jan 7	Thomas s of John & Ann NORMCOTT
Jan 7	Thomas s of Mary PERRY Illegitimate
Jan 24	Edward s of John & Ann TYSOE
Feb 6	Elisabeth d of Elisabeth FELLOWS illeg.
Feb 12	Richard s of Richard & Mary HARRIS
Feb 17	Sarah d of William & Sarah FOXALL
Mar 3	John s of John & Sarah BATE
Mar 24	Arthur s of William & Sarah KIDSON

Burials 1732

Apr 22	Mr John COMBER With Aff.
Apr 24	John s of John DAVIS With Aff.
May 31	Edward TAYLER With Aff.
Jun 5	John MOUNSTEVEN
Jun 17	Mary d of Thomas & Mary KNOWLES with Affidavit
Jul 17	Mary d of Simon & Jane WALKER with Aff.

Aug 27   Ann HOLLINS   with Aff.
Oct 3   Isabel the wife of George BAKER
Oct 4   William, Ann & Mary PARDOE   with Aff.
Oct 10   Ann CRANDAGE   with Aff.
Oct 12   Mary the wife of Christopher BROWN with Aff.
Oct 17   Hannah d of Mr [BT's: "Master"] John GROVE & Hannah his wife   with Aff.
Oct 22   Mary AUDEN   with Aff.
Nov 14   Humfrey COLEBORN
Nov 15   Sarah WHITE
Dec 18   Sarah BOWEN   with Aff.
Jan 8   Edward HILLMAN   with Aff.
Jan 27   Thomas SMALLMAN
Feb 8   Hannah the wife of John TROWMAN [BT's: "TRUEMAN"] with Aff.
Feb 8   Elisabeth FELLOWS
Feb 10   Mary ROBINSON   with Aff.
Feb 11   Mary HILLMAN   with Aff.
Mar 5   William DUCKHOUSE
Mar 13   Thomas s of William & Hannah BRICE
Mar 19   Thomas s of Mr [BT's: "Master"] John GROVE   with Aff.
Mar 20   Henry BARRET

Memorandum that I signified to Mr Thomas HATCHETT Church warden by a note under my hand March 21 that Isabel BARKER, Humfrey COLEBORN, Sarah WHITE, Thomas SMALLMAN, Elisabeth FELLOWS, William DUCKHOUSE were buried without Affidavits of their being buried in woollen.

Memorandum that I signified to Mr John HODGETS overseer of the Poor by a note under my hand March 21 that Thomas son of William & Hannah BRICE, Henry BARRETT were buried without Affidavits of their being buried in woollen.

Marriages 1732

Apr 8   Stephen HIGGS & Elisabeth TILLEY
Apr 17   Joseph PLANT & Ann PATCHET
Sep 3   Elijah WHITE & Mary FOURNACE
Nov 2   Samuel JEAVONS & Hannah DALE
Dec 23   Richard PRICE & Mary HILLMAN
Dec 26   Thomas SKINNER & Susanna SARBETT
Jan 6   Jonathan VEAL & Margery PERINS
Feb 3   Thomas PERINS & Sarah WALLIS

Burials 1733

Mar 25 [BT's: "26th"]   John s of John & Mary CLARKE
Apr 10   Edward DIXON   with Aff.
Apr 11   Mr [BT's: "Master"] John COMBER   with Aff.
May 2   Joyce PLANT   with Aff.
May 6   Edward s of John & Ann TYSOE   with Aff.
Jun 6   Sarah d of George & Mary BAKER

Jun 8	Lydia LINES
Jun 26	Elisabeth the wife of Joseph HILLMAN with Aff.
Jun 3	Sarah the wife of John BATE with Aff.
Jul 6	Mary WARREN
Jul 7	Mary HATTEN
Jul 14	Sarah wife of Mr [BT's: "Master"] John WHITE with Aff.
Aug 20	Joseph BROWN with Affidavit
Aug 23	Walter LITTLETON Esquire with Affidavit
Oct 28	Richard WARREN with Affidavit
Nov 8	Sarah JOHNSON with Affidavit
Nov 8	John s of John & Elisabeth PARKS
Dec 1	Frances COLTS
Jan 16	Elisabeth HARVEY With Affidavit
Jan 29	Joan d of William & Elisabeth ROBINSON With Affidavit
Feb 1	Sarah STOKES
Feb 10	Elisabeth SHAW With Affidavit
Feb 17	Elisabeth INCHMORE With Affidavit
Mar 5	Sarah the wife of William FOXAL With Affidavit

Baptisms 1733

May 5	Jarvis s of John & Frances BURFORD
May 6	Samuel of Samuel & Sarah PARDOE
May 14	Sarah d of Edward & Elisabeth BLUN
May 15	Hannah d of Benjamin & Sarah HALL
May 19	Betty d of Ann SMALLMAN Illegitimate
May 27	John s of John & Jane BROOK
Jun 2	Lydie d of Phebe LINES illegitimate
Jun 13	Ann d of William & Mary ESSELBY
Jun 17	Benjamin s of the Rev^d Mr [BT's: "Master"] William YATE & Martha his wife
Jun 24	Elisabeth d of James & Elisabeth LENNARD
Jul 8	William s of Thomas & Mary DUTTON
Jul 22	Betty d of William & Mary HORTON
Aug 5	Sarah d of John & Mary INCHMORE
Aug 18	John s of William & Mary SHELDON
Aug 19	Susannah d of Benjamin & Susannah PLANT
Sep 2	John s of Thomas & Hannah WARREN
Sep 19	Mary d of William & Mary HEMMINS
Sep 29	Hannah d of Samuel & Hannah JEAVONS
Oct 13	Edward of George & Catharine DUN
Oct 22	Mary d of William & Jane WALFOOT
Oct 31	John s of Richard & Margaret COOK
Nov 1	Elisabeth d of John & Katharine LOW
Nov 4	Eleanor d of Thomas & Sarah PERINS
Nov 3	John s of John & Elisabeth PARKS
Nov 10	George s of George & Mary BANES
Dec 8	Ann d of William & Eleanor HAINES
Dec 12	Mary d of Jonathan & Margery VEAL
Dec 23	Hannah d of James & Elisabeth NEWMAN
Dec 27	William s of Thomas & Jane KETLEY

Dec 31 Robert s of Richard & Mary SPENCER
Jan 16 Hannah d of Elisabeth BUCKSTON
Jan 23 Joseph s of Sarah COOK
Feb 2   Elisabeth d of Christopher & Elisabeth TOLLEY
Feb 23 Mary d of Harry & Mary CLARKE
Feb 26 Hannah d of Benjamin & Mary POTTER
Feb 24 Phebe d of Hannah LINES
Mar 3   Thomas s of Thomas & Ann BAYLIS
Mar 3   Hannah d of John & Ann TYSOE
Feb 18 Sarah d of William & Sarah VEAL misplaced
Mar 17 Amy d of William & Hannah BRICE
Mar 17 Betty d of Samuel & Elisabeth SMITH

Marriages 1733

May 12 William JOHNSON & Sarah KIDSON
May 13 John HOLLINS & Jane BEELEY [BT's: "BEELY"]
Jun 15 William VEAL & Sarah TROW
Sep 8   Joseph COOKSEY & Ann KETLEY
Sep 30 John LEA & Jane RICE
Oct 23 Joseph BEEMAN & Hannah NEW
Nov 4   John HARWOOD & Sarah BROOK
Nov 15 John TRUEMAN & Sarah SARBIT
Nov 19 William HAINES & Eleanor WHITE
Dec 23 Edward BANNISTER [BT's: "BANISTER"] & Mary EATON
Dec 26 James NEWMAN & Joanna ALLDEN
Dec 26 John TONKES & Ellen WALHOUSE
Feb 7   Christopher BROWN & Mary BROOK

Burials 1734

Apr 2   Betty NEWMAN
Apr 4   Mary d of John & Mary INCHMORE   with Affidavit
Apr 6   Margaret LOCKHART   with Affidavit
Apr 7   Thomas GITTINS
Apr 27 Richard s of William & Mary HADLEY with Affidavit
May 8   Edward BIRD   with Affidavit
May 30 Edward DUN   with Affidavit
Jun 7   Eleanor d of Mr [BT's: "Master"] John WHITE   with Affidavit
Jun 9   Samuel s of James & Elisabeth LENNARD   with Affidavit
Jul 12 Mary RAWLEY   with Affidavit
Aug 31 John s of Moses & Sarah DILWORTH   with Affidavit
Sep 5   Mary d of Thomas & Mary DUTTON   with Affidavit
Oct 12 John HORTON   with Affidavit
Oct 17 Betty d of Ann SMALLMAN
Oct 30 Eleanor the wife of William WHITE
Nov 8   William s of Thomas & Jane KETLEY with Aff.
Jan 15 Joan MATHERS   with Affidavit
Jan 20 Jane KETLEY   with Aff.
Jan 26 John s of John & Mary INSULL [BT's: "INSHALL"] with Affidavit

Memorandum that I signified to Mr Francis HATCHETT Overseer of the Poor by a note under my hand February 11 that Betty SMALLMAN and Eleanor WHITE were Buried without Affidavits of their being Buried in woollen

Feb 21 George DAVIES without Affidavit which I signified to John TIMMINS Church Warden by a Note under my hand March 4

Baptisms 1734

Apr 6	Margaret d of Charles & Mary JONES
Apr 6	Richard s of William & Mary HADLEY
Apr 6	Thomas s of Thomas & Margaret COOK
Apr 15	Sarah d of John & Ann BATE
Apr 15	Hannah d of Henry & Sarah SMITH
Apr 20	Hannah d of William & Sarah JOHNSON
May 5	Elisabeth d of John & Mary STOCKIN
Jun 9	Elisabeth d of George & Mary BAKER
Jun 11	Elisabeth d of Richard & Sarah BROOK
Jul 6	Benjamin s of Edward & Margery LINE
Jul 7	Mary d of John & Mary CLARK
Jul 7	John s of John & Jane LEA
Jul 14	Mary d of Moses & Sarah DILWORTH
Jul 17	Joseph s of John & Elisabeth NEW
Jul 17	Mary d of John & Elisabeth NEW
Jul 20	Thomas s of John & Jane HOLLINS
Jul 28	John s of William & Ann PERREY
Jul 28	Samuel s of Young & Elisabeth LAMBETH
Aug 11	Abraham s of John & Sarah CHAMBERLAIN
Aug 18	John s of John & Sarah SHINTON
Aug 21	Joseph s of Robert & Elisabeth MILLS
Aug 28	John s of John & Sarah TRUEMAN
Sep 3	Thomas s of Mr [BT's: "Master"] Thomas LOW & Sarah his wife
Sep 8	Ann d of John & Elisabeth PARKS
Oct 6	Mary d of John & Frances BURFORD
Oct 20	Prudence d of Edward & Mary BANNISTER [BT's: "BANISTER"]
Oct 22	Mary d of Edward & Elisabeth HOPKINS
Oct 23	John s of Samuel & Sarah OWEN
Oct 29	John s of William & Eleanor WHITE
Nov 1	William s of Joseph & Mary SMALMAN
Dec 11	Thomas s of James & Mary BARRET
Dec 14	Hannah d of John & Elisabeth POWEL
Dec 24	Betty d of Samuel & Mary WICKWARD [BT's: "WICKARD"]
Jan 9	John s of William & Elisabeth TAYLER
Feb 1	William s of William & Sarah ROBINSON
Feb 8	Martha d o John & Jane BROOK
Feb 21	Catharine d of [In OR looks like name "Jeremiah" was entered and then altered. BT's: "James"] & Elisabeth CASWELL
Mar 9	Benjamin s of Samuel & Elisabeth RAWLEY
Mar 10	Edward s of Christopher & Elisabeth TOLLEY

Mar 10 Sarah d of Joseph & Hannah BEEMAN
Mar 22 Sarah d of Samuel & Sarah PARDOE

Marriages 1734
May 12 John SIMS & Mary HARRIS
May 23 John CRUNDAL & Hannah DANCER
May 26 William WHITE & Eleanor LINES
Dec 27 Thomas FERIDAY & Susanna DUNN
Feb 10 Thomas LANDORE & Hannah JOICE
Feb 18 William CLEMSON & Elisabeth DARBY

Baptisms 1735
Mar 29 Joseph s of William & Alice AUDEN
Mar 30 John s of Thomas & Mary RICHARDS
Apr 20 Joan d of William & Mary HORTON
May 11 John s of George & Elisabeth JORDAN
May 11 Harry s of William & Hannah BRICE
May 21 Ann d of James & Joanna NEWMAN
May 31 John s of James & Catharine BECKLEY
Jun 28 Joseph s of John & Mary INSULL [BT's: "INSALL"]
Jul 12 Ann d of Philip & Elisabeth HAINS
Jul 26 Mary d of John & Mary SIMS
Jul 27 Mary d of Samuel & Hannah JEVANS
Aug 3   John s of Giles & Elisabeth LINGHAM
Aug 9   Mary d of Thomas & Dorothy HUGHES
Aug 24 Ann d of Richard & Mary HARRIS
Sep 9   Thomas s of James & Elisabeth TAYLER
Sep 13 James s of Sarah ROGERS Illegitimate
Sep 19 William s of Samuel & Sarah OWEN
Oct 12 Nathanael s of Joseph & Ann AUDIN
Oct 16 Elisabeth d of Thomas & Prudence HILL
Oct 18 Susanna d of John & Mary SUCH
Nov 15 Hannah d of Thomas & Mary MASON
Dec 10 Eleanor d of Richard & Mary LINE
Jan 10 Elisabeth d of Thomas & Hannah LANDORE
Jan 18 Joseph s of Joseph & Mary SMALMAN
Jan 18 William s of William & Eleanor HAINS
Jan 21 Catharine d of Mr John GROVE & Hannah his wife
Jan 24 Thomas s of William & Mary ESSELBY
Jan 8   Mary d of William & Elisabeth TAYLER
Feb 7   Betty d of William & Sarah JOHNSON
Feb 14 Robert s of John & Sarah SHINTON
Feb 23 Thomas s of Thomas & Hannah CLOWES
Feb 28 John s of Thomas & Margaret COOK
Feb 29 Mary d of William & Elisabeth CLEMSON
Mar 4   Harry s of John & Sarah BAYLIS
Mar 7   Nancy d of John & Lydie PARDOE
Mar 14 Thomas s of Thomas & Susanna FERIDAY
Mar 14 Thomas s of Thomas & Susanna WARREN
Mar 15 Edward s of Joseph & Ann LYE

Mar 24 Edward s of Edward & Mary DICKIN

Burials 1735

Apr 3 Joseph DAW buried without a regular Affidavit where of notice was given to John TIMMINS Church Warden by a note under my hand May 12
May 11 Francis s of William & Jane WALFOOT buried without Affidavit whereof notice was given to Mr John GROVE Overseer of the Poor by a note under my hand June 21
May 27 Mary d of John & Frances BURFORD buried without Affidavit whereof notice was given to Mr John GROVE Overseer of the Poor by a note under my hand June 21
May 31 Susanna HILLMAN   with Aff.
Jun 1 Sarah CRUNDALL   with Aff.
Jun 9 Susanna d of John & Mary HODGETS   with Affid.
Jun 21 Mary WHITE   with Aff.
Jul 3 Margaret d of Charles & Mary JONES   with Aff.
Jul 12 Mary d of Thomas & Ann BAYLIS   with Aff.
Jul 25 Susanna d of John & Mary SUCH buried without Aff. whereof I gave notice to John TIMMINS Sept 2
Aug 11 Richard s of Richard & Jane HOLLINS   with Aff.
Aug 11 Mary d of Thomas & Dorothy HUGHES buried without Aff. whereof I gave notice to John TIMMINS Sept 28
Aug 16 Ann the wife of Robert PARKS without Affidavit
Sep 1 William TAYLER without Affidavit
Oct 28 Sarah the wife of Samuel PARDOE   with Aff.
Nov 5 Elisabeth the wife of Gabriel MOILE   with Aff.
Nov 13 Mary d of John & Ann BATE   without Affidavit
Nov 27 Mary JEAVONS with Affidavit
Dec 2 William FOLEY Esquire with Affidavit
Dec 22 Henry WARD   without Affidavit
Dec 22 Abigail ROGERS widow without Affid.
I gave Notice January the 7th to Mr Shadrach CRUMP by a Note under my hand that Ann PARKS, William TAYLER, Mary BATE, Henry WOOD, widow ROGERS were buried without Affidavit.
Jan 22 William PERRINS   with Aff.
Feb 20 Samuel DAVIS   with Aff.

Marriages 1735

Apr 9 John BIRD & Elisabeth RICHARDS
Jul 2 Edward DICKIN & Mary TIMMINS
Oct 7 Robert TAYLER & Elisabeth ESSELBE
Nov 24 Joseph NEEDHAM & Sarah DUN
Feb 3 Joseph GALE & Betty BUXTON

Burials 1735

Mar 12 James s of Sarah ROGERS without Aff whereof Notice was given to Shadrach CRUMP May 5 1736
Mar 14 William HADLEY without Affidavit whereof Notice was given to Shadrach CRUMP Overseer of the Poor May 5 1736

Baptisms 1736

Mar 28	Mary d of John & Mary STOCKIN
Apr 5	Henry s of William & Sarah KIDSON
Apr 9	Joseph s of Joseph & Sarah LEABORN
Apr 11	Francis s of William & Jane WALFOOT
Apr 16	Sarah d of John & Sarah TRUEMAN
Apr 26	Betty d of Edward & Elisabeth BLUN
Apr 29	William s of Edward & Mary BANNISTER
Apr 30	Thomas s of Josias & Mary RAWLEY
May 15	Thomas s of Jonathan & Margery VEAL
May 22	William s of Joseph & Mary GREEN
Jun 6	Mary d of John & Jane LEA
Jun 13	Hannah d of Richard & Jane LAWRENCE
Jun 20	Charles General s of Charles & Mary JONES
Jul 3	Peter s of Moses & Sarah DILWORTH
Jul 3	Elisabeth d of Thomas & Mary DUTTON
Jul 17	William s of William & Mary HEMMIN
Jul 25	William s of William & Ann PERRY
Aug 1	Thomas s of John & Hannah CRUNDALL
Aug 1	William s of Christopher & Elisabeth TOLLEY
Aug 6	Samuel s of John & Margaret FARLEY
Aug 27	Elisabeth d of Jeremiah & Elisabeth CASWEL
Sep 4	Benjamin s of Benjamin & Mary POTTER
Sep 26	Henry s of John & Elisabeth BIRD
Sep 28	Phebe s of Mary WALL Illegitimate
Oct 9	William s of John & Eleanor COLEBORN
Oct 23	William s of William & Jane COATES
Oct 23	Samuel s of Samuel & Sarah OWEN
Nov 7	Sarah d of James & Joanna NEWMAN
Nov 21	Elisabeth d of William & Mary PUTSEY
Nov 28	Benjamin s of John & Jane BROOK
Dec 5	Mary d of Richard & Margaret COOK
Dec 18	Samson s of James & Elizabeth LENNARD
Dec 23	Ann d of John & Ann TYSOE
Dec 27	Susanna d of John & Sarah CHAMBERLAIN
Jan 8	Mary d of Elisabeth LOW illegitimate
Jan 16	William s of William & Mary HUTT
Jan 29	Elisabeth d of Robert & Elisabeth MILLS
Jan 30	Thomas s of William & Elisabeth PERIGO
Feb 1	Thomas s of Ann SMALLMAN illegit.
Feb 8	Jesse s of Benjamin & Mary GROVE
Feb 9	Catharina d of Edward & Elisabeth HOPKINS
Mar 1	Sarah d of Thomas & Mary GREEN
Mar 2	William s of Samuel & Hannah JEVANS
Mar 5	Philip s of Philip & Elisabeth HAYNES
Mar 6	Ann d of Richard & Mary SPENCER
Mar 6	John s of George & Mary BAKER
Mar 7	Benjamin s of Thomas & Mary RICHARDS
Mar 24	Mary d of William & Anna Elisabetha CHURCHARD

Burials 1736

Apr 7	Thomas s of Thomas & Susanna WARREN with Aff.
Apr 18	Robert FOLEY Esquire with Affidavit
May 8	Jane the wife of Humfrey BATE with Aff.
May 16	John s of John & Elisabeth POWEL without Affidavit whereof Notice was given to William PUTSEY Overseer of the Poor by a note under my hand July 22
May 31	Ann BROWN with Aff.
Jun 9	Betty d of Isaac & Elisabeth FRYER without Affidavit whereof Notice was given to William PUTSEY Overseer of the Poor by a note under my hand July 22
Sep 6	Thomas HILMAN without Affidavit whereof Notice was given to William PUTSEY Overseer of the Poor by a note under my hand Oct 16
Sep 8	Thomas s of John & Hannah CRUNDAL with Affidavit
Sep 8	Richard MORRIS without Affidavit whereof Notice was given to William PUTSEY Overseer of the Poor by a note under my hand October 16
Sep 23	Mr John COOK with Affidavit
Oct 4	Phebe d of Mary WALL with Aff.
Nov 4	Elisabeth SPENCER with Aff.
Dec 23	Samson s of James & Elisabeth LENNARD with Aff.
Jan 5	Lydia PARKER with Aff.
Jan 15	Elisabeth the wife of Thomas SIMS with Aff.
Jan 20	Richard COOK with Affidavit
Feb 6	Thomas s of James & Elisabeth TAYLER with Aff.
Feb 8	Mr William COLLEY with Affid.
Feb 9	Edward OLIVER with Affidavit
Feb 15	Mr Samuel BOWERS with Affidavit
Feb 26	Peter s of Moses & Sarah DILWORTH
Mar 7	Mary d of Humfry & Mary FRYAR
Mar 10	Benjamin s of Thomas & Mary RICHARDS with Affidavit
Mar 15	Rachel BECKLEY with Affid.
Mar 19	Edward HUTT
Mar 21	Mary BROOK with Affidavit

It was signified to Thomas HUGHES Constable by a note under my hand April the sixteenth 1737 that Peter DILWORTH Mary FRYAR Edward HUTT were buried without Affidavit

Marriages 1736

Apr 25	Samuel CARTER & Elisabeth SMITH
Jul 31	William HUTT & Mary WARD
Oct 2	Edward ALLEN & Mary BAKER
Oct 19	James COLES & Margaret BORE
Dec 8	John COATES & Hannah BRAZIER
Feb 2	William WHITE & Abigail LAMBERT
Feb 7	Gabriel MOIL & Mary WILKES

Baptisms 1737

Apr 23	Humfry s of Humfry & Mary FRYAR

May 9	John s of William & Mary HORTON
May 22	Ann d of John & Elisabeth NEW
May 22	Betty d of William & Hannah BRICE
May 29	Thomas s of Thomas & Susannah WARREN
Jun 19	Mary d of Thomas & Sarah LOW
Jul 1	William s of William & Eleanor WATKINS
Jul 12	Mary d of Thomas & Ann BAYLIS
Aug 26	Eleanor d of John & Mary CLARK
Aug 27	Thomas s of John & Mary SIMS
Aug 28	Benjamin s of Elisabeth POWEL illegitimate
Sep 10	Thomas s of Elisabeth MOSELEY illegitimate
Sep 24	Mary d of John & Katharine LOW
Oct 2	John s of William & Margaret EVANS
Oct 8	Mary d of Isaac & Elisabeth FRYAR
Oct 10	William s of John & Sarah KING
Nov 6	Richard s of Joseph & Mary SMALMAN
Nov 9	Elisabeth d of Joseph & Sarah LEABEN
Nov 23	Susanna d of Mary PENSON illegitimate
Dec 4	Richard s of Thomas & Ann BAYLIS
Dec 8	Harry s of Thomas & Mary RICHARDS
Dec 18	Sarah d of John & Hannah CRUNDAL
Dec 28	Mary d of John & Ann NORMCOT
Jan 15	Mary d of Anthony & Martha SMITH
Jan 15	Sarah d of William & Elisabeth TAYLER
Jan 16	Joyce d of Solomon & Eleanor BRASIER
Jan 28	Elisabeth d of Joseph & Hannah HILLMAN
Jan 29	Edward s of John & Elisabeth BIRD
Jan 30	George s of Joseph & Hannah BEEMAN
Feb 4	Richard s of Thomas & Margaret COOKS
Mar 12	Sarah d of James & Elisabeth LENNARD
Mar 14	Sarah d of Jeremiah & Elisabeth CASWEL

Burials 1737

Apr 21	John BRISCOE with Affidavit
Apr 26	Henry SMITH
Apr 26	Jesse s of Benjamin & Mary GROVE
May 8	Edward LYDAL with Affidavit
May 14	Elisabeth the wife of Michael SPARRY with Affid.
May 14	Elisabeth GRANGER
May 16	Jeremiah SMITH with Affid.
May 22	Anna Elisabetha the wife of William CHURCHARD with Aff.
Jun 3	Mary ROGERS

I signified to Mr Edward WALDRON Church Warden by a Note under my hand June 12 that Henry SMITH, Jesse GROVE and Elisabeth GRANGER were buried without Affidavits of their being buried in woollen

Jun 15	John PERINS with Aff.
Jul 5	Martha d of Thomas & Mary MASON with Affidavit
Jul 5	Jane the wife of Richard HOLLINS with Affidavit
Jul 18	Sarah NEWMAN

Jul 20 William s of William & Eleanor WATKINS
I signified to Mr Edward WALDRON Church Warden by a note under my hand July the thirty first that Sarah NEWMAN and William WATKINS were buried without Affidavits of their being buried in woollen
Jul 27 Joseph INSALL s of John INSALL   with Affidavit
The Affidavit of William BATKINS[sic] being buried in woollen was made in due time but did not come to my hands till after.
Aug 13 Mary LYTHALL   with Affidavit
Sep 13 Mrs Elisabeth FOLEY   with Affidavit
Oct 6   Mrs Margaret JUKES   with Affidavit
Oct 14 Mr Samuel COOK   with Affidavit
Oct 22 Mrs Margaret WOOD   with Aff.
Nov 7   Judith d of Henry & Judith PHINEY   without Affidavit where of notice was given to Mr Edward WALDRON by a note under my hand

Marriages 1737
Apr 12 John COOPER & Ann NEWMAN
Jan 6   William WHITTAKER & Ann HALL
Feb 1   John BRASIER & Hannah KIDSON
Feb 4   Thomas KETLEY & Merial NOXEN

Burials 1737
Nov 22 Sarah the wife of Thomas DARBY   without Affidavit whereof notice was given to Mr Edward WALDRON December the eleventh
Dec 9   Harry s of Thomas & Mary RICHARDS
Jan 10 Mary MOSELEY   with Affidavit
Notice was given to Mr Edward WALDRON that Harry RICHARDS was buried without Affidavit by a Note under my hand January the eighth
Jan 17 Mary ESSELBEE without Affidavit whereof notice was given to Mr Edward WALDRON by a note under hand January the twenty ninth
Feb 12 James LENNARD   with Affidavit
Feb 23 Abigail SMALLMAN   without Affidavit whereof notice was given to Benjamin DODSON Overseer of the Poor by a note under my hand April the sixth

Baptisms 1738
Mar 25 John s of John & Hannah COATES
Apr 2   Jane d of Richard & Jane LAWRENCE
Apr 8   Edward s of Edward & Elisabeth BLUN
Apr 9   Matthew and Samuel sons of John & Elisabeth POWEL
Apr 29 William s of John & Sarah BAYLIS
May 1   James s of James & Joanna NEWMAN
May 13 John s of Edward & Mary WILCOX
Jun 4   Mary d of Joseph & Ann LYE
Jun 9   Joseph s of Samuel & Sarah OWEN
Jun 11 Hannah d of Sarah TURNER Illegitimate

Jun 11   Thomas s of Christopher & Elisabeth TOLLEY
Jun 15   Thomas s of William & Eleanor WATKINS
Jun 21   Mary d of Richard & Elisabeth HORTON
Jun 29   Elisabeth d of William & Elisabeth CLEMSON
Jul 1   Richard s of John & Jane LEA
Jul 2   William s of George & Elisabeth JORDAN
Jul 18   Elisabeth d of Paul & Mary GARDINER
Aug 18   Jeremiah s of John & Sarah TRUEMAN
Aug 19   Sarah d of William & Sarah ROBINSON
Aug 29   Robert s of Samuel & Mary WHITTINGHAM
Sep 1   Joseph s of John & Sarah SHINTON
Sep 2   Elisabeth d of John & Sarah HARWOOD
Sep 12   Sarah d of Samuel & Mary PERINS
Oct 1   Elisabeth d of James & Elisabeth NEWMAN
Oct 1   Elisabeth d of Young & Elisabeth LAMBERT
Oct 7   John s of William & Martha CARTWRIGHT
Oct 11   Hannah d of Thomas & Hannah LANDORE
Oct 14   John s of John & Mary STOCKINGS
Oct 16   Mary d of Benjamin & Mary GROVE
Oct 20   Edward s of Elisabeth ROBINSON   Illegitimate
Oct 21   Jane d of William & Jane WALFOOT
Oct 23   Robert s of William & Elisabeth CHURCHARD
Nov 18   Hannah d of Humfrey & Hannah BROWN
Nov 18   Mary d of Thomas & Mary RICHARDS
Nov 25   Edward s of Edward & Mary BANNISTER
Dec 26   William s of unknown mother   Illegitimate
Dec 27   Martha d of Mary SUCH   Illegitimate
Jan 11   Arthur s of John & Hannah BRASIER
Feb 18   Sarah d of Josiah & Elisabeth RAWLEY
Mar 3   Mary d of Robert & Elisabeth MILLS
Mar 3   James s of Mary BARRET   Illegitimate

Burials 1738

Apr 8   John NICKOLS   without Affidavit whereof notice was given to Mr Edward WALDRON May the seventh by a note under hand
May 6   Ann the wife of Richard BATE   with Affidavit
May 8   Samuel s of John & Elisabeth POWEL
May 9   Francis WHITTAKER   with Aff.
May 27   Ann the wife of Timothy SUTCLIFF
Jun 27   Thomas s of William & Eleanor WATKINS   with Affidavit
Notice was given to Mr Edward WALDRON that Samuel POWEL and Ann SUTCLIFF were buried without Affidavits by a note under hand July the sixteenth
Jul 20   Elisabeth CROMPTON
Jul 27   Elisabeth OWEN with Aff.
Aug 27   Edward CHAMBERLAIN
Aug 30   Robert WHITTINGHAM
Sep 28   William BOWATER
Oct 2   Agnes PERRY   without Affidavit
Oct 9   Sarah PERINS   with Aff.

Oct 14   John BATE   with Aff.
Notice was given to Mr Thomas HILLMAN Church warden that Elisabeth CROMPTON, Edward CHAMBERLAIN, Robert WHITTINGHAM and William BOWATER were buried without Affidavit by a note under hand
Oct 22   William DUTTON with Aff.
Nov 3   Abigail BLACKMORE
Nov 7   Thomas HOLMES   with Aff.
Nov 8   Margaret STRINGER
Nov 10   Sarah ROBINSON
Nov 14   Alice the wife of Richard DUN
Nov 18   Margaret COOKSEY   with Aff.
Dec 1   Mary d of Thomas & Mary RICHARDS   with Affidavit
Notice was given to Mr John GROVE Church warden that Margaret STRINGER, Sarah ROBINSON, Alice DUN and Abigail BLACKMORE were buried without Affidavits of their being buried in woollen by a note under hand Dated December the sixteenth in the Year of our Lord 1738
Dec 22   John SINKLEY   without Affidavit
Jan 3   Mary d of John & Mary CLARKE   with Affidavit
Jan 16   Magdalen BROWN   with Aff.
Jan 24   Benjamin POWEL   without Affidavit
Jan 26   Mr Thomas WALDRON   with Affidavit
Feb 4   Margaret the wife of Thomas IDDINS   without Affidavit
Notice was given to Mr Thomas HILLMAN that John SINKLEY and Benjamin POWEL were buried without Affidavits of their being buried in woollen by a note under hand dated the eleventh day of February
Feb 8   Mrs Ann WORRAL widow   with Aff.
Notice was given to Mr Thomas HILLMAN that Margaret IDDINS was buried without Affidavit of her being buried in woollen by a note under my hand March 21
Feb 27   Thomas LAVENDER   with Affidavit
Feb 27   Robert HOLLINS with Aff.
Mar 1   John s of William WHITE   without Affidavit
Mar 5   Merial MOSELEY   withoutAffidavit

Marriages 1738

Apr 23   Job RAWLINS & Mary OLIVER
Apr 25   Henry YEATES & Sarah ROGERS
Jun 11   Richard OLIVER & Ann BROWN
Jul 2   James BURTON & Mary REYNOLDS
Jul 23   William MATTHEW & Elisabeth SMALLMAN
Dec 14   John HAND & Elisabeth HUGHS
Dec 24   George COWLEY & Mary TILLEY
Jan 28   John MOSELEY & Mary KITELEY
Mar 1   John BARRET & Hannah LINES

Burials 1738

Mar 22   Thomas s of George DODSON   with Affidavit

Notice was given to Mr Thomas HILLMAN that John WHITE and Merial MOSELEY were buried without Affidavit made by a Note under my hand dated
April 28

More Baptisms 1738
Mar 6   William s of Philip & Elisabeth HAINS
Mar 6   Mary d of John & Eleanor COBORN
Mar 10   Molly daughter of Humfrey and Mary FRYAR

Baptisms 1739
Apr 8   John s of Richard & Ann OLIVER
May 2   Elisabeth d of Edward & Elisabeth HOPKINS
May 3   Martha d of Henry & Sarah YATES
May 3   John s of George & Mary BAKER
May 5   Betty d of William & Sarah DAVIS
May 6   Thomas s of William & Elisabeth MATTHEWS
May 21   Jonathan s of Jonathan & Mary READ
Jun 1   Edward s of John & Ann TYSOE
Jun 2   Sarah d of Thomas & Mary DUTTON
Jun 9   Betty d of William & Mary HUTT
Jun 16   John s of John & Hannah BARRETT
Jul 1   John s of Josias & Mary RAWLEY
Jul 5   Salley d of Thomas & Mary MASON
Jul 29   Mary d of Richard & Sarah BEARDSLEY
Aug 12   William s of William & Hannah BRICE
Aug 13   Ann d of Solomon & Eleanor BRASIER
Aug 25   Sarah d of Jeremiah & Mary SCOT
Aug 29   Elisabeth & Margaret daughters of William & Mary HEMMING
Sep 3   John s of William & Jane TIMMINS
Sep 3   Elisabeth d of Benjamin & Mary POTTER
Sep 22   Elisabeth d of Samuel & Priscilla CRANE
Oct 2   Richard s of John & Mary MOSELEY
Oct 5   Sarah d of Joseph & Sarah LEABEN
Oct 10   John s of William & Sarah ROBINSON
Oct 13   Elisabeth d of John & Mary SIMS
Oct 24   Betty d of William & Ann PERRY
Oct 28   Major s of Richard & Jane LAWRENCE
Oct 28   Joseph s of John & Sarah CHAMBERLAIN
Oct 30   John s of George & Mary COWLEY
Oct 14   Mary d of Thomas & Mary RICHARDS
Nov 14   Sarah d of William & Sarah KIDSON
Nov 21   Hannah d of Harry & Mary BROWN
Dec 26   John s of John & Elisabeth BIRD
Dec 27   Mary d of Charles & Sobieski HILLMAN
Dec 27   John s of Joshua & Mary SIDDENS
Dec 29   Mary d of John & Hannah COATES
Jan 1   John s of William & Elisabeth CHURCHARD
Jan 1   John s of John & Rebecca DEAN
Jan 3   Sarah d of John & Sarah HAYWARD

Jan 6	Sarah d of Young & Elisabeth LAMBERT
Jan 19	Ann d of John & Mary INSALL
Feb 2	Thomas s of Samuel & Mary PERRINS
Feb 9	Mary d of Thomas & Mary GREEN
Feb 9	Thomas s of Martha DUN illegitimate
Feb 21	Mary d of John & Sarah KING
Mar 9	Sarah d of Adam & Mary HADEN
Mar 12	Sarah d of William & Mary PAR

Burials 1739

Mar 28	John WINFORD with Aff.
Mar 30	Catharine the wife of John TRUEMAN with Aff.
Apr 27	John HAYWOOD
May 14	Mary JOHNSON with Aff.
Jul 1	John CRANDAGE
Apr 2[sic]	Mary the wife of Humfrey BATE with Aff.
Jul 3	Robert s of William & Elisabeth CHURCHARD
Jul 22	John s of Samuel & Mary WHITTINGHAM
Aug 31	Sarah DUTTON
Oct 30	Margaret the wife of William CRUNDAL [BT's: "CRUNDALE"] with Affidavit
Nov 1	Elisabeth LAMBERT

Notice was given to Mr Shadrach CRUMP that John CRANDAGE, Robert CHURCHARD, John WHITTINGHAM and Sarah DUTTON were buried without Affidavits of their being buried in woollen by a Note under hand Dated the thirtieth day of October

Nov 9	Sarah d of John & Mary CLARK
Nov 23	Hannah d of Harry BROWN with Aff.
Nov 27	Joyce WHITE with Affidavit
Dec 3	Edward HILLMAN with Aff.

Notice was given to Mr Shadrach CRUMP that Sarah CLARKE was buried without Affidavit of her being buried in woollen by a note under hand dated the eleventh day of October

Jan 4	Thomas KETLEY with Affidavit
Jan 4	Sarah HAYWARD
Jan 16	Margaret NEWMAN
Jan 27	William BRICE
Feb 6	Sarah NEEDAM
Feb 16	Richard MOSELEY
Feb 19	Elizabeth KETTLEY with Affidavit
Feb 27	Margaret the wife of Herbert GROVE

Notice was given to Mr Shadrach CRUMP that Sarah HAYWARD, Margaret NEWMAN, William BRICE, Sarah NEEDHAM and Richard MOSELEY were all of them buried without Affidavits made of their being Buried in woollen by a Note under hand dated the fourth day of March

Mar 13	Elisabeth d of William & Mary HEMMING
Mar 13	Margaret d of William & Mary HEMMING
Mar 17	Richard BATE
Mar 21	William PUTSEY with Affidavit

Marriages 1739

Sep 30 Humfrey BATE & Mary RIDDING
Oct 20 Henry MOSELEY & Mary TOLLEY
Dec 23 Edward STOKES & Mary BACON

Baptisms 1740

Mar 30 Job s of Samuel & Elisabeth RAWLEY
Apr 5   Martha d of John & Jane LEA
Apr 5   John s of Mary CORFIELD illegitimate
May 1   Elisabeth d of William & Jane PLIMLEY
May 5   Joseph s of William & Eleanor HAYNES
May 6   Jane d of Benjamin & Mary GROVE
May 17 Eleanor d of Henry & Ann HELPS
May 23 Joseph s of Josias & Mary RAWLEY
May 31 Mary d of Thomas & Susannah WARREN
Jun 1   Mary d of Edward & Elisabeth BLUN
Jul 26 Jane d of William & Jane SMITH
Jul 27 John s of Joseph & Mary SMALLMAN
Jul 31 Joseph s of William & Sarah HILL
Aug 1   Hannah d of Humfrey & Hannah BROWN
Aug 20 Richard s of Humfrey & Mary BATE
Aug 29 Roger s of Mr William & Susanna HOLMER
Aug 30 John s of Anthony & Martha SMITH
Sep 28 Thomas s of James & Joanna NEWMAN
Oct 27 Thomas s of Edward & Mary STOAKES
Nov 2   James s of John & Elisabeth POWEL
Nov 10 Mary d of Samuel & Mary WITTINGHAM
Nov 24 Joseph s of Sarah KINDIN illegitimate
Dec 26 Richard s of John & Mary STOCKINGS
Dec 27 Ann d of William & Elisabeth THOMAS
Jan 7   Isaac s of Humfrey & Mary FRYAR
Jan 10 Hannah d of William & Hannah BRICE
Jan 10 George s of William & Elisabeth MATTHEWS
Jan 10 Sarah d of William & Elisabeth CLEMSON
Jan 11 Thomas Vincent s of Francis & Margaret BLACKMORE
Jan 18 Thomas s of Jane POWEL illegitimate
Feb 7   Thomas s of Robert & Elisabeth MILLS
Feb 15 Betty d of John & Sarah HAYWOOD
Feb 20 Samuel s of John & Sarah TRUEMAN
Mar 1   Jane d of Ann SMALLMAN illegitimate
Mar 7   William s of Thomas & Elisabeth COLEBORN
Mar 8   Mary d of Joshua & Mary SIDDINS
Mar 8   William s of Thomas & Ann WATKINS
Mar 15 Eleanor d of Thomas & Hannah LAUNDER

Marriages 1740

Jan 6   John FELLOWS & Mary LINE
Feb 8   Thomas IDDINS & Elisabeth HADLEY

Burials 1740

- Apr 4   Richard THICKS with Aff^d
- Apr 25   John s of Mary CORFIELD
- May 11   William HEMMING
- May 24   Ann GIBBS   with Aff
- May 26   Ruth GREEN   with Aff
- May 27   John s of William & Sarah ROBINSON

Notice was given to Mr Shadrach CRUMP that Margaret GROVE, Elisabeth HEMMING, Margaret HEMMING, Richard BATE, John CORFIELD, William HEMMING were all of them buried without Affidavits made of their being buried in woollen by a Note under-hand dated the third day of June

- Jun 13   Richard CORFIELD
- Jul 11   William CHAMBERS
- Jul 19   Eleanor BENNETT   with Aff
- Jul 28   Thomas KIDSON with Aff
- Aug 4   Ann the wife of John BATE   with Aff
- Sep 1   Edward SARBITT   with Aff
- Sep 4   Henry YORK
- Sep 9   John s of John & Rebecca DEAN
- Sep 28   Christian d of Herbert GROVE
- Oct 14   Mercy TURNER
- Oct 20   Joseph s of William & Sarah HILL
- Oct 21   Mary d of Richard & Elisabeth HORTON   with Aff
- Oct 31   Elisabeth the wife of John BATE   with Aff:

Notice was given to Mr Shadrach CRUMP that Richard CORFIELD, William CHAMBERS, Henry YORK, John DEAN, Christian GROVE, Mercy TURNER, Joseph HILL were all of them buried without Affidavit made of their being buried in woollen November the ninth

- Nov 3   John s of John & Elisabeth BIRD   with Affidavit
- Nov 5   William TURNER son of William & Mercy TURNER
- Nov 6   Hannah WALDRON   with Aff
- Nov 9   Richard WARREN
- Nov 16   Mary d of Samuel & Mary WITTINGHAM   with Affid
- Nov 22   John NORMCOTT
- Dec 3   Isabel SMITH
- Dec 4   William CRUNDAL   with Affid
- Dec 7   John s of William & Jane TIMMINS   with Affidavit
- Dec 9   Joseph HARRIS
- Dec 23   Richard s of John & Mary MOSELEY
- Dec 29   Elisabeth d of Thomas & Margaret COOK   with Affid
- Dec 30   Jane d of Benjamin & Mary GROVE
- Dec 31   Thomas s of Thomas & Margaret COOK   with Aff
- Jan 12   Hannah d of William & Hannah BRICE
- Jan 13   Elisabeth DUN
- Jan 27   Eleanor the wife of Mr William WATKINS   with Aff
- Jan 27   Martha d of John & Jane LEA
- Jan 30   Thomas s of Jane POWEL
- Feb 1   Samuel RAWLEY

Feb 8   Mary the wife of Thomas DUTTON   with Aff
Feb 15   Sarah NEWMAN
Feb 18   Betty d of John & Sarah HAYWOOD
Feb 27   Elisabeth the wife of Samuel GARDINER   with Aff
Mar 1   Mary d of Robert & Elisabeth MILLS
Mar 2   Sarah d of Young & Elisabeth LAMBERT
Mar 6   Elisabeth the wife of John POWEL
Mar 13   Thomas s of Robert & Elisabeth MILLS
Mar 14   Elisabeth MOUNSTEVEN

Notice was given to Mr CRUMP Church warden that William TURNER, Richard WARREN, John NORMCOTT, Isabel SMITH, Joseph HARRIS, Richard MOSELEY, Jane GROVE, Hannah BRICE, Elisabeth DUN, Martha LEA, Thomas POWEL, Samuel RAWLEY, Sarah NEWMAN, Betty HAYWOOD, Mary MILLS, Sarah LAMBERT and Elisabeth POWEL were all of them buried without Affidavits made of their being buried in woollen by a note under hand the twentieth day of March

Mar 15   Elisabeth the wife of John BIRD   with Affidavit
Mar 16   John HILMAN   with Affidavit
Mar 19   Elisabeth the wife of John JINKES   with Aff
Mar 23   Margaret d of Richard & Mary WOOD   with Aff

Baptisms 1741

Mar 26   Esther d of Joseph & Hannah BEEMAN
Apr 11   Mary d of William & Sarah DAVIS
Apr 1[sic] Samuel s of Jeremiah & Elisabeth CASWEL
Apr 11   John and Samuel sons of John & Mary FELLOWS
May 1   James s of Thomas & Margaret REYNOLD
May 10   Thomas s of George & Martha WALKER
Jun 13   Edward s of Edward & Mary PARKS
Jun 17   Ann d of Joseph & Ann LYE
Jul 4   Mary d of Thomas & Margaret COOK
Jul 12   Samuel s of Charles & Mary JONES
Jul 19   Jinny d of Benjamin & Mary GROVE
Aug 2   Ann d of John & Mary MOSELEY
Aug 10   Ann d of John & Rebecca DEAN
Sep 5   Helene d of John & Hannah CRUNDAL
Sep 9   William s of William & Jane TIMMINS
Oct 2   Mary d of William & Sarah HILL
Oct 8   Joseph s of William & Elisabeth CHURCHARD
Oct 14   Samuel s of Philip & Elisabeth HAYNES
Oct 26   William s of Richard & Jane LAWRENCE
Nov 9   Abraham s of Samuel & Priscilla CRANE
Nov 11   Mary d of Harry & Mary BROWN
Nov 22   Sarah d of William & Alice AUDIN
Dec 6   Joseph s of John & Jane LEA
Dec 13   John s of John & Eleanor COLEBORN
Dec 16   Ann d of William & Ann PAYNE
Dec 20   Catharine d of Solomon & Eleanor BRASIER
Dec 23   John s of Edward & Ann SARBIT

Dec 27   Eleanor d of John & Mary SIMS
Jan 24   Mary d of Jonathan & Mary READ
Feb 19   John s of Christopher & Elisabeth TOLLEY
Feb 21   Margaret d of Thomas & Elisabeth COATES
Feb 11   Thomas s of Samuel & Mary WHITTINGHAM
Mar 13   Richard s of John & Hannah COATES
Mar 14   William s of John & Ann TYSOE

Burials 1741

Apr 3   William MARTIN
Apr 12   George s of Joseph & Hannah BEEMAN
Apr 24   Mary the wife of Mr Thomas WORRAL   with Affidavit
May 2   Elisabeth PENSON
May 6   William DAVIS   with Aff.
May 14   Mary the wife of John HAYES   with Aff.
May 25   Richard s of Thomas & Dorothy HUGHS
May 30   Samuel s of Samuel & Elisabeth CARTER
Jun 1   Sarah d of the Widow HEMMING
Jun 7   Jane BRADLEY   with Aff.
Jun 7   Mary POWEL
Jun 7   Thomas LANDER
Jun 14   William TAYLER   with Aff.
Jun 23   Ann SMALMAN
Jun 23   Mary HILMAN
Jun 25   Simon WALKER
Jul 2   Ruth NEW with Affidavit
Jul 3   James CLAY
Jul 9   Richard HARRIS
Jul 10   Mary the wife of John HODGETS   with Aff.
Aug 13   Thomas COOK
Aug 30   Jinny d of Benjamin & Mary GROVE
Sep 6   Margaret the wife of Richard HILLMAN

Notice was given to Mr Richard HOLLINS Churchwarden the seventh day of September by a note under hand that Thomas MILLS, Elisabeth MOUNSTEVEN, William MARTIN, George BEEMAN, Elisabeth PENSON, Richard HUGHS, Samuel CARTER, Sarah HEMMING, Mary POWEL, Thomas LANDER, Ann SMALLMAN, Mary HILLMAN, Simon WALKER, James CLAY, Richard HARRIS, Thomas COOK were all of them buried without Affidavits made of their being buried in Woollen.

Sep 9   John WORRALL
Sep 15   Ann the wife of George WINFORD
Sep 17   Robert YORK   with Aff.
Oct 1   Richard s of John & Mary STOCKINGS
Oct 4   Samuel GRYFFIS
Oct 15   Elisabeth the wife of Isaac FRYAR
Oct 17   Richard HILLMAN
Oct 24   Susanna d of Mary PENSON
Nov 3   Thomas WINFORD   with Aff.
Nov 11   Mary d of William & Sarah HILL
Nov 16   John CLARKE

Nov 20   John BATE
Nov 25   Rachel CORFIELD
Nov 25   Edmund MASON
Dec 5   Mary ROBINSON
Dec 10   Susanna LINES
Dec 10   Ann SOUTHALL
Dec 12   Elisabeth HARWOOD
Dec 21   Ann d of Joseph & Ann AUDIN
Dec 23   Margaret WEB
Dec 30   Elisabeth the wife of John MOSELEY

Marriages 1741

Aug 24   Richard MOSELEY & Joan NEWMAN
Sep 14   Thomas BARNET & Jane MOUNTFORT
Oct 5   Joseph READ & Sarah DARBY
Nov 30   John ALLEN & Mary LINE
Jan 6   Joseph NEEDHAM & Jane ROWLAND

Buried 1741

Dec 30   Mary MASON
Jan 8   William HORTON
Jan 27   Margaret COOK
Feb 1   John MOSELEY
Feb 4   Samuel PERRINS   with Affidavit
Feb 13   John SARBET   with Affidavit
Feb 19   Mr William HURTLE   with Affidavit
Feb 23   Richard TROW
Feb 24   Elisabeth HAYWOOD
Feb 27   Sarah WOOLLOSTON   with Aff.
Mar 12   Mary d of Edward & Elisabeth BLUN
Mar 17   Edward s of Edward & Elisabeth BLUN both of them with Affidavit

Burials 1742

Mar 29   John WHITECRAFT   with Aff.
Apr 16   Mary BIRD   with Affidavit
Apr 20   John KING
Apr 24   Amy PROSSER
May 8   Sarah PEACH   with Affidavit
May 11   George POWEL
May 16   Thomas s of Samuel & Mary WHITTINGHAM
May 21   Elisabeth d of Paul & Mary GARDINER
Jun 8   John TRUEMAN
Jun 18   Elisabeth the wife of Samuel LIE   with Aff.
Jul 5   Hannah d of Harry & Mary BROWN
Jul 8   John GROVE
Jul 10   Mary SPENCER
Jul 27   John s of William & Elisabeth CHURCHARD
Aug 10   Mary BATE
Aug 21   Jane ALLEN

Sep 7	Mary d of Robert & Elisabeth MILLS
Sep 26	Bridget PRICE
Oct 13	Thomas GROVE
Nov 13	Elisabeth d of the Reverend Mr John PERRY Vicar of Clent with Affidavit

Notice was given to Mr Richard WORRALL Church warden the thirteenth day of November by a note under hand that Hannah BROWN, John GROVE, Mary SPENCER, John CHURCHARD, Mary BATE, Jane ALLEN, Mary MILLS, Bridget PRICE, Thomas GROVE were all of them buried without Affidavits made of their being buried in woollen.

Dec 4	Elisabeth WILLMOT of Stourbridge with Affidavit
Dec 7	William s of John CHARLETON with Affidavit
Dec 14	Phebe COLEBURN with Affidavit
Dec 21	Mary DEAKIN with Affidavit
Dec 29	Margaret d of George & Martha WALKER with Aff.
Jan 6	Edward & Mary son & daughter of Henry & Mary SMITH
Jan 8	Ann d of Elijah & Mary WHITE
Feb 12	Hellen d of Edward & Mary STOKES
Feb 23	Elisabeth PERRINS with Affidavit
Mar 2	William s of John & Ann TYSOE

Baptisms 1742

Apr 4	John s of John & Hannah CHAULTON
Apr 14	William s of Jonathan & Margery VEAL
Apr 20	Helen d of Edward & Mary STOKES
Apr 26	Helen d of Edward & Elisabeth BLUN
May 9	Edward s of Edward & Jane RICHARDS
Jul 7	Mary d of Thomas & Elisabeth KING
Jul 11	Mary d of George & Mary COLY
Jul 25	Humfrey s of Richard & Jane MOSELEY
Aug 28	Thomas Kidson s of John & Hannah BRASIER
Aug 29	Mary d of Joseph & Sarah LEABEN
Sep 18	Mary d of Jeremiah & Mary SCOT
Sep 29	Richard s of Richard & Ann OLIVER
Oct 5	Mary d of Paul & Mary GARDENER
Oct 7	Sarah d of Humfrey & Sarah BATE
Oct 9	William s of John & Mary ALLEN
Oct 24	William s of Thomas & Susannah WARREN
Oct 31	Richard s of John & Mary STOCKINGS
Nov 8	Margaret d of George & Martha WALKER
Nov 20	Edward s of Edward & Elisabeth HOPKINS
Nov 23	Anthony s of William & Sarah HILL
Dec 4	Catharine d of William & Ann PERRY
Nov 22	Sarah d of Thomas & Jane BARNET
Dec 12	Edward s of William & Elisabeth MATTHEWS
Dec 27	William s of William & Elisabeth CLEMSON
Dec 29	James s of Zachary & Sarah GROVE
Jan 1	Edward and Mary son & daughter of Henry & Jane SMITH
Jan 5	James s of Thomas & Mary RICHARDS

Jan 13   Joseph s of Joseph & Martha BAYNHAM
Jan 30   James s of Joshua & Mary SIDDINS [crossed out and possibly "SOWTHEREN" written at the side; BT's: "SIDDENS"]
Jan 30   Edward s of John & Mary FELLOWS
Feb 6   Hannah d of Robert & Elisabeth MILLS
Feb 7   Betty d of William & Elisabeth CHURCHYARD
Feb 19   Martha d of William & Jane PLIMLEY
Feb 23   Sarah d of Daniel & Hannah COLEBORN
Feb 26   Joseph s of Thomas & Mary GREEN
Mar 12   James s of James & Mary BURTON
Mar 13   Sarah d of Thomas & Elisabeth COLEBORN

Marriages 1742

May 10   Edward DAVIS & Mary FONES
May 25   John MOSELEY & Mary WINFORD
Jun 12   Thomas DUTTON & Jane HADEN
Jun 27   Foxhall CARTWRIGHT & Susanna OWEN
Jul 7   Isaac FRYER & Elisabeth GRIFFIS
Dec 23   Joseph HANCOX & Hannah WHITE
Dec 30   Humfrey KETLEY & Mary NOXON
Jan 31   Joseph SHAKESPEAR & Lydie MARTIN

More Burials 1742

Mar 3   John SOUTHALL
Mar 3   Rebecca LOVETT   with Affid.
Mar 8   Elisabeth WEB   with Affidavit
Mar 18   Catherine d of Solomon & Eleanor BRASIER
Mar 21   Isaac s of Hunfrey & Mary FRYAR
         Mary d of Humfrey & Mary FRYAR buri [Entry crossed out]
Notice was given to Mr Richard WORRALL Church Warden by a note under hand dated the twenty third day of April in the year of our Lord one thousand seven hundred and forty three that Edward & Mary SMITH, Ann WHITE, Hellen STOKES, William TYSOE, John SOUTHALL, Catherine BRASIER, Isaac FRYAR, Mary HUTT, Eleanor LAUNDER, Mary FRYAR, Ann MOSELEY, Sarah SHINTON were all of them buried with out Affidavits made of their being buried in woollen.

Burials 1743

Mar 25   Mary HUTT
Mar 26   Eleanor d of Hannah LAUNDER
Apr 7   Mary d of Humfrey & Mary FRYAR
Apr 9   Ann d of Mary MOSELEY widow
Apr 15   Sarah d of John & Sarah SHINTON
Apr 18   Sarah d of William & Elisabeth CLEMSON   with Affidavit
Apr 19   Richard OLIVER with Aff.
Apr 20   Elisabeth d of Christopher & Elisabeth TOLLEY
Apr 21   Anthony s of William & Sarah HILL
Apr 26   Mary the wife of Richard LINES   with Aff.
Apr 28   Mary d of John & Hannah COATES
Apr 29   Hannah the wife of John CHAMBERS   with Affid.

May 3   Elisabeth FERIDAY
May 4   Thomas s of Humfrey & Mary FRYAR
May 8   Ann d of William & Ann PAINE with Aff.
May 10 James TAYLOR with Affid.
May 19 Thomas SIMS   with Affidavit
May 30 Thomas VEAL
May 30 Sarah d of Thomas & Jane BARNETT   with Affidavit
Jun 3   Martha the wife of Joseph BAYNHAM with Affidavit
Jun 6   Betty d of William GROVE   with Affidavit
Jun 8   Elisabeth d of William & Elisabeth CLEMSON   with Aff.
Jun 14 William s of William & Elisabeth CLEMSON with Aff.
Jun 30 Sarah d of William & Ann PAYNE   with Affidavit
Jul 4   Ann TYSOE
Aug 14 Sarah the wife of William HILL
Aug 25 Mary WORRALL
Notice was given to Mr Jeremiah CASWELL Church Warden by a note under hand dated the fourteenth day of September that Elisabeth TOLLEY, Anthony HILL, Elisabeth FERIDAY, Thomas FRYAR, Thomas VEAL, Ann TYSOE, Sarah HILL, Mary WORRALL, were all of them buried with out Affidavits of their being buried in woollen.
Sep 14 John s of Charles & Sobieski HILLMAN   with Affidavit
Oct 2   Mary CARTWRIGHT   with Affidavit
Oct 5   Joseph s of Sarah KINDIN
Oct 9   Alice POWELL
Nov 2   Joseph s of Christopher TOLLEY
Nov 22 Elisabeth d of Richard & Elisabeth HORTON
Nov 27 Rebecca the wife of John BLACKBURN   with Affidavit
Dec 7   Lydia MARRIOT
Dec 19 Edward BIRD
Jan 5   Arthur s of John & Hannah BRASIER with Aff.
Jan 6   Mary BRISCOE
Mar 1   Jane WEBB   with Aff.
Mar 5   Mary TITLEY
Mar 15 William FORREST   with Aff.

Baptisms 1743
Apr 30 Samuel s of John & Betty BACHE
May 1   Jeremiah s of John & Sarah SHINTON
May 2   Isaac s of Isaac & Elisabeth FRYAR
May 22 Elisabeth d of Thomas & Susanna FERIDAY
Jun 23 Elisabeth d of John & Rebecca DEAN
Jun 19 Joseph s of Thomas & Margaret COOK
Jul 11 Joseph s of Christopher & Elisabeth TOLLEY
Jul 30 Sarah ONION d of Elisabeth ROBINSON Illegitimate
Aug 7   John s of Joseph & Margaret FOSBROOK
Aug 8   John Grove s of Richard & Jane LAWRENCE
Aug 11 Edward s of William & Mary HUTT
Aug 1   Thomas s of Joseph & Ann LYE
Aug 22 John s of Charles & Sobieski HILLMAN
Aug 27 John s of Philip & Ann HAYNES

Sep 10   William s of Richard & Rachel DUN
Sep 26   Betty d of William & Jane SMITH
Oct 8   Samuel s of Thomas & Jane DUTTON
Oct 28   Richard s of William THOMAS & Elisabeth his wife
Nov 6   Ann d of William & Hannah BRICE
Nov 20   Mary d of Richard & Joan MOSELEY
Nov 21   Elisabeth d of Richard & Elisabeth HORTON
Nov 28   Rachel d of John & Sarah CHAMBERS
Dec 11   Mary d of Thomas & Ann TOY
Dec 31   Jane d of John & Jane LEA
Jan 21   Hannah d of John & Hannah COATES
Feb 2   Elisabeth d of William & Elisabeth TAYLER
Feb 18   Edward s of John & Mary ALLEN
Mar 8   Edward s of Edward & Mary STOKES

More Baptisms in 1744[sic; entries placed out of order in OR]
Feb 2   William s of Edward & Elisabeth HOPKINS
Feb 10   Moses son of Thomas & Elisabeth KING
Feb 17   Sarah d of Robert & Elizabeth MILLS
Feb 23   Elisabeth d of Thomas & Mary LYNE
         [Page now badly stained]
[?; BT's: " Mar 6]   John s of William & Phoebe TAYLER
[?; BT's: "Mar 10"]   Sarah, d of [?; BT's "of William & Sarah JOHNSON"]
[?; BT's: "Mar 15"]   Mary d of Joshua & Mary SIDDENS
[?; BT's: "Mar 17"]   Sarah d of Thomas & Margaret COOK
[?; BT's: "Mar 23"]   Ann d of Joseph & Elizabeth SALE[?]

Marriages 1743
May 25   Samuel PARDOE & Jane BATE
Jun 5   William BECKLEY & Sarah BRASLER [BT's: "BRASIER"]
Jun 26   William NEWMAN & Sarah NOCKSON
Sep 19   William PERRINS & Margaret DAVIS
Sep 25   William TAYLER & Phebe CHAMBERLAIN
Dec 27   George RICE & Mary MATTHEWS
Jan 31   Thomas SIMS & Elisabeth BROOK

Marriages 1744
Mar 27   Humfrey TRUEMAN & Mary YORK
May 19   Richard FERIDAY & Hannah HILLMAN
Jun 3   Samuel BROOK & Mary EVANS
Jun 29   William TOYE & Mary LYE
Sep 16   Joseph PERRINS & Mary BRIDGINS
Feb 2   Francis LEWIS & Elisabeth TAYLER
Feb 5   Thomas HICKMAN & Sarah PENSON
Feb 7   Thomas CRANE & Mary OWEN
Feb 26   James PERRY & Elisabeth WINFORD

Baptisms 1744
Apr 14   Joseph s of William & Sarah NEWMAN

Apr 15	Jane d of Samuel & Jane PARDOE
May 1	William s of Humfrey & Mary KETLEY
May 3	Catharine d of William & Elisabeth CLEMSON
May 6	Edward s of James & Joanna NEWMAN
May 6	Martha d of Edward & Elisabeth BLUN
May 19	Betty d of Josias & Mary RAWLEY
May 21	Mary d of William & Sarah CHAMBERS
Jun 9	Joseph s of John & Eleanor COLEBORN
Jun 13	Ann d of William & Jane TIMMINS
Jun 17	Mary d of John & Sarah HAYWOOD
Jun 24	Mary d of John & Ann BROWN
Jul 7	Samuel s of Harry & Mary BROWN
Jul 14	Daniel s of William & Elisabeth MATTHEWS
Jul 21	James s of Jeremiah & Mary SCOTT
Aug 4	William s of William & Sarah BECKLEY
Jul 31	Elisabeth d of William & Margaret PERRINS
Sep 2	Sarah d of Edward & Ann SARBETT
Sep 7	Josua [BT's: "Joshua"] s of Zachariah & Sarah GROVE
Sep 13	Hannah d of Jeremiah & Elisabeth CASWELL
Sep 15	Benjamin s of Thomas & Elisabeth COATES
Sep 16	Paul s of Paul & Mary GARDENER
Sep 23	Mary d of John & Hannah CHAULTON
Oct 7	Mary d of Edward & Mary HAYES
Oct 7	James s of John & Mary STOCKINGS
Nov 3	Thomas s of Joseph & Hannah BEEMAN
Nov 5	Benjamin s of Daniel & Hannah COLEBORN
Dec 5	Mary d of Thomas & Elisabeth SIMS
Dec 29	Mary d of Henry & Mary PEALE
Jan 1	Humphrey s of Humphrey & Sarah BATE
Jan 5	Ann d of Henry & Jane SMITH
Jan 21	Richard s of Joseph & Ann LYE
Jan 20	Humphrey s of John & Sarah SHINTON
Jan 29	William s of William & Elisabeth CHURCHYARD
Jan 29	Sarah d of John & Mary SIMS

Burials 1744

Apr 20	James SMITH
May 8	Elisabeth d of William CLEMSON with Affidavit
May 22	Mary d of William & Sarah CHAMBERS
Jun 25	Mary d of John & Ann BROWN
Jul 10	Elisabeth BULLAS with Aff.
Jul 24	Samuel s of Philip & Elisabeth HAYNES with Aff.

Notice was given to Mr Jeremiah CASWELL Church-Warden by a Note under hand, dated the twenty ninth of July that James SMITH, Mary CHAMBERS and Mary BROWN, were buried without Affidavits of their being buried in woollen

Aug 8	Elisabeth PERRINS with affid.
Aug 23	Mary the wife of Richard PRICE
Aug 28	Mary d of Joshua & Mary SIDDINS
Sep 8	Thomas POWELL

Sep 16	Mary CLARKE widow
Sep 20	Elisabeth d of Thomas IDDINS [BT's: "IDDENS"]
Oct 24	Mary WORRALL with affid.
Oct 31	Ann BATE
Nov 1	William TOMBLINS [BT's: "TOMLINS"] with Affidavit
Nov 19	Charles General JONES with Affidavit
Jan 4	Henry s of Matthew & Mary MASON with Affid.
Jan 11	John s of John & Eleanor COLEBURNE [BT's: "COLEBORN"] with affid.
Jan 24	Thomas IDDENS
Feb 11	John LYE with affid.
Mar 5	Sarah the wife of Charles DAWS
Mar 13	Sarah the wife of Wm JOHNSON
Mar 15	Ann LOW [BT's: "LOWE"]
Mar 19	William BURTON
Mar 20	Henry FINEY [BT's: "FINNEY"]

Baptisms 1745

Apr 15	John s of William & Jane PLIMLEY
May 18	Jane d of Isaac & Elisabeth FRYAR
May 24	Sobieski d of Charles & Sobieski HILLMAN
Jun 5	Joanna d of William & Ann PERRY
Jun 9	James s of Christopher & Elisabeth TOLLY
Jul 13	Sarah d of Job & Mary RAWLEY
Jul 16	Mary d of Edward & Mary GROVE
Jul 30	Rebecca d of John & Rebecca DEAN
Aug 4	William Brown s of Richard & Elisabeth HORTON
Aug 16	William s of Jane POWELL Illegitimate
Sep 2	Mary d of Richard & Mary KIDSON
Sep 14	Thomas s of Edward & Mary PARKS
Oct 14	Hannah d of George & Mary COWLEY
Oct 20	Edward s of Thomas & Hannah WARREN
Oct 20	John s of Thomas & Sarah MORRIS
Oct 26	William s of Thomas & Ann TOYE
Nov 13	Elisabeth d of Humfrey & Mary KETLEY
Nov 16	John s of Thomas & Mary CRANE
Nov 16	John GUEST s of Mary DOOLITTLE Illegitimate
Nov 23	Rebecca d of Thomas & Mary RICHARDS
Dec 7	Prudence d of Thomas & Mary GREEN
Dec 17	Joan Grove d of Richard & Jane LAWRENCE
Nov 10	Mary d of John & Hannah BRASIER misplaced
Dec 26	William s of James & Sarah BAYLIS
Jan 11	Joseph s of John & Sarah PERRINS

Marriages 1745

Apr 29	Henry GUEST & Eleanor BANNISTER
Jun 5	James BAYLIS & Sarah DAVIES [BT's: "DAVIS"]
Aug 5	Richard KIDSON & Mary WHITE
Aug 13	Francis HANCOX & Sarah WHITE
Aug 29	Samuel BELL & Sarah TRUEMAN

Oct 7	John PERRINS & Sarah HARRIS
Dec 5	William GUEST & Mary DOOLITTLE
Dec 8	William BRIDGINS & Mary YAPP
Jan 2	William PARDOE & Ann WARREN
Feb 11	Robert SMITH & Ann DIXON
Feb 18	Joseph RADNOR & Mary TOMBLINS

Burials 1745

Apr 7	Hannah d of John & Hannah COATES	with Affd.
May 3	John HOLLINS with Affd.	
May 31	Joan GROVE Widow with Affd.	
Jun 4	Robert PARKS	
Jul 18	John OAK	
Jul 29	Mary the wife of Matthew MASON	
Sep 12	Sarah PARDOE	
Sep 29	James COOK	
Oct 2	John MOSELEY with Affd.	
Oct 7	Sarah d of Edward & Ann SARBETT	
Oct 9	Mr Thomas HATCHETT with Aff.	
Oct 24	Samuel CASWELL	with Aff.
Nov 9	Samuel GARDENER	
Jan 5	Gerard DAVIS	
Jan 5	Mary PERKS	
Feb 5	John FELLOWS	
Feb 21	Thomas GIBBS with Affidavit	
Mar 6	Mary d of Elijah & Mary PERKS	
Mar 8	Mrs Hannah COLLEY with Aff.	
Mar 14	Mary COATES with Aff.	
Mar 16	Jane WALKER	

More Baptisms 1745

Jan 12	Elisabeth d of Samuel & Jane PARDOE
Jan 19	Mary d of Edward & Sarah VEAL
Jan 19	Sarah d of John & Jane LEA

Burials 1746

Mar 27	George WALKER
Apr 10	Hannah FOSBROOK
Apr 11	Benjamin GROVE
Apr 22	Sarah LINES
May 6	William HILL
May 16	Henry s of William & Rosamond BROWN
May 17	Thomas BAYLIS
Jul 2	John INSULL with Aff.
Jul 21	Elisabeth d of Mr John PERRY Clerk & Agnes his wife with Aff.
Aug 4	Elisabeth d of William & Ann PERRY
Aug 18	John s of John & Sarah HAYWOOD
Oct 5	Elisabeth RICHARDS
Oct 11	Catherine ADAMS

Oct 20	Catherine LANE
Dec 14	Robert DALE
Dec 18	Mary d of Josuah & Mary SIDDINS
Dec 18	Susanna d of Matthew & Elisabeth UNDERWOOD
Dec 25	Elisabeth OLIVER with Aff.
Jan 4	William s of William & Sarah BECKLEY with Affd.
Jan 26	James BECKLEY
Mar 14	Joshua GROVE

Baptisms 1746

Mar 30	Mary d of Thomas & Susanna FERIDAY
Apr 12	Richard s of Richard & Rachel DUNN
Apr 12	Mary d of William & Sarah NEWMAN
Apr 13	Mary d of John & Hannah COATES
Apr 18	James s of William & Jane SMITH
Apr 18	Ann TOWNSEND d of Elisabeth DEAN Illegitimate
Apr 19	Benjamin s of Thomas & Jane DUTTON
Apr 26	Martha d of Henry & Mary PEALE
Apr 26	Mary d of William & Sarah VEAL
May 12	Henry s of William & Rosamond BROWN
May 17	Catherine d of Henry & Jane BAYLEY
May 18	Joseph s of Joseph & Margaret FOSBROOK
May 19	Elisabeth d of Philip & Elisabeth HAYNES
Jun 1	Richard s of James & Mary BURTON
Jun 3	Margaret d of Edward & Elisabeth BLUNN
Jun 4	John s of Humfrey & Sarah BATE
Jun 6	Ann d of Joseph & Sarah LEYBORN
Jun 13	Mary d of Samuel & Sarah BELL
Jun 22	Elisabeth d of Thomas & Jane BARNETT
Jun 28	Joanna d of James & Joanna NEWMAN
Jun 28	Damaris d of John & Mary STOCKIN
Jul 5	Elisabeth d of Jeremiah & Mary SCOTT
Jul 22	John s of John & Sarah HAYWOOD
Aug 3	Edward s of Mary JONES Illegitimate
Sep 7	Edward s of William & Mary HADLEY
Sep 10	Jane d of William & Jane TIMMINS
Sep 14	Catherine LANE a Foundling Child
Sep 30	William s of William & Phebe TAYLER
Oct 10	Thomas s of Thomas & Phebe HILL
Oct 18	Edward s of Edward & Ann SARBITT
Nov 1	John s of John & Eleanor COLEBORN
Nov 22	Samuel s of Richard & Joanna MOSELEY
Nov 23	William s of William & Elisabeth MATTHEWS
Nov 29	Samuel s of Robert & Ann SMITH
Nov 30	Elisabeth d of John & Mary ALLEN
Dec 16	Hannah d of Thomas & Elisabeth SIMS
Dec 24	Susanna d of Edward & Mary GROVE
Dec 24	Arthur s of Richard & Mary KIDSON
Jan 25	Thomas s of Thomas & Elisabeth COATES
Feb 19	Thomas s of William & Elisabeth CHURCHYARD

Mar 20   Henry s of Isaac & Elisabeth FRYAR

Marriages 1746
Jun 3   John ALLEN & Mary RICHARDS
Sep 15   Richard PRICE & Mary PERRINS
Oct 9   John TYSOE & Mary MOSELEY
Oct 9   Edward NEWMAN & Sarah FRYAR
Dec 27   John COPE & Margaret TAYLER
Jan 11   Peregrine LINES & Betty SALE
Jan 19   William HADLEY & Elisabeth WANNERTON
Feb 2   Thomas MASON & Jane ALLPOT

Baptisms 1747
Apr 3   John s of Richard & Grace INCHMORE
Apr 4   William s of Daniel & Hannah COLEBURN
Apr 1[sic]   Hannah d of James & Mary FORGEAM [BT's: "FORGHAM"]
Apr 8   Edward s of John & Hannah CHAULTON
Apr 12   Sarah d of Edward & Mary HAYES
Apr 24   Thomas s of Paul & Mary GARDENER
Apr 8   Mary d of Job & Mary RAWLINS
May 3   Elisabeth d of Thomas & Elisabeth KING
May 15   Matthew s of Matthew & Elisabeth UNDERWOOD
May 16   William s of Thomas & Mary LINE
May 23   Elisabeth d of Sarah BAYLIS illegitimate
Jun 23   William s of John & Rebecca DEAN
Jul 15   James s of John & Margaret ALLEN
Jul 22   John s of Edward & Isabel TOWNSEND
Jul 24   Henry s of Henry & Jane BEELY
Jul 26   Elisabeth d of John & Sarah HAYWOOD
Aug 2   Susanna d of John & Mary SIMS
Aug 8   Joan d of Edward & Sarah NEWMAN
Aug 17   Margaret d of William & Jane PLIMLEY
Sep 1   Richard s of Richard & Elisabeth HORTON
Sep 5   Sarah d of William & Sarah CHAMBERS
Sep 6   Mary d of John & Sarah SHINTON
Sep 17   Petronella d of Christopher & Mary BARNWELL
Sep 27   Jeremiah s of John & Mary TYSOE
Sep 30   Margaret d of Edward & Elisabeth HOPKINS
Oct 4   William s of Samuel & Jane PARDOE
Oct 18   Elisabeth d of Robert & Elisabeth MILLS
Oct 31   Sarah d of Henry & Jane SMITH
Nov 1   George s of George & Mary COLLEY
Nov 10   Edward s of Thomas & Jane MASON
Nov 28   William s of Thomas & Elisabeth HODGES
Nov 21   Ann d of Samuel & Sarah BELL   misplaced
Dec 9   Mary d of William & Elisabeth HADLEY
Dec 12   John s of Thomas & Ann DERRICK
Dec 27   Jane d of Thomas & Jane DUTTON
Jan 2   Sarah d of Humfrey & Mary KETTLEY
Jan 16   Daniel s of William & Hannah NORMCOTT

Burials 1747

Apr 1	Francis HATCHET	with Affidavit
Apr 12	Damaris d of John & Mary STOCKIN	
Apr 15	Mary MOUNTSTEVEN	
Apr 18	John s of Richard & Grace INCHMORE	
May 24	Matthew MASON	
Jul 20	Richard PRESTON	with Aff.
Aug 10	Joan d of Edward & Sarah NEWMAN	
Aug 21	Margaret d of Edward & Elisabeth BLUN	with Aff.
Sep 16	John KETLEY	with Aff.
Oct 25	Mary the wife of Joseph COLLEY	
Nov 17	Mr John GREEN with Affidavit	
Dec 19	Mary SMITH	
Jan 2	Susanna d of Edward & Mary GROVE	
Jan 5	Margaret JONES	
Jan 8	Edward WILLIAMS	with Affid.
Jan 15	Elisabeth the wife of Thomas SALE	
Jan 16	John HAYES	
Jan 18	Elisabeth d of John & Sarah HAYWOOD	
Feb 2	Elisabeth CHAMBERS	with Aff.
Feb 7	James s of John & Mary ALLEN	with Aff.
Mar 8	Elisabeth the wife of James PERRY	
Mar 11	Robert s of John & Sarah PERRINS	
Mar 16	Sarah the wife of Edward WALDRON	with Aff.

Marriages 1747

Apr 20	William LYTHALL & Dorothy OWEN
Apr 30	John SUCH & Ann PENSON
May 29	William LYE & Hannah FOWNES
Jun 18	Edward WALDRON & Martha WHITE
Nov 17	John DAVIS & Mary BAKER
Feb 23	William COWELL & Sarah LEANORD

More Baptisms 1747

Jan 17	Sarah d of William & Mary BRIDGINS
Jan 30	Ann d of Joshua & Mary SIDDINS
Feb 2	William s of William & Eleanor GUEST
Feb 7	Elisabeth d of Thomas & Mary CRANE
Feb 13	Hannah d of Joseph & Margaret FOSBROOK
Feb 20	Richard s of William & Sarah NEWMAN
Feb 21	Robert s of John & Sarah PERRINS
Feb 23	William s of William & Mary GUEST
Feb 27	Catherine d of John & Jane LEA
Mar 16	Ann d of Humfrey & Sarah BATE
Mar 19	Sarah d of Philip & Elisabeth HAYNES

Marriages 1748

Apr 12	John CHAMBERS & Mary SUCH
Jun 12	John WELD & Mary JOHNSON
Jul 9	Thomas ARNET & Mary INSUL

© Staffordhire Parish Registers Society

Jul 12	Benjamin TAYLER & Elisabeth JONES
Aug 9	William TOLLEY & Elisabeth SUCH
Oct 18	John JOYCE & Sarah CHAMBERLIN
Oct 30	Samuel GREEN & Ann LOWE
Dec 8	John JINKES & Mary RUDGE
Dec 27	John PEW & Sarah BANKS
Jan 31	Joseph COLLEY & Elisabeth LINE
Feb 5	Richard HAYWOOD & Mary JONES

Burials 1748

Apr 2	Ann the wife of Mr Thomas WALDRON
Apr 3	John CRANE
Apr 8	Mary BECKLEY
Apr 23	Mary HANCOX
May 17	John BLUN
Jun 9	Jane d of John & Sarah HAYWOOD
Sep 1	John s of John & Eleanor COLBORNE
Sep 6	John s of Edward & Isabel TOWNSEND
Sep 7	William JOHNSON
Sep 24	Margaret HAYNES
Sep 27	Elisabeth the wife of Thomas KING
Oct 12	Prudence d of Thomas GREEN
Oct 21	Humfrey FRYER
Nov 2	Joseph s of Joseph & Margaret FOSBROOK
Nov 17	Arthur KIDSON
Nov 20	Mary the wife of Henry PEAL [BT's: "PEALE"] with Aff.
Nov 28	Mary d of George & Mary BURFORD
Dec 29	Jane KETLEY
Feb 11	Sarah d of James & Mary FORGEAM
Feb 11	Mary MORRIS
Mar 13	Elisabeth ROBINSON
Mar 18	Ann d of Isaac FRYER

Baptisms 1748

Apr 4	Samuel s of Richard & Ann HIGGINS
Apr 6	William daughter[sic & also recorded the same in the BT's] of Elisabeth NORRIS Illegitimate
Apr 12	John s of Edward & Elisabeth BLUN
May 7	Richard s of Richard & Mary PRICE
May 8	Martha d of Thomas & Margaret COOK
May 20	Jane d of John & Sarah HAYWOOD
May 25	Mary d of Thomas & Phebe HILL
Jun 11	Thomas s of John & Hannah COATES
Jun 12	Mary d of Richard & Agnes TOWNSEND
Jun 17	Elisabeth d of John & Ann HOLLINS
Jun 18	Evans s of Evans & Mary REYNOLDS
Jun 25	Sarah d of William & Ann PERRY
Jul 17	Elisabeth d of Richard & Grace INCHMORE
Jul 20	Sarah d of John & Mary DAVIS
Sep 11	Richard s of Thomas & Hannah WARREN

Sep 18	Joseph s of William & Phebe TAYLER
Sep 24	John s of Thomas & Mary GREEN
Sep 24	John s of Humfrey & Sarah BAYLIS
Oct 9	Robert s of Robert & Ann SMITH
Oct 16	Mary d of James & Mary BURTON
Nov 4	John s of William & Elisabeth CHURCHYARD
Nov 6	Timothy s of William & Elisabeth MATTHEWS
Nov 17	Mary d of George & Mary BURFORD
Nov 18	Elisabeth d of Melicent BROOK illegitimate
Nov 20	Joseph s of Thomas & Jane MASON
Dec 3	Edward s of Richard & Rachel DUNN
Dec 11	William Holmer s of Edward & Mary GROVE
Jan 6	William s of Samuel & Ann GREEN
Jan 6	John s of Matthew & Elisabeth UNDERWOOD
Jan 7	John s of John & Mary ALLEN
Jan 8	John s of John & Mary ALLEN [sic; also entered twice in BT's]
Jan 12	George s of Christopher & Elisabeth TOLLEY
Jan 14	Sarah d of James & Mary FORGEAM
Jan 20	William s of Mary LAMBERT illegitimate
Jan 21	Susanna d of William & Elisabeth TOLLEY
Feb 20	Charles s of Joseph & Ann COALMORE
Feb 22	John s of Joseph & Sarah LEBAN
Feb 25	Ann d of Isaac & Elisabeth FRYER
Mar 7	John s of Robert & Elisabeth DANIEL
Mar 17	William s of John & Sarah HAYWOOD

Baptisms 1749

Mar 26	Benjamin s of John & Sarah SHINTON
Apr 22	Charles s of John & Mary TYSOE
May 14	Thomas & Joseph sons of Sarah TURNER illegitimate
May 14	Elisabeth d of Paul & Mary GARDENER
May 15	Jinny d of Edward & Sarah NEWMAN
Jun 14	Margaret d of George & Elisabeth DODSON
Jun 14	Mary d of Humfrey & Sarah BATE
Jun 17	John s of John & Sarah JOYCE
Jul 8	John & Jeremiah sons of John & Mary CHAMBERS
Jul 9	Betty d of Richard & Mary HAYWARD
Jul 19	Richard s of John & Ann HOLLINS
Jul 26	Joseph s of Eleanor BRIDGENS illegitimate
Aug 13	Benjamin s of Thomas & Mary RICHARDS
Aug 27	Mary d of Edward & Isabel TOWNSEND
Aug 29	Ann d of Samuel & Mary HOLLINS
Aug 29	John s of Edward & Mary HAYES
Sep 17	John s of Samuel & Jane PARDOE
Sep 30	Sarah d of Charles & Sobieski HILLMAN
Nov 1	Ann d of George & Mary WHITE
Nov 3	Richard s of Richard & Agnes TOWNSEND
Nov 4	Thomas s of John & Eleanor COLBORNE
Nov 6	Elisabeth d of John & Mary JINKES
Dec 3	Hannah d of William & Ann DUDDALL

Dec 5	Elisabeth d of William & Elisabeth HADLEY
Dec 5	Elisabeth d of Joseph & Elisabeth COLLEY
Dec 7	Joseph & Mary s & d of Humfrey & Mary KETLEY
Dec 26	Thomas s of Thomas & Ann DERRICK
Dec 31	William s of John & Mary SIMS
Jan 7	Benjamin s of Richard & Ann OLIVER
Jan 20	Sarah d of William & Jane SMITH
Jan 21	John s of William & Jane TIMMINS
Jan 28	Ann d of George & Mary COLY
Feb 5	Richard s of Thomas & Phebe HILL
Feb 12	Sarah d of William & Sarah NEWMAN
Feb 17	Thomas s of Benjamin & Esther WHITE
Feb 23	Richard s of Richard & Joan MOSELEY
Feb 25	John s of Thomas & Mary LINE
Feb 25	William s of William & Eno NORMCOTT
Feb 27	Mary d of John & Ann TIMMINS
Mar 10	Francis s of Thomas & Elisabeth COATES

Marriages 1749

Apr 6	John BEARD & Mary HILL
May 2	John TIMMINS & Ann MERCHANT
May 28	William GOLD & Mary TURNER
Aug 31	James PERRY & Mary MOSELEY
Sep 4	Thomas KING & Mary LAMB
Nov 16	Edward HILLMAN & Priscilla CHAMBERLIN
Dec 3	John EVANS & Mary DODSON
Dec 26	John LINE & Mary CRUMP [BT's: "CRUMPE"]
Jan 10	John JONES & Mary TOLLEY
Feb 6	Thomas REYNOLDS & Sarah VEAL

Burials 1749

Apr 29	William VEAL with Aff.
May 2	Edward WALDRON with Aff.
May 9	Jane the wife of John MOUNSTEVEN with Aff.
May 17	Joseph s of Sarah TURNER
May 29	William TOLLEY with Aff.
May 31	Thomas s of Sarah TURNER
Jun 13	Elisabeth DODSON with Aff.
Jun 19	John s of John & Sarah JOYCE with Aff.
Aug 31	Elisabeth the wife of William TIMMINS with Aff.
Sep 1	John DODSON with Aff.
Nov 8	Elisabeth PARKES
Nov 11	Sarah OWEN with Aff.
Nov 18	Edward s of Richard & Rachel DUNN
Dec 28	John s of John BARRETT
Dec 5	Margaret the wife of George DODSON
Jan 12	Hannah d of James & Mary FORGEAM with Aff.
Jan 18	John TRUEMAN
Jan 22	Benjamin COLLITwith Aff.
Mar 1	Mary MOSELEY

Mar 8 Michael SPARREY
Mar 20 Samuel MORRIS with Aff.

More Baptisms 1749

Mar 11 Eleanor d of Henry & Eleanor GUEST
[The writing changes at this point]
Mar 13 Elisabeth d of Thomas & Elisabeth SIMS
Mar 18 Betty d of William FRYER & Margery his wife

Marriages 1750

Apr 23 Joseph ROLES & Mary BROOK
Apr 29 Henry MOSELY & Ann MASON
May 26 John DUDLEY & Mary HICKMANS
Aug 21 John BRICE & Hannah SUTCH
Oct 1 Thomas FRYER & Betty CHAPMAN
Dec 12 Henry HADDOCK & Ann TILLEY
Jan 3 Joseph GROVE & Elisabeth ROBINSON

Burials 1750

Apr 14 Elisabeth WARD
Apr 18 John SMALLMAN   with Aff.
Apr 22 Thomas KETLEY   with Aff.
Apr 26 Francis HUGHES
May 4 Betty d of William FRYER & Margery his wife
May 5 Esther the wife of Benjamin WHITE   with Aff.
May 19 William TIMMINS
Jun 4 Thomas CHAPMAN
Jul 8 Mary the wife of Samuel HOLLINS   with Aff.
Jul 23 Mary d of Edward HILLMAN & Priscilla his wife
Aug 8 Edward BAKER   with Aff.
Aug 22 Sarah d of John LEA & Jane his wife
Aug 27 Samuel s of Thomas MASON & Jane his wife
Aug 30 Robert WHITTON & Sarah his wife were buried
Sep 1 Nicholas s of Joseph HANCOX & Hannah his wife
Sep 29 George GROVE
Oct 11 Edward GROVE
Oct 30 Hannah GREEN
Nov 2 Humphrey BATE

Baptisms 1750

Mar 28 Thomas s of Thomas KING & Mary his wife
Apr 16 Edward s of Samuel BELL & Sarah his wife
Apr 16 Benjamin s of John LEA & Jane his wife
Apr 18 William s of John CHALTON & Hannah his wife
Apr 27 Sarah d of John JOYCE & Sarah his wife
Apr 29 Cicely d of Christopher BARNWELL & Mary his wife
May 12 Edward SAUNDERS in the 51st year of his life
May 9 Edward s of John BENNISON & Martha his wife
May 20 Ann d of Thomas BARNETT & Jane his wife
Jun 5 Martha d of Joseph COALMORE & Ann his wife

Jun 16	Thomas s of Joseph FOSBROOK & Margaret his wife
Jun 24	Hannah, d of John MORRIS & Hannah his wife
Jul 6	Thomas s of Humphrey BATE & Sarah his wife
Jul 12	Ann d of William GOLD & Mary his wife
Jul 22	Humphry s of James PERRY & Mary his wife
Jul 22	Mary d of Edward & Priscilla HILLMAN
Jul 29	John s of John HOLMES & Mary his wife
Jul 29	Mary d of Willm GUEST & Mary his wife
Sep 2	Ann d of Samuel GREEN & Ann his wife
Sep 2	John s of Thomas MASON & Jane his wife
Sep 5	Ann d of John EVANS & Mary his wife
Sep 29	Shusannah d of William MATTHEWS & Elizabeth his wife
Sep 29	Samuel s of Philip HAYNES & Elizabeth his wife
Oct 6	Alice d of Richard & Rachel DUNN his wife
Nov 3	Thomas s of Richard PIERCY & Mary his wife
Nov 3	Richard s of Josiah SIDDINS & Mary his wife
Nov 4	John s of John PERRINS & Elizabeth his wife
Nov 10	James s of John COATES & Hannah his wife
Nov 17	James s of Robert SMITH & Ann his wife
Dec 5	Betty illegitimate d of Mary WILLIAMS
Dec 8	Phebe illegitimate d of Sarah TURNER
Dec 9	John s of Willm COATES & Mary his wife
Dec 15	Mary d of Thomas CRANE & Mary his wife
Dec 26	John s of John BRADSHAW & Sarah his wife
Jan 1	Margaret d of John HAYWOOD & Sarah his wife
Jan 6	Ann d of James BAYLIS & Sarah his wife
Feb 2	Mary d of John TYSO & Mary his wife
Feb 21	Isaac s of Edwd NEWMAN & Sarah his wife

More Burials 1750

Nov 8	Esther ye wife of Soley WELLS
Nov 10	Thomas s of Richard PIERCY & Mary
Nov 27	John BATE
Nov 29	John s of John HOLMES & Mary his wife with Affidavit
Dec 9	Sarah the wife of Mr Fra^s [BT's: "Francis"] HANCOX with Aff.
Dec 16	John s of Thos MASON & Jane his wife
Dec 25	Ann TWYCROSS
Jan 1	Samuel CARELESS
Jan 15	Wm COATES
Feb 4	Dorothy ALLEN with Aff.
Feb 16	Joseph MORRIS with Aff.
Feb 27	Alice ALDEN
Mar 3	Mary BROWN with Aff.
Mar 24	John s of John BRADSHAW & Sarah

More Baptisms 1750

Mar 3	Helen d of John ALLEN & Mary his wife
Mar 12	Thomas s of Willm TAYLOR & Phebe his wife
Mar 24	Sarah d of Joseph HILL & Betty his wife

Baptisms 1751

Apr 28	William s of John SUCH & Ann his wife
May 4	Joseph s of Edwd LINE & Mary his wife
May 25	Richard s of William GILES & Ann his wife
Jun 1	William s of Edwd STOKES & Mary his wife
Jun 2	Ann d of Samuel PARDOE & Jane his wife
Jun 13	James s of Edwd BLUNN & Elizabeth his wife
Jun 19	William s of John HOLLINS & Ann his wife
Jun 21	Martha d of Thos WHITTINGHAM & Martha his wife
Jun 29	Mary d of John ALLEN & Mary his wife
Aug 13	John s of Richard PRICE & Mary his wife
Aug 13	William s of John JENKS & Mary his wife
Aug 30	Letitia d of Willm CHURCHYARD & Eliz his wife
Sep 1	Bartholomew s of Thos FRYER & Betty his wife
Sep 1	Abigail d of Willm PERRY & Ann his wife
Sep 19	Sarah d of John BRASIER & Hannah his wife
Sep 14	William s of Evans REYNOLDS & Mary his wife
Oct 2	William s of Joseph GROVE & Elizabeth his wife
Oct 4	Thomas s of John JOYCE & Sarah his wife
Oct 5	Sarah d of Willm TOLLEY & Elizabeth his wife
	[The next entry is crossed through:]
	~~Mary d of William BEVAN & Martha his wife~~
Oct 12	Samuel s of Thomas COLBERN & Elizabeth his wife
Oct 19	Ann d of Thomas KING & Mary his wife
Nov 3	Thomas s of Richd MOSELEY & Joan his wife
Nov 5	John s of Richd HAYWOOD & Mary his wife
Nov 9	John s of Edward HILLMAN & Priscilla his wife
Nov 10	Margaret d of James BURTON & Mary his wife
Nov 18	William s of Willm CHAMBERS & Sarah his wife
Nov 26	Ann d of Thomas HILL & Phebe his wife
Dec 7	Sarah d of John BENNISON & Martha his wife
Dec 10	Sarah d of Paul GARDNER & Mary his wife
Dec 11	Margaret d of Joseph BROWN & Maria his wife
Dec 18	Richard s of Humphrey BATE & Sarah his wife

Marriages 1751

Apr 8	William ALLEN & Ann DUNN
Jun 1	John HAYNES & Sarah HILLMAN
Aug 5	William DAVIS & Mary PENSON
Aug 25	Gabriel MOYLE & Dorothy BOWER
Sep 26	Edward SILK & Catherine CLARKE
Oct 13	Soley WELLS & Sarah SMITH
Nov 5	John HIDSTONE & Hannah THOMMAS
	[One entry erased]

Burials 1751

Apr 12	William s of William & Elizabeth CHURCHYARD
Apr 19	Elizabeth LYE
May 2	John RAWLEY
May 18	Ann DOLPHIN

May 18	John s of James BAYLIS & Sarah his wife
May 20	Thomas s of Will[m] TAYLOR & Phebe his wife
Jun 22	Dorothy ADAMS
Jun 23	Phoebe illegitimate d of Sarah TURNER
Jul 7	Mary HILL
Jul 18	James s of Edw[d] BLUNN & Elisabeth his wife
Aug 3	William WARD
Aug 21	Edward WORRALL
Aug 29	Thomas TOY
Sep 20	Mary d of John ALLEN & Mary his wife
Sep 22	Evan EVANS
Oct 6	Mary d of William BIVAN & Martha his wife
Oct 27	Richard s of Joshua SIDDINS & Mary his wife
Nov 2	Thomas s of Humphrey BATE & Sarah his wife with Aff.
Nov 3	Mary PUGH
Nov 5	William TOWNSHEND
Dec 3	Benjamin HALLEN with Aff.
Dec 4	Francis HATCHETT
Dec 14	Ann COMBER with Aff.

The Year 1752 takes Date on ye 1st January according to an Act of Parliament made in ye 24th Year of ye Reign of our Sovereign [name erased] George ye 2^d in ye Year of our Lord 1751

Baptisms in 1752

Jan 6	Richard s of Rich[d] INCHMORE & Grace his wife
Jan 12	Jacob s of Isaac FRYER & Elizabeth his wife
Feb 19	George s George & Mary WHITE his wife[sic]
Feb 24	Edward s of Thomas DUTTON & Jane his wife
Feb 29	Elijah GROVE illegitimate s of Hannah CLARKE
Mar 14	Ann d of William HADLEY & Elizabeth his wife
Mar 14	William s of Rich[d] HASLEDINE & Hannah his wife
Mar 15	Ann d of Humphrey KETLEY & Mary his wife
Mar 30	Hannah d of John TIMMINS & Ann his wife
Mar 30	Sarah d of John MORRIS & Hannah his wife
Apr 3	John s of Mr John HOLMES & Mary his wife
May 2	Joseph d of Thomas COATES & Elizabeth his wife
May 9	Ann d of Edward HAYES & Mary his wife
May 30	Sarah d of Thomas LYNE & Sarah his wife
May 30	Mary d of William & Eno NORMCOTT
	[An entry has been erased]
Jun 5	John s of John HAYNES & Sarah his wife
Jul 6	William & Stephen sons of Joseph COALMORE & Ann his wife
Jun 10	Thomas s of John ALLEN & Mary his wife
Jul 21	Isaac s of Thomas & Jane MASON
Jul 21	Betty d of Thomas ROBINS & Elizabeth his wife
Aug 16	Margaret d of John SIMS & Mary his wife
Aug 21	Elizabeth d of Samuel BELL & Sarah his wife
Sep 16	Mary d of William GOSLIN & Elizabeth his wife

Sep 21	Nancy d of John DAVIES & Elizabeth his wife
Oct 17	Edward s of Oliver DIXON & Mary his wife
Oct 19	John s of John HAYWOOD & Sarah his wife
Oct 29	Mary d of James PERRY & Mary his wife
Nov 10	Eleanor d of Edward BLUNN & Elizabeth his wife
Nov 15	Thomas s of Thomas SIMS & Elizabeth his wife
Nov 19	Joseph s of John HIDSTONE & Hannah his wife
Dec 3	Francis s of Willm PLYMLEY & Jane his wife
Dec 2	Nancy d of William SMITH & Jane his wife
Dec 16	William s of Edward NEWMAN & Sarah his wife
Dec 28	Lucy d of John WILLIAMS & Susannah his wife

Marriages 1752

Jan 8	William GOSLIN & Elizabeth COLLIT [BT's: "COLLETT"]
May 15	James KNOTT & Margaret ORAM
May 27	Francis WARNEL & Mary JONES
Jun 15	Benjamin GAUNT & Isabel TOWNSHEND
Jun 15	Oliver DIXON & Mary HODGHES [BT's: "HODGES"]
Jun 29	Humphrey DUTTEN & Mary BROOKE
Sep 24	Samuel SUTCLIFF & Mary MASON
Oct 3	William PEACE & Sarah BLUNN
Dec 3	Benjamin SIMONS & Hannah PARTRIDGE

Burials 1752

Jan 1	John IMMS
Jan 11	Mary DUNNE with Aff.
Jan 22	Thomas JOHNSON
Jan 24	Elizabeth DOVEY with Aff.
Feb 9	Daniel HANCOX
Mar 24	Ann DERRICK
Apr 3	Ann TWYCROSS
Apr 15	John BRISCOE
Apr 18	Sarah CARELESS
Apr 20	Paul GARDENER
May 5	William JOHNSON
May 17	Elijah GROVE illegitimate son of Hannah CLARKE
Jun 5	Sarah HAYNES
Jun 22	William Holmer s of Edwd & Mary GROVE
Aug 6	Benjamin BECKLEY
Oct 3	Ann FRYER
Oct 18	Joyce DODSON with Aff.
Oct 26	John LYNE
Oct 29	Thomas KING
Nov 8	William s of Edward STOKES & Mary his wife
Nov 15	Eleanor the wife of William HAYNES
Dec 3	Joseph COLEBURN [BT's: "COLEBORNE"]
Dec 6	Evan REYNOLDS
Dec 9	John BARRETT
Dec 11	John HORTON with Aff.
Dec 18	John HOLMES with Aff.

Dec 17　Thomas BROOK
Dec 18　John COATES

Baptisms 1753

Jan 6　Thomas s of James BAYLIS & Sarah his wife
Jan 6　Ann d of Robert SMITH & Ann his wife
Jan 7　Sarah d of Henry GUEST & Eleanor his wife
Jan 9　Richard s of George COOLY & Mary his wife
Jan 13　Edward s of Richard DUNN & Rachel his wife
Jan 13　Samuel s of William GOLD & Mary his wife
Jan 20　Richard s of Joseph FOSBROOKE & Margaret his wife
Jan 20　Betty s of Joshua SOUTHERN & Mary his wife
Jan 25　Thomas s of William BIVAN & Hannah his wife
Feb 3　Thomas s of Thomas GREEN & Mary his wife
Feb 3　Thomas s of Thomas BARNET & Jane his wife
Feb 8　Ann d of William TAYLOR & Phoebe his wife
Feb 10　Harry s of Widow KING
Feb 18　Jeremiah of William MATTHEWS & Elizabeth his wife
Feb 25　Mary d of Samuel GREEN & Ann his wife
Feb 28　Bartley s of Thomas FRYER & Betty his wife
Mar 11　Mary d of William ALLEN & Mary his wife
Mar 12　Elisabeth d of John TILLEY & Agnes his wife
Mar 17　John s of Joseph GROVE & Elizabeth his wife
Mar 25　Sarah d of Widow COATES
Apr 14　William s of Simon NORMCOTT & Jane his wife
Apr 16　John s of John DEAN & Rebeckah his wife
Apr 28　Sarah d of William GUEST & Mary his wife
May 4　Sarah d of John PARR & Sarah his wife
May 27　Richard s of Thomas COLEBURN [BT's: "COLEBORNE"] & Hannah his wife
Jun 13　Ann d of John HOLLINS & Ann his wife
Jul 9　Martha d of Benjamin GAUNT & Isabel his wife
Jul 12　Edward s of Willm PEACE & Sarah his wife
Jul 30　Tryphena d of Benjamin DODSON & Mary his wife
Jul 31　Mary the illegitimate d of Mary HICKS
Sep 9　Robert s of Robert DANIEL & Elizabeth his wife
Sep 2　Margaret d of John CHALTON & Hannah his wife
Oct 5　Joseph s of Sarah BAYLIS illegitimate
Aug 21[sic]　Robert s of Meredith EVANS & Mary his wife
Oct 12　Mary d of Edward STOKES
Nov 5　Mary d of Samuel HIDSTONE & Betty his wife
Nov 9　Hannah illegitimate d of Margaret ROBINSON
Nov 10　Edward s of Edward HILLMAN & Priscilla his wife
Nov 13　William s James KNOTT & Margaret his wife
Nov 23　Ann d of Thomas ROBINS & Elizabeth his wife
Nov 23　Samuel s of William TOY & Mary his wife
Nov 26　Thomas s of Thomas WHITTINGHAM & Martha his wife
Dec 2　Thomas s of John SUCH & Ann his wife
Dec 2　Jane d of John HAYWOOD & Sarah his wife
Dec 2　Ann d of John JENKS & Mary his wife

Dec 2   Joseph s of Joseph COLLEY & Elizabeth his wife
Dec 16 William s of William NEWMAN & Sarah his wife
Dec 25 Martha d of John JOYCE & Sarah his wife
Dec 25 Mary d of Joseph HANCOX & Frances his wife
Dec 26 Ann d of John BENNISON & Martha his wife
Dec 26 John the illegitimate s of Ann TAYLOR

Marriages 1753

Feb 27 Samuel HIDSTONE & Betty BLUNN
Mar 5   John INCHMORE & Hannah BARRNETT
May 23 William POWELL & Mary HARRIS
Sep 2   Edward EVANS & Sarah KING
Oct 17 William HARES [BT's: "HAES"] & Frances GWYER

Burials 1753

Jan 19 Edward ALLEN
Jan 25 Humphrey KETLEY
Feb 9   Joseph FOSBROOKE [BT's: "FOSBROOK"]
Feb 12 William TRUEMAN   with Aff.
Feb 12 Bartholomew s of Thomas FRYER & Betty his wife
Feb 23 Catherine d of the Rev^d Mr PERRY
Feb 27 Thomas s of Thomas DERRICK
Mar 4   Eleanor d of Edward BLUNN & Elizabeth
Mar 8   William MATTHEWS
Mar 20 Ann d of James BAYLIS & Sarah his wife
Mar 28 Mary HARE
Apr 6   Judith FINNEY
Apr 16 Elizabeth MORRIS
May 3   Mary RICHARDS
May 6   John TILLEY
May 7   Samuel SMITH
Jul 20 Eleanor d of Mr Joseph HANCOX & Hannah his wife
Jul 24 Isaac s of Thomas MASON & Jane his wife
Aug 5   Sarah d of Hannah COATES Widow
Aug 11 Elizabeth the wife of Mr Jeremiah CASWELL with Aff.
Aug 15 Richard s of James BURTON & Mary his wife
Aug 18 Richard s of Richard OLIVER & Ann his wife
Oct 7   Robert s of Meredith EVANS & Mary his wife
Oct 12 Mary the wife of Edward STOKES
Oct 14 John CHALTON
Oct 28 John BROOK
Oct 29 Edward s of Edward GROVE & Mary his wife
Nov 4   Ann d of Willm GOLD & Mary his wife
Nov 18 Richard HILLMAN [19 may have been overwritten by 18; BT's: "18"]]
Nov 18 Mary TAYLOR
Nov 20 James s of Thos RICHARDS & Mary his wife
Nov 23 Margery LYNE
Dec 7   Elizabeth BROWN
Dec 12 John CRUNDALL

Dec 14   Thomas NORRIS
Dec 20   Mary MOSELEY
Dec 29   Mary d of Joseph HANCOX & Frances his wife   with Aff.

Baptisms 1754

Jan 6   John s of Benjamin SIMMONS & Hannah his wife
Jan 13   Thomas s of John ALLEN & Mary his wife
Jan 13   Elizabeth d of John ASHLEY & Hannah his wife
Feb 22   Catherine d of William LYE & Hannah his wife
Mar 12   Richard s of William POWELL & Mary his wife
Mar 17   John s of John TIMMINS & Ann his wife
Mar 17   Richard s of Richard HAYWOOD & Mary his wife
Apr 16   Sarah d of Thomas HILL & Phoebe his wife
Apr 19   Margaret d of John RAYBOULD & Rachel his wife
Apr 19   John s of Richard REYNOLDS & Mary his wife
May 19   Mary d of Richard CLIMER & Elizabeth his wife
Jun 2   William s of William GILES & Ann his wife
Jun 16   Margaret d of Samuel PARDOE & Jane his wife
Jun 16   Charles s of Thomas MASON & Jane his wife
Jun 18   Joseph s of Joseph CRANE & Ruth his wife
Jun 22   Mary d of John GROSVENOR & Mary his wife
Jul 14   William s of William FRYER & Margery his wife
Jul 21   Mary d of John TIMMINS & Jane his wife
Jul 27   Joseph s of John PARR & his wife
Jul 30   William s of Thomas DERRICK & Jane his wife
Aug 3   Sarah d of Joseph BROWN & Maria his wife
Aug 10   Betty d of John HIDSTONE & Hannah his wife
Aug 17   Catharine d of Thomas BIVAN & Mary his wife
Aug 28   Mary d of Oliver DIXON & Mary his wife
Sep 7   Ann d of John BAYLIS & Joan his wife
Sep 8   John s of Willm ROBINSON & Mary his wife
Sep 15   Sarah d of Thomas WESTWOOD & Sarah his wife
Sep 25   Jane & Keturah daughters of William GOSLIN & Elizabeth his wife
Oct 3   Mary d of John HOLLINS & Ann his wife
Oct 11   Elizabeth d of John OLDFIELD & Elizabeth his wife
Oct 12   Mary d of Robert SMITH & Ann his wife
Oct 20   Humphrey s of George WHITE & Mary his wife
Oct 26   Ann d of Samuel SUTCLIFF & Mary his wife
Oct 27   Mary d of Willm TAYLOR & Phoebe his wife
Oct 30   Mary the illegitimate d of Ann BROOK
Nov 16   Edward s of Edward HAYES & Mary his wife
Dec 14   Betty d of Henry GUEST & Eleanor his wife
Dec 5   Richard s of Joseph COLLEY & Elizabeth his wife
Dec 26   John s of John TILLEY & Agnes his wife
Dec 26   Richard s of Richard HASLEDINE & Hannah his wife
Dec 26   Thomas Turner s of John HAYWOOD & Sarah his wife

Burials 1754

Jan 5   Elizabeth DERRICK

Jan 6	Mary VEAL
Jan 16	Dorothy HARPER
Jan 25	Betty HIDSTONE
Jan 31	James RICHARDS
Feb 9	Susannah FEREDAY
Mar 2	Ann d of John HOLLINS & Ann his wife
Mar 14	Mary VEAL
Mar 19	Martha d of John JOYCE & Sarah his wife
Mar 26	Betty the illegitimate d of Mary WILLIAMS
Mar 31	Mary SMALLMAN
Apr 7	Mary d of Samuel HIDSTONE
Apr 25	Elizabeth WHITE
May 15	Harry PERRINS
Jul 19	John s of William INCHMORE
Jul 29	Ann MASON
Sep 3	Mary MUCKLESTONE
Oct 4	Mary d of John HOLLINS & Ann his wife
Oct 12	Joseph CHAMBERLAIN with Aff.
Oct 24	John s of Edward EVANS & Sarah his wife
Nov 16	Ann BAYLIS
Nov 23.	Eleanor RAWLEY
Dec 1	John s of John TIMMINS & Ann his wife
Dec 8	John TOWNSHEND

Marriages 1754

Jan 27	John BAYLIS & Joanna ALDEN
Feb 13	William HICKMANS & Ann JEVENS

More Burials 1754

Dec 9	William STOKES
Dec 29	Betty d of Henry GUEST & Eleanor his wife

Baptisms 1755

Jan 1	John s of Meredith EVANS & Mary his wife
Jan 2	Elizabeth d of George COLY & Mary his wife
Jan 5	Mary d of John PERRINS & Sarah his wife
Jan 25	Thomas s of Thomas NORRIS & Mary his wife
Feb 2	Samuel s of William NORMCOTT & Eno his wife
Feb 19	Benjamin s of Thomas ROBINS & Elizabeth his wife
Mar 7	William illegitimate s of Eleanor CRUMP [BT's: "CRUMPE"]
Mar 8	John s of James PERRY & Mary his wife
Mar 16	Samuel s of Thomas COATES & Elizabeth his wife
Mar 22	Thomas s of William GOOLD & Mary his wife
Apr 11	Ann d of Thomas FEREDAY & Mary his wife
Apr 12	James s of Bishop SMITH & Hannah his wife
Apr 26	John s of George SOUTHALL & Hannah his wife
Apr 27	Samuel s of Samuel GREEN & Ann his wife
May 1	Mary d of Thos LINE & Mary his wife
May 4	Jane d of William ALLEN & Mary his wife
May 15 [BT's: "16"]	Margaret d of Edward NEWMAN & Sarah his wife

May 3	Mary d of John EVANS & Mary his wife
Jun 1	Paul s of William MATTHEWS & Elizabeth his wife
Jun 7	Richard s of Thomas BARNETT & Jane his wife
Jun 7	Nancy d of William GUEST & Mary his wife
Jun 18	Elizabeth d of Humphrey BATE & Sarah his wife
Jul 6 [BT's: "20"]	Rachel d of Walter KIDSON & Margaret his wife
May 6[sic]	Sarah d of George STOKES & Sarah his wife
Jul 19	John s of William BIVAN & Martha his wife
Aug 9	Margaret d of Richard DUNN & Rachel his wife
Aug 31	John s of Joseph CRANE & Ruth his wife
Sep 6	Mary d of Thomas DERRICK & Jane his wife
Sep 9	Elizabeth d of John GROVE & Elizabeth his wife
Sep 19	Sarah d of Harry BROWN & Mary his wife
Sep 22	Mary d of George ECCLES & Catherine his wife
Oct 3	Ann d of Thomas SIMS & Elizabeth his wife
Oct 18	Sarah d of Benjamin SIMMONS & Hannah his wife
Oct 24	John s of John HOLLINS & Ann his wife
Nov 30	Elizabeth d of Richard MOSELEY & Jane his wife
Dec 7	James s of Joseph GROVE & Elizabeth his wife
Dec 27	Sarah d of Edward HILLMAN & Priscilla his wife
Dec 27	John s of John BENNISON & Martha his wife

Burials 1755

Jan 5	Robert SCOTT son of a travailing woman
Jan 22	Sarah JOHNSON
Apr 2	Edward BROWN with Aff.
Apr 12	Eleanor HOLMES with Aff.
Apr 21	Ann d of Thomas FEREDAY & Mary his wife
Apr 27	William the illegitimate son of Eleanor CRUMP
May 24	Margaret NOTT
May 25	James s of Widow COATES
Jun 3	Humphrey BATE
Jun 4	John LINE [BT's: "LYNE"]
Jun 13	William s of James NOTT
Jun 29	Samuel WHITTINGHAM
Jul 23	Sarah d of James CHAMBERS & Sarah his wife
Aug 6	Elizabeth d of George COLY & Mary his wife
Aug 6	Ann d of Samuel BELL & Sarah his wife
Aug 14	John CHAMBERS
Aug 18	Elizabeth BACHE
Sep 11	John RICHARDS
Sep 21	William s of William GILES & Ann his wife
Sep 25	Mary FELLOES
Sep 30	Thomas s of Thomas WHITTINGHAM & Martha his wife
Oct 9	Edward VEAL
Oct 30	John s of John HOLLINS & Ann his wife
Dec 5	Margaret LOWE
Dec 6	Elizabeth the wife of Mr Richard WORAL with Aff.
Dec 10	Elizabeth WARBURTON
Dec 30	William FOLEY Esq[r]

Baptisms 1756

Jan 1	Sarah d of John ASHLEY & Susannah his wife
Jan 6	Elizabeth d of Richard RICKETTS & Mary his wife
Jan 12	Henry s of Henry GUEST & Eleanor his wife
Feb 4	Mary & Lucy daughters of Samuel HIDSTONE & his wife
Mar 2	Thomas s of William HARPER & Nancy his wife
Jan [sic] 26	William s of John TIMMINS & Ann his wife
Mar 20	Samuel s of Jacob GARDENER & Sarah his wife
Mar 24	Margaret d of William TOY & Mary his wife
Mar 28	Mary d of John JENKS & Mary his wife
Apr 2	Esther d of Benjamin DODSON & Mary his wife
Apr 19	Elizabeth d of Richard CLIMER & Elizabeth his wife
Apr 23	Ann d of John RAYBOULD & Rachel his wife
May 8	Mary d of John ALLEN & Mary his wife
May 9	Ann d of John COLLINS & Elizabeth his wife
May 15	Benjamin s of John PARR & Sarah his wife
Jun 8	Violetta d of Benjamin GAUNT & Isabel his wife
Jun 6	Betty d of William NEWMAN & Sarah his wife
Jul 4	Sarah d of George COLY & Mary his wife
Jul 4	Martha d of John EDSTONE & Hannah his wife
Jul 9	Elizabeth d of Meridith EVANS & Mary his wife
Jul 10	Mary d of John MUCKLESTONE & Ann his wife
Jul 14	Catharine d of Thomas HASLEDINE & Ann his wife
Jul 24	Mary d of Richard HAYWOOD & Mary his wife
Aug 1	Betty d of Thomas JORDAN & Mary his wife
Aug 14	Nancy the illegitimate d of Betty SMITH
Aug 23	Thomas s of Benjamin GROVE & Martha his wife
Sep 17	Thomas s of John TILLEY & Agnes his wife
Sep 18	Mary d of William CHAMBERS & Sarah his wife
Sep 19	Benjamin s of Thomas HILL & Phoebe his wife
Sep 26	James s of William DUDLEY[?] & Hannah his wife
Sep 29	William s of William GILES & Ann his wife
Oct 2	Elizabeth d of William GOSLIN & Elizabeth his wife
Oct 6	Frances Davey s of Thomas BIVAN & Mary his wife
Oct 30	Nancy d of James BAYLIS & Sarah his wife
Nov 7	James s of Richard REYNOLDS & Mary his wife
Nov 9	Ann d of John ALLEN & Mary his wife
Nov 13	John s of Robert SMITH & Ann his wife
Nov 15	Thomas s of Samuel PARDOE & Jane his wife
Nov 21	Thomas s of Job HOGHETTS & Ann his wife
Nov 21	Richard s of Thomas FEREDAY & Mary his wife
Nov 27	Thomas s of William ROBINSON & Ann his wife

[The next entry appears to have been added at the bottom of the page]
Jun[sic] 26   Elizabeth d of Mr George STOKES & Sarah his wife

Burials 1756

Feb 8	Martha RADSTONE
Feb 15	John RADSTONE
Mar 1	Joseph WHITE

Mar 5	Margaret GROVE
Mar 16	Mary HORTON with Aff.
Mar 30	Sarah d of Philip HAYNES & Mary his wife
Mar 31	Elizabeth POWEL
Apr 6	Thomas s of John FELLOWES & Mary his wife
Apr 11	Lydia SHAXSPEAR
Apr 21	Elizabeth TAYLOR
Apr 29	John s of John FELLOES & Mary his wife
May 6	Elizabeth CHAMBERLIN with Aff.
May 20	Mary WATKINS
May 27	Margery TAYLOR
May 30	Mrs Hannah HANCOX the wife of Jos: HANCOX Kidd[r]
Jun 8	John COLY
Jun 22	Meriall KETLEY
Jun 24	Thomas s of John HAYWARD & Sarah his wife
Jul 18	Richard PRICE
Jul 23	Sarah d of George COLY & Mary his wife
Aug 10	Edward NEWMAN
Aug 18	Mary POWELL
Aug 23	Hannah FEREDAY
Sep 7	Sarah MILLS
Sep 1	Thomas s of Benjamin GROVE & Martha his wife
Oct 3	Joan NEWMAN
Oct 9[?]	John TIMMINS with Aff.
Oct 9	Joseph COOKE
Oct 21	John ALLEN
Oct 28	Benjamin DUTTON
Oct 29	Thomas HILL with Aff.
Nov 9	John DERRICK
Nov 18	Elizabeth ALLEN[?]
Nov 18	Thomas BROWN
Nov 18	Ann HUTT
Nov 20	Ann d of William HADLEY & Elizabeth his wife
Nov 25	Thomas s of Thomas BARNETT & Jane his wife
Nov 25	Mary d of Thomas DERRICK & Jane his wife
Nov 26	Francis Devey[?] s of Thos BIVAN & Mary his wife
Nov 28	Samuel s of Jacob GARDINER & Sarah his wife
Nov 28	Catherine d of Thomas HASLEDINE & Ann his wife
Dec 16	Henry WALLINS
Dec 16	Mary COOKE
Dec 18	John s of Samuel PARDOE & his wife
Dec 19	John ERLAM
Dec 24	William MARTEN
Dec 28[?]	John s of Joseph GROVE & Elizabeth his wife

Baptisms 1757

Jan 9	Jonathan s of Thomas VEAL & Elizabeth his wife
Jan 12	Thomas s of Humphrey BATE & Sarah his wife
Feb 5	Thomas Allport s of Tho[s] MASON & Jane his wife
Feb 9	Sarah d of James CORNFORTH & Eleanor his wife

Feb 17	John d of John THOMAS & Priscilla his wife
Feb 18	Francis s of Francis HOMFRAY & Catharine his wife
Feb 22	Richard s of Henry PEALE & Mary his wife
Mar 17	Samuel s of Samuel LEWIS & Mary his wife
Apr 2	Maria d of Joseph BROWN & Maria his wife
Apr 2	Sarah d of Joshua SOUTHERN & Mary his wife
Apr 2	Sarah d of Thomas DERRICK & Jane his wife
Apr 11	Susannah d of John OLDFIELD & Elizabeth his wife
May 11	Sarah the illegitimate d of Sarah BAGOT
May 31	Mary d of John CRUNDALL & Phoebe his wife
Jun 8	Edmund Wells s of John GROVE & Elizabeth his wife
Jun 18	John BARNETT illegitimate s of Phoebe LINES
Jul 6	Sarah d of John COLLINS & Elizabeth his wife
	[An entry appears to have been erased]
Jul 9	Parren[?] s of Richard HASLEDINE & Hannah his wife
Aug 27	Joseph s of Joseph FORSBROOK & Margaret his wife
Aug 28	John s of John SUCH & Ann his wife
Sep 4	Joseph s of William ALLEN & Mary his wife
Sep 7	Abraham s of Mr George STOKES & Sarah his wife
Sep 25	Joseph s of George FLETCHER & Hannah his wife
Oct 16	Ruth d of Joseph CRANE & Ruth his wife
Nov 30	Letitia d of Thomas TIMMINS & Jane his wife
Dec 2	Catherine d of Thomas HASLEDINE & Anne his wife
Dec 9	Mary d of William PEACE & Sarah his wife
Dec 11	John s of Thomas SIMS & Elizabeth his wife
Nov 10[sic]	Benjamin s of John DUDLEY & Elizabeth his wife
Dec 30	Martha d of John BENISON & Martha his wife
	[then apparently added at the bottom of the column:]
May 20	Mary d of Thomas LINE & Mary his wife
	[Two entries appear to have been erased]

Burials 1757

Jan 2	Ann TIMMINS
Jan 15	Mary LOWE
Feb 11	Abigail GIBBS
Feb 19	Thomas Allport s of Thomas MASON & Jane his wife
Feb 27	Samuel s of William NORMCOTT
Mar 11	A woman who was found dead on Iveley common
Mar 23	Mary DIX alias THICKS with Aff.
Mar 27	Hannah TYSO
Mar 29	Mary d of Mary ALLEN
Apr 5	John NEW
Apr 8	Catherine BECKLEY
Apr 21	Richard s of Joseph COLLEY & Elizabeth his wife
May 5	Joseph s of Joseph COLLEY & Elizabeth his wife
May 11	Thomas NEW
Jun 3	William FOXALL
Jun 8	Major LAWRENCE
Jun 9	John MUCKLESTONE
Jun 10	Elizabeth NEW

Jun 18   Mary RAWLEY
Jul 8   Ann DAVIS
Jul 14   Goodwife SPARREY
Aug 12 John s of John THOMAS & Priscilla his wife
Aug 30 Thomas VEAL
Oct 13   Mary GROVE
Oct 16   Nicholas LEACH
Nov 28 John s of Benjamin SIMMONS & Hannah his wife
Dec 2   Sarah d of Benjamin SIMMONS & Hannah his wife
Dec 15 The Rev^d Mr. Richard BATE Minister of Kinver   with Aff.
Dec 19 Margaret NEW
Dec 27 Betty CHURCHYARD

Baptisms 1758

Jan 1   Sarah d of John ROWLEY & Mary his wife
Jan 1   George s of George SOUTHALL & Hannah his wife
Jan 19   William s of Samuel EDSTONE & Joyce his wife
Jan 22   John s of John ASHLEY & Hannah his wife
Jan 28   Henry s of Henry SCOTT & Sarah his wife
Feb 5   John s of Jacob GARDENER & Sarah his wife
Feb 7   Margaret d of John REYNOLDS & Ann his wife
Feb 8[?] James s of William PORTMAN & Mary his wife
Feb 9   Mary d of Charles BROOKSHAW & Mary his wife
Feb 11   William s of Thomas TALBOT & Mary his wife
Feb 12   William s of James BATE & Esther his wife
Feb 15   Mary d of Richard TIMMINS & Elizabeth his wife
Mar 8   Jane d of George WHITE & Mary his wife
Mar 11   Joseph s of Samuel GREEN & Ann his wife
Mar 12   Thomas s of William TIMMINS & Jane his wife
Mar 27   Margaret d of Thomas MASON & Jane his wife
Mar 28   Ann d of John PARR & Sarah his wife
Mar 28   John s of Richard CLYMER & Elizabeth his wife
Apr 23   John s of John TIMMINS & Mary his wife
Apr 29   Betty d of Edward HAYES & Mary his wife
May 12 Sarah d of Constantine TIMMINS & Mary his wife
       [An entry at the top of the column appears to have been erased]
May [?] Sarah d of Mr Henry BATE & Mary his wife
Jun 4   Catherine d of William GUEST & Mary his wife
Jun 5   Joseph s of John TILLEY & Agnes his wife
Jun 10   John s of Richard DUNN & Rachel his wife
Jun 12   Joseph & Mary s & d of Benjamin GAUNT & Isabel his wife
Jul 9   Sarah d of Thomas NORRIS & Mary his wife
Jul 15   Edward s of Edward MATTHEWS & Jane his wife
Jul 22   Sarah d of Thomas BARNET & Jane his wife
Jul 23   Edward s of Henry GUEST & Eleanor his wife
Jul 23   John s of Thomas BLUNT & Sarah his wife
Jul 30   William s of James LEES & Jane his wife
Aug 3   Martha d of Joseph WALTON & Sarah his wife
Sep 3   Edward s of James CORNFORTH & Eleanor his wife
Oct 7   Sarah d of Robert SMITH & Ann his wife

Oct 8   Sarah d of John SHINTON & Sarah his wife
Oct 8   John s of John EDSTONE & Hannah his wife
Oct 15   Elizabeth d of Joseph GROVE & Elizabeth his wife
Nov 11   John s of John JENKS & Mary his wife
Nov 15   Mary d of Edward LYE & Margaret his wife
Nov 18   Benjamin s of Benjamin SIMMONS & Hannah his wife
Nov 19   Hannah d of George STOKES & Sarah his wife
Nov 28   Benjamin s of William TAYLOR & Phoebe his wife
Dec 26   Thomas s of Thomas DERRICK & Jane his wife

Burials 1758

Jan 18   Mr John HOLLINS
Jan 31   Jonathan s of Elizabeth VEAL Widow
Feb 7   Mary BROWN
Feb 7   Joyce BRASIER
Feb 11   Thomas s of Richard TILLEY
Feb 16   Mrs Margaret ELTON
Feb 22   Thomas LYE
Mar 20   Sarah d of John COLLINS & Elizabeth his wife
Mar 26   Mary SPENCER
Apr 7   Francis d of Mr Joseph HANCOX
Apr 19   Mrs Elizabeth BATE   with Aff.
Apr 21   Margaret d of Richard DUNN & Rachel his wife
Apr 22   Catharine LOWE with Aff.
May 12   Joseph HILLMAN
May 15   Joseph s of Joseph FELLOES & Mary his wife
May 16   Humphrey MILLS
Jun 6   John JENKS
Jun 7   Hannah TRUEMAN
Jun 7   John DIX alias THICKS
Jul 4   Mary d of Benjamin GAUNT & Isabel his wife
Jul 6   Joseph s of Benjamin GAUNT & Isabel his wife
Jul 17   Ann OLIVER
Aug 10   Mary CLARKE
Sep 24   Ann MORRIS
Oct 1   Ann BIVAN
Oct 7   Robert WHITTINGHAM
Nov 13   Richard WOOLDRIDGE
Nov 19   Elizabeth BROOKE
Nov 22   Mary HORTON
Nov 22   Hannah d of George STOKES & Sarah his wife
Dec 20   Sarah LAVENDER

Baptisms 1759

Jan 5   William s of William ROBINSON & Mary his wife
Feb 7   Margaret d of James PERRY & Mary his wife
Feb 9   Richard s of John COLLINS & Elizabeth his wife
Feb 24   Joanna d of William GOSLIN & Elizabeth his wife
Feb 24   James s of Richard HAYWARD & Mary his wife
Feb 24   Elizabeth d of Edward HILLMAN & Priscilla his wife

Feb 27	Betty d of George COLEY & Mary his wife
Mar 7	Jeremiah s of Mr Francis HOMFRAY & Catherine his wife
Mar 28	Sarah d of Thomas LAMBETH & Mary his wife
Apr 13	William s of John ALLEN & Mary
Apr 17	Jane d of [BT's: "Mr"] Thomas ROBINS & Elizabeth his wife
Apr 15	William s of Thomas FEREDAY & Mary his wife
Apr 28	Mary d of Samuel LEWIS & Mary his wife
Apr 28	Ann d of Thomas FRYER & Elizabeth his wife
May 12	Thomas s of William NEWMAN & Sarah his wife
Jun 4	Francis s of Francis MEDLICOTT & Mary his wife
Jun 16	Mary d of William GILES & Ann his wife
Jun 24	Thomas s of Samuel PARDOE & Jane his wife
Jul 28	Mary d of Joseph BROWN & Maria his wife
Sep 2	William s of Thomas BROOK & Hannah his wife
Sep 8	William s of William DAVIS & Martha his wife
Sep 16	Elizabeth d of William SMITH & Hannah his wife
Sep 10	Joseph s of John GROVE & Elizabeth his wife
Sep 22	William s of William EVANS & Sarah his wife
Sep 22	Edward s of Thomas BIVAN & Mary his wife
Sep 23	John s of John CRUNDALL & Phoebe his wife
Sep 23	Mary d of Joseph PORTMORE & Mary his wife
Oct 17	Benjamin s of Benjamin DODSON & Mary his wife
Oct 14	Joseph s of John COOKES & Elizabeth his wife
Oct 24	Edward s of Humphrey BATE & Sarah his wife
Nov 4	Samuel s of John ASHLEY & Hannah his wife
Nov 6	Benjamin s of John HAYWARD & Sarah his wife
Nov 22	Nelly BRETTELL illegitimate d of Phebe HILL
Nov 24	Maria d of William HEMMING & Betty his wife
Nov 20	Henry s of Henry EVANS & Mary his wife
Dec 2	James s of George LITTLEWOOD & Sarah his wife
Dec 28	Maria the illegitimate d of Mary WILLIAMS

Burials 1759

Jan 5	Sarah CASWELL
Jan 22	Hannah ERLAM
Jan 28	Elizabeth HAYWOOD
Feb 9	Ann TYSO
Feb 16	Charles JONES
Mar 5	Mary PERRY
Mar 12	Edward BROOKE [BT's: "BROOK"]
Mar 14	Mrs Mary HANCOX
Mar 27	Mary MOSELEY
Apr 16	John SHINTON
Apr 28	Margaret BARNETT
Apr 30	Mrs Elizabeth HODGETTS
May 16	Sarah BROOKE
May 17	John WALDRON
May 21	John BATE
May 27	Elizabeth FRYER
Jun 5	Benjamin RENSHAW

Jun 6	Richard BROOKE
Jun 19	Ann LYE
Jun 19	Joseph NEEDHAM
Jun 26	Christopher BROWN
Jul 12	Mary BRADLEY
Jul 24	The Rev^d Mr. John Comber RAYBOULD with Aff.
Jul 24	Mary POWELL
Aug 9	Elizabeth MATTHEWS
Aug 23	Betty d of George COLEY & Mary his wife
Oct 22	Harry CLARKE
Nov 18	John RICE
Nov 20	William FIELD
Nov 30	Joseph s of John GROVE & Elizabeth his wife
Dec 2	Thomas PADDOCK
Dec 28	John BARNETT
Dec 29	Sarah BAYLIS
Dec 30	William BROOKE

[The bottom half of the page is blank but written obliquely across the page is the comment:]
"Descendant of John LONGFORD"

Baptisms 1760

Jan 5	Thomas s of Richard HASLEDINE & Hannah his wife
Jan 5	John s of Jervis BURFORD & Hannah his wife
Jan 20	John s of James CORNFORTH & Ellen his wife
Jan 26	Thomas s of George FLETCHER & Hannah his wife
Jan 25	Benjamin s of John BENNISON & Martha his wife
Jan 29	William Silvester s of George STOKES & Sarah his wife
Feb 10	John s of William ALLEN & Mary his wife
Feb 10	Benjamin s of John REES & Susannah his wife
Feb 12	Betty d of Samuel EDSTONE & Betty his wife
Feb 16	Susannah d of John PARR & Sarah his wife
Feb 24	John s of John ROWLEY & Mary his wife
Feb 27	Mary d of John PAGETT & Hannah his wife
Mar 8	Eleanor illegitimate d of Phoebe LYNE
Mar 8	Joseph s of Samuel HADDOCK & Elizabeth his wife
Mar 22	Thomas s of Samuel ADAMS & Mary his wife
Mar 23	Rebekah d of Joshua SOUTHERN & Mary his wife
Apr 7	Joseph s of Richard CLIMER & Mary his wife
Apr 7	John s of John JOYCE & Sarah his wife
Apr 8	Richard s of John BROWN & Mary his wife
Apr 20	Margaret d of John TIMMINS & Ann his wife
May 7	Ann d of Edward LYE & Margaret his wife
May 10	Benjamin s of Joseph FORSBROOKE [BT's: "FOSBROOK"] & Margaret his wife
May 21	John s of Benjamin SIMONS & Hannah his wife
May 24	Ann d of Thomas LYNE & Mary his wife
Jun 1	Sarah d of Wm AINSWORTH & Elizabeth his wife
Aug 9	Margaret d of Richard DUNN & Rachel his wife
Aug 17	Laetitia d of Robert GREEN & Elizabeth his wife

Aug 24	Samuel s of John EDSTONE & Hannah his wife
Aug 30	William s of Robert SMITH & Ann his wife
Aug 31	Mary d of Thomas NORRIS [BT's: "MORRIS"] & Elizabeth his wife
Sep 17	Sarah d of Edward MATTHEWS & Jane his wife
Oct 8	Elizabeth d of Lashfoot PERKS & Ann his wife
Oct 29	Sarah d of John COLLINS & Elizabeth his wife
Oct 30	Catherine d of John GROVE & Elizabeth his wife
Nov 8	George s of John WITTAKER & Ann his wife
Nov 9	Josiah s of John JENKS & Mary his wife
Nov 15	Thomas s of Thomas MASON & Jane his wife
Nov 16	James s of John HAYWOOD & Sarah his wife
Nov 21	Sarah d of Thomas SIMS & Elizabeth his wife
Nov 29	Thomas s of Thomas TALBOT & Elizabeth[crossed out; BT's: "Elizabeth"] Mary his wife
Nov 30	William s of John PERRY & Mary his wife
Dec 30	Sarah d of Willm ROBINSON & Mary his wife

Burials 1760

Jan 12	William BAKER
Jan 12	George WINFORD
Jan 15	George BAKER Senr
Jan 17	Edward VEAL
Jan 17	Mrs Martha WALDRON
Jan 23	Benjamin s of John HAYWOOD & Sarah his wife
Feb 11	Margaret COOKE
Mar 11	Martha d of John RAWLEY & Martha his wife
Mar 13	Ann WARD
Mar 13	Charles MUCKLESTONE
Mar 21	William Silvester s of George STOKES & Sarah his wife
Apr 11	Mary LEWIS
Apr 13	Mary INCHMORE
Apr 30	Mrs Martha YATE the wife of the Rev^d Mr William YATE
May 15	Samuel CRANE
May 22	Edward s of Edward MOYLE & Hannah his wife
May 25	Susannah d of Wm BEDALL & Susannah his wife
May 30	Mary d of Jacob GARDENER & Sarah his wife
Jun 2	Margaret GROVE
Jun 20	John COLEBOURN
Jun 22	Sarah GAMSON
Jul 6	Jacob GARDENER
Jul 9	Elizabeth HARRIS
Jul 11	Mary PENSON
Aug 5	Isaac COLLEY
Sep 8	Jane RENSHAW
Oct 19	John FLETCHER
Oct 20	Elizabeth WORRALL
Nov 7	Margery LEECH
Nov 9	John COOKE
Nov 15	Amy WILLIAMS

Nov 20	Mary HARPER
Dec 6	Mary ALLEN
Dec 16	Mr. John BACHE
Dec 16	Harry MOSELEY
Dec 21	Martha RAWLEY
Dec 26	William of William DAVIS & Martha his wife
Dec 29	Catherine d of John GROVE & Elizabeth his wife

Baptisms 1761

Jan 11	Sarah d of George WHITE & Mary his wife
Jan 18	Hannah d of Richard HAYWOOD & Mary his wife
Jan 28	Ann d of John TILLEY & Agnes his wife
Feb 7	Mary d of John REYNOLDS & Ann his wife
Feb 14	Martha d of James PERRY & Mary his wife
Feb 15	John s of James BAYLIS & Sarah his wife
Feb 16	George s of George STOKES & Sarah his wife
Feb 21	Nancy d of William GOSNEL & Elizabeth his wife
Feb 28	William s of Richard REYNOLDS & Mary his wife
Feb 28	Thomas s of Thomas TIMMINS & Jane his wife
Mar 4	Martha the illegitimate d of Elizabeth SIMS
Mar 7	Joseph s of Edward HILLMAN & Priscilla his wife
Mar 14	Ann d of William DAVIS & Martha his wife
Mar 23	Humphrey Bate s of William TIMMINS & Jane his wife
Mar 28	Martha d of William COATES & Mary his wife
Mar 28	Thomas s of John PARR & Sarah his wife
Apr 3	Betty d of Thomas COWHORN & Betty his wife
Apr 11	Hannah d of John CRUNDALL & Phoebe his wife
Apr 12	Sarah d of Joseph COLLEY & Elizabeth his wife
Apr 24	Thomas EVANS the illegitimate s of Mary RUSSELL
Apr 27	Susannah the illegitimate d of Sarah BAGOTT
Jul 26	Samuel s of Richard LEES & Rebeckah his wife
Aug 3	George s of William EVANS & Sarah his wife
Aug 29	Mary d of Thomas BARNETT & Jane his wife
Sep 3	Eleanor d of John GROVE & Elizabeth his wife
Sep 5	Henry s of Henry PEALE & Mary his wife
Sep 25	Helen d of James CORNFORTH & Helen his wife
Sep 29	Mary d of Edward HOBSON & Mary his wife
Oct 11	Mary the illegitimate d of Margaret POTTER
Oct 14	Abigail d of Thomas FRYER & Elizabeth his wife
Oct 16	Margaret the illegitimate d of Margaret BLACKSHAW
Oct 16	Thomas s of Mr. Thomas ROBINS & Elizabeth his wife
Oct 17	Joseph the illegitimate s of Susannah PENSON
Oct 18	Charlotte d of Joseph PORTMAN & Mary his wife
Oct 24	Mary the illegitimate d of Martha SUCH
Oct 28	Benjamin s of Thomas FEREDAY & Mary his wife
Oct 31	Sarah d of John PERRINS & Sarah his wife
Nov 5	Sarah d of John COOKE & Elizabeth his wife
Nov 8	Elizabeth d of Edwd EVANS & Nancy his wife
Nov 22	Hannah d of John BROOK & Sarah his wife
Nov 22	Mary d of Jervis BURFORD & Hannah his wife

Dec 6 Betty d of John ALLEN & Mary his wife
Dec 26 Susannah d of John WHITAKER & Ann his wife
Dec 30 Joseph s of Joseph BROWN & Maria his wife

Burials 1761

Jan 31 John s of Mr Moses HARPER
Feb 9 Mary CLARKE
Feb 23 Martha d of Mr Moses HARPER
Mar 24 William WHITE
Mar 26 Ann TOWNSHEND
Mar 29 Elizabeth the illegitimate d of Phoebe HILL
Apr 7 John SIMS
Apr 15 Richard CARELESS
Apr 17 Thomas BAYLIS
Apr 21 William BECKLEY
Apr 23 Martha BROOKE
Apr 30 Mr Thomas JACKSON
May 1 William TURNER
May 13 Joseph MASON
Jun 2 Elizabeth d of John TILLEY & Agnes his wife
Jun 21 John TILLEY
Jun 22 Mr John GROVE
Jul 3 Mrs Sarah WALDRON
Jul 24 Samuel WHITE
Jul 27 Sarah LAVENDER
Aug 1 George DODSON
Aug 3 Jane GEARY
Sep 20 John HODGES
Oct 24 Margaret d of Joseph BROWN & Maria his wife
Nov 2 Elizabeth TOYE
Nov 3 Benjamin s of Joseph FORSBROOKE & Margaret his wife
Nov 18 Bridget CLEWES

Baptisms 1762

Jan 5 William s of Thomas MEDDEAGE & Mary his wife
Jan 10 Joseph s of Thomas BLUNT & Sarah his wife
Jan 12 Eleanor d of John BROWN & Mary his wife
Jan 16 William s of John EDSTONE & Hannah his wife
Jan 16 Margaret d of John BARNETT & Ann his wife
Jan 16 Elizabeth d of Samuel ADAMS & Mary his wife
Jan 29 Susannah d of Joseph ALDEN & Jane his wife
Feb 6 John s of George FLETCHER & Hannah his wife
Mar 16 Samuel s of Samuel HIDSTONE & Joyce his wife
Mar 27 Samuel the illegitimate s of Elizabeth SMITH
Apr 24 John the illegitimate s of Elizabeth VEAL
Apr 30 Richard PARKS the illegitimate s of Mary VEAL
May 15 Hannah d of Samuel WALL & Sarah his wife
Jun 5 John s of Richard HASLEDINE & Hannah his wife
Jun 11 Sarah d of Richard CLYMER & Elizabeth his wife
Jun 27 Sarah d of Edward MOYLE & Hannah his wife

Jul 5	William s of George STOKES & Sarah his wife
Jul 23	Sarah d of Benjamin DODSON & Mary his wife
Jul 24	Benjamin s of John PARR & Sarah his wife
Jul 25	Joseph s of Robert SMITH & Ann his wife
Jul 28	Sarah d of Richd TIMMINS & Elizabeth his wife
Aug 8	Sarah d of William HEMMING & Betty his wife
Aug 28	Richard s of William COATES & Mary his wife
Sep 11	Sarah d of William ALLEN & Mary his wife
Sep 11	John the illegitimate s of Mary COLEBERN
Sep 11	Joseph the illegitimate s of Sarah INCHMORE
Sep 25	Thomas s of John REEVE & Eliz: his wife
Sep 25	George s of George LITTLEWOOD & Sarah his wife
Sep 25	Edwd s of Verral ADAMS & Margaret his wife
Oct 2	Joseph s of William GILES & Ann his wife
Oct 4	Joshua s of Joshua SOUTHERN & Mary his wife
Oct 23	Edward s of William NEWMAN & Sarah his wife
Oct 31	Jane d of John COLLINS & Elizabeth his wife
Nov 13	Samuel s of William STOCKIN & Elizabeth his wife
Nov 24	Hannah d of Benjamin SIMMONS & Hannah his wife
Dec 19	George s of Jarvis BURFORD & Hannah his wife
Dec 26	John s of J^{no} PERRY & Mary his wife
Dec 27	Jane d of Thomas MASON & Jane his wife
Dec 28	Walter s of Richard DUNN & Rachel his wife

Burials 1762

Jan 2	Mary d of Jervis BURFORD & Hannah his wife
Jan 17	Mary d of Thomas BARNETT & Jane his wife
Jan 18	Mary the illegitimate d of Martha SUCH
Jan 30	Elizabeth ROBINSON
Feb 2	Mr Richard WORRALL Junr
Feb 8	Thomas s of Thomas MASON & Jane his wife
Feb 12	Jane BANNISTER widow
Feb 26	Ann BAYLIS
Mar 9[?; BT's: "1st"]	John FORESBROOKE
Mar 10	Thomas GREEN
Mar 10	Mary SARBETT
Mar 10	Richard HORTON
Mar 22	Mary MOSELEY
Mar 23	Margaret d of Samuel PARDOE
Apr 25	Hannah POSTON
May 8	Elizabeth d of Joseph GROVE & Elizabeth his wife
Jun 14	Eleanor d of John GROVE & Elizabeth his wife
Jul 8	Betty SMITH
Jul 23	William s of Thomas MEDDEAGE & Mary his wife
Jul 24	John s of John COATES & Mary his wife
Jul 25	Richard POWELL
Jul 30	Sarah KIDSON
Aug 2	William THOMAS
Aug 5	Edward PIERCE
Aug 23	James NEWMAN

Sep 10 Thomas SALE
Sep 21 Edward BLUNN
Sep 26 Edward JONES
Oct 20 Francis SIMS
Oct 27 Hannah EDSTONE
Nov 9   Elizabeth d of Samuel ADAMS & Mary his wife
Nov 11 Martha GROVE
Nov 26 John GREEN
Nov 26 John MOSELEY
Nov 26 William s of John EDSTONE & Hannah his wife
Dec 9   Mr. John COOKE of Stourton-mill
Dec 20 Elizabeth NEWMAN

Baptisms 1763

Jan 1   Mary d of Thomas BAYLIS & Sarah his wife
Jan 3   Mary d of Samuel HOLLINS & Ann his wife
Jan 5   Richard s of John HAYWOOD & Sarah his wife
Jan 6   Matthew s of John REYNOLDS & Ann his wife
Jan 16 Hannah d of Edward HOBSON & Elizabeth his wife
Jan 23 Martha d of Thomas SIMS & Elizabeth his wife
Feb 2   Benjamin s of James REYNOLDS & Susannah his wife
Feb 11 Martha d of William DAVIS
Feb 12 Thomas s of Thomas LINE & Mary his wife
Feb 15 Thomas s of Lashfoot PERKS & Ann his wife
Feb 16 Hannah d of John PAGETT & Hannah his wife
Feb 19 Betty d of Henry GUEST & Eleanor his wife
Feb 20 Margaret d of Richard HAYWOOD & Mary his wife
Mar 3   Hannah the illegitimate d of Elizabeth BROOK
Mar 19 Betty d of William ROBINSON & Mary his wife
Mar 27 Mary d of Thomas JORDEN & Martha his wife
Apr 5   Thomas s of John BENNISON & Martha his wife
Apr 13 Mary d of William POWELL & Mary his wife
Apr 24 Thomas s of Francis MEDLICOTT & Mary his wife
Apr 24 Sarah d of Thomas PERRINS & Elizabeth his wife
Apr 29 Betty d of Constantine TIMMINS & Mary his wife
May 1   William s of John SOUTHERN & Eliz^b his wife
May 16 Elizabeth d of Richard BROOK & Elizabeth his wife
May 24 Richard s of Mr. Richard MARSTON & Barbara his wife
Jun 4   Thomas s of John JENKS & Mary his wife
Jun 5   Mary d of Joseph COLLEY & Elizabeth his wife
Jun 12 Susannah the illegitimate d of Sarah JONES
Jun 19 Benjamin d of Thomas MILWARD & Mary his wife
Jun 25 Ann d of John BARNETT & Ann his wife
Jun 29 Joseph s of William GOSNELL & Elizabeth his wife
Jul 2   Martha d of Thomas TIBBETS & Mary his wife
Jul 19 William s of Edward MATTHEWS & Jane his wife
Jul 22 William the illegitimate s of Mary COOKE
Jul 27 Mary d of Richard FOXALL & Ann his wife
Sep 3   Benjamin d of George STOKES & Sarah his wife
Sep 28 Benjamin s of Edward HILLMAN & Priscila his wife

Sep 9	Catharine d of James CORNFORTH & Helen his wife
Oct 1	Edwd s of Samuel ADAMS & Mary his wife
Oct 1	John s of John COOKE & Elizabeth his wife
Oct 2	Thomas s of Thomas BACHE & Ann his wife
Oct 8	Hannah d of John ASHLEY & Hannah his wife
Oct 8	William s of George FLETCHER & Hannah his wife
Oct 11	Thomas s of Thomas BOOTH & Betty his wife
Oct 10	Robert Philimore s of John GROVE & Elizabeth his wife
Oct 15	William s of Samuel FRANK & Mary his wife
Oct 15	Fanny d of Joseph PORTMAN & Mary his wife
Oct 25	Thomas s of Joseph RAWLEY & Elizabeth his wife
Nov 5	Mary d of William COATES & Mary his wife

Burials 1763

Jan 1	Alice RICHARDS
Jan 5	Thomas s of Thomas BACHE & Ann his wife
Jan 13	Sarah d of William, HEMMING & Betty his wife
Jan 31	Ann HIGHERES[?]
Feb 4	Samuel s of John BRISTONE[?]
Feb 11	Martha DAVIS
Feb 25	Mary d of Samuel LEWIS
Mar 5	Abigail WHITE
Mar 3	Joseph s of Joseph FORSBROOK
Mar 10	Edward s of James CORNFORTH & Eleanor his wife
Mar 18	Mary MATHER
Apr 25	Samuel illegitimate s of Betty BARROW
May 4	Mary d of Willm CHAMBERS & Sarah his wife
May 7	Mary WILLMOTT
Jun 7	Richard KIDSON
Jul 28	Hannah FINNEY
Aug 27	John TIMMINS
Sep 15	Joseph BATE
Oct 2	Betty [crossed out] Elizabeth SMITH
Oct 7	Mary SIMS
Oct 26	Mary DAW
Oct 24	William CANDY
Nov 27	Elizabeth STOCKIN
Dec 13	Samuel DUTTON
Dec 16	Thomas PERRY

More Baptisms 1763

Nov 6	Robert[crossed out] Richard s of William[crossed out] Thomas SANXAY & Ann his wife
Dec 25	Mary d of Edward HUGHES & Mary his wife

Baptisms 1764

Jan 1	Hannah d of Thos COWHORN & Elizabeth his wife
Jan 14	William s of Paul BOWATER & Sarah his wife
Jan 22	Josiah d of Robert GARDENER & Elizabeth his wife
Jan 22	Elizabeth d of Thomas MOYLE & Frances his wife

Mar 3   William s of William MORGAN & Mary his wife
Mar 3   John s of William EVANS & Sarah his wife
Mar 18   Abel s of Thomas DERRICK & Jane his wife
Mar 23   Elizabeth d of John REEVE & Elizabeth his wife
Apr 2   John s of John BROOK & Sarah his wife
Apr 5   Sarah d of John ALLEN & Mary his wife
Apr 10   Hannah d of Thomas ROBINS & Elizabeth his wife
Apr 14   Thomas illegitimate s of Elizabeth IDDINS
Apr 23   John Mucklestone s of Joseph FORSBROOKE & Marg^t his wife
Apr 24   Mary d of Samuel PARDOE & Elizabeth his wife
May 19   Hannah d of John PARR & Sarah his wife
May 26   Sarah d of Samuel WALL & Sarah his wife
Jun 6   Jane d of Mr. Samuel HOLLINS & Ann his wife
Jun 11   Joseph s of Thomas FEREDAY & Mary his wife
Jun 29   Mary d of John BROWN & Mary his wife
Jul 29   Susannah d of Robert SMITH & Ann his wife
Aug 10[?]   Joseph s of Richard REYNOLDS & Mary his wife
Sep 10   Susannah d of Benjamin EDWARDS & Elizabeth his wife
Sep 15   Thomas s of Benjamin SIMMONS & Hannah his wife
Sep 22   Thomas s of Samuel EDSTONE & Betty his wife
Oct 5   John s of Mr. John BACHE & Ann his wife
Oct 6   William s of William HUMFRIES & Hannah his wife
Oct 13   Job s of John EVANS & Mary his wife
Nov 11   Thomas s of Thomas LANGLEY & Mary his wife
Nov 17   John s of Thomas BAYLIS & Hannah his wife
Nov 18   Thomas s of James REYNOLDS & Susannah his wife
Nov 19   James s of John COLLINS & Elizabeth his wife
Nov 27   Lydia NAILER illegitimate s of Martha BLUNN
Dec 1   Ann d of Joseph BROWN & Maria his wife
Dec 7   Betty d of John REYNOLDS & Ann his wife
Dec 16   Richard s of the Rev^d Mr. John WORRALL & Susannah his wife
Dec 26   Mary Maria d of Richard HASLEDINE & Hannah his wife
Dec 27   Barbara d of Mr. Richard MARSTON & Barbara his wife

Burials 1764
Jan 2   Mr. Richard HOLLINS of Stourton Castle
Feb 24   Mrs Elizabeth CASWELL
Feb 26   Joseph s of Sarah INCHMORE
Feb 26   Joseph s of Thomas BLUNT
Apr 24   Mr. John WHITE
Jun 2   Thomas s of John DUDLEY & Elizabeth his wife
Jun 9   Elizabeth PUTSEY
Jun 24   Jane GREEN
Aug 3   Ann ALLERTON
Sep 2   Joseph illegitimate d of Susannah PEARSON
Sep 9   Elizabeth LEWIS
Sep 13   Martha PRICE
Oct 14   Sarah BAYLIS

Oct 20   Ann PALMER
Nov 4   Ann PARKES
Dec 13   Amy BRICE
Dec 19   Richard s of the Rev^d Mr. Jno WORRALL & Susannah his wife
Dec 22   Thomas s of Thomas BACHE & Ann his wife

Baptisms 1765
Dec 25   Judith Elizabeth d of Willm BLUNN & Mary his wife
Dec 26   Elizabeth Barnett d of John ALDEN & Sarah his wife

Baptisms 1765
Jan 1   Ann d of Richard TIMMINS & Elizabeth his wife
Jan 19   Richard s of John BYNIAN & Mary his wife
Jan 20   Letitia d of Richard BAKER & Jane his wife
Jan 21   Betty d of John REYNOLDS & Ann his wife
Jan 24   Mary d of John FLETCHER & Elizabeth his wife
Jan 26   John s of John BARNETT & Ann his wife
Feb 10   Joseph s of John PERRY & Mary his wife
Feb 20   Mary d of John & Mary HOPKINS
Feb 20   Francis illegitimate s of Mary MASSEY
Feb 22   John illegitimate s of Sarah BAGOTT
Feb 23   Ann d of John BENNET & Rose his wife
Feb 23   Jenny d of Richard HAYWOOD & Mary his wife
Mar 3   Thomas s of Edward DOUGHTY & Eleanor his wife
Mar 13   Betty illegitimate d of Mary HOCKIN
Mar 31   Robert s of George LITTLEWOOD & Sarah his wife
Apr 13   Sarah d of George FLETCHER & Hannah his wife
Apr 14   James s of John SOUTHERN & Elizabeth his wife
Apr 17   Mary d of Thomas MASON & Jane his wife
Apr 25   Samuel s of Thomas PERRINS & Elizabeth his wife
Apr 25   Jervis s of Jervis BURFORD & Hannah his wife
May 5   John s of Richard FOXALL & Ann his wife
May 11   Thomas s of John GREEN & Hannah his wife
May 22   Elizabeth d of Charles GREEN & Elizabeth his wife
May 26   Lucy d of Thomas BOOTH & Elizabeth his wife
Jun 14   James s of Willm HEMMING & Mary his wife
Jun 15   Thomas s of Thomas MEDDEAGE & Mary his wife
Jun 22   Elizabeth d of Samuel FRANKS & Mary his wife
Jun 22   William s of William ALLEN & Mary his wife
Jun 22   Mary d of James AKERMAN & Sarah his wife
Jul 1   Mary d of Richard BROOKE & Elizabeth his wife
Jul 3   Richard s of Thos COWHORN & Mary his wife
Jul 14   William illegitimate s of Mary STORY
Jul 20   Martha d of Thomas EDWELL & Martha his wife
Aug 10   John Cotton s of Thomas TIBBETTS & Mary his wife
Aug 31   John s of William GILES & Ann his wife
Oct 5   William s of William GOSLIN bap & Elizabeth his wife
Oct 5   Mary d of John COOKE & Elizabeth his wife
Oct 7   Elizabeth d of Edward HOBSON & Mary his wife
Oct 16   Elizabeth illegitimate d of Mary COLEY

Oct 19	Richard s of Lashfoot PERKS & Ann his wife
Oct 20	Sarah d of Joseph RAWLEY & Elizabeth his wife
Oct 25	Sarah illegitimate d of Eleanor GROVE
Oct 26	Margaret d of Thomas BACHE & Ann his wife
Oct 27	Sarah d of Thomas JORDAN & Martha his wife
Nov 2	Samuel s of William MORGAN & Mary his wife
Nov 16	Henry s of Samuel ADAMS & Mary his wife
Dec 3	Phoebe d of George STOKES & Sarah his wife

Burials 1765

Jan 9	Thomas ARNOTT
Feb 1	Ann FREEMAN
Feb 9	William JENKS
Mar 10	Mary CRANE
Mar 18	Mary PUTSEY
Mar 28	John SUCH
Mar 30	Hannah BRICE
Apr 3	John BAKER
Apr 20	Richard LYNE
May 7	Edward UNDERWOOD
May 11	Keturah GOSLIN
May 22	Thomas s of Samuel HEADSTONE & Betty his wife
May 26	Sampson SPENCER
May 30	John illegitimate s of Mary COLE
Jun 1	Elizabeth d of William GOSLIN & Elizabeth his wife
Jun 29	William s of William EVANS & Nancy his wife
Jul 2	Mary TILLEY
Jul 3	John s of William EVANS & Nancy his wife
Jul 13	Hannah HILLMAN
Jul 15	Ann PARDOE
Jul 16	Thomas COOKE
Aug 3	Thomas PRICE
Aug 24	Francis illegitimate s of Mary MASSEY
Oct 15	Catherine HICKMANS
Oct 22	Mrs Susannah WORRALL
Oct 26	Sarah BECKLEY
Nov 15	Eleanor HIGHERY
Nov 20	The Reverend Mr. William YATE Schoolmaster of Wolverley
Dec 23	Daniel DUNN
Dec 26	Samuel MOSELEY
Dec 31	Elizabeth UNDERWOOD

Baptisms 1766

Jan 4	John s of Benjamin COLLET & Sarah his wife
Feb 5	John s of John PATCHETT & Hannah his wife
Feb 9	Joseph s of William ROBINSON & Mary his wife
Feb 9	Francis s of Benjamin EDWARDS & Elizabeth his wife
Feb 11	Walter s of Francis MEDLICOTT & Mary his wife
Feb 15	John s of Thomas DUTTON & Elizabeth his wife
Mar 3	Humphrey s of Mr. John BACHE & Ann his wife

Mar 4	Fanny d of Mr. Thomas ROBINS & Elizabeth his wife
Mar 8	William s of John PARR & Sarah his wife
Mar 8	James Tilley s of Edward MATTHEWS & Jane his wife
Mar 16	Frances d of Thomas MOYLE & Frances his wife
Mar 18	Robert s of Lazarus ADAMS & Catherine his wife
Mar 31	Elizabeth d of William COATES & Elizabeth his wife
Mar 31	Mary d of Edward HILLMAN & Priscilla his wife
Apr 1	Thomas s of John BROOK & Hannah his wife
Apr 1	William s of William JENKS & Elizabeth his wife
Apr 19	Elizabeth d of John COLLINS & Elizabeth his wife
Apr 20	James s of James CORNFORTH & Helen his wife
Apr 26	Mary d of Thomas BAYLEY & Betty his wife
May 3	Sarah d of John HAMMOND & Margaret his wife
May 14	Joseph s of Thomas STOKES & Sarah his wife
May 20	George s of Richard DUNN & Rachel his wife
May 30	Elizabeth d of John FLETCHER & Elizabeth his wife
May 31	Thomas s of Harry BRICE & Susannah his wife
Jun 7	Benjamin s of John LEES & Jane his wife
Jun 11	John s of Robert PIPER & Mary his wife
Jun 27	Richard s of Richard CLYMER & Elizabeth his wife
Jul 5	Richard, s of John JENKS & Mary his wife
Jul 12	William s of William EVANS & Mary his wife
Jul 27	Nelly d of Thomas MILLARD & Mary his wife

Gave in a Copy of the Register at the Bishop's Visitation of the above names

Aug 9	Jane d of John ASHLEY & Hannah his wife
Aug 9	Jane d of Samuel FRANKS & Mary his wife
Aug 10	James s of John ALLEN & Mary his wife
Aug 13	Kitty d of William HUMFRIES & Hannah his wife
Sep 9	Fanny d of Mr. Richard MARSTON & Barbara his wife
Sep 14	John s of John SOUTHERN & Elizabeth his wife
Sep 20	Thomas s of Samuel WALL & Mary his wife
Oct 16	Hannah d of Thomas LINE & Mary his wife
Oct 28	John s of John BROWN & Mary his wife
Nov 28	William illegitimate s of Sarah MORRIS
Dec 7	Sarah d of Bridget LOXLEY a traveling woman
Dec 27	Edward s of John REYNOLDS & Martha his wife
Dec 25	Jane d of Thos COWHORNE & Elizabeth his wife

Burials 1766

Jan 7	Mary BARNETT
Jan 20	The Rev^d Mr. John WORRALL Clerk
Feb 23	Mr. Thomas WORRALL
Feb 25	Elizabeth FRYER
Feb 27	Mrs Catherine HOMFRAY
Mar 3	Joseph RICHARDSON
Mar 5	Mary DIXON
Mar 10	Ann LAVENDER
Mar 11	Edward WHITTON
Mar 23	John KETLEY

Apr 8   Elizabeth KETLEY
Apr 11   Ann MOSELEY
Apr 14   William CHAMBERS
Apr 16   Elizabeth Barnett d of John ALDEN & Elizabeth[crossed out]
           Sarah his wife
May 4   Jeremiah TYSO
May 7   Mary RICHARDS
May 19   The Rev^d Mr. Benjamin YATE
May 25   Matthew UNDERWOOD
May 27   Mary MASON
May 30   Sarah CHAMBERLAIN
Jun 2   Mary SMITH
Jun 7   Mary TRUEMAN
Jul 10   Thomas DAVIES an Exciseman
Jul 13   Henry HACKETT
Jul 18   John COLLINS
Jul 18   Elizabeth GROVE
Jul 20   George DUNN
Jul 24   Elizabeth BROOKE
Jul 25   Thomas FERADAY
Jul 27   Samuel TAYLOR
Aug 1   William ROBINSON
    Gave a Copy of the Register at the Bishops Visitation of the above
Aug 26   Mary PIPER
Sep 9   James SMITH
Sep 25   Catherine DUNN
Dec 2   Thomas NEWMAN
Dec 14   Jane d of Samuel FRANKS & Mary his wife
Dec 29   Thomas s of Harry BRICE & Hannah his wife

Baptisms 1767

Jan 1   Mary d of John CHALTON & Margaret his wife
Jan 24   Eliza-Maria d of Samuel EDSTONE & Betty his wife
Jan 31   Elizabeth d of James REYNOLDS & Susannah his wife
Feb 18   Fanny illegitimate d of Helen CRUNDALL
Feb 28   Sarah d of Thomas BLUNT & Sarah his wife
Mar 3   Edward s of George STOKES & Sarah his wife
Mar 3   Sarah d of John BENNETT & Rose his wife
Mar 7   George s of John & Ann WHITAKER
Mar 20   Thomas s of John BARNETT & Ann his wife
Apr 10   Mary d of William AINSWORTH & Eliz^h his wife
Apr 19   Mary d of William CHAMBERLIN & Mary his wife
May 6   Peggy d of Joseph BROWN & Maria his wife
May 12   Lydia d of John & Mary HANSON
Jun 6   Catharine d of John PARR & Sarah his wife
Jun 8   Edward s of James AKERMAN & Sarah his wife
Jul 1   Sarah d of John HOPKINS & Mary his wife
Jul 18   James s of John PERRY & Mary his wife
Jul 31   Joseph s of Edward HOBSON & Elizabeth his wife

Jul 31   Joseph illegitimate s of Mary COOKE
Aug 1   John s of Thomas BOOTH & Betty his wife
Aug 8   Susannah illegitimate d of Mary WARREN
Aug 19   Humphrey s of Richard TIMMINS & Elizabeth his wife
Aug 26   Sarah d of Mr. John REEVE & Elizabeth his wife
Sep 12   George s of George BAINES & Martha his wife
Oct 4   Elizabeth d of Henry PARKER & Elizabeth his wife
Nov 3   Thomas s of William JENKS & Mary his wife
Nov 5   John s of John REYNOLDS & Ann his wife
Nov 10   Sarah d of Samuel ADAMS & Mary his wife
Nov 24   Martha d of Thomas MASON & Jane his wife
Nov 28   Esther d of Benjamin COLLETT & Sarah his wife
Dec 2   John s of John POINTER & Sarah his wife
Dec 12   William s of Francis TAYLOR & Elizabeth his wife
Dec 27   Abraham s of Rich HASLEDINE & Hannah his wife
Dec 30   Ann d of Lashfoot PERKS & Ann his wife

Burials 1767

Jan 4   Mary IMMS
Jan 11   Ann FOXALL
Jan 18   Sarah d of George STOKES & Sarah his wife
Jan 26   Ann HAMMOND
Feb 1   Joseph LYANE
Feb 1   Sarah illegitimate d of Eleanor GROVE
Feb 23   Richard NELSON
Mar 6   Joseph COLLETT
         Elizabeth PARKES [entry crossed out]
Mar 21   Elizabeth PARKES
Mar 31   John FREEMAN
Apr 2   John LOWE
Apr 28   Ann DAVIS
         Mrs Mary WORRALL died May the 2^d & was buried May the 5th
May 10   Samuel LYE
Jun 10   John JENKS
Jun 18   Ann EVANS
Jun 21   Edward LYNE
Jul 5   Ann NORMCOTT
Jul 25   George s of George BAYNES
Aug 4   Mary LAMBETH
Aug 7   Thomas STOKES
Aug 25   William REYNOLDS
Aug 29   Joseph s of Edward HOBSON & Elizabeth his wife
Sep 15   Benjamin s of James REYNOLDS & Susannah his wife
Sep 7   Ann HADDOCK
Sep 19   Ann BARNETT
Sep 24   Hannah SIMMONS
Oct 7   Margaret BARNETT
Oct 21   Frances BURFORD
Nov 5   Mary MORRIS

Nov 21 Jane POWELL
Dec 9 Thomas HUGHES

Baptisms 1768
Jan 2 Jane d of James FRANKS & Mary his wife
Jan 30 Thomas s of John JOHNSON & Mary his wife
Feb 6 John s of John EDWARDS & Ann his wife
Feb 19 Elizabeth d of Benjamin EDWARDS & Elizabeth his wife
Feb 24 Sarah d of Thomas GIBBITS & Mary his wife
Apr 2 Ann d of Thomas JORDEN & Martha his wife
Apr 3 Gamaliel s of John BRICE & Elizabeth his wife
Apr 5 Elizabeth d of Isaac FRYER & Margery his wife
Apr 9 John s of John COOKE & Elizabeth his wife
Apr 11 Betty d of William GOSNELL & Elizabeth his wife
Apr 23 Hannah d of Harry BRICE & Hannah his wife
Apr 27 Richard s of Samuel HOLLINS & Ann his wife
Apr 29 Hannah d of John ALDEN & Mary his wife
May 7 George Grove s of Edward MATTHEWS & Jane his wife
May 9 Betty d of John LOWE & Betty his wife
May 14 Benjamin s of Thos DUTTON & Elizabeth his wife
May 14 Nancy d of Richard BOOTH & Ann his wife
May 25 Elizabeth d of John BACHE & Ann his wife
May 28 Eleanor d of Edwd DOUGHTY & Eleanor his wife
Jun 18 Thomas s of Thomas BAKER & Margaret his wife
Jun 19 John s of William HEMMING & Betty his wife
Jul 16 Ann d of George LITTLEWOOD & Sarah his wife
Jul 22 William s of James CORNFORTH & Helen his wife
Aug 21 Phoebe d of Thomas HARRISON & Ann his wife
Aug 24 Henry s of Joseph ALDEN & Jane his wife
Aug 28 Joseph s of Thomas BACHE & Ann his wife
Sep 4 Aniesia d of John REYNOLDS & Martha his wife
Sep 4 Nancy d of John HARRIS & Catherine his wife
Sep 10 Mary d of William ROBINSON & Mary his wife
Sep 16 Edward s of Edward HOBSON & Elizabeth his wife
Sep 16 Thomas s of Richard MARSTON & Barbara his wife
Sep 25 John s of Joseph MORECROFT & Mary his wife
Sep 30 Joseph s of William COLEBOURN & Jane his wife
Oct 2 Elizabeth d of John BARNETT & Ann his wife
Sep 20[sic] John s of George STOKES & Sarah his wife
Oct 22 John s of Edward BEARD & Elizabeth his wife
Nov 27 Jane d of John ALLEN & Mary his wife
Dec 5 David s of John WHITTAKER & Ann his wife
Dec 10 John s of John LEES & Jane his wife
Dec 30 John illegitimate s of Mary JENKINS
Dec 30 Mary d of Tho: LANGLEY & Mary his wife

Burials 1768
Jan 12 Moses HARPER
Jan 25 James s of John ALLEN & Mary his wife
Feb 12 Mary WEBB

Feb 21   Mary d of John GROVE & Elizabeth his wife
Mar 7   Samuel NEW   with Aff.
Mar 14   John HARPER
Apr 13   Mary d of John EDWARDS & Ann his wife
Mar 14   Benjamin WHITE
Apr 17   Mary SIMS
Apr 21   Sarah d of John HOPKINS & Mary his wife
May 1   Samuel s of Thomas PRICE & Elizabeth his wife
May 12   John EVES
May 17   William POWELL
Jun 6[?] Thomas CLEWES
Jun 23   Win: JONES
Jul 12   Humphrey BATE
Jul 17   Mary d of Samuel HOLLINS & Ann his wife
Jul 19   Thomas BAYLIS
Jul 21   Elizabeth IDDINS
Aug 5   Mary TOWNSHEND
Aug 18   Elizabeth TAYLOR
Sep 3   Lot s of [blank] ROCK
Sep 21   John HANCOX
Oct 2   John HAYWARD
Nov 11   Mary PERRINS
Nov 16   Priscilla FIELDHOUSE
Nov 29   Hannah d of Lashfoot PERKS & Ann his wife
Dec 2   Thomas MEDLICOTT
Dec 6   William s of Samuel ADAMS & Sarah his wife
Dec 11   Mr Thomas WALDRON
Dec 13   Eleanor NORMCOTT
Dec 17   Mary TIMMINS
Dec 29   William s of William BLUNN & Elizabeth his wife

Baptisms 1769
Feb 4   George s of Richard NIGHTINGALE & Hannah his wife
Feb 11   Nancy d of Samuel HEATH & Susannah his wife
Feb 18   William s of James ACREMAN & Sarah his wife
Feb 19   Thomas s of James STOCKIN & Ann his wife
Mar 4   John s of William EVANS & Sarah his wife
Mar 27   Peter s of James REYNOLDS & Susannah his wife
Mar 27   John s of Samuel WALL & Sarah his wife
Mar 28   John s of John REEVE & Elizabeth his wife
Mar 29   John s of Thomas FLETCHER & Sarah his wife
Mar 29   Hannah d of John GREEN & Hannah his wife
Apr 16   Betty d of Thos PERRINS & Elizabeth his wife
Apr 16   Sarah d of John HOPKINS & Mary his wife
Apr 21   Edward s of Isaac FRYER & Margery his wife
Apr 23   Richard s of John BROOK & Sarah his wife
Apr 30   Edward s of Thomas MILLARD & Mary his wife
May 14   Sarah d of Tho: STOKES & Mary his wife
May 14   Ann d of Jervis BURFORD & Hannah his wife
May 15   Peter s of John SOUTHERN & Elizabeth his wife

May 16   Beatrix d of William SMITH & Beatrix his wife
May 24   Jeremiah s of Thomas ROBINS & Elizabeth his wife
May 27   Esther d of William ALLEN & Mary his wife
Jun 3   Charles illegitimate s of Margaret HAYWOOD
Jun 10   Edward s of Richard REYNOLDS & Mary his wife
Jun 25   Thomas s of Thomas MOYLE & Frances his wife
Jul 8   Violetta d of John PARR & Sarah his wife
Jul 25   Jonathan s of John GROVE & Elizabeth his wife
Jul 30   Mary d of John BENNETT & Rose his wife
Aug 15   John s of Thomas & Mary BIGLEY
Sep 3   Joseph s of Joseph WILLIAMS & Hannah his wife
Sep 10   Thomas s of Willm CHAMBERLIN & Sarah his wife
Sep 15   Robert s of Robert SMITH & Sarah his wife
Sep 17   William s of David LEOUT[?] & Sarah his wife
Sep 21   John MORRIS illegitimate s of Sarah TROW
Sep 23   Richard illegitimate s of Sarah HILLMAN
Sep 30   Richard s of Benjamin BAYLIS & Ann his wife
Oct 28   Charles s of Lazarus ADAMS & Catherine his wife
Oct 28   Thomas s of Aaron FELLOW & Sarah his wife
Nov 18   Thomas KENDRICK illegitimate s of Mary COOK
Nov 18   Lydia d of John GUEST & Hannah his wife
Nov 21   Sarah d of Charles GREEN & Elizabeth his wife
Dec 2   Jane d of Harry KIDSON & Mary his wife
Dec 3   William s of John CHALTON & Margaret his wife
Dec 3   Samuel s of John CARTWRIGHT & Mary his wife
Dec 6   Elizabeth d of Philip BAKER & Ann his wife

Burials 1769
Jan 1   Mary POWELL
Jan 4   John s of Edward MOYLE & Hannah his wife
Feb 2   John STOCKINS
Feb 5   Thomas s of John GREEN & Hannah his wife
Feb 8   Sarah NEW
Feb 26   Elizabeth d of Edward HOBSON & Eliz: his wife
Mar 2   John s of George STOKES & Sarah his wife
Mar 12   Blower DAVIS
Mar 14   Mary KING
Mar 16   Abigail BATHAM
Mar 30   William s of Richard THOMAS & Mary his wife
Apr 19   Joseph s of John PERRY & Ann his wife
Apr 25   Sarah TAYLOR
Apr 26   Mary LAMB
May 2   Sarah d of Joseph & Elizabeth COLLEY
May 4   Sarah d of Sam: ADAM & Elizabeth his wife
May 20   Priscilla CRANE
May 22   Joseph s of Joseph GOLD & Mary his wife
Jun 3   John s of Willm EVANS & Mary his wife
Jun 4   William TAYLOR
Jun 6   William PARDOE
Jun 8   Jane d of John ALLEN & Mary his wife

Jun 13   Mary BECKLEY
Jun 30   Elizabeth CHURCHYARD
Jul 9   Elizabeth MOLE
Jul 9   Francis MATTHEWS
Jul 9   David ADAMS
Jul 11   Mary TURNER
Jul 17   John PARDOE
Jul 22   John s of Edward BEARD & Eliz: his wife
Jul 23   Jane DUTTON
Jul 24   Phoebe HILL
Jul 27   Jane MORRIS
Jul 29   Edward BEARD
Aug 16   Mr. Jeremiah CASWELL of the Hyde
Aug 25   Elizabeth JONES
Aug 31   Mary CARELESS
Sep 5   Mary BIGLEY
Oct 11   A poor traveling man was buryed
Oct 21   John JOYCE
Nov 29   Moses DILLWORTH
Nov 30   Elizabeth MARSH
Dec 12   Hannah d of Thomas KELLAM & Hannah his wife

Baptisms 1769

Dec 10   Hannah d of William GUEST & Esther his wife
Dec 16   Sukey d of Joseph BROWN & Maria his wife
Dec 27   Sarah d of John LOWE & Betty his wife
Dec 30   Mary d of Francis MEDLICOTT & Mary his wife
Dec 31   Betty d of John BRICE & Betty his wife
Dec 31   Nancy d of Richard THOMAS & Mary his wife

Baptisms 1770

Jan 19   William s of William AINSWORTH & Elizabeth his wife
Jan 25   Hannah d of Richard MARSTONE & Barbara his wife
Feb 24   Philip s of Edward MATTHEWS & Jane his wife
Apr 16   Violetta d of John WHITTAKER & Ann his wife
Apr 16   Samuel s of Samuel PARDOE & [blank] his wife
Apr 17   Joseph s of John PERRY & Ann his wife
Apr 17   Richard s of Samuel ADAMS & Elizabeth his wife
Apr 25   Betty d of John COOKE & Betty his wife
Apr 28   Ann d of John POINTER & Ann [crossed out] Sarah his wife
May 1   Sarah d of Thomas RICHARDS & Sarah his wife
May 11   Martha d of Thomas COWHORNE & Elizabeth his wife
May 15   Thomas s of George STOKES & Sarah his wife
May 24   Martha d of Edwd HILLMAN & Priscilla his wife
Jun 16   Benjamin s of John REYNOLDS & Ann his wife
Jun 16   Sarah d of Thomas MASON & Jane his wife
Jun 19   John s of Daniel PIPER & Betty [altered in different hand to "Rebeckah"] his wife
Jun 24   Richard illegitimate s of Isabel [crossed out and altered to [?] HUBBALL

Jul 6   Henry s of Richard NIGHTINGALE & Hannah his wife
Jul 11   Esther d of Richard TIMMINS & Elizabeth his wife
Jul 15   George s of Lashfoot PERKS & Ann his wife
Jul 20   Tryphoena d of Thomas BAGLEY & Betty his wife
Jul 18   Sarah d of Samuel ADAMS & Elizabeth his wife
Aug 5   John s of Richard CHIDLEY & Elizabeth his wife
Aug 19   Mary Richards d of John ALLEN & Mary his wife
Aug 26   Ann & Sarah daughters of John BROWN & Mary his wife
Aug 26   Mary d of Francis COOKSON & Elizabeth his wife
              Mem   Gave in a Copy of the above at the Bishop's Visitation
Sep 9   Ann d of Joseph TOW & Mary his wife
Sep 9   John s of John BAYLIS & Jane his wife
Sep 29   Jane d of John LEES & Jane his wife
Oct 28   Sarah d of John WOOD & Sarah his wife
Nov 5   George s of John MIDDLEMORE & Alice his wife
Nov 10   Mary d of Thomas BUSH & Mary his wife
Nov 18   Mary d of John SOUTHALL & Elizabeth his wife
Nov 18   John s of Richd BAYLIS & Mary his wife
Dec 2   Ann d of Hum^y SHOTTON & Jane his wife
Dec 7   Enoch TURLEY illegitimate s of Elizabeth HAYWOOD

Burials 1770

Jan 8   Hannah LYE
Jan 19   Elizabeth BEELY
Jan 26   Mary HADLEY
Jan 27   Hannah CLEWES
Feb 7   Amy HACKETT
Feb 8   William BROWN
Feb 8   Mary ALLEN
Feb 11   Benjamin s of John EDSTONE & Ann his wife
Mar 5   John WALLENS
Mar 11   James NEWMAN
Mar 30   John MOUNTSTEVEN
Apr 28   Edward s of Isaac FRYER & Margery his wife
May 6   Mary BEST
Jul 6   Humphrey GOODMAN
Jul 15   Betty ALLEN
Jul 22   Samuel LEWIS
Aug 13   William CLEMSON
Aug 13   Betty GOSNELL
Aug 25   Sarah BAYLIS
Aug 25   Joseph s of Thomas BACHE & Ann his wife
              Mem: gave in a Copy of the above at the Bishop's Visitation
Sep 6   Sarah POSTON
Sep 9   Martha WHITTINGHAM
Sep 16   Richard LAWRENCE
Nov 23   Jane MATTHEWS

More Baptisms 1770

Dec 25   Mary d of Harry BRICE & Hannah his wife

Dec 26   Sarah d of Thomas BATE & Margaret his wife
Dec 26   Samuel s of Willm EVANS & Sarah his wife
Dec 30   Martha d of Joseph REYNOLDS & Martha his wife

Baptisms 1771

Jan 2   Isaac s of Thomas CALLAM & Hannah his wife
Jan 6   Mary d of James CORNFORTH & Helen his wife
Jan 23   John s of William JENKS & Mary his wife
Jan 27   Elizabeth d of Edward STEPHENS & Eliz: his wife
Feb 2   Betty d of Thomas WILSON & Mary his wife
Feb 8   Edward Conwood s of J^no REEVE & Elizabeth his wife
Feb 17   Margaret d of Saml SMITH & Elizabeth his wife
Feb 23   George s of John EVANS & Ann his wife
Feb 24   William s of George BENNETT & Elizabeth his wife
Feb 24   Elizabeth d of Joseph RAWLEY & Elizabeth his wife
Mar 8   Mary d of Tho: FLETCHER & Sarah his wife
Mar 9   Benjamin s of James REYNOLDS & Susannah his wife
Mar 17   Thomas s of Thomas JORDEN & Martha his wife
Mar 21   Thomas s of Thomas DODD & Sarah his wife
Mar 22   Ann d of John BROWN & Ann his wife
Apr 12   Samuel s of Richard HAYWOOD & Sarah [lightly crossed out & "Mary" entered] his wife
Apr 19   Edward s of Samuel WALL & Sarah his wife
Apr 21   Joseph s of John BROOKE & Sarah his wife
Apr 23   Dorothy d of Richard MARSTON & Barbara his wife
May 1   Thomas s of Thomas KERSHAW & Mary his wife
May 4   James s of John GUEST & Hannah his wife
May 23   William s of John BACHE & Elizabeth his wife
May 31   Francis s of Edward HOBSON & Elizabeth his wife
Jun 23   Sarah d of John CARTWRIGHT & Mary his wife
Jun 30   William s of William BLUNN & Mary his wife
Jul 13   Thomas s of Humphrey SHINTON & Alice his wife
Jul 20   Jane d of Aaron FELLO & Sarah his wife
Jul 24   Edward s of Francis LEWIS & Elizabeth his wife
Jul 21   Sarah d of Richd PALMER & Mary his wife
Jul 22   Benjamin s of Willm GOSNELL & Elizabeth his wife
Jul 28   Nelly d of Wm ROBINSON & Sarah his wife
Aug 4   Ann d of John PARKS & Susannah his wife
Aug 18   Samuel s of Abraham CRANE & Ann his wife
Aug 24   John s of James AKERMAN & Sarah his wife
Sep 1   Penny d of Thomas MILWARD & Mary his wife
Sep 7   Mary SILK aged eighteen years was bap
Oct 6   John s of John GREEN & Hannah his wife [an alteration appears to have been made above Hannah]
Oct 20   Elizabeth d of John BENNET & Rose his wife
Nov 1   Martha d of Wm HEMMING & Betty his wife
Nov 16   Nancy d of Benjn BAYLIS & Nancy his wife
Nov 22   Thomas illegitimate s of Sarah FELLOWS
Nov 31   Mary d of John BUTTERY & Rebeckah his wife
Dec 4   Catherine d of John LOWE & Betty his wife

Burials 1771

Jan 2	Samuel GREEN
Jan 5	Jane BROOKE
Jan 6	Eleanor WHITE
Jan 14	Jane COLLINS
Jan 17	Josiah RAWLEY
Jan 26	Sarah KIDSON
Feb 1	Nancy d of Richard THOMASON
Feb 14	Edward POWELL
Feb 14	Elizabeth JENKS
Feb 17	Dorothy HUGHES
Feb 18	William WATKINS
Mar 1	Sarah PERRINS
Mar 10	Elizabeth THOMAS
Mar 18	Hannah REWBERRY
Mar 20	Sarah d of John BROWN & Mary his wife
Mar 29	George BAKER
Apr 12	John s of John REEVE & Elizabeth his wife
Apr 24	Edward s of Samuel WALL & Sarah his wife
Jun 3	James PERRY
Jul 8	Sarah OLIVER Widow
Jul 28	John s of Daniel PIPER & ~~Betty~~ [crossed out and entry made in different hand] Rebeckah his wife
Aug 5	Thomas HASLEDINE
Aug 21	Elizabeth JORDEN
Aug 30	Ann LYTHALL
Sep 10	Benjamin s of Wm GOSNELL & Elizabeth his wife
Oct 30	Susannah MASON[?]
Nov 15	Ann illegitimate d of Margaret CLARKE
Nov 19	Joseph SHAKESPEAR
Dec 12	Beatrix d of Willm SMITH & Beatrix his wife
Dec 13	Martha d of Joseph REYNOLDS & Barbara his wife
Dec 14	Mary BROWN

More baptisms 1771

Dec 7	Nancy d of Jno WHITTAKER & Ann his wife
Dec 24	William s of Richard THOMAS & Mary his wife
Dec 26	Ann d of John HOPKINS & Mary his wife
Dec 27	Sarah d of George STOKES & Sarah his wife
Dec 28	William s of William JOHNSON & Elizabeth his wife
Dec 28	John s of Isaac FRYER & Margery his wife

Baptisms 1772

Jan 10	Mary illegitimate d of Mary HARRIS
Jan 10	Ann d of John HOLLY & Ann his wife
Jan 17	Samuel s of John BARNETT & Ann his wife
Feb 1	Thomas s of John PERRY & Mary his wife
Feb 8	Mary d of Samuel MOSELEY & Jane his wife
Feb 23	Thomas s of Thos [entered in different hand] STOKES [rubbed through] & Mary his wife

Feb 25	Edward s of Edward DOUGHTY & Eleanor his wife
Feb 26	Mary illegitimate d of Martha FELLOES
Feb 28	Charles s of Samuel ADAMS & Mary his wife
Mar 1	Thomas s of Robert SMITH & Sarah his wife
Apr 1	Daniel & William sons of Daniel PIPER & Rebekah his wife
Apr 5	William s of Thos TIMMINS & Jane his wife
May 3	James s of John TURNER & Ann his wife
May 22	Thomas s of John ROWLEY & Mary his wife
May 24	Mary d of Thomas BIGLEY & Mary his wife
Jun 8	William s of Samuel PARDOE & Elizabeth his wife
Jun 8	Elizabeth d of Thos FORESBROOK & Jane his wife
Jun 8	Mary d of Thos TIBBETTS & Mary his wife
Jun 26	Elizabeth d of John REYNOLDS & Ann his wife
Jul 23	John s of John FLETCHER & Elizabeth his wife
Jul 25	Elizabeth d of Henry KIDSON & Mary his wife
Jul 31	Betty d of Jno SOUTHERN & Betty his wife
Aug 2	Thomas s of John EDWARDS & Ann his wife
Aug 18	Eleanor d of Richd BELCHAM & Mary his wife
Aug 19	Hosannah & Susannah daughters of Jo: WILLIAMS & Hannah his wife
Sep 5	Richard s of James BATE & Sarah his wife
Sep 18	Betty illegitimate d of Sarah HARRISON
Oct 3	Margaret d of John COOKE & Betty his wife
Oct 4	Elizabeth d of Richard BAYLIS & Mary his wife
Oct 14	Richard illegitimate s of Mary COOKE
Oct 23	Ann illegitimate d of Sarah HILLMAN
Oct 31	Benjamin s of Benjamin EDWARDS & Elizabeth his wife
Nov 14	Sarah d of Philip BAKER & Ann his wife
Nov 14	James illegitimate s of Mary DUCE
Nov 22	Edward s of Edward BAYLEY & Ann his wife
Nov 13[sic]	Martha d of Tho: MOYLE & Frances his wife
Nov 13[sic]	Sarah d of Joseph PERRINS & Ann his wife
Dec 19	Ann d of Thos RATCLIFF & Elizabeth his wife
Dec 26	Daniel s of Rich: MARSTON & Barbara his wife
Dec 27	Thomas s of Tho: DODD & Sarah his wife
Dec 30	Mary d of Wm COPE & Mary his wife

Burials 1772

Jan 3	Mr. Richard WORRALL of Stourton
Jan 11	Mrs SHUTT of Hafcott
Jan 14	Mary HARRIS
Jan 30	Margaret REYNOLDS
Feb 1	Joseph s of John PERRY & Mary his wife
Feb 8	Thomas s of Jno PERRY & Mary his wife
Feb 13	William s of John DUDLEY & Elizabeth his wife
Feb 14	Mary illegitimate d of Mary HARRIS
Feb 14	Barbara HACKETT
Feb 14	Mary MONAM
Feb 21	Edward s of William BLUNN & Mary his wife
Mar 23	Sarah HALL

Apr 8 Sarah WARREN
Apr 22 Thomas BAKER
May 17 Elizabeth s of John BARNETT & Ann his wife
May 18 Mary HEMMING
Aug 3 Richard TIMMINS
Aug 30 Sarah EVANS
Sep 18 Mary STOKES
Sep 21 Richard DUNN
Nov 19 James illegitimate s of Mary DUCE
Nov 21 Elizabeth GROVE
Nov 26 Mary ROWLEY

Baptisms 1773

Jan 1 Sarah d of Thomas ROGERS & Mary his wife
Jan 11 Thomas s of Edward HOBSON & Eliz: his wife
Feb 2 Edward s of Lashfoot PERKS & Ann his wife
Feb 6 John s of Jeremiah CHAMBERS & Sarah his wife
Feb 7 Edward s of John CARTWRIGHT & Mary his wife
Feb 22 John s of John ALDEN & Sarah his wife
Mar 5 Thomas illegitimate s of Ann HAY
Mar 6 John s of John GUEST & Hannah his wife
Mar 17 Mary d of George STOKES & Sarah his wife
Mar 19 Betty illegitimate d of Mary PERRINS
Mar 20 William s of Wm SMITH & Beatrix his wife
Mar 24 Sarah Lightfoot d of John BACHE & Ann his wife
Apr 4 Joseph s of Thomas HARRIS & Catherine his wife
Apr 11 William s of Richard WALTERS & Ann his wife
Apr 12 William s of Jno GROSVENOR & Sarah his wife
Apr 16 Mary d of Tho: PERRINS & Elizabeth his wife
Apr 16 Jenny d of Richd NIGHTINGALE & Hannah his wife
May 9 Joseph s of Joseph RAWLEY & Elizabeth his wife
May 16 Mary d of John GROVE & Elizabeth his wife
May 21 Sarah d of Harry BRICE & Susannah his wife
May 20 Elizabeth d of John THOMAS & Margaret his wife
May 29 Sarah d of John BAYLIS & Jane his wife
Jun 1 Joseph s of James CORNFORTH & Helen his wife
Jun 16 Thomas s of Thomas & Sarah FLETCHER
Jun 11 Elizabeth d of William JOHNSON & Elizabeth his wife
Jun 25 John s of Wm AINSWORTH & Eliz his wife
Jun 10 Sarah d of John PARR & Mary his wife
Jul 3 Hannah d of Aaron FELLOES & Sarah his wife
Jun 27 Jane s of John BROWN & Ann his wife
Jul 18 Samuel s of Samuel FELLOES & Sarah his wife
Aug 8 John s of George BENNETT & Elizabeth his wife
Aug 15 Sarah d of John BROOK & Sarah his wife
Aug 22 Sarah d of Tho: CASSHEYE & Mary his wife
  Memorandum delivered in a Copy of the above at the Bishop's Visitation
Aug 29 Mary d of James CORBETT & Elizabeth his wife
Aug 22 William s of Jno WHITTAKER & Ann his wife

Sep 11   Sarah d of Joseph OSBORNE & Ann his wife
Oct 1   John s of Daniel PIPER & Rebecca his wife

Burials 1773
Jan 5   Catherine COLLETT
Jan 13   Mr. Thomas HILLMAN of Dunsley
Feb 4   James s of Thos WILSON & Sarah his wife
Feb 6   Eleanor CRUMP
Feb 21   Sarah WILSON
Mar 10   Richard HASLEDINE
Mar 11   Ann SOUTHALL
Mar 25   George BATE
Mar 25   Mary d of George STOKES & Sarah his wife
Apr 28   Mary HADDOCK
May 25   Elizabeth d of Jno THOMAS & Margaret his wife
May 30   Ann REYNOLDS
Jun 12   Mary DODSON
Jun 12   Harry LAMBERT
Jul 13   Thomas s of John ROWLEY
Jul 16   Mary d of Thomas FLETCHER & Sarah his wife
Aug 2   Richard CLYMER
Aug 5   Mary SMITH
Aug 10   John s of Richard BAYLIS & Mary his wife
         Memorandum delivered in a copy of the above at the Bishop's Visitation
Sep 15   James NEWMAN
Sep 15   Hannah BROWN
Sep 17   Elizabeth TAYLOR
Sep 18   Mary d of Thomas LANGLEY & Mary his wife
Oct 1   Mary HOPE
Oct 15   Thomas BARNETT
Oct 19   Ann WARREN
Oct 27   Mary JORDEN
Oct 31   Elizabeth CASWELL
Nov 11   Lydia NAYLOR
Nov 27   Sarah REDSTONE
Dec 8   John HOPE
Dec 21   William MEDLICOTT
Dec 26   Jane HILLMAN

More Baptisms 1773
Oct 3   Mary d of Edward HITCHCOCKE & Ann his wife
Oct 3   Richard s of Samuel MOSELEY & Jane his wife
Oct 9   Sarah d of Joseph GOULD & Mary his wife
Oct 13   Ann d of John PAGETT & Hannah his wife
Oct 31   Jane d of Thomas WILKES & Ann his wife
Oct 31   Rosannah Amelia d of John REYNOLDS & Martha his wife
Nov 5   Samuel s of Joseph ROWLEY & Sarah his wife
Nov 26   James s of John BURNAGE & Sarah his wife
Dec 27   William s of Joseph CRANE & Mary his wife

Dec 28 Richard s of Richard THOMAS & Mary his wife

Baptisms 1774

Jan 1	Sarah d of George BURGESS & Martha his wife
Jan 1	Ann d of William EVANS & Sarah his wife
Jan 14	Elizabeth d of Wm KETLEY & Sarah his wife
Jan 14	James s of James AKERMAN & Sarah his wife
Jan 16	Richard s of Jno GREEN & Hannah his wife
Jan 16	John s of Edwd STEPHENS & Elizth his wife
Jan 23	Joseph s of John SOUTHALL & Ann his wife
Feb 6	Mary d of Joseph FIELDHOUSE & Sarah his wife
Feb 13	Elizabeth d of John MIDDLEMOR [BT's: "MIDDLEMORE"] & Alice his wife
Feb 20	Elizabeth d of Thos MILWARD & Mary his wife
Mar 20	Samuel s of Robert SMITH & Sarah his wife
Mar 20	Sarah d of John MALPASS & Eliz: his wife
Apr 4	Richard s of Willm PALMER & Mary his wife
Apr 4	Mary d of John PERRY & Mary his wife
Apr 6	Thomas s of Edwd BAYLEY & Ann his wife
Apr 9	Susannah d of Benjn EDWARDS & Eliz: his wife
Apr 9	John s of William DUNN & Mary his wife
Apr 10	Mary d of Richd BAYLIS & Mary his wife
Apr 21	Ann d of George STOKES & Sarah his wife
Apr 22	Frances d of Jervis BURFORD & Hannah his wife
Apr 27	Mary d of Richd REYNOLDS & Mary his wife
May 15	Sarah d of Wm PARKES & Sarah his wife
May 15	Sarah d of John SOUTHERN & Elizabeth his wife
May 29	Mary d of Richd HOLLOWAY & Alice his wife
Jun 4	Mary d of Jno THOMAS & Margaret his wife
Jul 4	John s of John CHAMBERS & Sarah his wife
Aug 13	John s of John HOPKINS & Mary his wife
Aug 14	Philip s of John MATTHEWS & Catharine his wife
Aug 28	Ann d of Nathaniel JONES & Mary his wife
Sep 11	Mary d of Thos ROGERS & Mary his wife
Sep 27	John s of Jo^n NEWE & Eliz: his wife
Oct 9	Betty d of John BROWN & Mary his wife
Oct 14	Ann d of Isaac FRYER & Margery his wife
Oct 18	Joseph SILK illegitimate s of Elizabeth NEWMAN
Nov 5	John s of John BENNETT & Rose his wife
Nov 8	Elizabeth d of James BATE & Sarah his wife
Nov 9	Thomas s of Wm HEMMING & Betty his wife
Dec 4	Thomas s of Frances LEWIS & Elizabeth his wife
Dec 11	Joseph s of Joseph ROGERS & Elizabeth his wife
Dec 26	John s of Joseph CRANE & Mary his wife
Dec 26	Joseph s of Wm JENKS & Mary his wife
Dec 27	Sarah illegitimate d of Catharine PERRY
Dec 28	Sarah d of Thomas STOKES & Sarah his wife

Burials 1774

Jan 19   Elizabeth d of Wm KETLEY & Sarah his wife

Jan 23   Ann MORGAN
Jan 31   Martha TIBBETTS
Feb 13   Mary TIBBETTS
Feb 15 [BT's: "13"]   Esther TIMMINS
Feb 15   Wm Thos s of Jno HIDSTONE & Ann his wife
Apr 2   Mrs Ann COMBER
Apr 4   Sarah FOXALL
Apr 5   Joseph s of John BROOKE & Sarah his wife
Apr 6   Mary FELLOWES [BT's: "FELLOWS"]
Apr 14   Benjamin PERRY
Apr 16   Elizabeth BRICE
May 2   Betty RAWLEY
May 8   Mary d of Richd BAYLIS & Mary his wife
May 10   John CHAMBERLAIN
May 10   William PEARCE
May 16   Sarah TIBBETTS d of Thos TIBBETTS [BT's: "TIBBITTS"]
Jun 19   James s of John TURNER & Ann his wife
Jun 21   Ann ALLDEN
Jun 26   Joseph ALLDEN
Jul 11   William STOKES
Jul 11   Sarah d of John BROOK & Sarah his wife
Jul 27   Richard DUNN
Aug 17   William HICKMANS [BT's: "HICKMAN"]
Aug 30   Samuel MORRIS
Sep 8   Ann d of Edwd NEWMAN & Eliz: his wife
Nov 1   John POWELL Esqr
Nov 23   John MIDDLEMORE
Nov 26   John HARWOOD
Dec 3   Elizabeth BRADELEY
Dec 10   Elizabeth DEANE

Baptisms 1775
Jan 4   Harriott d of William COPE & Mary his wife
Jan 15   William s of Thomas JORDEN & Martha his wife
Jan 11   Sarah d of Thomas ROWLEY & Ann his wife
Jan 28   William s of John COOK & Betty his wife
Jan 29   Betty d of Willm ALLEN & Mary his wife
Feb 1   Catherine d of Edwd HOBSON & Eliz: his wife
Feb 18   Mary d of John GUEST & Hannah his wife
Feb 28   Mary d of John WHITAKER & Ann his wife
Mar 5   William s of William MARTIN & Penelope his wife
Mar 12   William s of Samuel BRETTELL & Mary his wife
Mar 12   James s of James REYNOLD & Susannah his wife
Mar 12   Thomas s of Edwd BODDISON & Joanna his wife
Mar 18   William s of William TAYLOR & Mary his wife
Mar 19   Hannah d of the Widow FELLOES
Apr 2   Sarah d of Thomas BACHE & Eliz: his wife
Apr 17   Sarah d of Joseph FIELDHOUSE & Sarah his wife
Apr 23   Aaron s of Aaron FELLOES & Sarah his wife
Apr 23   Benjamin illegitimate s of Abigail PERRY

Apr 26   Sarah d of Thos FLETCHER & Sarah his wife
May 17   Sarah d of Edwd HITCHETT & Ann his wife
May 17   William s of Thomas RATCLIFF & Elizabeth his wife
May 27   William s of Thomas PEARCE & Martha his wife
Jun 11   Philip s of Thomas MOYLE & Frances his wife
Jun 16   Ann d of Daniel PIPER & Rebeckah his wife
Jun 18   Joseph s of Thomas DODD & Sarah his wife
Jun 25   Elizabeth d of Jno GROSVENOR & Sarah his wife
Jun 28   Mary d of Humphrey SHINTON & Alice his wife
Jun 29   Shusannah d of Lashfoot PERKS [BT's: "PEARKES"] & Ann his wife
Jul 9   Thos s of Joseph WILLIAMS & Hannah his wife
Jul 9   Joseph s of John BROOKE & Sarah his wife
Jul 19   Jeremiah s of Jeremiah CHAMBERS & Mary his wife
Jul 28   John s of Eleanor DOUGHTY Widow
Jul 30   Sarah d of Edwd TIMMINS & Hannah his wife
Aug 27   William illegitimate s of Sarah HARRISON
Sep 12   Thomas s of John POYNTER & Sarah his wife
Sep 13   Ann d of Walter SHUTT & Phoebe his wife
Sep 15   Mary d of Richd NIGHTINGALE & Hannah his wife
Sep 17   Lucy d of Thos COX & Elizabeth his wife
Sep 20   Elisha s of Edwd NEWMAN & Eliz: his wife
Oct 28   Ann d of George BURGESS & Martha his wife

Burials 1775

Jan 4   John BAYLIS
Jan 5   Lydia PARDOE
Jan 10   Samuel BRISCOE
Jan 6   Edward NEW
Feb 23   Isaac FRYER Parish Clerk
Mar 3   Jemima REYNOLDS
Mar 7   Edward DOUGHTY
Mar 10   Frances BROWN
Apr 27   Sarah HASLEDINE
May 5   John CRANE
May 11   Thomas ALLEN
May 21   Ann ALLDEN
May 31   William SMITH
Jun 13   Mary ALLEN
Jun 14   Philip HAINES
Sep 14   Ann HOLLINS
Sep 14   Eleanor BROWN
Oct 3   Elizabeth SIMS
Oct 8   Christopher BARNWELL
Oct 11   Margaret RUSSELL
Oct 20   Mary DAVIS
Nov 14   Thomas BATE
Nov 14   Elizabeth MARKES
Nov 17   Mary SITCH
Dec 3   Jane GOSNEL

Dec 19 Humphrey FRYER
Dec 21 Joseph GILES
Dec 31 Hannah HARRIS

More Baptisms 1775
Nov 12 Sarah d of Samuel MOSELEY & Jane his wife
Nov 12 Mary d of Francis NIXON & Mary his wife
Nov 25 Ann Sophia d of Henry KIDSON & Mary his wife
Dec 17 Samuel s of John BROWN & Ann his wife
Dec 27 William s of James CORBETT & Elizabeth his wife